My Camp
Life in the French Foreign Legion

J. R. Lawrence

Contents

1: Escape to the Legion

Buy the ticket, take the ride.
Hunter S. Thompson

What follows is my account of the French Foreign Legion, for the period of my engagement: Starting in August 2007, and ending in September 2011.

It was a crisp, sunny morning in August, when I arrived at Ashford International train station. All I had with me was a small rucksack with my passport, a packed lunch, and around £300 in cash inside. This would be the first time that I had left my country. I was both anxious and excited about the journey that lay ahead. I had recently been released from serving twenty-one months of a three and a half year prison sentence for robbery, and was still on licence.

I had returned home, after nearly two years away in Her Majesty's Prison Rochester YOI (young offenders institute), to the council estate where I lived in East Sussex, which is in the southeast corner of England. I soon discovered that not much had changed while I had been away; everyone was still doing exactly what they had been doing when I left: living with their parents, playing computer games, and smoking weed.

I had decided, during my time in prison, not to let myself slip back into my old lifestyle, and that now things had to change. It may sound a bit cliché, but prison, for me, was a blessing in disguise. Yes, I hear you; living with, to put it frankly, a bunch of fucking violent loons in a cage and having people watch you take a dump is not ideal, but it got me off drugs, made me give up smoking, start going to the gym, and introduced me to some good people.

It was while in prison that I first met Frank. Frank had been in the British parachute regiment. He was a funny guy and he had a lot of interesting stories. Frank didn't think he would be able to get back into the parachute regiment after being in prison, but he missed the army life. His new idea was to join the French Foreign Legion. He would talk about it all the time. I had no idea what he was going on about at that period in my life. I had never considered joining the army. To hell with getting shot, I thought. Frank was not on a long sentence, it was around two months if I remember correctly. His time soon passed and he was gone.

Several months after Frank had been released, I was in my cell watching Channel 4 when an advert came on for 'Escape to the Legion,' a four-part TV series starring survival expert Bear Grylls. In that show Bear takes eleven people to an old Legion fort near Tazzougerte, which is on a high plateau in the Sahara desert, and puts them through their paces.

I remembered what Frank had said about the Foreign Legion and decided to watch it. The show was entertaining enough. They had three ex-legionnaires taking part: a short, obnoxious, loudmouth American sergeant; a corporal from the UK; and a German sergeant-chef. The show consisted of the eleven volunteers going through a four week boot-camp style program to test their resolve. It had its funny moments: like when one guy, Terry, couldn't even do a single chin up, then got frustrated and kicked the wall like a zeta male; or when one slimy guy tried to pretend that he had a bad back, got found out, and put in jail for 24 hours with people throwing buckets of water over him on a regular basis. The show looked ridiculous at first, but by the end I was starting to feel the pull of the Foreign Legion and the fresh start it could offer to someone like me.

It was the last episode in the series that got me though, when they showed the modern day Legion in action. I thought to myself, this could be the way to escape my unpromising existence in England, get away from my past of criminality, and actually do something meaningful. That was the moment I went down the Foreign Legion rabbit hole, and it would be a long time before I came out the other end.

Once my mind was made up, I began preparing myself so as to have the best chance of passing the selection. I started going to the gym, and I went to the library and got out a book called 'Legionnaire' by Simon Murray, which was a good read, but a bit outdated as the author joined in 1960. I also began learning French in my cell. I would copy out from a French book, into a note book, for a couple of hours over lunchtime each day, while I was locked up. I kept this routine up over the last ten months of my sentence.

It was a grey, drizzly, autumn day when I was released from Rochester prison. I had been up since the break of dawn with all my stuff packed into large plastic bags ready to go. There was one other lad who was getting released on the same day as me. I can't remember his name, but he had the dishevelled appearance of an alcoholic, or junkie. After a brief exchange of words I established that he was, to put it mildly, not very clever, but one is a prisoner of one's circumstances and we set off for the train station together.

I should explain that when you leave prison in the UK, you are given a free rail ticket home and around forty pounds in cash, plus whatever you have saved through earnings from work done whilst in prison. My new travel buddy, fresh out of prison, decided that he wanted to use some of this cash to buy some alcohol, so he went in an off-licence and got an eight pack of inexpensive Australian lager. I stood outside the shop thinking to myself, this guy is a fucking train wreck. On your first day out of jail you are required to report to probation, and you can't be intoxicated for that, so it wasn't boding well for him already.

We, eventually, reached the train station at the bottom of Rochester high street, got our tickets, and sat down on a bench to wait for the train. It turned out that we would be travelling part of the way together. Our train arrived after roughly thirty minutes and we went aboard. My travelling companion had already demolished two cans of beer by this point. There were plenty of free seats on the train, so we each took a seat next to the window, on different sides of the carriage.

It was about an hour into the journey when a skinhead-looking type, with prison tattoos on his face and hands, came walking down the isle of our carriage. The man, who had been released with me, and who was by now quite drunk, began to shout, 'easy mate, easy,' to this guy for no reason other than that he was being a drunken idiot. The skinhead took umbrage at this and unleashed a tirade of punches into his face. From his slumped position on the train seat, the man, who I had only met that morning, stretched out his arm and pointed at me. The skinhead looked at me and barked, 'You fucking want some too?' I answered that it was nothing to do with me, then he turned and apologized to the other train passengers for pummelling a man in their presence, and got off at the next stop. I couldn't believe it. I had only been out of jail a few hours and this cretin had almost got me into a fight. Luckily, it was just two more stops until I changed trains, so I sat their quietly and waited for my stop, then left without a word.

It was late afternoon when I arrived in Lewes, East Sussex, for my probation meeting. I had told the probation service, six months prior to my release that I would have no fixed address upon being let out. My reason for claiming 'no fixed abode' was that I didn't want to expose myself to the same people and influences that had landed me in prison in the first place. There were no hostels in the town I came from, so I assumed that this would be a good way to avoid going back there.

However, when I arrived for my first meeting the lady who was my probation officer had completely neglected to arrange anything. According to my licence conditions, I had to have a fixed address, so I needed to find somewhere fast; otherwise I would be recalled back into custody. My probation officer rang round every homeless shelter in Sussex. The only one that had a spare bed was in Crawley, which was almost thirty miles away.

I used the last of my money to get the train from Lewes to Crawley, and it wasn't until late at night that I finally got to my destination. What a first day out that had been. The homeless shelter where I was staying was a large Nissan hut with around ten rooms, and a large living room area that had a TV. The people there were all alcoholics, drug addicts, or sex-offenders. They absolutely stunk, and I had to share a room with four of them. The smell of stale urine and body odour gave me a headache after a while. I would have to go outside and get some fresh air every couple of hours. The food that we received was all expired cakes and pastries, donated by local supermarkets. I hated the homeless shelter from the moment I walked in there, and after a couple of weeks I had had enough, so I phoned my parents and asked them to come and get me. I would have rather been sent back to jail than spend another moment in that place with those flee-bitten, skanky bastards. I packed my bags, told the shelter staff I was leaving, and waited outside by the road for my step-father to come pick me up.

Not long after returning back home with my parents, I managed to get some work helping a friend build his house. It wasn't the best paying job, at twenty pounds a day, but for an ex-convict just out after a fairly long stretch, it was alright. Over the next three months I went to work and continued going to the gym. I went on long runs when I woke up in the morning down the local back lanes, and tried my best to abstain from drinking alcohol, although I did smoke cannabis a few times. I do enjoy a good bong to relax at the end of a hard day. I also tried my best to stay out of trouble, and to avoid certain people.

After a fairly long wait, and a lot of paperwork, I finally got my first passport. I was ready to go. I had already saved up some travelling money, checked out all the relevant information on the internet about joining the Legion, and printed off a couple of maps of where to go once I was in France. So, I said goodbye to my family and left.

Now that we are up to speed, I will continue where I left off (at Ashford international train station). I went inside, walked up to the desk, and checked in. It is a fairly new station at Ashford, which is a small town in Kent near the British end of the channel tunnel, in Folkstone. I had a two hour wait for my train to arrive, so I sat down to read. I try to always have a book handy on long journeys.

My new-looking Eurostar train arrived, and I embarked upon the first leg of my journey. I had never seen the Eurostar up close and it is an impressive feat of engineering, to say the least. It looks like an airplane that is stuck to the ground, which can lean like a motorcycle in the bends. As I travelled along towards the tunnel entrance in Folkstone, I thought about what France would be like, if I would understand any French, and what the plants and trees would be like. I had never really been anywhere you see. My family is quite poor, by British standards at least, so we never went on vacation. There wasn't even a holiday in the UK. All the same, I have always been interested in the world and did have ambitions to travel at some point. I am a lover of animals and nature in general, and had always dreamed of going to Africa to see all the big game.

After what seemed like only a few minutes, large metal fences appeared at the sides of the track, then, with a whoosh, the train entered the tunnel. After that it was thirty minutes of darkness, before the train emerged on the French side. From my inquiries online, I had decided that I would enlist at the recruitment centre in Lille, as it was the nearest. My plan was, to go to Lille, find the Legion recruitment centre, and voila. But alas, as with all plans, mine too would not survive contact with reality.

The Eurostar pulled up into the expansive Lille international train station, which looked more like an airport. It was so big that it took me a while just to get out of the place. When I stepped outside, I was struck by the distinctive French architecture, and the tall narrow buildings which lined the streets. Everything looked much older here than it did in Britain. I had printed out a map to the Legion recruitment centre, and it was just over a mile from the train station, next to the town's citadel.

I set off through the wide streets of Lille, stopping briefly to buy some pastries from a street vendor. I quickly arrived at the park where the citadel is located, but it was from this point that things started to go wrong for me. The park around the citadel in Lille is fairly large. It even has a zoo in it! It is also completely encircled by a river, so as to make it into an island. I thought that I could cut across the park and get to the recruitment centre faster. Well, after an hour of walking around this park, I was starting to recognize certain features of it, and concluded that I was going in a circle. I tried to ask a French family, who were walking past, if they could point me in the right direction, but I couldn't understand what they were saying. Their speech was too fast for me to keep up. I did, however, manage to discern 'pont noir (black bridge),' so off I went again, this time in search of a 'pont noir.'

After another half hour of circling the park, I came out of the trees and into a grassy area. There was a river about twenty meters in front of me. Great, I thought, if I follow the river then eventually I will find this black bridge. A short while later I saw it in the distance. An old iron bridge, with a centimetre thick layer of black paint all over it from the many years of successive coats that had been applied. As I looked away from the bridge and across the street. I saw it; there directly opposite me was Rue Princesse and the recruitment centre.

I took a few minutes to gather my courage, then went over to the gate and rang the bell. I waited, but there was no answer, so I rang again…and again. By the fourth time I was getting a little worried; what the hell was I going to do if they weren't in? It couldn't be closed, as it was only two o'clock in the Afternoon. Then I heard footsteps on the other side of the door, and a tall thin man in combat fatigues opened the gate. I tried to explain to him, in my broken French, that I wanted to join the Legion. He listened, then shook his head at me and said, 'Here we don't take legionnaires. You must go to Paris or Marseille,' then he closed the door. Shit! What am I going to do now, I thought. It is just as expensive here as in England and I don't have much money.

I walked back towards the train station mulling my situation over; Paris or Marseille...Paris or Marseille. I knew that if I went to Paris it would cost me more time in the long run, as all volunteers have to go to the main recruitment centre in Aubagne, near Marseille, anyway. I had to get into the Legion before my probation officer noticed that I was gone, and a warrant was issued for my arrest. I didn't want anything to come up when they checked for my name in any police databases, or whatever, during interview, so I decided that Marseille it was.

After getting lost again, and walking what seemed like ten miles, I finally got back to the train station. There were regular trains to Marseille, so there was no problem there. However, when I arrived at the ticket counter to pay, I discovered that it would cost me all but €30 of my money. Desperate times call for desperate measures; plus, I assumed that the Legion would accept me and then everything would be alright (I know better than to assume such things now).

Another wait for another train. When the train arrived, it had smart looking double-decker carriages. I had never seen a double-decker train before. I climbed aboard and went upstairs. The train started up and slowly screeched out of the station. France is a big country and as you travel across it, you start to notice the difference in the environment. The countryside outside of the window starts to look more arid, and more mountainous the further south you go. It took roughly four hours to get to Marseille. The trains in France travel at 200mph which is astonishing. Especially when compared to the UK, where you are lucky if they do half that, and we invented the damn things!

Arriving at St Charles station, in Marseille, I was struck by the grandeur of the place. It is a huge stone building with a commanding view straight down one of Marseille's main boulevards to the bottom of the hill, on which it sits in the centre of the city. I quickly found a taxi and asked the driver if €30 was enough to get me to Aubagne. He seemed happy enough and motioned me into his cab. The traffic in Marseille was terrible: The French have a style of driving, of which, I am not very fond. Soon we were clear of the city centre and on our way to Aubagne. This time I hoped there wouldn't be any problems, as Aubagne is the main recruitment centre. On the way there I stared out of the window at the silhouettes of the hills in the distance. Trying to imagine what the Foreign Legion would be like. I knew it couldn't be like that show on Channel 4.

The taxi pulled up at a large double gate just outside the small town of Aubagne. I gave the driver all my money and he pointed me in the direction of a door. At the front of the Première Régiment Étranger (1RE) there is a large entrance with a set of rising arm barriers. To the left of the barriers is a long building that runs the length of the entrance, which I assumed was the guardhouse. I walked up and approached the first window, a sergeant in a black kepi was in there. I tried to tell him what I wanted using my limited French, but this didn't appear to have the desired effect. The sergeant disappeared then emerged through a side door and I walked over to meet him. He asked if I was sure that I wanted to join the Legion, and if I had given it proper consideration. I replied that I was indeed sure. On hearing that, the sergeant asked for my passport, which I handed over promptly. He studied it for a moment then asked if I had any toiletries with me. 'Toiletries,' I repeated, 'no...I don't' (all the information I had looked at online said that all I needed was a passport, so that's all I brought with me). He then told me in no uncertain terms that, I must go get: a towel, toothbrush, toothpaste, razor, etc. When I had got all that, I could come back, but not tonight, because it was too late now. I would have to wait for tomorrow.

My heart sunk. What the hell am I going to do now, I pondered: I had no money, no change of clothes, no phone credit, and no idea how I was going to go about getting the things that I needed in order to be let in. I walked back to the small town of Aubagne. Aubagne is one of those single high street towns, not much, I imagine, ever happened around there, so I decided that I would have to go back to Marseille. It was late already, maybe

10:00pm, and there were no trains that I could bunk, so I would have to walk it. It was around twenty kilometres to Marseille and the only way to get there, that I knew, was along the motorway. There wasn't much point staying in Aubagne, and besides I had some time to kill.

I started off, walking along the edge of the motorway. It was very dark out there on the road and there wasn't much of a verge to walk on. I had remembered, from gazing out the window during the taxi ride that about half way through the journey the factories and industrial parks stopped and gave way to trees. So, I knew that when I started seeing factories, and alike, I would be roughly half way there. It's always good, on a long journey, to set up smaller goals. It makes the whole thing seem less daunting.

I had been walking for what felt like hours, and there was still no sign of any factories. Just the dark silhouettes of the hills in the distance. All of a sudden a French police van flew past me then slammed on its brakes. It skidded to a halt at the side of the road. The reverse lights flashed on and the driver was coming at me full speed in reverse. Unfortunately, for him, he failed to notice a large plastic sand filled barrier just off the back corner of his van, and smashed into it with a very loud bang, which sent it spinning along the road. Two policemen then got out of the car and called over at me. They appeared to be quite angry, but after establishing that I was a foreigner, they calmed down. One of the officers explained to me that it was illegal to walk next to the motorway in France. I was aware of this, in the UK we have the same law, but I find it is always better to nod politely, apologize, and play the ignorant fool in these situations. After telling me what I was doing wrong the policemen asked me where I was going. I told them that I was trying to get to Marseille. They decided that the best option was to put me in their van and drive me there themselves.

Not long after embarking with the two police officers, I saw the industrial estates come into view. I was only half way! Thank God I didn't have to walk it all, I thought. The policemen dropped me off somewhere around Hôpital de la Timone, in central Marseille. It was probably around one in the morning and

Marseille was dead. I had to find a place to sleep. I decided that the best option would be an abandoned car, and set out to search for one.

After an hour, or so, of roaming the streets without even the faintest whiff of an abandoned car, I came across a disused car lot. It had been fenced off, and the gate was chained and padlocked, but inside I could see a small portable office building and next to that an old car. Great, that's just what I need. I scaled the fence and went over to inspect the vehicle. It was up on blocks, so it definitely wasn't being used. I checked the door and to my relief, it was open. At this point I could have curled up and gone to sleep anywhere. I was exhausted. What a day, what a fucking day! Before I went to sleep, I made a promise to myself that tomorrow I would get all the stuff that the sergeant had asked for at any cost. I would not be defeated.

Morning broke over the south of France and I awoke from my slumber. Sleeping on chairs, be they car, bus, or airplane; always gives you an aching back in the morning. I sat up in the car and collected my thoughts; today is the day, either I get those things, or I walk back to England. I decided that the first thing I should do is check the office building next to the car. I went round the back and forced open one of the windows. Inside it was a right mess. It looked like there had been a group of homeless people living in there at some stage, it certainly smelt like there had been. I had to watch where I stepped because there was green fuzzy shit and screwed up newspaper all over the floor. I walked through into what appeared to be the kitchen. There was a lot of cupboards in this room and I set to work checking them. After fifteen minutes in this foul smelling building I had managed to find a towel and a face cloth. It wasn't much, but it was a start. Now I just needed to get my hands on all the toiletries that the sergeant had mentioned.

I walked the streets of Marseille weighing up my options. In the end I decided that there was nothing else for it: I would have to go into a shop and just steal the things that I needed. If you are thinking, wow, this guy just got out of jail and now he's planning to break the law, what an animal. Then I can understand that, but I really didn't give a rat's ass by this point. I had already broken the terms of my licence by leaving the UK and I was tired, fed up, and desperate. It made no difference what I did now. I would have my licence revoked and be sent back to jail for leaving the country anyway, so I was fucked every which way. At times life is like a poker game, and right now I was all in: Legion or bust.

I drifted through the city and ended up near the port, where I came across a mini-supermarket. Excellent, I thought, this place should have everything I need and they won't have the security that a supermarket has. I found a plastic bag to put the towels in and went over to the shop. Entering the store I saw an old man at the checkout and no security guard. I went down the aisles just taking what I wanted and slipping it into the bag with the towels. I decided to go hell for leather and just steal everything from one shop. I got: shampoo, soap, toothpaste, and a toothbrush; But there was one thing missing…a razor.

The razors were kept behind the counter. I left the shop with all my free goodies. No one had spotted me and I was on my way again; this time in search of razors. They were the only thing left to get. I check several other stores, but again, and again, I encountered the same problem. I would have try something far bolder than before. The next shop I went into was a small convenience store run by a middle aged Arab gentleman. I approached the counter in a friendly manner, squinted my eyes in the direction of the razors, and made shaving gestures with my hand. The store owner smiled, grabbed a packet of razors from the shelf behind him, and held them up smiling. I nodded my head enthusiastically and motioned for him to let me have a look. To my amazement he handed the razors to me. I examined them for a second, they were cheap single blade disposable razors, but I had no choice. I looked up into the shop keepers eyes. He smiled at me and I smiled at him and with that I bolted out the door. The last thing I can remember as I broke eye contact with the shopkeeper to run away, is seeing the smile drop from his face. That image will be with me until the day I die.

As I pounded the pavements of Marseille in my escape from the shopkeeper, a sudden rush of adrenaline came over me. I know it's wrong, but boy was that exhilarating to blatantly disregard the norms of society for a moment. After covering a couple of blocks I slowed down to a walk. Yes! I said to myself, I've fucking done it. I have everything that the sergeant had asked for. Now my only problem was how to get back to Aubagne. I didn't want to walk alongside the motorway for fear that if the cops stopped me this time, they might match me with the description of a thief in Marseille.

I went to a small regional train station called 'Gare de la Blancard,' which was not too far from where I had slept the previous night. I walked into the station, found the platform for Aubagne and sat down to wait for the train. As I was waiting something caught my eye. There was a plump dark skinned man, an employee of the train station, making sexual gestures at me. He was raising his eyebrows in suggestive manner, pointing to his office, and motioning for me to go inside. Hells fucking bells, I thought. I have been in some dangerous situations before, but the thought of being raped by a pervert at a train station in France terrified me. I gave that guy the middle finger and continued to wait for my train. I thought to myself, if that gay sexual predator comes over, just run, don't bother fighting him: It isn't worth the risk, just fucking run.

It wasn't long before the train pulled up at my platform. As the doors opened I discovered why, in France, bunking the train was not a viable option. Out from both ends of the train stepped two ticket inspectors and they were looking at everyone who got on. This wasn't going to work, so I got up and left. I decided that there was only one thing for it: I would have walk back along the motorway, but I decided that it was better to wait for night to fall before starting on my journey. I thought this would protect me somewhat from detection by the police, and I also had no water with me, so I had to be mindful of that too. I walked to the outskirts of Marseille and waited for it to get dark.

As the sun set and the dark of night covered the sky I set off again. Back on the road, walking along AutoRoute 50. I had been walking for not much more than an hour when another police van came past, and, sure enough, the brake lights came on and it pulled over. I walked up to the van and two officers got out. They shouted something at me French. I just repeated, 'English, English,' and pointed to myself. One of the officers asked me, what I was doing. I told him that I wanted to go to the Foreign Legion base in Aubagne. Legion! He exclaimed, oh good, good. Come with us, we will take you, it is dangerous out here on the AutoRoute. Yet again, I climbed aboard a French police van, but this time, I hoped, would be the last. As I sat there in the back of the police van, with the two officers chatting amongst themselves, I was thinking, would this really be it? After all that bullshit, would I finally get past the front door of the French Foreign Legion?

2: Engagé Volontaire

Nothing can stop the man with the right mental attitude from achieving his goal; nothing on earth can help the man with the wrong mental attitude.
Thomas Jefferson

The police van drew up right out front of the main gate. I hoped that I wouldn't be seen as I couldn't imagine it's every day that perspective legionnaires turn up with a police escort, then nor could I imagine that it was the first time either. I got out of the van, thanked the two officers for their kindness, then turned and walked up to the guard house. To my surprise, when I arrived at the window I discovered that it was a different sergeant on duty. I went through the same procedure as last time: The sergeant came out of the guard house, checked my passport as before, then looked up and asked me if I had the necessary things to clean myself with. 'Yes I do,' I replied with confidence, as I began opening my bag to show him. 'OK, follow me,' he said. The sergeant had a quick word with one of the other legionnaires in the guard house, and we were off.

We started walking along a narrow path, which wound its way through the regiment. After passing the mess hall, we cut across some grass and came out in front of a large, rectangular, concrete building. I followed the sergeant up a series of steps and into the building. On entering we took the corridor to our left and stopped outside the first door on our right. The sergeant entered, and a few minutes later came out to usher me inside.

Inside the office there sat a rather fat, red faced, and short tempered corporal-chef (corporal-chef/Cch is a rank between corporal and sergeant, it has no equivalent in the British or American armed forces. It is a rank given to corporals who are not deemed sergeant material, for reasons of: age, intelligence, physical fitness, etc. It is a dead end, career wise, as it's a rank you cannot be promoted from). I stood there in front of the corporal-chef's desk while he looked at my passport, which the sergeant from the gate had just handed to him (I wouldn't see that particular passport again until I left). He looked up at me and told me to sit down. He spoke some English, and as far as I could tell from his accent he was a German. Once I sat down the questioning began. He asked for my name, age, and address. Then he confirmed that I wanted to sign a five year contract, and that I fully appreciated what that entailed, for example: I would not be permitted to travel outside of France for five years, own a car, or live outside of base. He then asked if I would like to keep my name or take one from the Legion. 'From the Legion,' I replied. He warned me that I would not be able to contact anyone or reveal my true identity for the length of my contract if I went through with this. I told him that my mind was made up. I didn't worry about the not being able to contact people part anyway, how the fuck was the Legion going to know if I called my family from a payphone. Having spent the last two years in prison, where there are no mobile phones, meant that I had everyone's number stored in my brain. Not like now, I couldn't even tell you my own phone number. Besides, I had no choice but to join up; I was homeless, penniless, and hungry. The corporal-chef then looked at his computer and said, 'your new name is John Moo-rye.' John Moo-rye, I repeated. It must be a

French name, I thought, because that doesn't sound like an English surname.

Once the interview was out of the way, the corporal-chef informed me that tomorrow I would start the selection process. However, for tonight, as it was Sunday, I would sleep in a room just down the hall. He got up and showed me to the room I would be staying in. Inside there were a few people installed already: three Brazilians, who had travelled together; a Portuguese man; and a guy from Kazakhstan. The Brazilians and the Kazak were friendly enough. The Brazilians were all ex-military. I couldn't find out much about the Kazak, as he spoke no English, but he looked quite old to be starting something like this. He must have been close to the age limit of forty, and he didn't look in great shape either: His face was red with varicose veins, and his teeth were yellow from nicotine stains. I didn't speak with the Portuguese man, he only spoke with the Brazilians.

Later, at around 9:00pm, the corporal-chef came into the room to tell us to turn off the lights and go to bed. 'Tomorrow you will go over to the selection centre and then the real fun begins,' he said with a wicked smile. So we turned off the lights and bedded down. I was so happy to be in an actual bed, but my happiness soon turned into shock: It wasn't more than twenty minutes after we had turned the lights off, when I noticed that the Portuguese man was masterbating furiously in one of the top bunks. Oh my fucking god! What have I got myself into, I thought, what kind of person masterbates in a room full of strange men. I rolled over, faced the wall, and tried to ignore it. Fortunately, I was exhausted from the escapades of the last two days and fell asleep in minutes.

The next thing I knew, the lights came on and the German corporal-chef was standing in the doorway bellowing, 'Portugal, Portugal, wake up.' The Portuguese man awoke, sat up in his bed, and gave him one of those 'chocolate wouldn't melt' looks. The corporal-chef continued, 'you had a car crash in Portugal, you killed somebody, and you cannot stay here. The police are waiting for you at the gate.' The Portuguese guy tried to explain himself, but the corporal-chef cut him off, 'no talk, get your things and come with me.' He jumped down from his bed and gathered his things while the corporal-chef waited at the door, watching him like a hawk and making sure he didn't dawdle. After a few minutes his stuff was packed and he left, never to be seen or heard of again. I, for one, was grateful: That man was clearly deranged and should never be allowed near weapons. So there's the proof that the Legion has changed since its inception. If you are wanted by Europol, then you can't get out of it by going to France and joining the Foreign Legion. After this short episode we settled back down to sleep. This time without anyone jacking off.

The next morning, at six o'clock, the door flew open and the corporal-chef shouted, 'Reveille'. We all sprang out of bed and leapt to attention. He told us that we should get washed and dressed, because we would be heading over to the mess hall for breakfast.

The mess hall looked like your average school cafeteria. You entered one end, lined up, took a plastic tray, plate, cutlery, and a small glass, then you passed in front of the servers, who would dump a ladle of whatever was being served that day on your plate. Breakfast in the Legion is notoriously bad; it consisted of a mini baguette, a single serving of jam, and black coffee. You might get lucky and have a different flavour of jam every now and then, but essentially it's the same breakfast every day. While we were eating breakfast, I saw a legionnaire enter the mess hall wearing his guard uniform. He looked around forty years of age, and I noticed he only had one medal. I can remember thinking, wow, if this guy only has one medal, it must be really hard to get decorated here. How naïve I was. I now understand that Aubagne (1RE), is the administrative hub of the Legion. The legionnaires who are assigned to that regiment are either bureaucrats, sportsmen, or musicians. That is why the legionnaires there have nothing but the defence medal, which you receive for a years' service in the military. They have, most of them, never even been near combat and rarely, if ever, shot a gun. Because of this they are looked down on by the other regiments. They are described as, 'civilians who wear army boots.'

After a short breakfast we were told to go back to the room and get ready to move. The corporal-chef delighted in telling us that we had 'had it easy' up until that point, and that soon the real fun and games would begin. We went back to the room and began to pack. I didn't have much so I was finished in five minutes. While we waited to leave we discussed, as best we could not having a common language, what would happen over in the recruitment centre. No one knew very much except that we needed to complete some physical tests involving chin ups, rope climbing, and a multi-stage fitness test, commonly known as the 'beep test'. We were in the middle of discussing what to expect at the induction centre, when the door flew open, and the corporal-chef beckoned us to follow him.

It was only a short walk past the cafeteria to the induction centre. The centre was located in a large two story building, with a basketball court sized parade ground in front of it. Round the back there was a dusty yard with a few chin up poles and some fig trees littered around the edges, and a shabby looking concrete area down the bottom end. The corporal-chef took us around the side of the building to the basement. We were led into a large rectangular room which looked like a gym changing room. Inside there were rows of benches with coat pegs, and large metal pipes running all over the ceiling. At the far end was a desk, and behind that desk was a large doorway that led to a store room. There were already a load of people waiting in their underwear. We entered with the corporal-chef and he handed us over to the NCO (non-commissioned officer: In the Legion 'NCO' applies to all grades of sergeant, but for this book I will use the term to describe the grades of corporal and corporal-chef as well), who was sitting behind the desk. Before he left, the corporal-chef told us to find a peg and get undressed, then wait for further instruction. He informed us that we would be getting issued with clothes to wear while we underwent the induction process.

The other people in the room were, I discovered, from Paris. They had enlisted at fort de Nugent, and spent a week there working, before being loaded on the train and sent to Marseille. The

NCO started calling out names from a list. When my name was called I went up to the desk, took my kit, and returned to my place to get changed. The kit we had been issued consisted of: a pair of ball-hugging shorts that looked like they were straight out of the 70's, blue track suit, black t-shirt, black socks, black Y-fronts, and some Chinese sweatshop trainers. After we had all been issued with our new clothes, we were given a black travel bag and told to put all of our civilian clothes and other possessions inside. We would get it back after our basic training. Those who had money on them were told to hand it over to the NCO. He assured us that we would get it back, but for now we were forbidden to have any money until we received our first pay check.

Now that the kit had been given out we were told to go to the tarmacked area in front of the induction centre and await further instruction. The NCO began shouting, 'allez, allez, vite, vite.' The room broke into a frenzy and everyone was rushing, trying to get through the door at the same time. I did likewise and once I was outside, I followed all the other blue tracksuits up to the parade ground. The first people to arrive had already started to get into rows, and I took my place amongst them. I always tried to get in the middle or towards the back when we were lined up like this. As it turns out, it wasn't difficult to stay away from the front: The legion, like everywhere else, has its fair share of brown noses, who think they can butt-kiss their way through anything.

Another NCO, a well-built black guy who looked like the perfect stereotype of the tough old drill sergeant, came out of the building and began looking us over. He walked around the square formation, stopping every now and then to scream at someone and order them into press-up position. After he had given us the once over, he stood in front of us and began the same speech that he probably gave every new bunch of recruits here: 'we would be here for fifteen days, during those fifteen days we would undergo a series of tests, as well as a medical examination. If we failed any of these, we would be out the door that same day. If we passed, we would be issued with a red arm band to signify progression to the next stage. During the second week. We would be issued with the kit that would see us through instruction, and we would take up service in the regiment. On the final day there would be one last selection, only those who were picked would go to the 4ème Régiment Étranger (4RE), in Castelnaudary, South-west France, to start basic training. While here, we were to obey the Legion's every command and do nothing else besides.' After that he told us that, if we did as he said, then all would pass well. If anyone stepped out of line then they would be out the door before they knew it. There weren't any threats of violence at this stage. Just a lot of being yelled at and made to do press ups.

After he was finished talking, he told the four or five people who were still doing push-ups, to retake their places, then pointed to the far end of the building, and told us to go inside and line up. We walked single file into the corridor and lined up along the wall. The NCO entered the building through the main door and immediately started going berserk at two people, who he promptly made do press-ups. It quickly became apparent that the reason for this outburst was that he had seen them leaning against the wall. Lesson one: Don't lean against the wall.

Once all the drama had died down, I noticed that there was a legionnaire with a set of hair clippers waiting at the end of the corridor (no prizes for guessing what was coming next). We all went in, one by one, and got our hair cut by those god awful clippers, which did more plucking than cutting.

After the hair cut we were told to go outside and wait in the yard until further notice. The yard round the back was a complete dust bowl. There were roughly a hundred people standing around in groups chatting and trying to pass the time. All with the same shorts and t-shirts on. In the centre of the yard there was a set of chin up bars, which always had people hanging around, showing off their gymnastic abilities. In the top corner of the yard there was a couple of logs to sit on, but you would have to be very quick in order to get a place. The yard's perimeter fence had seen better days and was lying in a tangled mess in the dust. I guess the legion didn't care too much about people deserting at this point, because all you had to do was step over the small wall, where the fence should be, and walk down the side of the camp to the road.

While waiting in the yard I got talking to a French-Vietnamese guy who spoke excellent English. His name was Ho and he told me that he had been a nuclear engineer, and had spent the last twenty years working in Britain. Ho was thirty-eight years old, so quite close to the age limit of forty. I found it odd that someone in his position would want to join the Foreign Legion, but he explained to me that it was a dream of his from adolescence. He wanted to accomplish this ambition before he retired to running the hotel he owned in Peru. It was good to have someone to talk with, it helped pass the time.

A loud whistle sounded and everyone in the yard stampeded for the parade ground. It was lunchtime and everyone had to get lined up. Once we were nicely lined up on the parade ground one of the NCOs from the centre took us to eat. During the selection process, and all the way through basic training you are required to go to lunch accompanied by an NCO (normally a corporal). The accompanying NCO is supposed to take his meal last. When he is finished eating the time is up, you must clear up your plate then line up at the exit. This normally passes well, but you do get the odd person who has already stuffed his face on chocolate bars, doesn't take a meal, and gives you a minute and a half to eat your food, clear your tray, and be at the door waiting to go. There are definitely some in the Legion, as there must be in every army, who enjoy wielding their power just a bit too much. The armed forces, I would guess, is a very desirable occupation for psychopaths.

After lunch we returned to the induction centre. I and the other new arrivals were shown upstairs and put into dormitories. There were six people to a dorm. The rooms had terracotta tiled floors, hospital beds with steel lockers beside them, a single separate toilet/shower room, and windows at the far end which could be opened. The orange blankets that we used were those itchy asbestos wool things that looked like they dated from the First World War. Everything in the Legion is painted the same colour: The walls, beds, and armoires are all the same yellowy cream. The

NCO, who had brought us up, told us that it was 'siesta time.' In the Legion everyone sleeps for two hours at midday. I think this dates from the time when the Foreign Legion was based in Algeria and it was too hot to work at that time. I have never taken a nap during the day in my life, so I normally used the siesta time to get things done.

Soon after the door was closed, the other people in my room were snoring away. I sat up in my bed, which was next to the window, and stared out to the main road that ran past the camp to watch the cars go by. I was thinking how strange it was that the free democratic society of France and the totalitarian world of the Foreign Legion could exist side by side, separated by only a chain-link fence.

At 13:45 a whistle was blown to wake everyone up so that they had time to prepare for the assembly at 14:00. Being already awake, I was the first into the bathroom (the others were busy frantically making their beds). I had a quick wash then walked down to the assembly ground, before the second whistle blew. You didn't want to be late for assembly. On the parade ground one of the NCOs was waiting for the stragglers, who he would make do laps of the building.

After the assembly, some were dismissed to go wait round the back, in the yard. However, I and a bunch of others were told to go into the building and line up in the hallway again. This time it was to take an IQ test. The test was a pretty standard thing with simple problems to solve and patterns to find. The test was available in your mother tongue (at this stage the Legion doesn't expect you to understand any French).

After completing the test, the corporal, who was instructing us, explained what we would be going through over the next two weeks. He told us that we would be tested both mentally and physically, and that we would also be interview by an officer to determine if we had the right character to be a legionnaire. If we passed the tests we would be given a red arm band and asked to sign a provisional five year contract. Then over the course of the remaining week we would be issued with all our kit, and put to work in the regiment. He stressed that it was important that we followed orders and worked our hardest, because the smallest thing could make the difference between us staying and going.

After the classroom stuff was done, we were returned to the yard. I can't remember how it happened, but I met an Irish fellow there called 'Doyle.' He was the same age as me, but a little bit taller and heavier built. He had joined the Legion to be a soldier and fight in war. He was in great shape physically. We got chatting and instantly clicked. He had gone to Paris to sign up, and had been with me earlier in the classroom, so it looked like we would be going through selection together. That was good news as both of us had come alone.

I spent the next few days at Aubagne in the infirmary. Every time we entered the infirmary we were made to strip down to our underwear and stand in the hall waiting. Every scar and tattoo on your body was noted down in your file. A lot of people got shown the door at this stage in the selection process, especially during the dental inspection. They conducted a very thorough examination of us that even included full body x-rays. The last thing we had to do at the infirmary was be checked for any signs of sexually transmitted infections, or drug use.

The yard at Aubagne was constantly changing; people were always coming and going. There was a group of people, who hung around near the building in combat fatigues. They were new recruits in their second week of induction. They had on the coveted red arm band. They were called 'rouge' by the NCOs, who would constantly be messing with them. Barely ten minutes would go by without someone shouting 'rouge' at the top of their lungs, followed by a stampede of boots running for the parade ground to line up. This made it difficult to talk with any of them, but I did find out that there were three Brits among them: Greg, Utton, and Frazer. Greg was an ex-con like me, he was tall, balding on top, with a beer gut, and a baby face. Greg was completely doolally and gave zero fucks about everything. Utton was around six foot with narrow eyes, and he was a heavy smoker. He was a veteran of the RAF's airborne unit, and had seen action in several places and knew how to play the game better than most of the NCOs. Frazer was short and fat with a huge nose. He used to wash dishes in civilian life (which would prove handy in the Legion), and legend has it he used to walk to work with night vision goggles on.

They were all friendly enough, but they were almost finished with the induction process and would depart for Castelnaudary to begin basic training soon. So we never got to talk much, but Utton did give me one piece of advice. He told me to ask for 2REP when it came time to choose a regiment. 2REP was considered the Legion's foremost regiment, and it was where all three of them were going. Doyle and I made a pact that we would both ask for 2REP at the end of instruction, but that was still a long way off. We had barely gotten a toe in the door.

The next day I was taken over to what the Legion calls 'The Gestapo.' This is really just an administrative department that liaises with Europol and other law enforcement agencies, as well as dealing with the signing, and terminations, of contracts. Over at the gestapo you are taken into an office and interviewed by an NCO. The guy I sat down with was British. The conversation started pleasantly enough with him asking me if Bruce Forsyth was still alive. I confirmed that he was. He then made a joke about the Chinese and pointed to a picture on the wall behind me that looked like a blown up Charlie Hebdo cartoon. I stood there in front of his desk and he began asking me about my past life: If I had taken drugs and what sort; whether I had ever been in trouble with the law; what was my profession in civilian life; and why did I come to the Legion. I was upfront with him about my criminal record and told him that I had joined the Legion to change my life. He pressed for details and when he was satisfied that I was telling the truth, began to sum up my situation. I can't remember what it was, but I disagreed with something he had said and went to interject. That's when he snapped, 'shut your fucking mouth and listen when I am talking, OK.' I nodded and he continued with his speech for about fifteen minutes, during which I didn't say a word (I was later to see that he had written on my dossier 'good listener', which made me smile).

In the afternoon, after the mandatory siesta, everyone was lined up on the parade ground again. We were informed that straight after the assembly we would be doing the physical tests. These tests are not difficult and can be done by most able bodied young men. The physical requirements are: four chin ups; level seven on the beep test; and climbing a five meter rope with only your arms. Though these are not difficult, you must complete them in quick succession. It is therefore advisable to only expend about 75% of your maximum, on any one test. I for example was able to do around twenty-five chin ups, but on that day I stopped at ten. Others were not so forward thinking and went flat-out on everything. They had built up such an oxygen debt after the beep test that they could barely walk (some were even being sick in the bushes).

After these tests were done, another assembly was called and the NCO, who had conducted the tests, called out the names of those who had passed. My name was called and I followed the others round to the yard. We assembled on the concrete area at the bottom and waited for further instruction. Those who had failed were never seen again. They were marched to the basement, made to change into their civilian clothes, and ejected from the regiment.

A few minutes later a different NCO emerged from the building in sports gear. This guy's legs were rippling with muscle like those of a sprinter. I got the feeling we were about to burn a whole load of calories. He began chatting to one of the new recruits. It looked like they knew each other. Then, before I knew it, he shouted something and we were off. We ran out of the regiment and across the road to a large park with tree-lined paths that ran all the way around it. This guy ran like a gazelle, and so did that recruit he had been talking to. They must know each other from running competitions, or something like that, I thought. We ran round that park for well over an hour. Then we noticed that we were coming up to lap some of the people from our group. Stopping to look around we could clearly see people, in various stages of exhaustion, strewn all over the park. Less than twenty had managed to keep up, and I, for one, was glad that we stopped when we did. We turned around and jogged slowly through the park, collecting the stragglers. Once we had rounded everyone up, we formed a line and walked back to the regiment.

At the parade ground we were made to do a few sets of press-ups, before stretching. After the stretching, everyone was excused; except for a small group of people, which conspicuously contained the most notable slowpokes form the park: We wouldn't be seeing them again. We had lost quite a big chunk of our group during the physical tests, and the run in the park had shrunk it even further. However, It was hard to tell exactly how many, as people were constantly arriving too.

My clothes were now sweaty and dirty from running and washing clothes in Aubagne was not very convenient. During the first week of the selection process you only have one set of everything. Normally you wash your laundry in the sink before you go to bed and dry them overnight. But now I would have to put them on wet. However, this wasn't too bad as August in the south of France is fairly hot and after half an hour they were dry.

That night after diner we were lined up on the parade ground and I could see that we were about fifty in number. We had all finished the first week of induction and had completed the necessary tests and interviews. The NCO, who was in charge of the centre, emerged from the front door and began to call out names from a list. If he called your name, you were to leave the formation, go to him, and collect your red arm band. After that you went straight round to the yard at the back. After an anxious few minutes, my name was called, and I left the rows to go receive my red arm band.

Ten or fifteen people did not make the grade, they had done all the tests, but were not picked. After the tests of the first week are done, a committee made up of Officers and senior NCOs convenes. This group is charged with the duty of examining the dossiers of the prospective legionnaires, and making the final decision on who stays and who goes. People with offensive tattoos, criminal pasts, and ugly faces, are often weeded out at this stage. A German with 'born to kill' tattooed on his shoulder did not receive his arm band even though he had done well all the way through selection. It's worth bearing in mind that even if you pass all the tests, there is still no guarantee of getting in.

Everyone who passed was issued with two complete sets of combat fatigues and a pair of boots. Now, for the first time, I felt like I was in the army, and now that the first week was out of the way I could relax a little. Those who get through to week two, have a very high likelihood of going to Castelnaudary. Only injury or our own poor judgment could let us down now. I was delighted at passing selection and receiving my red arm band; especially considering what my situation was like only a week before. I was overdue for a little bit of success.

The weekend was now upon us, but don't think that in the Legion you get to rest. It may be a Catholic institution, but they desecrate the Sabbath more than that man caught picking up sticks in the book of numbers. The regiment works every day of the week. At the weekend people come to collect new recruits for menial labour. This is another reason why the 1RE is hated by the other regiments. Not only do they not do any military training, but they also don't even do their own cleaning up. It's all done by the new recruits, so if you want an easy life in the Legion you should ask to be sent to Aubagne after basic training.

I was taken off with Doyle, and three others. We had to clean one of the company buildings. The corporal who took us, and the other three guys were all Arabs (as are three-quarters of the legionnaires in Aubagne). They stayed on the ground floor together, so that they could talk and drink coffee in the club. I didn't mind this, because me and Doyle were sent to clean upstairs, and left alone. We went up to the first floor, and our plan was to work quickly from there to the top floor, then find somewhere to hide, and wait to be called.

On Monday, we were introduced to one of the most dreaded aspects of Legion life: Regimental service. The Foreign Legion doesn't employ any civilians, so all the work has to be done by legionnaires. This regimental service comprises of guard, mess duty, and being a general dogsbody in parts of the regiment where there are no low-ranked legionnaires to do the crappy jobs. There are other things, which I will get to, but for the most part service is either mounting guard or washing dishes (at Aubagne there is no guard duty for new recruits, as they haven't yet received weapons training). My first time doing service I was in the kitchen scrubbing pots and pans. The legionnaire cooks (all Chinese) were hard to understand; their French was terrible, but the work was simple enough and we could steal some extra food when they weren't looking. I have to admit that I fucking hated working in the kitchen. It's not what you think of when you consider joining up.

On Tuesday of my second week, I and one other recruit, a German, were taken to work at the vineyard and retirement home for legionnaires, in Puyloubier. This is where the Legion makes its official wine that is sold all over the world. We were taken there by a stocky Moroccan corporal. It was around five o'clock in the morning when we left. It is an hours' drive north from Aubagne to Puyloubier. When we got there the corporal set us to work loading wine bottles into trucks. The trucks were fairly big and this task lasted all morning. At lunchtime we went into the mess hall where all the old legionnaires were. It fucking stunk of stale piss in there. The German who came with me tried to help one of the old guys with something, and he went crazy. The retiree began shouting at, and hitting him. The corporal managed to step in quickly and calm it down. He warned us not to interact with the people staying at the home.

After lunch we went into the gift shop to wait out the midday break. The corporal began asking us some questions in a friendly manner. He inquired as to our nationalities. After hearing that I was British and the other guy was German he made some remark about the Second World War. I smiled to humour him, and in a flash his personality flipped. He lurched forward, grabbed me by the lapels, and pulled me towards him. With his face only a couple of inches from mine; he screamed at me, 'you never laugh at me, do you understand.' I stared back at him wandering what was going to happen next. What the fuck was going on with this guy, I

33

thought. This had to be the reason why he had been removed from the active regiments and tucked out of the way here. He was young, physically able, and not noticeably stupid, but he clearly had some anger issues, and thought that I had disrespected him. Then just like that he let me go and left.

In the afternoon the corporal set us to work cleaning and arranging things at the vineyard. At around 5:00pm, he returned to give us a baguette each, and informed us that we would be going back soon. We were to go wait for him in the car park at the entrance.

After a fairly long wait the corporal eventually arrived and drove us back to the regiment. Thank fuck that's over, I thought, as I sat in the back of the van on the way back to Aubagne. I hoped that I would never have to go back there and see that asshole ever again and those crazy, stinky, old men too.

The next day, following breakfast, I was told to wait by the parade ground with four others. A corporal-chef came in a small white van to collect us. He was Polish, and for a relief, after yesterday, seemed to be a normal human being. He took us to the house of a high-ranking officer. Our task was simple: weed the garden. I couldn't complain about being used as slave labour, because it was a beautiful sunny day and the garden was full of trees that provided plenty of shade. The officer's wife brought us out some water and snacks at midday and we had lunch in the garden beneath the thick leafy boughs. The afternoon rolled on and we finished our gardening duties. Then the corporal-chef arrived to take us back to the regiment, and I was back to waiting around that dusty old yard.

Every night during induction at Aubagne you have to clean and arrange your room for inspection. At around 9:00pm an NCO (normally a corporal-chef) comes round to inspect the rooms. Everyone must stand and wait at the foot of their bed. When he enters, the room snaps to attention. He then passes a quick inspection of us and the room, and once everything is to his satisfaction, stands near the door and bids us goodnight, before flipping the light switch. It's a funny part of Legion tradition that

34

you are required, on hearing this, to shout at the top of your lungs 'Bonne nuit caporal-chef.' It always seemed a bit silly to me, but whatever; when in Rome.

Thursday, we were told that we would be going to the store room to get our kit. The stores are on the opposite side of the regiment. Located somewhere behind the museum. The buildings over there looked really old. From their appearance I would guess that they used to be stables, because the bottom floor was full of large wooden doors that were big enough to drive a car through. From the outside they looked deserted; most of the windows were blacked out like they were expecting the Germans to come and blitz them at any moment. We entered one of the buildings via a huge stone doorway. Inside on the second floor there was a long thin room. Inside the long thin room was a counter running the length of one wall, with about five NCOs on the other side. On the floor near the opposite wall was a painted line. We had to walk in along the line, stop, turn right, and face the counter.

Once we were lined up, the measuring began, and we were called up one at a time to get measured. The instructions were quite simple: lift your arm, put your foot here, and try this on, etc. Many of the people in my group were from Eastern Europe and Russia, there were some Asians too. They got their first real taste of the Legion here. The NCOs doing the measuring had no time for anyone who didn't understand the orders, and they didn't mind giving you a shot to the body if you didn't do as they wanted quickly enough. Sometimes they would be walking up and down the line making sure you arranged your things neatly, and making you do press-ups if you didn't. Seeing a few people get screamed at and beasted made you pay attention to what was going on. There was no indiscriminate violence, or bullying (yet). If you ran all the time, understood French, and paid attention to detail. You didn't get hit. Simple as that.

I stood in that room all day, there is of course the obligatory siesta at midday, but apart from that I spent the whole day waiting for my name to be called out, then rushing to get my kit and bring it back as fast as possible. All the while being constantly harried by

the NCOs. Here is a list of some of the items that you get issued in
Aubagne:

- Leather driving gloves
- Great coat
- Green beret
- Poncho
- 2 Rucksacks (large & small)
- Fleece jacket
- 2 sets of Combat fatigues
- 2 sets of Guard uniform
- Metal gourd
- Cooking pots
- Gore-Tex jacket
- 2 pairs of Boots
- Green tracksuit
- Black leather shoes
- Running shoes
- Toiletry bag
- 2 sleeping bags (summer & winter)

There are probably a few things that I have missed out, but
that is most of it. This kit is really old and half of it never gets used
after basic training, but you have to keep it and guard it in mint
condition, because they expect it back when you leave. If it isn't,
you will be charged for it, and I would bet my arm that they adjust
for inflation.

I had managed to stand next to Doyle and Ho while we were
getting our kit, which was a life saver for me and Doyle, as Ho
could translate at lightning speed. Being able to talk also staved off
boredom, but we had to be careful. Since becoming rouge the
Legion had banned the use of our native languages. If you were
caught speaking your mother tongue, you would be punished.
About a quarter of the people in the Legion are French, and if I had
to guess, I would say that around fifty percent are from French
speaking countries, so for most this isn't a problem. However, if,
on the other hand, you hail from China it can be a daunting
experience.

On Friday we were taken back to the gestapo. This time it was
to sign a provisional five year contract. The contract would only
become valid if we completed basic training. It was while looking

at this contract, for the first time, that I noticed what my name was. It was 'Murray' not 'Moo-rye'. I was called John Murray. It wasn't a bad name as far as things went. You could tell that the people who worked at the naming department liked to have some fun at times. I have seen whilst in the legion a: D. Beckham; N. Bonaparte; C. Klein; M. Jackson; and many more.

That afternoon we were taken into a classroom to watch a video about basic training at the 4e Régiment Étranger, in Castelnaudary. The video was full of the usual stuff: people doing obstacle courses, hand to hand combat, abseiling, stretcher bearing, etc. When the video was over, the NCO in charge told us what to expect in Castelnaudary. I didn't understand much of it. However, I did manage to discern something about snow. Fortunately, Ho kindly filled me in about the rest. The NCO had apparently said that, on Monday the corporals who would take us through basic training, would arrive to accompany us on the train, and he had warned us to be on our best behaviour, as they would be looking for any excuse to beast us.

That Saturday I didn't get picked for any work and was left to loiter about in the yard. Somewhere next to the entrance of the induction centre there was a sailor's bag that was filled with sand. This ridiculously heavy bag was christened 'Bernadette' in honour of the wife of Jacques Chirac, France's former president who had stepped down earlier that year. During that weekend the steady hum of people chatting away in the yard was frequently punctuated by the tremendous roar of 'Bernadette' coming from one of the NCOs, then there would be a moment of silence as everyone looked to see what was going on. A few seconds later you would see some hapless individual come running round the corner with that bag on his shoulders. The NCOs would make you do laps of the building, and I will tell you, as someone who is reasonably fit, after three laps with that thing you were knackered. Plus it made you filthy, so you had to wash your clothes after you were done. They made people do this most days, but today was just a constant stream of guys running around the building. We all avoided contact with the NCOs as much as we could, but they would call improvised assemblies, make you line up round the front, and search for reasons to punish you. If they found nothing amiss, they would make everyone run round the building, or do press-ups, and the last to arrive, or the first to give up, would get to carry Bernadette.

During one of these improvised assemblies, after making us do press-ups, and run round the building a few times, one of the NCOs shouted out, 'we didn't ask you to come here. If you don't like it you can go home.' He then asked if there was anyone who wanted to leave, and told us to raise a hand if we felt like quitting. To my surprise, someone did raise their hand. I turned my head to see who it was, and the look on the guy's face said it all; he was pissed! I could actually hear him hyperventilating with rage from where I was stood, a few meters away. The NCO called him out and sent him to the office inside. I found it quite funny just how pissed off that guy had looked. He wasn't having any second thoughts. They had pushed him too far that day.

The next morning I was sent with a few others to work in the kitchen all day; and I mean all day. I went over before breakfast and didn't get back until almost eight o'clock in the evening. While I was over there, scrubbing baked on food off the cooking pots, I realized that I had caught a cold from one of the other lads. It's to be expected in those cramped conditions, but I really didn't need a cold now. Basic training was going to be hard enough and I knew they wouldn't let me rest just because I had a fever. I would just have to suck it up. It was around this time that I also realized that I was constipated. I was incredulous as to how almost two weeks' worth of food could fit inside me. Where was it all going?

That night, when I got back to the induction centre and the corporal-chef came round to turn off the lights, he reminded us that our corporals would be coming tomorrow, and warned us to be up and ready to leave earlier than usual, then he turned out the lights. We shouted goodnight to him and went to bed. I was very happy that this was my last night here in Aubagne. I couldn't wait to get to Castelnaudary and begin the real training.

The next morning, when reveille was sounded, I jumped out of bed and started arranging my things, then went and had a wash and shave. Those razors I had stolen in Marseille were already starting to get blunt, and somewhat uncomfortable to shave with. I had just come out of the toilet when the door flew open and slammed into the foot of the first bed. Like a shot this tall, wiry man with olive skin entered the room. 'Garde-à-vous,' he shouted, which is French for 'stand to attention.' We all leapt to the ends of our beds and stood there silently. It was one of the corporals from the 4RE; they were here.

Suddenly, his eye caught sight of something, and like a flash he crossed the room, grabbed the foot of the bed at the far end near the window, and lifted it high into the air. One of the men in our room had still been asleep! We had all been so preoccupied that no one noticed. The man, who was asleep in bed, rolled down to the head, and landed in a heap. The corporal then dropped the bed and no sooner had it come crashing down to the floor, than he was round the side next to him, unloading a flurry of punches into his face. He then dragged him from the bed, kicked him and made him do some press-ups. The corporal then addressed everyone in the room, 'wake up bitches, wake up, or I will wake you up, and you won't like it at all.' He then advised the man he had just rudely awoken, that he was to get his shit together and fast, and with those words he left. We had a bit of a chuckle about what had just happened. The face that a man makes, when he awakes to find his bed perpendicular to the floor and a stranger punching his face, is priceless. The guy who had been on the receiving end saw the funny side of it too.

We were told to line up on the parade ground with all of our kit. There were only two corporals (Cpl) there to collect us: Cpl Dino; who I had already met in my room, was from Brazil. He was a sniper from the 2e Régiment Étranger d'Infanterie (2REI). This is the Legion's largest regiment with 1230 men and ten companies. It is stationed at the old Roman city of Nîmes, in the south of France. It is second only to the parachute regiment in its reputation for harshness and discipline. Cpl Dino was a prime example of that.

The other Corporal: Cpl Kamel; was also from Nîmes. He was an Algerian. He was slightly younger than Dino, in his mid-twenties, and was also rather stern looking. They both were heavy smokers, as were many in the Legion. I would estimate that over half of all legionnaires smoke.

Once everyone was out on the parade ground, we were taken to breakfast, which lasted all of two minutes. Then it was back to the parade ground to await the bus that would take us to Marseille. While we were waiting for the bus to get ready we were set to work cleaning every inch of the rooms we had just vacated. They had been cleaned three times daily and scrubbed the night before, and were therefore not dirty to start with. That though was not the reason for the order. They just needed something to occupy us while we waited, and it gave them time for a coffee.

After a couple of failed reviews, we finally received the approval of the NCOs and were told to go wait in a bare room at the side of the induction centre. In there we were made to line up in rows. An old green bus pulled up outside; It looked like it came straight out of the sixties and was similar in appearance to a VW camper van. One of the NCOs from Aubagne came and stood in front of us and began to speak, 'Ok, now listen to me. When I call your name, you stand to attention, state that you are present, wait for me to check you off the list, then grab your things, and get on the bus. Do you understand?' 'Oui,' we replied. He began to call out the names. After a dozen or so names had been called, I heard mine and went to get on the bus. Doyle arrived shortly after and sat next to me. Ho was there too. I guess that in spite of his age, a guy with those kinds of qualifications doesn't turn up every day. To my surprise the old Kazak was there also, but only one of the Brazilians, who I had met that first night had made it. A group of people were still standing there in the room when the two corporals boarded and told the driver to depart. For whatever reason, the Legion didn't want those people. They had passed all the tests and done everything that we had done. Maybe someone had reported them as lazy or deceitful. Maybe there weren't enough places. Again, there is no guarantee of success when joining the Legion.

Sure one can stack the odds in one's favour by having youth or experience on one's side, but there will always be that element of luck in there; it's inescapable.

The bus lurched off and we made our way slowly down to the gate. Then we were on our way to St Charles train station in Marseille. As we travelled along the, by now familiar, Auto Route 50 between Aubagne and Marseille. I was astonished at the contrast between how I felt at that moment, full of hope, anticipation, excitement, and fear; to how I was the last time I came along this road. After that Sergeant had turned me away for not having brought toiletries with me. I had been in a very low place then, my mind was in panic mode, racing to try and come up with a solution to my problems. It was also the first time I had travelled along this road in the daylight. I could clearly see the tall hills that had just been dark silhouettes before.

It wasn't long until traffic started getting heavier, then, I was back in Marseille. We pulled up next to La Gare de Marseille Saint Charles, and unloaded the bus as fast as we could, then stood in formation and waited for our next order. Looking around I would guess that we now numbered somewhere between twenty and twenty-five in total. Cpl Dino told us to stand at ease. We were allowed to smoke, but we weren't to sit down, or to stray too far from the bags. Marseille, he said, was full of thieves, so we should be vigilant. Cpl Kamel was a francophone, so he went to get our tickets.

He returned a short while later. Called an assembly and handed the tickets out. We were under strict instructions not to lose them, or there would be hell to pay at Castelnaudary. We were in combat fatigues and beret for this journey. I was feeling exhausted from the cold that I had caught and was happy for some time to rest on the train.

The journey would take around eight hours in total. In the carriage rumours of the brutality we would encounter at the other end abounded. There was talk of hundred kilometre kepi marches, sleepless nights spent scrubbing toilets, and of scavenging food from the bins. The train journey took a rather scenic route. The tracks passed by the magnificent wetlands of Le Parc naturel régional de Carmague; where I saw a huge flock of flamingos wading. That was the first time I had seen flamingos in the wild. I wasn't aware they inhabited Europe. Then the train followed the coast along past Montpellier and Béziers, before taking a right at Narbonne and heading inland towards Castelnaudary. The Aude was the department we were heading for. It is named after the River Aude, which runs all the way from its source, the aptly named 'Lac d'Aude,' two kilometres up in the Pyrenees, to its mouth at Narbonne. The department is situated between the Pyrenees and the Mediterranean, and is bordered to the West by Toulouse.

Eventually our train pulled up to a station, as it had many a time on this journey, except that this time the sign read 'Castelnaudary.' We had arrived. We were rushed off the train and made to line up on the platform. The two corporals made sure our uniforms were correct before we set off. The buses that arrived this time were almost brand new. It was a shame that we would only be in them for five minutes.

Castelnaudary (Arrius' new castle) is a quiet market town. It is the capital of the Lauragais region, in the south west of France, close to the border with Spain. It covers nearly fifty thousand square kilometres and has roughly eleven thousand inhabitants. Its biggest claim to fame is the invention of cassoulet, a fancy-pants version of baked-beans and sausages. The town itself is medieval looking, with plenty of old stone buildings. The town's most prominent feature is the canal du midi, built in the 1700's, which runs straight through the middle of it. This one hundred and fifty mile long canal has its 'Grand Basin' in the centre of town. The Grand Basin is a breathtakingly beautiful and peaceful place, lined with trees and benches. The basin itself covers an area of several hectares, and there is a single red brick island in the middle, which was made to moor boats, but is now primarily a refuge for waterfowl.

Our bus left the town centre, went over a round-a-bout, and a few minutes later the regiment came into sight. It is a reasonably large camp there at Castelnaudary. The camp has been home to the legion since the 1970's. The layout is simple enough; there is a huge parade ground in the centre, and at each corner is an L-shaped building. These are where the three companies of new recruits are lodged. At the back of the regiment, opposite the gate, is the colonel's building. To the right of the central area are another four L-shaped buildings where the specialized training courses that the Legion conducts, are carried out. Past them is the officer's mess, which is fenced off from the rest of the regiment, and, for some reason has a load of tame fallow deer in its grounds. To the left of the central area is the rank and file's mess hall. In the same building as the mess hall are the foyer (Legion shop), and the corporal-chef's club. Behind that are the running track and gym, and behind the gym is the technical zone (where they keep all the vehicles and machinery). Finally, stretching from the technical zone all the way to the canal du midi at the far edge of the regiment is the driving centre, where all legionnaires come to do their tests.

It's rather eerie as you enter the regiment. There is not a person to be seen, it appears dead like a ghost town, but immaculately clean. The bus entered the main gate, turned left and parked outside the first building we came to. We got off and lined up with our bags. Once we were in formation, Cpl Dino told us not to move a muscle. He then went inside the building while Cpl Kamel watched over us. My new army boots hurt like crazy. They were those traditional tough leather boots with hard rubber soles. They were basically a direct copy of the American WW2 boots (hence the nickname: 'Rangers'). They made standing in place for more than ten minutes rather painful; the bottoms of my feet were used to soft cushy trainers. Walking on the other hand would cause the leather to fold inwards and jab into your ankle with every step. The other guys in my platoon tried everything to make them more comfortable. Soaking them in water over night, beating them with stones, and smothering them in boot polish, but nothing worked. You just had to get used to it. Eventually you would wear them in, and they would take the form of your foot, but the first couple of months were torture.

A tall slender man with blond hair stepped out of the company building and came towards us. 'Garde-à-vous,' shouted one of the corporals. We all snapped to attention. The tall man was our second in command, a Sergeant-chef (Sch: pronounced 'chef'), which is equivalent to the rank of staff sergeant in British/American forces. His name was Sch Popadynets, he was Ukrainian and he looked it with his blond hair and blue eyes. He was from the parachute regiment (2REP). I think he had recently injured his back (not uncommon for paratroopers), and was on his way out of the Legion. He told us we were to answer him at all times with 'Oui Chef'. He then tested our comprehension, and asked if we had understood what he had just said. 'Oui Chef,' we thundered back at him in unison. He smiled, then told the corporals to move everyone into one of the classrooms on the ground floor.

We went into the classroom, stacked our bags neatly in one corner, and sat down at the desks in silence. While waiting we were joined by two more corporals, making four in total. The first: Corporal Novak, was a Pole and a monster of a man. He was well over six foot and roughly a hundred and twenty kilograms in weight (he had rolls of fat on the back of his neck). His face bore resemblance to that of a pig's, and was of a similar complexion too. He was immensely strong, but useless at everything else. That didn't matter to him though, as he hailed from the 1er Régiment Étranger de Cavalerie (1REC) stationed in Orange. He just sat on his butt and drove all day. The last corporal was, Cpl Pillqu. He was from Peru, and was a small man; standing at around five and a half feet tall. He was from the 1st 1er Régiment Étranger de Génie (1REG), stationed at Laudun, in southern France. He was the most relaxed of our corporals, but only so long as you did what you were told.

I was just settling into the classroom when someone shouted 'Garde-à-vous' again, and at that moment a five foot nothing, Portuguese, fire-breathing dragon, by the name of Sgt Dsouza, entered the classroom. He looked similar to the rapper Marshall

Mathers (Eminem). He was a jumpmaster from the parachute regiment, and he embodied its harsh discipline to a T. He wasted no time in explaining exactly what he expected of us, and what would happen if we failed to live up to his expectations: We were not in Kansas anymore. Sergeant Dsouza then gave us a demonstration of what was in store for us. He pointed at a random recruit and told him to stand up and present himself. The legionnaire got up and said some stuff in French, which he approved of. He then asked him if he knew his service number. This time the legionnaire did not respond so readily. The sergeant approached and asked again, and again there was no reply. The sergeant punched him in the chest, the thud from which could be heard from across the classroom. He then screamed 'Pompe' at him ('Pompe' is the French word for push-ups). Sgt Dsouza then instructed us as to where we could find our service number. He told us that it was very important for a soldier to remember this. Then before he could go any further, one of the corporals said something to him, and it was 'Garde-à-vous' again. This time a middle aged man, with greying hair, entered the classroom, and the sergeant handed the room over to him. His name was Adjutant O'Malley and we were to address him as 'Mon Adjutant' (It's a strange thing about the French army that you have to address all the officers, plus adjutant (warrant officer) and adjutant chef (senior warrant officer) as 'Mon'. So it's: my captain; and my warrant officer).

The adjutant (Adj) told us that he had served in the Legion for sixteen years. He was from the third company of the parachute regiment, which specialized in amphibious warfare. He had recently injured his back (another one) and was on his way back to civilian life. He would be our 'Chef de section' (platoon commander) for the course of our instruction. He told us that this first week would be relatively relaxed compared to what was to come. This was because we would have to wait for another group to come from Aubagne, and take our numbers up to around fifty. While we waited we would learn a bit of French, marching, singing, and how to iron (the basics of Legion life). We would also not escape the dreaded service either.

When the next group arrived to complete our platoon, we would go to somewhere the Legion called 'the farm.' At the farm we would do the bulk of our basic training. The work load would start off impossible and quickly get worse, and we were to receive very little food and sleep. The culmination of our month on the farm would be the infamous kepi march, after which we would receive the white kepi and officially become legionnaires. After the farm we would be going to the Pyrenees for a week long adventure holiday. The remaining three months would be spent here in the main camp interspersed with trips to various training grounds. At the end of the four months we would be tested on everything that we had been taught. Those who came top would be able to choose which regiment they went to. Those who finished last would go where they were sent.

After his talk the adjutant ordered that everyone take their belongings upstairs and get set up in the rooms. He dismissed the classroom; except that was for me, Doyle, and one other chap. He called us over to sit in front of him and began to speak to us in English. He told us that he was from Ireland (in case we hadn't already guessed from his surname). He then told us that Anglophones were a minority in the Legion. There were no more than a hundred people from English speaking countries serving in all the different regiments. He then proceeded to offer us some advice. He told us to learn to speak French as fast as we could, because that was the single thing that would help us the most; to memorize everything that was in the field manuals that we would get; and to obey all the orders, and never answer back. Then finally he asked us which regiment we were thinking of going to. We all gave the same answer: 2REP. The Adjutant smiled, said good, and then told us that this was the last time that he would speak English with us, and that we were never to speak English to him again.

After the classroom I headed upstairs to go get installed in my room. The rooms were more of the same terracotta tiles and cream walls like they had been in Aubagne. There were five people to a room. Some of the rooms had an extra bed at the far end for the corporal to sleep in. My room didn't have a corporal in it, but Doyle's did. There was also a balcony at the back of each room and a toilet with four sinks and a single shower cubicle. The toilets were all the way down the opposite end of the corridor near the office, which led to the sinks being used as urinals during the night. The balcony in my room faced the parade ground. We were told that we had to remove all our laundry before the assemblies that took place each morning. If one of the officers was to look up and spot someone's dirty briefs flapping in the wind, it would not be good.

In my room were four people, including me: first off there was Maachi, a Moroccan, who was an excellent long distance runner. He was twenty years old and incredibly thin. He didn't have an ounce of fat on him. He was the guy that the NCO was chatting to in Aubagne. He was returning to Aubagne after instruction to join their running team. His older brother was already there and had won many trophies for the Legion, but in order for Maachi to join officially, he would have to do basic instruction, and become a legionnaire. He had no interest at all in the military and got frustrated with the orders, but Maachi was basically untouchable. It was clear that the NCOs had been told to leave him alone. Sometimes he would downright refuse an order, and nothing was said. He just got dismissed. I liked Maachi and got on well with him. We both shared a love for drinking tea, but I was astonished when I found out that he had scored zero on the IQ test, I didn't think that was possible (I discovered that when I had to clean the office one day and I looked through the files in there).

Then there was, Mejri, a Tunisian. He was a bit older, in his mid-twenties, and he bore a striking resemblance to Mehdi Hassan, the journalist. Also like Mehdi Hassan, he was a pompous, pseudo-intellectual arsehead at times. Mejri had also joined with the intention of going to Aubagne, but in his case it was to work for 'La Deuxième Bureau' (B2), which handles administration (the Gestapo is a part of B2. The name comes from: 'Deuxième Bureau de l'État-major général', which was France's external military intelligence agency from 1871 to 1940. This agency had a hand in the notorious 'Dreyfus affair' 1894 – 1906). Unlike Maachi, Mejri did not have immunity from punishment. He could speak English fairly well, and was friendly, but I could never understand why someone would join the Legion to work in an office, but someone's got to do it I suppose, and rather him than me.

Lastly there was Banica, a Romanian. He was small and a bit chubby looking. He spoke near perfect English and had a good sense of humour. Banica loved to wind people up and play practical jokes. He wanted to go to 2REP, like me, but had joined partly for financial reasons. His plan was to save up as much money as he could in five years, then go back to Romania and start a business. At the REP you get paid more than at the other regiments; you get what's called a jump bonus, which amounts to around €600 extra a month.

The sound of the whistle for dinner echoed through the corridors of our building. We had to go down and assemble in the carpark area. To the side of the carpark was a grassy area with two chin up bars and a rope. Before you can eat in the Legion you must do what is referred to as an 'aperitif.' This is basically a ten minute workout that mainly comprises of chin-ups, sit-ups, push-ups, and rope climbs. We did a few sets of each, then assembled in the carpark again. Normally, when you go for your meal in the Legion, you must go there marching and singing. However, we didn't know any marching songs yet so we were exempted for the moment.

When we got to the mess hall, I was shocked to see that there was no queue. Everyone else had eaten and gone. The mess hall here was much larger than the one at Aubagne. After eating we exited out of the fire door and walked down the steps at the side of the building. My company building was opposite the mess so we didn't have to march far at all. The first company was the furthest away from the mess. Those poor bastards must have had to sing two or three songs when they went for their meals.

The third Company of volunteers (3CEV), was my company. The company colour was yellow and the company symbol was a vintage, six wheeled, Dodge Power Wagon. There were three companies of volunteers at the Quatrième Régiment Étranger in total. The 1CEV was blue and the 2CEV was red. The second Company looked the worst out of the three. With their green track suit bottoms and red jumper it looked like permanent Christmas time over there. It didn't help matters that the singing was reminiscent of Christmas carols either (Incidentally red and green are also the official colours of the Legion). Each company had three platoons of forty to fifty men. To signify which company you belong to, you have to wear a yellow band that attaches to your shoulder when you are in combat gear. If you are in sports gear then your jumper, t-shirt, or vest, would correspond to your company colour.

The next day after breakfast we went for our first run as a group. There is a gate at the back of the regiment that opens out onto the Canal du Midi. The canal has a path on either side and trees line the banks making it a very pleasant place to go jogging. I was still feeling under the weather from my cold, and had started getting that dreadful throbbing in my ear that signals an infection, so I was glad that the run wasn't very long.

After the short run we went over to the building opposite us to receive the rest of our kit. The kit we got this time was new and half decent. It was mostly things you needed for use out in the field. We got a: basha, compass, gas cooker, head-torch, pen knife (with fork and spoon attachments), and a lighter. We also received two little books: the 'Carnet de Combat,' which was a small white book that contained everything you needed to know about the Foreign Legion. It had a section on the history of the Foreign Legion, and another about the battle of Camerone. This book contained all the standard operating procedures that the Legion used, with handy acronyms to remember them by, and there was also a section on all the different regiments that we could choose from at the end of instruction. The other book was 'Chants de la Légion Etrangère.' It was the same size as the other book, but with a black cover and it was filled with all the songs that the Foreign Legion sung. I found the front cover of this book very amusing.

There was an image of a Legionnaire singing very enthusiastically. His mouth was open in a perfect circle and let's just say many phallic references were made. I would prank my comrades by drawing cartoon penises entering, or ejaculating, into this man's mouth, which they would then have to work hard effacing. When I pranked Doyle's book he dealt with the problem by simply tearing off the cover along with my artwork and chucking it in the bin. We also got a bi-lingual dictionary, in everyone's mother tongue, which was much needed. I had, after two weeks, just started to understand spoken French. It wasn't great, but I could get the gist of what was being said, which was more than could be said for the majority of the other foreigners, who had trouble understanding the most basic of instructions.

I had started to get to know the others in my platoon and I had found out that the other person in the room with me and Doyle, when the adjutant had spoken to us, was from Finland. He spoke perfect English (not uncommon for Finnish people). His name was Raikkonen, and he was a strong, stocky man. In civilian life he had been involved with a motorcycle club. He joined the Legion to see action in war, and 'kill some motherfuckers.' He was friends with a Ukrainian, who also spoke English, called Chekov. Doyle and I linked up with them and formed a small Anglophone clique. However, the two main cliques that were forming in our platoon were the French, and the Russians. There was also a small gang of Romanians.

After receiving our new kit, and packing it away in our bags. We were told to go upstairs and line up against the wall. We were taken into the foyer, but we weren't allowed to purchase anything (we had no money anyway). Instead, we would be measured for our kepis and pick up all the small metal badges that are required for your dress uniform. We would not be allowed more than a brief touch of our kepis for the moment. That would have to wait until after the kepi march: We were still lowly engagés volontaires at this point.

After we had got our kit back to the rooms, someone called an assembly in the corridor and we lined up to await the news. It was

Sch Popadynets who had called us. He wanted to impress on us the importance of locking our stuff away in the armoires that we had been provided with. If someone were to lose something they might look to steal a replacement, so while we waited for lunch we had to put our names on everything we owned. We even put folded bits of paper with our names on them in our biros. He wasn't wrong and it didn't take long for things to start going missing.

That afternoon we were taken to the classroom to learn our first song. After being made to do an uncountable number of press-ups because of our lack of melody, and being punched for not knowing the words. We were deemed good enough to go outside and try it on the march. This didn't work out too well, and we quickly became familiar with the infamous 'marche canard.' The duck walk sent lactic acid surging into your thighs and the burn soon becomes unbearable. Cpl Novac, who took us marching, delighted in our suffering, but even he got tired and gave up eventually. The singing would have to wait.

The next morning we didn't go running instead we were taken to the running track behind the mess hall. We would be doing the Cooper test (the Cooper test measures cardiovascular fitness. You are given twelve minutes to do as many laps of a 400 meter running track as you can). That day I clocked up 3,300 meters, which is not bad considering I was nursing a cold. Maachi, the thunderbolt, lapped me twice, so he must have got at least 4,100 meters, which is insanely good. I could see why the Legion wanted him on their sports team, and he was a long distance runner so he could keep that pace up for a long time. After the cooper test we did the rope and chin-up test again, before heading back to our rooms.

Once everyone was showered and in combat fatigues, we went to the classroom for our first French lesson. This lesson was to be given by Sgt Dsouza. He taught us the names of some items that we would be dealing with day to day. He would hold up a pair of boots, for example, and say the name in French. We would then repeat it back three times. After that he would pick people at random and ask them to repeat the word again. If they couldn't answer, it was press-ups. If they couldn't answer after the press-ups, it was a punch; followed by press-ups. This went well at first with most people getting it right on their first or second try. Until he pointed at Nemet. Nemet was from Hungary, and as far as I am aware he used to be a farm hand in civilian life. He was in his mid-thirties and couldn't speak a word of any language except Hungarian. After the fifth or sixth time of screaming, hitting, and kicking the hell out of him the sergeant realized it was no use terrorizing Nemet and he dismissed him back to his place, with the caveat that he should seriously consider learning some French or he would become an Olympian at doing press-ups.

At that moment blood started to poor from my ear onto my vest. Before I could say anything the whole class was staring at me. The sergeant, in English, asked me, 'what the fuck was up with my ear.' 'I think it's infected,' I replied. 'Fucking hell Jonny!' he exclaimed, 'that's not good.' He then got one of the French speakers to take me over to the infirmary straight away.

Walking over to the hospital was difficult, I was on the verge of collapsing; because I hadn't had time to rest, my immune system had been over powered by the infection and I was in a bad way. I got to the infirmary and went straight in to see the doctor. He took my temperature and seeing that it was in excess of forty degrees-Celsius, ordered that I stay there for the time being. He prescribed me a course of antibiotics and put met on a IV-drip, then I was sent upstairs, given some strong sleeping pills, and left in the ward to sleep.

After four days of near continuous sleep I was feeling much better. It was nice not to wake up more tired than I had gone to sleep for a change. Sch Popadynets came over to visit me at lunchtime to ask how I was feeling, and see if I was ready to re-join the group. I told him that I felt fully rested and ready to rejoin the platoon. He smiled at me and said, 'OK I'll go talk to the doctor about you.' I liked Sch Popadynets, he was decent human being, and it felt like he actually cared about the welfare of the people under his command. He would often have a word with the sergeants, and corporals, if he thought the beasting was getting a bit out of hand. I also got the impression that he didn't think that he had anything to prove by being loud or aggressive, and I admired that.

That afternoon I went to see the doctor who gave me the once over. He told me that everything was in order, and I was free to go. My little vacation in the infirmary was over. I had gotten rid of my cold and the infection, and I had also managed to take my first shit in nearly three weeks. I think my body was just reacting to the change in my environment and trying to keep hold of all the energy it could.

I returned to my platoon just after the new group from Aubagne had arrived. We now numbered somewhere around fifty. There were a few new NCOs too: Sgt Flaubert, a tiny Frenchman, who came from 2REI; and Cch Jacques Laplace, who was the strangest son of a bitch you could ever hope to meet. Everything about him was odd, starting with his name, because it was clear that he was Polish. He was a bit like Jack Nicholson's character in The Shining crossed with Hannibal Lecter. He even spoke in a strange manner. There was also another corporal; Cpl Sonking, who was also from the infantry regiment at Nîmes. He was a medic and would not be too involved with the actual instruction. If one of the other corporals was occupied, he would fill in, but normally he just assisted the NCOs, and taught us the occasional bit of first aid. He was a French-African, in his mid-twenties, fairly short, with a bit of a pot belly, and was fairly laid back.

By being ill for a week I had missed out on a fair bit. How to iron the shirt for guard and how to do the double time march, for example. My comrades had also been taught a couple of songs from that little black book to sing. Now, every time we went to the mess hall, would mean marching and singing, and not knowing the song was a punishable offence. Unfortunately for me there was no time to catch up, as we had to prepare ourselves for departure. We had to get all the food and equipment for our month long stay at the farm. I and nine others jumped in the back of an army truck with Cpl Kamel and drove to the mess. We filled the truck to the brim with huge cans and cartons of food, then we got another truck and half-filled that too. After the food we went to get the weapons and ammunition. Everyone was ordered to remember their rifle number and we were warned that losing or damaging the gun, or any part of it, would result in a beasting so severe and long that we would have no choice, but to desert.

That night a guard was mounted around the trucks. All, except the guard, were set to work cleaning everything on our floor of the building. There was a list of things that were to be taken to the farm, I copied the list, then translated it with my dictionary. It was important not to miss anything from the list, because that would land you in serious trouble. All the rest of our belongings were to be locked away in our armoires.

Once we had cleaned the rooms and packed our rucksacks into the trucks, I could at last ask about what was going to happen at the farm. No one knew very much at all. The Legion, whenever possible, gives you the minimum amount of information they can, and we were all completely in the dark about the farm. That didn't stop the rumours though, which seemed to get more extravagant every time they were told. The kepi march, for example, got longer every time it was mentioned, and the description of what damage it would wreak on your feet got more graphic; boots that poured with blood when taken off, and soles of feet that had no skin on them. There was also now talk of how much the rucksacks would weigh, but we still had one last night in the camp before we had to deal with any of that. That night we talked until ten o'clock, when the lights went out.

I woke up to do my guard duty in the small hours of the morning. I enjoy the night-time very much, I find the quiet, and the darkness, very serene. It's also the only time that you are free from the NCOs. I was thinking about what the training at the farm would be like, but, in the end, I decided not to worry too much about it, I would see what it was like soon enough. Besides, plenty of people had been through it before me, so it couldn't be that bad.

The next morning I woke at six o'clock as usual. Every Monday in the Legion there is an extra-long assembly for all the regiment. The colonel reads out a twenty minute speech (that no one gives a damn about) and then the whole regiment goes on a long run together to start the week off. However, we did not join the run that day. Instead our company captain made us assemble behind our building and offered us some words of encouragement for the journey that lay ahead. At that point I didn't understand much, but it was something along the lines of: '*You are not children anymore. The Legion is your home now and the men around you are your family. During the next month you will live like those who went before you. You will be tested to the limits of your endurance. It is for your own good that we do this. We will turn you from civilians into legionnaires. I wish you all good luck.*' After those words from the captain, Cpl Novak gave us his version, just to make sure we understood, '*No more PlayStation, no more pizza, no more mamma and papa; bitches.*' When the assembly was over, we were herded onto the trucks and, once a final count was made, the engines started and we were off.

The town of Castelnaudary and the surrounding area is pretty flat, but just twenty kilometres away is where the Pyrenees begin. Our farm 'La Ferme de Raissac' was situated about twenty-five kilometres south of Castelnaudary, in the commune of Lafage. Our old Renault GBC 180 truck sped (I use the term loosely) out of Castelnaudary along one of its perfectly straight, roman roads. After a while the foothills appeared in the distance. The truck slowed to a crawl as we wound our way up the steep, narrow road that led to our new home. After the climb we carried on straight for a while, then the truck began to slow. We turned off the main road and drove down a country lane, then the truck turned again. This time we were entering a driveway. We travelled down this dirt road for five hundred meters, past a line of trees, then there she was: The farm of the third company.

3: The Farm

*This is no time for ease and comfort. It is
time to dare and endure.*
Winston Churchill

Our trucks pulled up alongside the long stone farmhouse, and then the fun began. A couple of the NCOs had gone on ahead and were waiting for us to arrive. As soon as the vehicles stopped, they were yelling at us to disembark and assemble. We poured out of the trucks and lined up, but it wasn't quick enough. Sgt Dsouza pointed to the hill behind us and directed our gaze to a large Foreign Legion logo made out of painted stones arranged on the ground. It was fifty meters up an extremely steep slope. "Go" barked the Sergeant. We all sprinted for the hill. I ran up there as fast as I could and was among the first to the top, but as the last person arrived he began calling us to assemble in the parking area again. We repeated this several times until we all were thoroughly exhausted. The sergeant then handed us over to the corporals, who took us over to a set of climbing ropes. Everyone was to climb five times, without the use of their legs. If you could not reach the top, then you would have thirty seconds to run up the hill and touch the logo again.

Once the rope climbs were done we thought it was over, but Cpl Novac had other ideas. He made us do press-ups on our knuckles in the car park, which doesn't sound too bad, until you realize that the car park was covered with gravel. The tiny sharp stones dug into your hands, and with the weight of your body pressing down it quickly became painful. When we had finished the press-ups, he told us to stand up and walk single file round to the other side of the building. Waiting for us on the other side was Sch Popadynets. He explained that now we had to unload all the trucks and install ourselves in the rooms. I helped load the food into the kitchen stores, while others took care of the armoury and sleeping quarters.

The farm of the third company is located deep in the French countryside, hidden away down a long dirt driveway. It is surrounded by woodland; no one can see out and no one can see in. One could almost say it was its own little kingdom, where the Legion reigned supreme. The farm complex itself wasn't very sophisticated: There was one long rectangular building, which was the farmhouse; then there was a breeze-block barn with an asbestos roof; and a couple of parking areas. We slept on the top floor of the farmhouse, in three separate rooms. The building was built on a slope and was wedge shaped. Under our sleeping quarters was a classroom, and at the thin end of the building was a shower room and toilets. The toilets on the farm were just holes in the ground, I had never seen toilets like that before (as far as I am aware we don't have them in the UK), and the showers were just a couple of shower heads attached to the ceiling that everyone had to huddle under. At the opposite end of the building, on the top floor, were the NCO's quarters; the kitchen and armoury were beneath them. Behind the farmhouse there was a flat grassy area with a flag pole, which was our parade ground. The only modern convenience we had while at the farm was electric lighting. Deserting from there would have been difficult. It was a long march to the main road, where you would have to hitch a ride, before anyone noticed you were gone and came looking. It was a good place to administer some harsh discipline.

After unloading the trucks we sat down outside to eat lunch. Today it was army rations, because the kitchen was not yet operational. I would like to be able to say something good about the French army rations, and coming a country famed for its cuisine you would think that would be easy, but they were pure excrement. I have seen and smelt roadkill that is more appetizing. In each ration you got: two large oval tins, which contained the main courses; two small tins of ground up animals; salty and sweet biscuits; the blandest hot chocolate known to man; and chewy toffees that pulled the fillings out of your teeth. Plus the bloody thing weighed a ton with all those tins. I once saw Doyle offer one of the tins of pâté to a dog. It took one sniff and turned its nose up in disgust.

After lunch we started setting up our rooms. The rooms we stayed in were pretty barren. They had bare stone walls and floors, and no ceiling, if you looked up you could see the rafters and roof tiles. The layout was strange: there was a single door at one end of the building and you had to walk through each room to get to the next one. I was in the last room, at the very end. In there with me was Cpl Novak, which sucked a bit as he was a sadistic bastard, but he was also very lazy and liked to sleep or play on his laptop when not required to work. He also snored like a rhinoceros, which is not what you want when you are dog-tired and have precious little time to sleep. Doyle was in the same room as me, but at the opposite end. Cpl Novak didn't want us speaking English with each other; we had to concentrate on learning French. Each person was given a fold-up camping bed, and there was a wooden cupboard (with no door) above each bed space for us to put our clothes in. We were told how to fold everything correctly and what order it should be placed in. There would be regular surprise inspections from the sergeants. If we failed, everything would be thrown out the window and we would have to go collect it and start again, all under a strict deadline. There were tales of past platoons who messed up so bad that they were made to march back to Castelnaudary carrying everything in their room. I did not want to march anywhere with the room so I always kept my things folded and arranged neatly.

After we had sorted the rooms out, we were told to go wait in the classroom with our songbook. It was good to be able to sit down in a nice, heated classroom, but it didn't take long before heads started bobbing and people were passing out on the desks. Sgt Flaubert and Cpl Sonking would be teaching us the songs tonight, as they were both Francophones, and Cpl Sonking had a good singing voice. When they entered the classroom everyone stood to attention, except that was for Doyle. He was fast asleep on his desk. The Sergeant noticed this and told the guy next to him, to give him a prod. Doyle woke and quickly sprang to his feet, but he wasn't going to get off that easy. The Sergeant called him to the front of the room and then directed his gaze out of the door. 'You see that hill over there,' he said. 'Oui Sergeant,' replied Doyle. 'OK, and can you see that hill behind it? You have three minutes to get there; GO!' Off he went running into the distance. While we waited for him to get to the hill, the Sergeant asked for a bucket of water. Anyone who was caught nodding off was to stick their head in it. Doyle eventually emerged on the hilltop and was summoned back. On returning to the classroom he was made to dunk his head in the bucket for good measure, then told to go stand behind his desk. There would be no more sitting for him that day.

We began to learn one of the songs from the book; one line at a time. It was difficult at first, especially for us non-French speakers, and we would forget the words as soon as we had finished singing. I didn't understand most of the words, it was just noise to me, so it was difficult to remember. Luckily there were enough Francophones to mask my, and others, ineptitude. I am not going to lie, I found the singing to be the most ridiculous shit ever, and I hated it from day one. I didn't join up to sing fucking carols, I thought, but I can understand the importance of it in bringing about group solidarity. All the same, looking around that room at people being made to sing under threat of severe punishment conjured up images of North Korea. It was pure madness, some were simply moving their mouths like goldfish hoping no one would notice.

In spite of our lack of understanding, after a few hours of this we were actually sounding pretty good and the sergeant told us to get into rows outside for some marching. When you sing and march in the Legion everything has to be timed off the left foot. Breaks between verses were two paces of the left foot long, for example. There would always be someone who screwed this up and started singing at the wrong time, which was very embarrassing for them (funny for the rest of us), and would result in the sergeant yelling out: 'shut your mouth Mongol' ('Mongol' in Europe means idiot. It comes from John Langdon Down, the first person to classify and describe what is today known as 'Down syndrome', but which he called at the time 'Mongolism', because he thought people from Mongolia looked like they had Down syndrome. Today this language would make the social justice warriors' heads explode with indignation, but the Foreign Legion has so far remained impervious to political correctness).

I was not very good at marching in step at first, and would often fall out of sync; earning me a punch from one of the NCOs. After a couple of hours practice, however, we had pretty much nailed it. Although, I was still not great and would fall out of step if we marched for too long. We marched back to the farmhouse and were told to go get our cutlery and line up outside the mess hall. We were told to go inside, collect our meal, then find a place at the table and stand behind our chair. No one was to sit, or to touch their food, until given the order. A few of the lads evidently did not understand what had been said and started chowing down straight away. When the corporals caught sight of this they ordered everyone to leave their trays at the table and reassemble outside. It was made clear to us that if the same thing happened again the food would go in the bins and we would not eat until tomorrow. Once again we entered the mess and, this time, those of us who had understood made sure no one started eating until we were told. Normally before beginning a meal in the Legion it is tradition to sing 'voila le boudin,' but we hadn't learnt that yet. Cpl Novak told us that because of our fuck-up earlier, we only had one minute to eat our food and be lined up outside. On his mark we sat down and attacked the food like wild dogs, and sure enough in under a minute there was nothing left.

Once dinner was over it was back to the classroom. We were informed that every night there would be a guard mounted, starting at eight in the evening and ending at six in the morning. Each person would take an hour and we would rotate by rooms. Luckily for me this first night was not my room, but there was still some work to be done before we could sleep. We would have to learn 'voila le boudin'. It was unacceptable that we ate without singing it. The song wasn't very long and didn't have to be performed while marching, so it wasn't too bad. We finished choir school at around eight o'clock and were told to shower and go revise from our little field manual until lights out at nine. Our first day at the farm was over, and all in all it wasn't that bad, but I had a feeling that things would get a lot worse.

The following morning we were up at six; there was no time to hang about. It was get up, get dressed, and line up for roll call, then we had a few minutes to get washed and shaved (my razors had started to get a bit rusty by this point and were getting rough on my face, leaving me looking rather red and sore). After that we had breakfast: black coffee and baguettes. At seven o'clock we had our main assembly (the one where we raised the flag).

Today we would be going on our first run. We were split into three groups according to ability. I was in the top group with Sgt Dsouza setting the pace, and boy could he run. Cpl Dino was bringing up the rear making sure no one slacked off. I was glad when a few kilometres into our run one of our group peeled off and began throwing up at the side of the road. The sergeant and corporal wasted no time in setting about him. They managed to harass him into running another 500 meters before he was throwing up again. This time Sgt Dsouza told Cpl Dino to take him back, but not before telling him, in no uncertain terms, that this would be the last time he ran with our group. He didn't want weaklings slowing us down. Being in the top group was not really that great as we had to run longer and faster than the others, which gave us less time to get showered and ready for instruction, and it made you super hungry.

A typical day at the farm consisted of classroom instruction on things like French, weapons training, and singing. Although the classroom stuff wasn't that difficult, there were still plenty of opportunities to get beasted. Learning the names of the different parts of the gun, for example. If you were called upon to name a certain component, and couldn't, you would have to do fifty push-ups while repeating the name of whatever it was at the top of every rep. For the French speakers this was child's play, but they were expected to help the rest of us. There were also two assault courses that we would have to do from time to time. The first was the standard French army 'parcour d'obstacle' which could be done individually and wasn't that difficult. It consisted of twenty obstacles and no one took over six minutes to complete it. The second was further off in the woods and was much larger, it took around thirty minutes and had to be done in a group. Sometimes we would go outside to be instructed on various pieces of equipment. The NBC (nuclear biological chemical) suit, for example, was taught outdoors. We would practice putting it on and taking it off, until we were fast enough to meet the standard time requirement set by the French government. I, forever the pessimist, couldn't fail to notice that these suits looked like they had seen better decades. They would probably offer little to no protection in the event of having to enter an irradiated zone. Also if you happened to be of Asian descent the mask was completely useless. Asian people have flatter faces than Africans or Europeans and the mask would not conform, leaving big gaps in places. We also received first aid training from Cpl Sonking, which included a lot of running around with stretchers. I noticed that the bandages we had been given were leftovers from the French-Indochina war! I believe the oldest ones were from the 1940's (I once saw one of these bandages in a Second World War display, in a museum in Narvik, Norway. If you want to see what I am talking about, then type 'pansement individuel' into a search engine).

On our second day at the farm the colonel in charge of the 4RE would be coming for our morning assembly. He would offer some words of advice and encouragement, as well as letting us know what was expected of us, before buggering off to do sod all in his office again. Cpl Kamel would be playing the trumpet, but we needed two people to stand either side of the flag pole. One of whom would have to raise the flag in time with the music. There were a lot of rules concerning the raising of the flag. You had to stand to attention facing the pole, then the highest ranking person would shout: 'prepare for the raising of the colour.' You would then have to put both hands on the drawcord and shout, 'ready,' plus the rank of whoever was giving the orders 'ready captain,' for example. The adjutant made it clear that at no point during the flag raising were you to turn your head towards the person shouting the orders: You had to keep facing the mast. After that 'send it up' would be shouted and at that moment the trumpet would start and so would the raising of the flag. Both had to finish at the same time. It was no use going too fast and then noticeably slowing down and lingering near the top, a steady pace was called for. Unfortunately, for this task the adjutant had chosen Kuzma: Kuzma was from Poland, he was nineteen and a full blown retard. He was really weird too, but that story is for later.

We got in rows, in front of the flag, and waited for the brass to arrive. The colonel turned up in his jeep with a little triangular flag on the back of it and spoke with the adjutant. The adjutant walked back in front of us and snapped us to attention. He then faced the colonel, saluted, and handed us over to him. The colonel began the flag ceremony (this is where it all went wrong). First Kuzma called the colonel 'mon adjutant.' The colonel shouted back in fury 'c'est mon colonel espèce d'abruti (Colonel! You fucking brute).' Then when he gave the order to raise the flag, Kuzma, like a dumbass, turned his head and stared at the colonel while hoisting the flag as fast as he could, then just kept on staring at him like a dumb dog. The Colonel stopped the trumpet short and shot daggers at the adjutant, this was not acceptable. Kuzma couldn't have screwed it up more if he tried. When he re-joined the rows, Cpl Novak gave him a bollocking in Polish, which sounded funny to me, it went something like: 'neep neep wurp kurva wurp wurp neep kurva matj.' I found the whole thing hilarious, but I had a feeling that I was in a minority.

The colonel was visibly pissed now, and his face was turning red. He ranted at us for five minutes or so, with veins protruding on his neck and forehead, then got in his jeep and left. As soon as he was gone Kuzma got an arse kicking to remember. The NCOs will never hit you in front of the officers, but once they have gone anything goes. Corporal punishment is as much a part of the Legion as marching, shooting, or singing. I personally didn't have a problem with it as long as it wasn't gratuitous (it was better than the singing), and that day, in my opinion, Kuzma had fully warranted it. He wouldn't make the same mistake again that was for sure, but he also received a beasting from hell for good measure.

Later that week, we were assembled outside the farmhouse, when Doyle lent over and said to me, 'Murray I think that Cch Laplace is a racist.' 'Why do you think that?' I replied. 'Well he keeps calling Tossy, blackie.' 'Yes, that is racist,' I concurred (Tossy was a thirty-something-year-old, former NCO, from the Ivory Coast). No sooner had Doyle told me this, than Tossy stuck his head out of the toilets, he had not heard the call for assembly. 'Come here blackie,' said the corporal-chef. 'Oh shit!' I whispered, 'you're right.' The Legion as it turns out is not only one of the most diverse institutions in the world, but it is also one of the most racist. Most of this is the standard black-white variety of racism, but there were definitely some Arabs who hated anyone who came from an English speaking country (especially if that country was the USA). There was, of course, some light hearted teasing between the British and the French lads, but it was all in good jest. I found being called a 'roast beef,' or 'Prince Charles' pretty funny, and I would tease them back about inventing homosexuality, and torturing farm animals.

At the end of each week at the farm we were taken on a march. The marches normally started in the evening and went on throughout the night. There was always a list put out before hand of the things that you need to take with you. You were given a short time to prepare and get lined up in front of the flag pole. Then you were led down to the armoury to collect the guns.

I was excited about the first march as it would be the first time that we would do something that involved the FAMAS (French assault rifle). It felt good to have an assault rifle in my hands at last. We were reminded, by the NCOs, that it was very important to take care of the gun and not lose anything or damage it. If we did, then our lives would not be worth living. It was advised that at night we put the gun in our sleeping bag with us. The corporals would be on lookout for any unguarded guns they could take during the night.

Before we set off, Adj O'Malley made us empty our rucksacks for a kit inspection, those who had tried to cheat by not including all the required kit were made to run up a few hills and given rocks to carry in their bags. I must admit this gave me some schadenfreude, especially as one of those caught was a notorious liar, cheat, and bastard: A Romanian man by the name of Barius, who looked like Boy George. He was such a shit that even his own countrymen disliked him. He was always on the take and cared for no one except himself.

After the inspection the adjutant made us form a single column and we set off. He had insisted that Cpl Novak accompany us. It was clear that the adjutant disliked him. If I had to guess, this was because Cpl Novak was a lazy fat turd. We marched off into the woods behind the farmhouse. After maybe an hour we emerged onto a small country lane. I enjoyed marching at night. It was peaceful and out here in the countryside there was no light pollution so you could see the Milky Way really well.

After a couple of hours marching my shoulders and back started to ache from the weight of the bag. The added weight of the gun made one side worse than the other, and walking on the hard road with my new boots was murder on my the feet. If this is what it feels like after a few kilometres, then what is the kepi march going to do to me, I thought.

We eventually came upon a small village (The small villages you find in rural France are like something off a postcard: The colonial era yellowing buildings with their wooden shutters drawn and a rusty Citroën 2CV parked in front, just smack of Frenchness). We turned off the road and entered a farm. It felt nice to be walking on soft ground again. We walked through some woods and a couple of fields before emerging on the road again. A few hundred meters up the road we entered a strangely familiar drive way: We were back at our farm. We had, in fact, just walked in a big circle. Even though we were back at the farm, we would not be sleeping in the rooms. Just in front of the farmhouse is a small field with a wooded area and a pond at the far end. This would be our camp for the night. I found a couple of trees to attach a rope to, and set up my tarpaulin. Once my shelter was sorted out I started cooking some rations. The march had only lasted three or four hours, and we had covered no more than ten kilometres of distance, but it had made me really hungry.

I really enjoyed this kind of thing: camping out and cooking food on a gas stove. It was a lot better than a prison cell that's for sure. While I was cooking my dinner Cpl Novak came over and told me that our room would be doing guard tonight and that I had the 3-4am slot. I never seemed to get the cushy first or last slot, which was fine, because in the early hours of the morning everyone would be asleep and I could get some serious thinking done. Also there was a fig tree nearby, which I could raid while the others slept. We had been forbidden from eating the figs, but no one gave a fuck. It was one of the perks of doing guard in the dead of night, well that and going off into the bushes to argue with Henry Longfellow. Yep, wanking on guard duty is an army tradition that is as old as war itself.

At six the next morning, the last guard woke everyone up. While I was taking down my basha and packing my bag, Doyle came running over. He was in a right state of panic. He told me that he had lost his gun during the night. Oh dear, I thought, one of the corporals must have taken it when he was asleep. I asked him where he had put the gun last night when he went to sleep, and he told me that he had initially put it in his sleeping bag, but found it too uncomfortable, so he had slipped it underneath his sleeping bag instead. It was clear that he must have rolled over during the night and left it exposed in the grass next to him. I sure wouldn't have wanted to be him at that moment.

Just as Doyle finished telling me what had happened, the adjutant called an assembly. Stop packing your things and come line up with your gun, he shouted. Once we were lined up he stood in front of us, held up a rifle, and demanded to know who didn't have their gun. Doyle reluctantly raised his hand. The adjutant called him out of the line, and as he approached, he struck him in the chest with the rifle stock, then in the stomach. Doyle doubled over, and then the sergeants who had come from the farmhouse set to work hitting and kicking him. They beat him for a couple of minutes before handing him to the corporals for a traditional beasting. The adjutant then addressed the rest of us, *'let this be a lesson to you, I don't say things for the fun of it. If I tell you to put your gun in your sleeping bag, then that's what you do. You are here to be soldiers, and soldiers follow orders. If they don't then the whole thing falls apart. Now go pack up your things and go to the farmhouse, get washed and shaved, and ready for your run.'*

I should mention at this point about '*bananes* (bananas)' which is the Legion euphemism for a blunder. If you make a mistake in the Legion, you have committed a 'banane.' If you keep on making mistakes you will be labelled as a 'bananier (banana tree)' because the mistakes fall from you like fruit from a tree. This is most definitely not what you wanted. If you were labelled as such you were effectively branded an idiot. You would only be given the simplest of tasks, like sweeping and mopping. Also you would be first on the list for any shitty jobs that had to be done. There is one other word which the Legion likes to use a lot, and that word is: 'corvée.' This is used to denote any kind of menial labour, but its precise definition is more telling. The exact definition of corvée is: 'a day's unpaid labour owed by a vassal to his feudal lord.' For a legionnaire there is always lots of corvée to be done, it is his bread and butter.

Doyle didn't come on the run with us that morning. When we got back he was scrubbing the toilets. I tried to ask him what was going to happen to him, but he was sent to go work in the armoury. After the shower we had to clean the guns. They weren't dirty but it kept us occupied. Today we all got to have the two hour siesta at midday, except for Doyle who was working in the kitchen. When I went back to my room I noticed that his things had been moved. I was worried that he might be getting sent back to the regiment, but I later discovered that he was not being sent back to Castelnaudary. He had just been moved into the first room, to a bed next to Cpl Sonking, who was tasked with watching him and making sure he didn't make any more bananes.

When I saw Doyle later, I noticed that he had acquired a new friend; in the form of a ten kilogram rock. He was to take this rock everywhere with him for the next week, and I mean everywhere: he ate with it, went to the shower with it, went to the toilet with it, and slept with it in his bed. Being seen without the rock would result in severe punishment. This seemed a little harsh to me, but I think the adjutant had chosen to punish him so strongly because they were both Irish, and Doyle had given his country a bad name by playing into the stereotype about Irish people being stupid.

The second week at the farm started in the same vein as the first. Half classroom learning and half practical. We started learning the legionnaire's code of honour, which went like this:

- Legionnaire, you are a volunteer, serving France with honour and fidelity.
- Each legionnaire is your brother in arms, whatever his nationality, his race, or his religion. You will express to him the same close solidarity that unites the members of a family.
- Respect the traditions of your leaders, discipline and camaraderie are your strengths, courage and loyalty are your virtues.
- Be proud of your status as a legionnaire, display it in: your uniform, always elegant; your behaviour, always dignified, but modest; and your barracks, always neat.

- Elite soldier, you train with rigor, you treat your weapon like it is the most precious thing, you maintain your physical fitness at all times.
- The mission is sacred, you will execute it at all costs, and if necessary, on operation, you will risk your life for it.
- In combat you act without passion and without hate, you respect your vanquished enemy, you will never abandon your dead, your wounded, or your weapons.

Everyone had to take turns leading this. You would shout out the first word or two of each verse and then everyone would join in to complete the rest. I would amuse the others from time to time by parodying the code, but this was risky: If I was caught making fun of the code of honour, then I would join Doyle in having a new friend to take care of. I always found it strange how the last part (your dead, your wounded, your weapons) got louder with each thing. It was like it was adding more emphasis and the thing they valued most was the weapons. I would parody it like this: to hell with the dead, take the wounded if you can, but for god's sake don't leave your weapons behind, they're expensive!

During the second week we started to learn basic military tactics. We learnt: fire and movement (leapfrogging), and how to use suppressive fire, contact drills, ambush drills, and patrolling. At this stage though we were only allowed to fire blanks, they didn't trust us enough for real ammunition. We also learnt how to fire the 40mm FAMAS grenade, which is placed over the end of the barrel and shot with a special bullet. It's very important to have a firm grip of the gun when firing the grenade as it kicks like a mule. A couple of lads didn't heed this warning and ended up with bloody noses from the hand rail smashing into their faces. There is also a pin you must pull out before firing, if you don't then it won't go off, and you would just clobber the enemy on the head. For the moment we were only using an orange practice grenade, but it was important we got the procedure right for when we used real ones in the future. Doyle forgot to pull the pin and had to do a few laps of the field. He wasn't alone, many made the same mistake. We also learnt how to camouflage ourselves and use the terrain in the most effective way. We also had our first taste of map reading. A lot of the guys were very bad at this, including some of the corporals, they found it difficult to locate themselves and couldn't understand the concept of true north. This was probably due to their French skills, or lack thereof. I was starting to be able to understand spoken French pretty well by this point, and everything we were being taught was in the little white book they had given us at Castelnaudary anyway, so you just had to read it. It wasn't as if there was much else to do in your free time.

As Friday of our second week arrived we were told to get ready for our second march. I assumed it would be longer, but exactly how long only the NCOs knew and they weren't saying a word. Once again they handed out a list of stuff we needed to pack in our bags. This time we had to take the NBC suit with us. As evening crept in we got our guns and bags, and lined up in front of the flag once more. No one tried cheat on the equipment list this time, it just wasn't worth the hassle. Doyle had finished his punishment and did not have to carry his rock with him anymore.

We lined up and began to march. This time we walked down the long drive and straight across the road into the field opposite. At the end of the field was a small river, a couple of meters wide, which we would have to ford. There were a couple of large stepping stones that could be used to cross without getting wet. The adjutant led the way. I managed to sneak my way to the front and cross. My reason for getting across early was that with each person the stones were getting wetter and wetter. I concluded that it wouldn't be long before they became slippery and people started to fall in. Sure enough somewhere after the fifteenth person accidents began to happen. Doyle, true to form, leapt at the first rock and went arse over tit into the river. This was bad on a number of levels, not least because all of your sleeping gear was in the bag, but also, marching with wet feet was not very pleasant. Cpl Novak, who was bringing up the rear, accepted that he wouldn't be able to hop across and just waded across like a hulking buffalo.

We continued on through the fields until we reached a large wooded area. So far this march didn't seem that bad, my boots were a bit more worn in than last week and we didn't walk on the hard road nearly as much. Sometimes we would pass through farms, which had fruit orchards. We stole whatever we could from the trees. There were also plenty of sunflowers around. I snapped the head off one and ate the seeds as I marched. This was not allowed by the NCOs, but they weren't paying much attention. The adjutant and Sch Popadynets were busy reading the map at the front, and the two Corporals were talking, and smoking cigarettes, at the back. For the rest of us it was forbidden to smoke while marching. Not that this bothered me. On this second march we were given five minute breaks every hour or so, unlike last time. Walking around in the woods completely disorientated me and after a while I had no idea where we were in relation to our farm.

After a few hours of traipsing through woods and fields we emerged onto the road. I recognized it from our daily runs with Sgt Dsouza. We were still a fair distance from our destination. The adjutant, instead of following the road back to our base, turned off and started heading away again. An hour or so later we passed through the same village as on the first march, and it became clear that we were going to enter our farm from the back; and sure enough we retraced our first march in reverse, and entered the trail that we had used the previous week.

Once we had walked half a kilometre into the woods, the adjutant stopped us and called an assembly. Tonight we would be staying on a wooded hill, which was at the intersection of two paths. Our job for the night was to stop anyone from travelling past us, and to defend our hill. The NCOs taught us the correct procedure for challenging an intruder. This was done in groups of three. First you would order the intruder to stop and state their name and purpose, then you would order them to advance to a distance of three or four meters from you and get on their knees with their hands on their head, then, while two of you had your guns trained on the intruder, a third would approach from behind, grab the person's hands and pull them back (this took the intruder off balance). The individual would then be frisked and taken prisoner. If at any time the intruder failed to comply we were to open fire on them. Each group of three was assigned a fox hole. In our groups we each took it in turn to watch guard while the other two slept. It must have been around one o'clock in the morning by the time that we got set up on the hill, so it was clear that we wouldn't be getting much sleep.

After a couple of hours sitting in our holes, a voice cried out in the darkness 'halte qui va là? (halt who goes there).' There were a few seconds silence, then the sound of automatic rifle fire erupted: rat-tat-tat-tat-tat-tat-tat. Then everyone began firing in the direction of the path. Powder grenades flashed and exploded on the path below. Then just as suddenly as it had started, it stopped, and the night fell back into silence.

The adjutant called an assembly down on the path. He demanded to know who had initiated the contact and why. It turned out that upon being challenged the intruders had opened fire and the legionnaire who had stopped them shot back in response. The adjutant commended us for successfully defending our position and ordered us back to our places as there might be another attack: There was no further action that night.

In the morning we took a role and made sure we had all our equipment (luckily no one had lost their gun this time). Adj O'Malley handed us over to the corporals and headed back to the farm with Sch Popadynets. We were ordered to clean our weapons out there in the woods. The Legion has severe OCD when it comes to cleaning weapons, and the inspections are never passed first time round. The duty NCO will come round with a sewing needle, or tooth pick, and dig around in the deepest darkest corners of the FAMAS (of which there are many). Any dirt that is found is wiped on your face. You will then be given another deadline for inspection and the process repeats itself. The guns are cleaned so vigorously that there is hardly any rifling left on the inside of the barrel, which makes the gun less accurate. We spent most of the morning cleaning our weapons.

After the inspection was passed we cooked our rations and slept in the undergrowth for a couple of hours. In the evening we were instructed to disassemble and reassemble our weapons until it became second nature; once this was achieved we blind-folded ourselves and continued as before. It didn't take that long to master this way of taking the gun apart, but there was always the danger of dropping one of the smaller parts and losing it in the leaf litter. That would result in a monumental beasting lasting for a few days.

We walked back to the farm later in the afternoon, just in time for dinner. After dinner, as usual, we were in the classroom learning another song. We had learnt maybe ten songs by now and it was helping us to learn French, but after the previous night, which had been almost devoid of sleep. The warm classroom with its candescent lighting made it impossible to stay awake. I think everyone stuck their head in the bucket that day (I was twice made to dunk my head). It got so bad that we were ordered to stack the chairs outside and stand behind our desks.

With every passing day now the work load was increasing. This coupled with the lack of sleep made everyone constantly hungry, sometimes we would sit and fantasize about the food we would eat the first time we were let out on town leave. There was also no shortage of people attempting to feign illness of injury, so that they would, in the best case be sent to the infirmary back at the regiment, or at least receive exemption from sport for a few days. Cpl Sonking was having none of it, he had far too much experience to be hoodwinked so easily. The most common complaint you would see was about the feet. Some guys did have some nasty blisters, but it wasn't going to kill them.

That night, after the march, I was on guard duty in the middle of the night again. I was starving hungry and the fig tree was almost bare by now. However, I spotted some stale baguettes in the bin. I fished one out, broke it up, and ate it during my guard. Taking food from the bins was risky. If I was caught I would be punished. They would make sure that whatever extra calories I had gained would be burnt off during my punishment.

The next day, Sunday, we were given a little treat. Someone had been to the regiment and brought a load of paintballing equipment back with them. I had never been paintballing before, but I had heard plenty of stories about how much the balls stung when they hit you. We put on the protective gear, and learned how to operate the guns, then the adjutant led us to the far end of the field we had camped in after our first march, where there was a wooden five bar gate. On the other side was a small enclosure, no bigger than half a football pitch. Scattered around inside were a few shipping containers, with doors and windows cut into them. There were also plenty of walls and points of cover, made out of tyres and wooden pallets, and along one side of the field was a huge mass of brambles that could be crawled through. All in all, it was a pretty decent course.

We split into two groups, with a couple of NCOs on each side, and went to opposite ends of the arena. A powder grenade signalled the start of each round. We charged forward, trying our best to shoot the opposing team and reach their side. It was great fun, and the paintballs didn't hurt at all: You hardly notice them with all the adrenaline rushing through your system. We played all morning, until our stock of paintballs ran out. When the adjutant called an end to the last round, I stood up, and just as I was lifting my mask off, Cpl Kamel shot me straight in the face. A fraction of a second later and I would have had no protection. I can only imagine what sort of damage it would have done to my eyes. But that was a minor down point in, what had been, a thoroughly great morning.

Week three arrived and after the morning flag ceremony, Cpl Kamel asked for a few volunteers to accompany him to Castelnaudary in order to pick up some supplies. There is a saying in the Legion 'legionnaire est toujours volontaire (legionnaires are always willing volunteers).' What this means in practice is that whenever someone asks for some people to do a job, no matter how shitty, everyone must put their hand up in a flash. If you don't, or if you appear reluctant, than you will get picked. This time it was different, everyone sincerely wanted to go. You could actually hear people sigh with disappointment when they weren't chosen. Me too, I was bummed that I didn't get to go, because the rest of us poor bastards would have to go on a run.

However, today's run was slightly different, we all ran together in one big group, instead of by ability. We set of at a steady pace led by the adjutant. I started off at the front, but it wasn't long before the apple-polishers were barging me out of the way, trying to run next to the NCOs and show off. I eventually gave up and went to the back of the group. Doyle was already there and he had noticed the same thing going on. We found it quite funny and began mocking the people who were currently busy conducting their own ass-kissing contest by making slurping noises and cocksucking gestures at them with our hands. However, it wasn't long before the joke was on us. When you are at the back of a large group of men running, who for the last couple of days have been dinning on that dog food pâté, and the various bits of offal you get in the mess hall. It generates a great amount of flatulence, and the smell smelt like it came straight from Beelzebub himself. Sometimes a fart would hit you just as you were inhaling and the retched gasses entering your lungs would almost cause you to projectile vomit. Some farts were so bad that it was like someone had just shit in your mouth when they hit you. The best solution, I could find, was to run slightly to one side of the main group, but I still got the occasional gassing.

After the run we stopped at the entrance to the farm and formed rows, the adjutant gave us the order to march and sing our way down the drive. We were actually getting quite good at this, and starting to show the first inklings of cohesion as a group. We belted out our repertoire of ten songs and the adjutant seemed pleased. Once we were back the order was to clean the farmhouse and all its facilities, then wait for the truck to arrive from Castelnaudary.

When the truck arrived everyone set to work unloading it. Most of the stuff they had picked up was food, but at the back there was a load of green foldable tables, and behind that was a large quantity of beer. Unfortunately the beer was Kronenbourg, but hey, beggars can't be choosers. I guessed that the beer was for the graduation ceremony that would take place after we had completed the kepi march. The smokers among us were pleased as they had been able to order two hundred cigarettes each (the money would be taken out of their first pay check).

Once the truck was unloaded, and all the beer and food was locked away in the store room. Cpl Novak took us for an extra-long workout session before lunch that day. We did ten rope climbs, fifty chin ups, and god knows how many push-ups and sit-ups. Most were able to climb the rope with relative ease by now. However, this was mostly to due to severe weight loss, rather than improved upper body strength.

After lunch we were given the standard two hour siesta. During the brake Cpl Kamel made the rounds of the rooms with a huge sack of chocolate bars and a pen and paper. He had stopped at the supermarket on the way back and brought a load of chocolate bar multipacks, split them open, and was now selling the individual bars for €1.50 (that was almost the same cost as the multipack itself). I didn't buy anything from him, but he soon sold all that he had. I must admit that it did piss me off a little that he was exploiting our situation and making a nine hundred percent profit on fucking chocolate bars, but what can you do. It's the same shit that theme parks get up to, besides, the rest of the guys were happy to get some extra food, and as it turned out this kind of thing was rife at Castelnaudary. The corporals and corporal-chefs would sell the new recruits anything they could, with a serious mark-up of course. Sometimes they would sell their old kit to naïve new-comers, telling them that it was reglementary, and that they would suffer when they went off to their regiments if they didn't have whatever piece of crap they were hawking.

That afternoon we went over to the field next to the obstacle course, to practice our combat drills some more. We also practiced throwing grenades into these concrete circles (sewer pipes stuck vertically in the ground). I was good at this: I guess all those nights in my youth, when I would go around with my friends and throw eggs at people's windows, had been good practice.

When night began to set in we went on a small patrol around the farm grounds. We stopped in a little wooded area and were told to clear a patch of ground and gather some firewood. We build a fire and dragged some logs around it for everyone to sit on. Sgt Dsouza sent a couple of guys off, and when they came back, they each had a crate of beer in their arms. We sat round the fire drinking the beers and singing the songs we had learned in the classroom. Once we had gone through the Legion songs Sgt Flaubert told us to get into our respective nationalities. Each group would have to sing their national anthem. It was the only time during instruction we would be permitted to speak in our mother tongue. The Francophones had it easy as there were loads of them. I was the only Brit there and the only time I had heard God Save the Queen was at the start of football matches. Fortunately, Doyle crept over and asked if he could sing with me, as he didn't know the Irish national anthem and he didn't want to get branded an idiot again. So when our time came, we sang God Save the Queen together; well the first verse at least. Sgt Dsouza found this highly amusing. He spoke English, and was well aware of the history between Ireland and Britain. He remarked that it must have been a cold day in hell, if an Irish man was singing the British national anthem. It was a good job the adjutant wasn't there or Doyle might have found himself lugging around another rock for a few weeks.

The most impressive bit of singing that night was, without doubt, from the Russians. There was seven or eight of them in our group, and they sang like a professional choir. First they sang the modern Russian Federation anthem and then the old Soviet Union version. It's a really catchy tune, not like God Save the Queen, which I find dreary and lacklustre. After that they sung Kalinka, which I knew from the game Tetris. All it needed was someone to be playing a balalaika and accordion, and it would have been perfect. There is something primordial about sitting round a campfire. Our genus has been doing it since Homo erectus discovered fire roughly one and a half million years ago on the African Savanah. I felt like it helped cement our bond as a group (this is what I took from it at least). Maybe it was just the fact that this was the first time since joining the Legion that we had been given the chance to relax a little. The beer undoubtedly helped too. I felt sorry for the poor souls who had to take guard that night. It must have been difficult to stay awake. It wasn't much better for me, though: Corporal Novak, due to his weight, snored like a banshee, and Tossy, who was also in my room, seemed to be suffering from sleep apnoea, and would make very weird noises in the night, so I wasn't getting off that lightly. Sometimes it seemed like Tossy and the corporal were having a competition to see who could make the most noise. However, It wasn't so bad with Tossy as we could wake him up and tell him to change his sleeping position, which normally sorted the problem out, but there was no way we could do this with Cpl Novak. The people in the other two rooms even complained about his snoring! You wouldn't want him in your fox hole, that's for sure, he would signal your position to everyone in a three mile radius.

During the third week we learned about land mines, but because of something called '*the Ottawa Treaty,*' which prohibits the use of certain types of mines (anti-personnel, and mines with anti-handling devices), we could only learn about anti-vehicle/tank mines. However, we did learn how to use trip flares and make booby traps with grenades, which is great fun and quite scary at the same time. I really enjoyed making booby traps, but they are fucking evil things. An interesting side note about the Ottawa Treaty is the world's three major superpowers (Russia, China, and the USA), have not signed it. That's why the Americans can still use Claymore mines.

On one of the mornings, after our run, we were doing some group exercises, such as stretchering people, and fireman's carry. One exercise involved us all lying on the floor next to each other, then the person at the end would get up and run over the stomachs of the rest of us and lie down again at the other end. In this way we moved along like caterpillar tracks. Cpl Novak thought it was funny to join in as well. He easily weighed 120 kilos, the fat fuck. I thought my eyes were going to pop out when he trod on me. When it was Doyle's turn, he got up and started making his way across.

However, unbeknownst to him, Tossy had lain down on top of an ants nest and they had got inside his clothes and began to bite him. Just as Doyle was stepping on to him, he began to move and jerk around causing Doyle to step right on his balls. Tossy let out a yell and jumped up. The NCOs had no idea what had just happened. They thought Tossy was just being unruly, so they gave him a kicking and ordered him to lay back down on the ants nest, shut up, and stop being a pussy. Afterwards, in the showers, when Tossy explained why he had acted as he did, we all found it very amusing, but he didn't find it so funny.

At the end of the third week we again prepared to go on another march. This march should have been even longer than the last, so we were looking forward to a sleepless night of constant walking, but it turned out to be pretty much identical to the last one we had done. The only difference was that instead of sleeping in the woods we went to the trenches that were just past the barn, not far from the farmhouse. Our mission was to defend the trenches from intruders. This time, however, we had some trip flares to help us secure a perimeter. The trenches were not very nice to say the least, the bottom was all muddy and you had to sleep sitting up as there was not much space. Again we took guard in groups of three and after a couple of hours there was a loud pop. Someone had tripped the flare, but the bloody thing didn't light up. It was a dud. We all began firing in the direction of the sound and after a couple of minutes the adjutant called a ceasefire. He went over to inspect the flare and indeed it had been tripped, but it had failed, through no fault of ours. The rest of the night passed without issue.

In the morning we packed up and went down to our assembly area. The adjutant ordered us to leave our bags on the assembly ground, and go hand our guns in. This was strange, I thought, every time we had gotten the guns out previously we had been made to vigorously clean them before handing them back to the armoury. Something was afoot! Once the weapons had been handed in we were split into our three groups, and our respective sergeants came and collected us. We started jogging around the bottom field, then formed a circle and did a comprehensive warm up. This doesn't look good, I was thinking. Then we were off jogging again. This time we jogged into the woods at the back of the farm. That's when it hit me, we are going to do that huge assault course.

Sergeant Flaubert led us up to the start point, then ordered us to sit down in the bushes next to the track. Almost as soon as we sat down, half of the lads fell asleep (I envy people who can just fall asleep like that, it takes me ages to drop off and the slightest noise will wake me). We sat there waiting in the bushes for nearly an hour, which made the warm up we had done pretty much useless. Eventually our sergeant came back and took us off to start the course. The adjutant informed us that this obstacle course was named '*la piste du silence* (The silent path)' and that while doing it, we were forbidden from making any noise. The other two groups had already gone at ten minute intervals from each other, and we still had a few minutes before we could start. Sgt Flaubert informed us that the point of this exercise was to develop team work. No one was to be left behind and we could only go as fast as our slowest member. That being said, he added that anyone who he thought was not giving 100 percent would receive his boot up their backside.

The obstacle course was not that difficult. It had the normal stuff: mud, barbed wire, water filled tunnels, balance beams, cargo nets, walls, etc. I found out the reason we had waited so long at the start. The NCOs had been busy placing car tyres along the route and setting them on fire. To me it seemed like a bit of a waste of time. You didn't have to jump over, or through, them. They were next to the path, and it was no more daunting than running past a camp fire. My group soon caught up with the guys in front of us. So we were treated to a break while they attempted to scale the next obstacle. Admittedly, it was the most difficult part of the course. The obstacle they were having difficulty with was a four meter high wall made out of wooden planks. The wood had become slimy so it was near impossible to scale, plus the rope that was supposed to help was snapped and frayed. The only solution was to make a human pyramid. They had made their pyramid using six people, the remaining members of the group clambered over them to get to the top. During this one of the guys at the bottom was evidently feeling the strain and began making shrieks of pain. The adjutant took umbrage at this and ran over to him. He began punching him in the kidneys and back of the head, while screaming at him 'it's the fucking piste du silence, do you understand that, stop your crying.' Poor bastard just had to stand there and take it. Finally they got over the wall and it was our turn. Not surprisingly we all kept out mouths shut.

At the end of the assault course we all assembled in rows and the adjutant addressed us. He had been less than impressed at our performance. Our punishment was to be handed over to the corporals for some more physical activities. Cpl Dino came over and asked us if anyone was feeling tired. The NCOs often asked this after any kind of strenuous activity, and of course we were all tired, but you could never say that, or you would get smoked. It was very sadistic. The closest thing I can liken it to in civilian life is when you are on a date and you have to pretend to like and be interested in things that you couldn't give a rat's arse about if you tried, just to try and score, except for in the Legion your prize for appeasement was a slightly less severe punishment. Anyway, we were run ragged for another hour or so, with different corporals taking the lead when one of them got tired, then everyone was led back to the farm.

Returning to the farmhouse I could see a lot of mess outside, as I drew closer it became apparent that all of our stuff had been thrown out of the windows into the yard. There was an audible collective groan from everyone as we realized what had happened. We assembled in front of the flag and Cpl Dino gave the orders. First we were to collect all the stuff that had been thrown out and arrange it back in the room ready for inspection, then once the inspection was passed we had to get the guns, clean them, and pass a review; then shower, and wash our combat fatigues. Only after all that was done would we be allowed to eat.

Everyone went over to find their things in the big pile outside the farm building. Those who had neglected to write their name on everything were in a world of shit. They had to fight it out amongst themselves for ownership of what had been tossed out into the jumbled heap. The rest of us collected what was ours and entered the rooms. Inside the building was another treat. The rooms, at first glance, looked like a bomb had gone off in there. It was noticeable that the NCOs had used this opportunity to really fuck with the guys they didn't like. For example: Mejri and Barius. Mejri pissed off the NCOs, because he thought that he was smarter than everyone. He especially annoyed the non-French speaking corporals (most notably Cpl Pillqu), by trying to correct them when they misspoke, or got elements of grammar wrong. Most people's beds had been turned over and their shelves emptied onto the floor, but those two had had every bag opened and all their things spread about the farm, inside and out. They never recuperated all their kit.

Everyone was dog tired and at the end of their wits. You could hear people cursing at the top of their lungs in their native language. Though I did not understand what they were saying their feelings were clear. You could hear people's hearts break as they entered the building and saw the mess. For the thieves among us this was the perfect opportunity to steal, and steal they did. Tossy discovered that someone had stolen a few pairs of his briefs, I only remember this because it was so funny. The look of sheer disbelief on his face was priceless. He couldn't comprehend what would possess someone to steal another mans used pants. I postulated that they might have been taken to be used as a masturbatory aid.

We eventually sorted the room out, and passed the inspection, then went down to the armoury, got the guns, and cleaned them in the classroom. Some idiots decided to try and sleep in the back of the room. They inevitably got caught and earned us all a run up the nearest hill. After that we were made to take all the tables outside and clean the guns standing up, outside of the NCO's quarters so that they could watch us from the window.

Week four, the final week at the farm. I knew the last week at the farm would be the hardest. However, I had gotten used to being tired and hungry all the time, having fifty plus assemblies a day, and being beasted permanently. I had acclimatized to life on the farm, so in a way the last week was no worse than the first. Guard duty at night had become something to look forward to, as it was the only time you had to yourself. Living for the past few weeks without any modern electronic devices was not that bad either, you realize just how much of your time you spend staring at a screen. All the same, I still was eager to get the farm over with. On return to the regiment I would receive my first pay check, and the first thing on my shopping list was a Mach3 razor: Those orange disposable ones that I had stolen in Marseille were just ridiculously blunt and rusty by this point. They had also given me a rash on my face. Oh, how I dreamt of having a descent shave that didn't make me wince with pain.

For most of the week we were tested on our firing drills and patrolling. Normally one of the corporals would lead us on these, but this week we were expected to take it in turns commanding the drill. Most of my comrades had learned a fair bit of French by now, but there was still a group of several people who just didn't seem to get the hang of it. I know it's mean spirited, but I was grateful for them as they would always be making mistakes, and this drew the attention of the NCOs away from the rest of us. Unfortunately for Doyle, he was one of the aforementioned group. This was strange as he wasn't dumb at all, in fact he was much better educated than I was. My theory was that maybe he had had a cushy life at home, where his parents had coddled him a bit too much, and this was probably the first time he was made to fend for himself. He wasn't getting beasted so much now, the NCOs had tried that, many a time, to little or no effect. Now they just accepted that he would make some silly blunders and automatically added him to the list for any undesirable work.

After all the drills were out of the way, we had to do some more physical tests. Who could do the most chin-ups and rope climbs, etc. The chin-up competition was impossible to win. The Eastern bloc guys looked like they had all done gymnastics at school. Instead of doing chin-ups the normal way they would flick themselves up. In this way they would do around fifty repetitions.

However, on the rope where you couldn't cheat like that, they were remarkably ordinary. After that we went down to the small obstacle course near the farmhouse. This was the standard course that every army camp in France has. It is five hundred meters long and has twenty obstacles. The national record for this was about 2:45, which should give you an idea of its difficulty. After being shown how to correctly pass each obstacle we were sent off at two minute intervals. I came first on this test finishing in three and a half minutes. Alas, no one else that day finished in under four minutes and the adjutant flew into a rage. We all had to run off to our rooms, put on our NBC suits, and do it while wearing that a few times; and by Jove is it difficult to do anything exerting with that gas mask on. It starves you of Oxygen. After a few of the lads collapsed on the course, we were told to take the mask off and just do it in the suit. This was still quite bad as it is incredibly hot. My prize for coming first that day was extra portions at lunch, and boy did I appreciate it. The extra protein was badly needed.

Eventually, the week drew to a close and we began to think about the kepi march. One of the French lads had found out that it would be sixty kilometres long, and we would complete it in two parts, over two days. That didn't sound too bad to me; thirty kilometres a day. The list for this march was huge. I am sure the NCOs had a great time thinking up all the things they could make us carry. There was so much stuff that it barely fit in the rucksack. My estimate is that our sacks probably weighed twenty-five kilograms, then you could add another five for the gun and webbing (tactical vest), so around thirty kilos in total. I could tell that this march was going to be painful. It was a different story for the corporals: Cpl Novak took only his food, a sleeping bag, and a waterproof Gore-Tex cover. He had obviously not heard about leading by example, or, more likely, he just didn't give a fuck.

The time of depart had arrived. Today we would be leaving early. This was the first time we had marched in the daytime. I didn't mind walking in the daytime. At this time of year (late September) it was starting to get cold so there wasn't any danger of getting heat stroke. In any case the sky was overcast that day. An army Chaplain arrived at the farm that day to march with us. France is a predominantly Catholic country, and the officers, being from the aristocracy, are all Catholic too: There is even a church in every regiment, for God's sake (sorry about the pun, but I couldn't resist).

We lined up and marched out of the farm to begin our two day journey. I was concentrating on the fact that by the end of these two days I would officially be a legionnaire: No more engagé volontaire bullshit. The adjutant, as always, led the way. After an hour or so the weight of the rucksack was compressing my back and making it ache. Fortunately, I could always rely on someone else to cause a stop before it got too bad. The people who had picked up blisters from the other marches were suffering right from the start. The workload at the farm combined with inadequate nutrition and lack of sleep, meant that your body took longer to heal, so if you got a blister from one march, it wouldn't be healed in time for the next.

It's a good idea, on long marches like this, to find something to think about to take your mind away from the monotony walking, and staring at the rucksack of the person in front. I usually daydreamed about my first holiday: where I would go, what I would do, and what I would eat. Simple things like this can help a lot.

It seemed like we were marching forever. We travelled through forests and fields. If we came across any fruit trees then they got stripped bare as usual. We were like a plague of human-sized locusts. It was somewhere along the first part of this march that I found a tree with strange yellow fruit on it. I couldn't tell what the fruit was exactly, it looked like a cross between an apple and a pair, but whatever it was, it was amazing. It tasted like the yellow starburst sweets. It was a bit risky taking fruit straight from the tree like that as you couldn't wash it first and were thus risking an upset stomach. During a march like this one, was definitely not when you wanted to have diarrhoea.

Sometime around midday, we arrived at the small village of Pech-Luna and sat down on its outskirts to have lunch. I had boudin and mashed potatoes in my ration pack (boudin is basically black pudding, which I like, but in the UK it's normally eaten as part of a fry-up breakfast).

After the short lunch break we were back on our way. This time we were walking alongside the road. I would advise anyone who has to go on a long march in boots to keep to the grass verge. While it is more work for your ankles walking on the uneven dirt, it saves the bottom of your feet: The grass almost acts like an insole.

The weather was slowly getting worse as the march wore on, and it eventually began to drizzle with rain. This was rather refreshing and it didn't get heavy enough to seep through our bags or soak our clothing. After another couple of hours we had reached the edge of the plateau that the farm was on. Below was the Lauragais valley with Castelnaudary right in the middle of it. It was about this time that some of the guys were beginning to fall behind. This was good for the rest of us, as we had to stop and wait for them to catch up. When they did catch up, they would receive a torrent of abuse from the NCOs. There was no rest for them, as we would be ordered to our feet as soon as they arrived. The slackers were told that if they wanted a rest then they should keep up.

For the next couple of hours we marched down from the plateau into the valley, accompanied by the intermittent rain. You might think that going downhill made it easier, but anyone who has done some mountaineering can tell you that it's just as hard, albeit in a slightly different way. When you walk along a flat or inclined surface it is your glutes that do most of the work, whereas on a decline it's your quads that bear the brunt. It is also a lot harsher on your knees, and if that wasn't enough with your feet now pressing against the front of your boots. You would develop sores on the tops of your toes.

There was now a group of maybe seven or eight people lagging behind, and they got slower and slower. The ground had evened out now, which made marching easier. At the start of the march everyone looked happy. Their heads were up and some were talking quietly amongst themselves, but now there was silence.

Everyone's head was down and their face either sported a grimace, or a look of sheer hopelessness. My bag was murdering my shoulders. Each time we got a chance to rest it was heaven to dump it. However, it didn't take long after putting it on again for the pain to come back.

By late afternoon, I was pretty damn hungry. We came upon the village of Sainte-Camelle (another tiny French village with a population of no more than a hundred). The name made me chuckle. I had images of the anthropomorphic smoking camel, from the cigarette adverts, dressed like the pope, with people worshipping him. Again we stopped near the village to eat, and to let the others catch up. We were told not to heat anything up as we would soon be at our destination for day one, and we would have more time there to cook and relax for the night. Cpl Sonking made the people who had been falling behind take off their boots so he could inspect their feet. Some of them had enormous blisters. Large areas of skin were sheared off, leaving red, sore looking skin in its place. It made you wince just to look at it. Cpl Sonking did what he could with his plasters and iodine antiseptic fluid (Betadine), but it can't have done much for the pain. The adjutant, did his part by scolding them for not taking better care of their feet. I felt some empathy for them, because it was hardly their fault for getting blisters, they just weren't used to walking so far, but this was the Legion and they knew what they were signing up for. Luckily for me I had plenty of practice walking back and forth between Marseille and Aubagne a month ago. Adj O'Malley did, however, show some compassion. He emptied the rucksacks of the three who were worst off, and divided their things among the rest of us. No one was happy about the extra weight, but they were slowing us down too much. If we had carried on like this we would hardly get any time to sleep. The person who was in the worst state was a Frenchman by the name of Gallineaux. His feet were torn to shreds and even without his bag he struggled. He was clearly in a lot of pain, and every step was agony for him.

A while after starting to march again, I was beginning to think that the adjutant was lying to us, about how far was left to go.

Maybe he was just trying to boost our morale. We had been marching for around two hours since our stop in Sainte-Camelle, and it was starting to get dark now. Then, up ahead, I saw an enormous reservoir with woods and camping areas all around it. Surely this must be it, I thought to myself. We crossed over the road and entered a small woods beside the lake. Thank goodness for that, now I can relax, I thought, and I am sure that I wasn't the only person to feel that way.

We picked our sleeping area for the night and began installing our tarpaulins. Everyone had to sleep in pairs. I paired up with Banica, the Romanian who was in my room back at Castelnaudary. We had just sorted out our bivouac, when an assembly was called. Surprise, surprise, it was to do with guard duty. I did have one bit of fortune, which was that Banica was on guard after me, so I wouldn't have to go searching around in the woods, in the dead of night for the next person.

After the assembly we all retired to our shelters to cook up our rations. I ate everything that was left in my ration box; and half of the next days' too. Those awful pâtés tasted a great deal better now that I had the kind of hunger a day's marching gives you. After scoffing down a load of food, I climbed into my sleeping bag.

The next thing I knew, I was being woken up for guard. Banica was cursing the guy who came to wake me, as not being able to tell who was who, he had woken him first. It was nice being beside the lake at night. There was a little grassy area between the lake shore and the woods, which I spent my time pacing up and down. Unfortunately there were no stars to be seen as the sky had clouded over. Please don't fucking rain, I pleaded with the sky, that's definitely not what I needed right now, but, It was all in vain. I could hear the distant rumblings of a storm approaching.

When my hour of guard neared its end. I went back to my bivouac to wake Banica, before resuming my pacing. The normal practice on guard duty is to wake the next person five minutes before change over time to give them a chance to get dressed, but it had been nearly ten minutes since I had woken Banica and he still hadn't emerged. I assumed that he must have fallen asleep again, so I went back over to where he was sleeping to check on him, and to my surprise there was no sign of him. Where the devil has he got too, I wondered, he can't have deserted, not from here, not now. I went back out to the lake's edge to try and find him, but to no avail. Shit, I thought, am I going to have to wake one of the corporals and tell them that I've lost Banica. Then, just as I was losing hope, there was a rustling in the bushes and out he popped. 'Hi Murray, you can sleep now,' he said nonchalantly. 'What were you doing over there? I was looking for you,' I asked him. He replied, in a manner of fact way, that he had felt the urge to go Hans Solo with Darth Vader's head and that was the reason for the delay. I just laughed, and bid him good night, then went back under my basha and tried to get some sleep.

It wasn't long after returning when I began to hear the first few droplets of water hitting the roof of my shelter. What started off as a light shower soon grew into a torrential downpour, accompanied by flashes of lightning and roars of thunder. What luck that I had finished guard when I did. I love the sound of rain hitting the top of a tent or a tin roof. It has a calming effect on me. Banica soon came back to the tent to wait out the rest of his guard, there was no point standing out in the rain. When his time was up he dashed across to the next guy's tent and gave him the guard list, and after that I fell asleep.

I don't know how long I had been asleep for when I was woken by a loud scream, followed by the wailing of: 'It's wet, it's all wet AAAAARRHH!' I looked round to see Mejri with his hands on his head in complete despair. His shelter was completely destroyed. What had happened was that when he had installed his bivouac, he hadn't angled the sides enough. The rainwater had collected on his tarpaulin and formed a pocket of water that kept on growing. It built up to the point where the weight of it had collapsed his shelter; dumping its contents on Mejri. It wasn't long before one of the corporals heard him, and shouted for him to shut up and quit his complaining before he really gave him something to complain about.

In the morning it was clear that Mejri had had an awful sleepless night, and he looked like a broken man. I busied myself trying to get some hot coffee going before we set off. I desperately needed some energy. Waking up more tired than when you went to sleep is no fun, but today was the final day of marching. This evening I would be a legionnaire, and tomorrow we would pack up, say goodbye to the farm, and leave for the 4RE, in Castelnaudary, with its heated rooms that were free from guard duty. There was, however, one small piece of good news that came out of last night: Cpl Novak, who had taken next to nothing with him, had been thoroughly drenched during the downpour. His sleeping bag and all his equipment was wet. He also had to march in wet clothes that day. This put him in a fouler mood than usual, but it was well worth it. Doyle, in particular, found this immensely entertaining.

We held an assembly and the adjutant tried his best to raise our spirits: 'There was 'only' another thirty kilometres to go, if we held a pace of five kilometres an hour, we would be finished by early afternoon.' Thirty kilometres sounded much more daunting than it had done the previous day. I couldn't see how the people who were struggling would cope. We had taken their bags and guns, but the pain from walking on the raw exposed skin left behind by the burst blisters was obviously causing them a great deal of pain.

We set off, walking alongside the reservoir and after an hour we arrived at the village of Cumiès, which is situated at the end of the lake. It is hardly worth calling a village though. It is a farm and three or four houses. Undoubtedly a lovely place to retire to, but raising children in a place like this would be a sure-fire way to encourage them to commit incest. We made our first stop here. The usual suspects had, once again, fallen behind. A couple more had joined their ranks, bringing their numbers to around ten. You have to bear in mind that there was fifty of us in total, so ten people is quite a big chunk and it is far too many to lose during a single march. The adjutant would probably get a bollocking from higher up for being too harsh on us, if one in five didn't make it through the march and get their kepis. So, once they arrived, we again split up their things. Now even some of the NCOs were now carrying two guns! My bag was now so heavy that I struggled to heave it onto my back.

After a good long pause, we re-embarked on our journey. The roads so far had been twisting country lanes, which was good because it stopped you from getting bored and kept morale up. Now, however, the roads began to straighten out and you could see for about a mile in front. At the speed we were going, these long straight roads seemed to last forever.

A while later we arrived at Villeneuve-la-Comptal, which is more like a town than a village. We stopped again on the fringe of the town to wait for the others, but by this time they were so far back we couldn't see them. It took maybe thirty minutes for everyone to arrive. When they did catch up the adjutant called an assembly for the sergeants and corporals only. While that was going on the Catholic priest was going around offering everyone sugary sweets. That was very thoughtful of him to bring a huge bag of sweets along for the march (It wasn't enough to ever make me want to go near a church, but a kind gesture none the less).

A short time after the meeting, we were off again, walking through the town centre. I noticed that it felt strange seeing civilization after nearly two months behind the walls of the Foreign Legion. It was as if somehow I didn't belong. It had been a while since any of us had seen shops, or people going about their daily lives. It didn't last long though, we turned right somewhere in the town and headed back out into the rolling fields. We found ourselves walking down another long, straight road. The march was really starting to drag on now, it felt like it took hours to cover a mile stretch of road (with all the stops we had to make to allow the walking dead to catch up). The people who were suffering with blisters and alike, really did look like zombies at this stage. I think that if you had handed certain of them a pistol, they would have put a slug through their own brain just to end their suffering and misery. That's what I got from the expressions on their faces anyhow. At the end of the long straight road we turned left and passed through another small town, and after we had gone past the town, the road started to incline more and more. Right, I thought, if we are going back up onto the plateau then we must be on the home stretch. The road became windier now as it ascended the plateau and it was easily another two or three hours before we were at the top.

Once we got to the top, we turned onto a small side road and paused at the entrance to a large farm to wait for everyone to catch up. After a, not so short, wait the stragglers began to slowly trickle in. We were told that the march was now over and a truck would be here to pick us up shortly. I have to admit that I was feeling rather good about myself. The march was over and I had earned my kepi. I was a Legionnaire. My feet and back were not so jubilant though, they were in bits, and I wouldn't be walking correctly for a week. However, I was sure that we hadn't walked thirty kilometres. What kind of march ended outside a farm, in the middle of nowhere. Surely, it had been intended that we would march back to our farm. I think that because of the walking wounded we had taken too long. We had to get to the graduation ceremony on time, because the brass was going to be there. It wouldn't have been good if we had made the colonel wait. My estimate was that we had marched around twenty kilometres on this second, and final, day.

Everyone was overjoyed to know that we had finished. It was well known that the kepi march was the most difficult thing in basic training. In theory it was all downhill from here. After a short wait, the truck arrived and we helped those who were having difficulty walking to climb aboard first, then the rest of us boarded and we set off for the farm.

When the truck pulled up in the car park we were called to assembly. The adjutant explained what we had to do. There was no time to relax; we had to get changed into our good set of combat fatigues, which had been ironed with all the creases in the right places. There were two main badges that we had to put on our uniform: the regiment badge, which went on your left breast; and the company badge, which normally went on the right, but which, for now would have to go inside the right breast pocket (the sergeants would take it out and pin it on us during the ceremony). After that was done, we put on our second pair of boots, which were nice and shiny and had never been warn. These really hurt your feet, especially after what we had just been through, but they looked nice. Once we were suited and booted, we lined up outside. The corporals handed us our white kepis with strict instructions not to put them on our heads until it was time. With that we climbed aboard the truck again and set off for the ceremony.

We only went a short distance, to the nearby village of Cahuzac. The truck stopped in front of a field, on the far side of the village. There was nothing special about this field except that there was an old stone tower in one corner. A tent had been set up at one side and there were a load of civilians milling around inside it. For us, the tent would have to wait. Our orders were to line up in rows and do a couple of dry runs of the ceremony, before the colonel turned up: He attended all the 'remises des képis blancs'. After what had happened at the flag ceremony, we couldn't afford to mess up in front of him again.

The ceremony went something like this: first the colonel would approach with his flag boy by his side; then the adjutant would hand over the section to him; after that, the colonel would stand us to attention, and tell us to put on our kepis; then we would recite the legionnaire's code of honour; lastly the sergeants would go from person to person, taking the company badge out of our pocket and pinning it on our chests. I was feeling quite nervous, as it was me who had been chosen to lead us in the code of honour. I had to say the first part of each verse, seven in total. If I fucked this up in front of the colonel, it would not be good for me. I was wondering why they didn't pick a French guy, but I suppose it is the 'Foreign' Legion after all.

I needn't have worried though, the ceremony passed without a hitch. Sgt Dsouza pinned my badge on me. I was glad about that because I respected him, and he was from the parachute regiment, which was where I aspired to go. During the pinning on of the badges, I heard Sgt Flaubert's voice coming from behind me.

Doyle had put his badge in the wrong pocket, but the Sergeant saw the funny side of it, and joked with him that he had a fifty/fifty chance and still got it wrong.

After all the pomp was finished with, we went over to the tent. It was full of food (crisps, cheese, saucisson), and beer. We all grabbed a bottle and, on the adjutant's mark, downed it in one. Then we, of course, had to sing one of the crappy, gay legion songs, before we were allowed to attack the food. Doyle and I were scoffing our faces like a couple of pigs, when one of the corporals came over and introduced an elderly British couple to us. They were expatriates who lived nearby. The conversation wasn't great. After exchanging pleasantries there was an awkward silence before they made their excuses and buggered off again. Doyle and I just laughed, these old toffs were form a different world to us. What did they think we were going to chat about, the annual yield of our vineyards? We wasted no time getting stuck back into the food. I didn't care about the beer. I am not a drinker, and neither was Doyle, if they had supplied a couple of bongs and some white widow, then that would be a different story. However, there were some who seemed to be enjoying the alcohol a bit too much. Groso, the old Kazak who I had met that first day in Aubagne was knocking them back like no one's business. Raikkonen, the Finn, came over to join Doyle and me. He was certain that Groso had been an alcoholic bum in civilian life. He pointed to his permanent red face and varicose veins as evidence for his theory. The corporals did eventually notice his excessive drinking and told him to lay off.

Meanwhile, Sgt Flaubert noticed that Doyle and I weren't drinking. He remarked that it was the first time he had seen a Brit and an Irishman refuse beer, and he soon put an end to that: Placing another bottle in our hands he ordered us to down them at once.

The party only lasted a couple of hours. Everyone helped to clear the tables away and take down the tent. Then we were back on the trucks heading to the farm. The people who had walked without rucksacks, or guns, were made to take guard that night, which I though was fair. We carried their shit for them on the march, so it was time to reciprocate. Having drunk a few beers and also being dead tired I fell asleep as soon as I lay down.

The next morning we were treated to a lay in and allowed to sleep until eight o'clock. All we had to do was clean the guns and the farm, then load the trucks and go. That was it, the farm was over.

4: Formiguères

On the mountains of truth you can never
climb in vain: either you will reach a point
higher up today, or you will be training your
powers so that you will be able to climb higher
tomorrow.
Friedrich Nietzsche

We arrived back at the 4RE, sometime in the mid-afternoon.
The first thing we had to do was hand the guns and left over
ammunition back in in. After the weapons were back in the
armoury, and the camp beds and other equipment that we had used
while at the farm were sent back to their respective stores, we went
for dinner in the mess. It felt good to be back at the regiment. Even
though we had ample time to eat, everyone was so traumatized
from the three minute meal times we had been given at the farm
that we just wolfed our food down like savages. Cpl Dino had to
came over at one point and tell us to calm down. Doyle had
developed the habit of eating his dessert first. His reason for this
was that if he ate it first, there was no way he could be deprived of
it, and he was then at ease to eat the main course. Out of the corner
of my eye, I saw, what must have been, a bunch of fresh recruits

from Aubagne, staring at us in horror. Little did they know, that they would be exactly the same in a months' time.

After dinner we went back to our section and were allowed to change into our sports gear. Everyone was ordered to pass by Cpl Sonking's room to be examined. He would determine who needed to visit the infirmary tomorrow. All in all, about ten people were ordered to go see the doctor. For the rest of us it would be business as usual, and we would have to go jogging in the morning. That night I was very uncomfortable sleeping in the heated rooms at the regiment. They felt so hot. I had become accustomed to the coldness of the farm, and had to sleep without a cover for the first few nights.

The next day we were up at six, and in our sports gear. We had breakfast, then after the company assembly, went for a run. It was clear that some of the NCOs were feeling the effects of the march too. We trotted along the canal for fifteen minutes, then turned round to head back. Today we would be getting our first month's salary. We didn't have bank accounts yet, so we would have to do it the old fashioned way. The adjutant took us over to the room below the mess hall and we lined up in front of a small table. An NCO entered with a metal safety box and sat down behind the table. When he called your name, you were to go up to him, salute, and give your name and number. He would then count your money in front of you, and ask you to confirm that it was correct and sign the registrar. After that you took off your kepi, and he placed your money inside of it. You then flipped it back on your head, saluted, and went to wait at the back of the room. It felt great to have some money again, but I still didn't know when I would get the chance to spend it. I was also worried about carrying my whole month's wages around on me. If I had learned anything at the farm, it was that there were some people among us that would rob their own grandmother. But there was nothing I could do. Our accounts were still in the process of getting made. The adjutant had assured us that we would have our bank cards by later that week, and that when they were ready we would go to 'La Banque

Postale,' in town, to deposit our money, so I would just have to be careful for a few days.

The next day I was sent to work over at the mess. They had a dish washing machine there, but unfortunately for me it was broken. This meant washing everything by hand. It took so long that by the time I had finished the cleaning from breakfast, it was lunchtime, and so on. The worst part of working in the kitchens is emptying the bins; they fucking stunk of rotting food. My way of not breathing in the foul air was to get to about fifteen metres from the bin area, take a big gulp of air, then run, dump the bag, and run back to where I was out of range of the smell. The only good thing about working at the mess was stealing extra desserts. That day it was chocolate éclairs, one of my favourites; second only to the mille-feuille (custard slice).

I didn't get back to the section until late that evening. On returning the others told me that tomorrow we would be going into town to deposit our money, and that I had to go iron my dress uniform. There was a room set-up for ironing downstairs. Everyone else had finished already, it was just me and a few others who had been on service that day left (plus a couple of guys who couldn't iron for toffee). The irons that we had were not very good to put it mildly: The years of constant use by people who had never ironed before had almost completely destroyed them. I wasn't great at ironing myself, the only time I had done it before was when I had visitors in prison. However, in spite of my lack of ironing skills I was making good progress, but I had to stop at nine and go upstairs for assembly (while at the 4RE you have an evening roll call, every weekday, at 9:00pm. This is when, the final count is made and you receive the orders for the next day. It's normally after this that people desert, as you have until 6 o'clock the next morning before anyone notices).

After the assembly I went back downstairs to finish my ironing. I didn't pass the first review of my clothes, but there was nothing majorly wrong; just a few double creases and rough patches, but I persevered and passed the second review. Eventually getting to bed not long after 10:00pm.

In the morning, after the assembly, we got changed into our 'tenue de sortie' (going out dress). Adj O'Malley called us into the corridor and handed us an envelope with our bank card and pin number in it. He gave us strict instructions to memorize the number then burn the letter in a bin on the balcony. He warned us that if he saw anyone, after today, with that letter he would punish the hell out of them; and he would have no sympathy for the fool who kept it and got their money stolen. With that said, he told us to retire to our rooms and wait for the bus.

When our transport arrived, I was glad to see that it was one of the nice busses again. The corporals told us to take our bags with us, and this could only mean one thing: They were going to let us do some shopping. We drove to Castelnaudary town centre, which is not far from the regiment, and stopped in front of the bank, on a beautiful tree lined street. Then we lined up in the bank and deposited our cash. The other people who wanted to use the bank that day must have been pissed, because the line stretched all the way out of the door!

After the banking was done Adj O'Malley called an assembly. He told us that we would have until 3:00pm to go do what we wanted in town (which gave us about five hours in total), and then we were all to meet back here outside the bank. If anyone was late he would not give us another chance to go out for the rest our basic training. However, I couldn't head for the shops straight away because, being the dumbass that I am, and lacking in foresight, I had deposited all my money in the bank without keeping any for shopping. So, I now had to go to the cashpoint, but I wasn't alone, and there was now a big line for that too. After getting some money, I teamed up with Doyle and we went off to find some shops. I told him that before anything else, I had to get a razor. There was no way I was using those blunt pieces of dog shit again.

I went into the first general store that we came across. I brought two Mach3 razors and some shaving cream (I had been using soap to shave with at the farm). After that was done I could relax. We found a small supermarket in town and filled our bags with goodies. I brought: an iron, hair clippers, electric kettle, a disposable camera, a pair of insoles for my boots, and loads of food. I wanted to get an iron because the ones at the regiment were awful; and it saved me from having to wait with all the others.

After the shopping was done, we went to a pizza restaurant that was next to the town square. The French make excellent pizzas, good enough to rival the Italians in my opinion. We ordered the biggest pizzas we could with plenty of extra toppings, and three desserts each. This made the waitress raise her eyebrows a bit, but we didn't care if she thought we were pigs.

It was after midday when we left the restaurant. We decided to walk around the town and see what else they had on offer. The only things we were forbidden from purchasing were computers and mobile phones (the Legion doesn't want you communicating with your family and getting homesick). However, we soon got bored. There simply wasn't much else to see in Castelnaudary. I did, however, manage to pick up a better English to French dictionary, than the Legion had provided me with, and a nice little phrase book too.

After all the eating and shopping, Doyle and I slowly made our way back down towards the bank. We were an hour early, but that was alright. We had done all we could in this small town. I went back into the bank to deposit the rest of my money. I didn't want to give the thieves a chance to steal it. People began slowly drifting in as the deadline approached. We hoped that no one had taken this opportunity to desert. That would have really sucked, but I needn't have worried; everyone turned up, although some did cut it close. It was apparent from some of the faces that there had been some drinking going on: One of the Brazilians could barely stand up.

A couple of days before the weekend, an assembly was called in the corridor. We received orders to pack our things and prepare to leave. There was a list of what we had to take with us, and, as usual, everything on our floor of the building had to be scrubbed clean. We were going to a place called Formiguères for a week long adventure holiday. Formiguères is a tiny village a hundred and twenty kilometres south of Castelnaudary, high in the

Catalonian Pyrenees (it is only a stone's throw from the border with Spain). The village sits in the middle of the Catalonian Pyrenees National Park, which is bordered to west by Andorra. The village itself only has 441 inhabitants, which meant that our visit would raise the population by ten percent. Formiguères sits a kilometre and a half above sea level with the surrounding mountain peaks reaching up to nearly three kilometres. The main attractions are its ski resort, and Romanesque church which was first built in the year 843. The village is your standard, picturesque, ski resort complete with cosy looking wooden chalets.

Everyone in my section was excited about going. It was a chance for us to have some fun and relax after the stress of the farm. Not surprisingly, those who had been taken off physical activities after the kepi march, suddenly got better. I think it was a Sunday when we departed the regiment to begin the long journey south. I noticed that Sgt Flaubert was not coming with us and now that I thought of it, I hadn't seen him since we had got back from the farm. He was my chef de groupe and I got on well with him. He had a good sense of humour, was competent, and never hit anyone. The most he would do is give you a cuff on the back of the head. I asked Doyle, who was in the same group, if he had seen him, but he hadn't seen him for a while either. I wondered what was up, and if he was gone, who would replace him. I hoped it wouldn't be that weirdo Cch Laplace. In fact, his replacement was much worse than the corporal-chef.

The driver started the bus, drove it round the corner, and stopped just before the main gate. Why have we stopped here? I was thinking. That's when I saw him, our new group leader: Sgt Rakoto. He was from Mayotte or Madagascar (if I had to guess). It would be easy to write him off as just a horrible person, but I don't know what was going on in his life, maybe he had a reason for being the way he was. The first impression I got from him was that he didn't want to be here, and was super pissed off that he was. In fact, I can't remember him saying one thing to me during the three months he was with us (he normally spoke to one of the corporals, but hardly ever directly to us legionnaires; unless he was really angry). He wore a permanent scowl, and was completely unapproachable. He treated us like he had caught us in bed with his wife. His normal response to a question was to shoot daggers at you, tut, look up to the sky as if to say kill me now, and walk off. He was just not interested in training us and, in effect, for the last three months my group leader was one of the corporals. In spite of his foul mood, there was one good thing about him, and that was that he didn't care enough to punish us, so no more beastings. Maybe I am being a bit harsh on him, he never actually did anything bad to me (he didn't do anything good either). He was just a miserable son of a bitch, who hated his life and took it out on everyone around him.

The bus left the regiment and drove in the direction of the farm, but instead of turning off, we kept to the big, departmental road. We began climbing higher and higher into the Pyrenees. Somewhere around halfway into the journey we stopped in a small town. While the bus driver had a rest we were allowed to go to the shops. I brought a whole black forest gateaux to myself, and Doyle had some other type of cake. We were getting stuck into our cakes on a bench, when Cpl Kamel came along and scolded us. He informed us that it was against the rules to eat with you beret on. We were oblivious to this, we knew that you had to have your beret on if you went outside, but the eating thing was news to us. He told us that it wasn't a problem to take the beret off outside if we were eating (it was hard to tell which rule should take precedence sometimes). Before going on his way, he called us a pair of tramps. Once he was out of sight, we burst out laughing, we weren't aware that in France only tramps ate with their hats on.

Back on the bus we really started climbing the mountains now. The roads were windy as hell and there was a huge drop to one side. The Pyrenees are really old mountains and they have a prehistoric feeling to them; it's not difficult to imagine dinosaurs roaming about in them. The mountains kept getting bigger and bigger, and pretty soon white, snow-capped peaks appeared in the distance. There were also signs along the road reminding people to use their snow chains. This was all new for me, we don't have any real mountains in the UK (yes Scottish people I know about Ben Nevis, but come on; it's just a glorified hill. If you can run up it in an hour, or carry a piano up it, then it's not a proper mountain). I was born in North Wales and grew up in the Snowdonia national park region, in sight of Mount Snowdon (Wales' highest mountain), but it had nothing on this, and no one ever needed snow chains around there. Condensation soon began forming on the windows of the bus, this meant I could no longer enjoy the view as much, everyone else was asleep by now and therefore didn't wipe it off, but I still had my window. I don't normally sleep on new journeys, I am quite childlike in that way, and I get excited and want to look at everything.

We passed a sign for 'Les Angles' and the adjutant woke everyone. It wouldn't be long now before we arrived, I guessed, and sure enough fifteen minutes later we entered Formiguères. It's a lovely little place with narrow streets and chalets, surrounded by mountains and pine forests. There was no snow in the town at this time of year; you had to go a bit higher for that. Our chalet was tucked away behind the Gendarmerie, on the edge of town. Looking at the Gendarmes milling around, I couldn't help thinking that I wouldn't like to be posted here. Sure the view took your breath away, but in the summer it would be dead, and in the winter you would be swamped by wankers with stupid hats and Oakley sunglass, who like to pull up on their skis and spray snow in your face.

The bus dropped us of in the car park behind our chalet. We sat and waited, while the adjutant went inside with the other NCOs to sort out the rooms. There was a couple of Renault army trucks parked next to the building, so no more comfy busses for us. One of the corporals came out with a box of rations and told us to eat while we waited. There was a kitchen with a cook there, but he hadn't prepared anything for today, as he needed two legionnaires to help him with the work (you can never escape the corvée in the Legion).

It was not long after eating that the corporals came to take us inside. The rooms were on the first floor, and they were nice enough, each one had two bunk beds, a shower, and toilet in it. On the ground floor was a lounge area with sofas, chairs, and a TV, and outside the lounge was a grassy area with picnic benches and a payphone. On our first evening we were given time to relax. I sat outside and chatted with some of the others until it was time for bed. The rooms had decent central heating, none of us were used to this sort of thing by now, and as a result had to sleep without covers and with the window wide open.

The next morning we were up bright and early. Today we would be going to visit some caves. We took the trucks to the Arbas Forest in the Haute-Garonne department, which is quite a distance away from where we were staying. We would be exploring the famous Felix-Trombe cave system (the Felix-Trombe cave system is pretty big: It is made up of ten inter-connected caves, which have a surveyed length of thirty kilometres, and a depth of around nine hundred meters).

The trucks pulled up in a forest car park. Our guides were already there with all the equipment we needed for the day. They gave everyone a rock climbing harness and a bunch of carabiners. Then we followed them through the woods to an inconspicuous hole in the ground. We all put on our head lamps and entered one by one. We had to abseil down a little bit at first, then we were in. The part of the cave that we were in was narrow and wet, and the walls were covered in a layer of slime. The only sound down there was the dripping of water, and we were walking in a small stream. It was amazing to realize that this tiny gentle stream had cut its way through all this solid rock over the ages, and created this whole cave system. This place had everything you could wish for in a cave, narrow parts to squeeze through, huge open chambers full of stalactites and stalagmites, crystal clear pools of water, and slime (lots of slime). There were sections where we had to climb, and parts to abseil down. It was all great fun. One of my favourite parts was when our guides told us to turn off all the lights and grab the harness of the person in front, then we moved through the cave, like a giant centipede, in perfect darkness.

We spent five or six hours exploring the subterranean world of the cave, before popping out another hole in the woods and walking back to the car park. After handing the equipment back, our guides produced a range of headlamps from their van. They asked if we were interested in buying them. They told us that they had tested loads of headlamps, and decided that these were the best on the market. Well, you could have bloody told us you had these before we went down the cave, I thought. The headlight that the Legion had given us was a big, heavy, unwieldy thing that still used a traditional bulb, had poor battery life, and wasn't that bright. These on the other hand were super bright LED lamps with red and green filters, which weighed a fraction of what ours did. They were a bit pricey at €45, but I brought one from them that day (it turned out that their judgment was sound, my lamp performed well and lasted me all the way through my service).

That evening after dinner I was hanging out in the chalet garden with a few others. A couple of guys had just finished kitchen duty and were complaining about the cook. He was an Asian corporal-chef, who didn't speak very good French. Apparently he flew off the handle if you made the smallest mistake (lighting the back left hob, instead of the back right, for example). He would start cursing and throw things at you. Someone made the remark that the reason for him being bald was that he had torn all his hair out.

As we were laughing about the cook, Doyle came up to me and demanded to have a word in private, so I walked over to the car park with him to find out what the problem was. He began explaining to me that he had lost his bank card. 'Alright,' I said, 'so what's the fuss, no one can use it without the pin (our bank cards weren't credit or debit cards, they were for ATM use only), if you need money while we are here I can lend you some.' He then explained to me that it wasn't that simple, because he had not burnt away the letter with his pin number on it, out of fear that he would forget his pin. I immediately realized that we had another situation like the missing FAMAS on our hands. The adjutant explicitly told us to get rid of that letter, and it was a safe bet that he was going to go completely ape shit if he found out. I asked Doyle to think carefully about the last time he could remember having it in his possession, and told him to go double check all his bags for it, but if he couldn't find it, then he would have to tell the adjutant and take punishment, because there was a cash point in town and someone could easily slip out each night and empty his account.

Doyle told me that he had already checked and double checked everything, and with his head hung low, he went to tell the adjutant the news. It was heart-breaking, because I could see the anguish on his face, he didn't want to be responsible for another banane, but there was no getting out if it. I returned to the picnic tables to await the coming storm, and sure enough, after five minutes a call for assembly rang out.

We lined up in the car park, Sgt Dsouza came out and informed us that someone had lost their bank card, and as a result we, and all our things, would be getting searched. We were to go upstairs and stand by the door to our rooms. No one was to enter or touch anything. As I walked along the hall to my room, I saw Doyle standing in his room with two corporals going through all his stuff. I stood by my door and waited for the search to begin. Cpl Dino came to my room. First he patted us down and made us turn out our pockets then he went in the room and began searching. He was busy searching our bags when Cpl Kamel came out of Doyle's room and declared that he had found the bank card and letter in the small side pocket of Doyle's duffle bag. Sgt Dsouza flew to the room and began kicking Doyle's ass, but the adjutant came up and stopped him. He then ordered us all downstairs. The ass whupping Doyle was going to get was not for our eyes, but we could hear it through the floor. The adjutant and sergeant went to town on him that day. Shortly after this fiasco we were ordered to go to bed early, and I, for one, was glad: That was definitely enough drama for one day.

Tuesday's activity was rock climbing. We boarded the trucks and headed off. Doyle was with us (there are many punishments in the Legion, but ostracism isn't one of them). We drove to the village of Llo, just thirty kilometres south of Formiguères, on the border with Spain. Again we met our guides on location, and got harnessed up. The rock we had to climb was a four hundred meter tall cliff. However, It wasn't exactly rock climbing. It was, what is known as 'via ferrata (iron road).' Via ferrata is what could be described as assisted climbing. The climbing route has steel cables running along it that are fixed to the rock every meter or two, so it doesn't have much slack in it. If you were a really crap climber, you could climb the whole thing using the cable, but that would definitely make you a pussy. There were also what look like giant staples that had been driven into the rock for you to step up like a ladder whenever there was a vertical ascent, or a slight overhang, to get up. The only part that was slightly dangerous was when you needed to transition from one cable to another, but even this was pussified, because you had a backup rope and carabiner on your harness. You simply attached the backup line to the new cable, and then switched your main to be your backup. At no time during the climb could you fall (nine year old girls were allowed to climb this particular route, so that should give you an idea of the difficulty).

I don't want to bitch too much though, the view was nice and I had plenty of time to appreciate it, as there were a few people among us who were scared of heights. They kept freezing every time we arrived at a tricky part of the route and holding everyone up. This did grate on my nerves a bit, because the climb was ridiculously safe. If they wanted to make it any safer we would have to be shrouded in bubble wrap. Luckily there weren't any nine year old girls climbing that day to laugh at us.

Even with all the hold ups we got to the top in under two hours. Unfortunately, for the wussies, that was not the end. There was another fun activity for those who don't like heights: The longest zip-line I had ever seen. It stretched from our peak, over the road, all the way to another mountain. It was easily three hundred meters across. There was no brake on it either, and I could imagine that you would have built up a fair bit of speed by the time you reached the other side. The only way to stop was by hitting a cargo net at the other end. Our instructors told us to grab hold of the net with both our arms and legs, as it would rebound and if you didn't have a good grip, it would fling you back out and you would get stuck in the middle. This wasn't too bad as the instructors could get you back in (I forget exactly how they done this, they sent you a line somehow and hauled your ass back). The real problem was if someone had started off behind you and you collided with them. That could potentially cause serious injury.

Sergeant Dsouza stepped up to go first and got across without a problem. Then the rest of us formed a queue and waited for our turn. It wasn't long before Murphy's Law struck our group. A few people ahead of me, someone had just sailed down the line and hit the net. When the guide saw him make contact with the net, he gave the next guy the signal to go, and just as he left the launch platform, the person at the far end lost grip of the net and began heading in reverse. I can only imagine that this was what witnessing a train crash feels like. Everyone could see what was going to happen, but there was nothing we could do about it. They hurtled towards each other, picking up speed all the time. Then they collided with each other back on back. There was a loud thud as they collided that echoed through the valley. It didn't stop us zip lining though, we waited for them to get hauled in and then continued. I went up, attached myself, and stepped out. When I hit the net at the other end it knocked the wind out of me, but I held on. Once across I asked the crash victims how they were feeling. Both complained of pain in the back and ribs. It wouldn't have surprised me if they had broken a rib or two. Luckily for them, all that was left to do was walk down a trail to where the trucks were parked and go back to our chalet.

Arriving back at Formiguères, I was really hungry. We hadn't been able to eat during the day's activities. Doyle's punishment, for misplacing his bank card, and not burning the letter with his pin on it, was to work in the kitchen all week. This was good as there was only one additional person per day who had to do corvée cuisine (kitchen duty). We could hear the bad tempered cook cursing Doyle and throwing pots and pans at him, but he would soon wear himself out. It did no good to stress Doyle out, he would just make more mistakes. Not everyone reacts the same way under pressure.

Wednesday, day three, was canyoning. As the name suggests canyoning is travelling in canyons. This turns out to be a rather difficult thing, which requires you to use a variety of techniques, such as: abseiling, jumping, climbing, and swimming. This is a useful activity for testing your resolve, because once you are down in the canyon, the only way out is to complete the course. The sides are normally so steep and the location so remote that there really is no backing out. So you just have to conquer your fear and get on with it. Our destination for today was 'Le Canyon du Llech,' which is just outside the town of Parades, on the eastern boundary of French Catalonia.

We met our guides (in another car park) and got kitted up. This time we had to wear a life jacket and helmet, as well as a climbing harness. After a short walk from the car park, we began our climb down into the gorge. We stopped about half way down, on a small ledge with the river forty feet below. We would have to jump from here into the canyon. There was quite a drop and the pool at the bottom didn't look that big. Needless to say I was a little nervous. The guides told us not to worry. All we had to do was approach the edge and step out. It was important that we looked straight ahead, pointed our feet down, and folded our arms across our chest. If you looked down the water would give you a good hard slap in the face, just like belly flopping in a pool.

The NCOs from the parachute regiment went first. When it was Sch Popadynets' turn, he leapt from the edge, and because he was around six foot six, he leapt so far that he almost hit the other side of the canyon, even the guides looked worried for a moment. After a few people had gone it was Kuzma's turn, and he was obviously shitting himself: it was written all over his face. He looked like he was going to cry, but Cpl Novak was having none of it. He wouldn't have him portraying Poles as pansies in front of the other nationalities, and ordered him to the ledge. Kuzma approached the jumping off point quivering with fear. The guides did their best to calm him and talk him through it, but no one was ready for what happened next. Kuzma tentatively stepped up to the ledge and the guides started the count, one…two…three! On three Kuzma's nerves got the better of him and he turned back to chicken out, but lost his footing and slipped. He fell and the top of his body slammed into ledge and rebounded, sending him flipping backwards through the air. While falling he let out a continuous blood curdling scream, ending only when he hit the water with a forty foot belly flop. Just hearing the slap from his impact with the water told me that it must have hurt. It was one of the funniest things I have ever seen in my life, I couldn't breathe from laughing so hard. What topped it off was the look on his face in that split second between slipping and bouncing off the rock. He had that 'terror of death' look on his face that people get when things are happening to fast for their brain to process, and they just look stupid. It was ironic how his fear of falling, had caused him to panic and fall: His worst nightmare had come true. Everyone was pissing themselves laughing, it was amazing.

I went over to the ledge and got ready to jump, and it did look like a long way down, but I try not to dwell on thoughts like that; they will consume you if you do. I stepped out straight away and came crashing down into the water a couple of seconds later. It was a bit nippy in the river, I'm guessing that it must have been meltwater.

Once everyone was down, we swam on a bit and went down a natural waterslide carved through the granite by the water. Then we came to our next drop, a reasonably high waterfall. We had to swim up to the waterfall, climb on the rock face, and lay supine on it. You then edged yourself forwards until the water swept you away. It was great fun, the rock went down a couple of meters and at the edge was a lip (like a ski jump). It shot you right out into the middle of the pool below.

We continued our travels by swimming, sliding and jumping until we came upon a really tall waterfall. This thing was too high to jump from, so we abseiled down it. One of the guides went first and showed us how it was done and we followed suit. I was feeling confident about this as I had abseiled a few times when I was a teenager. I got myself attached to the rope and walked over the edge. Once clear of the rock I let the rope run fast, trying to show off my skill, but after a couple of meters the rope disappeared and I fell, arms and legs flapping, into the water below. Those fuckers had played a trick on us: The rope only went down halfway. My face must have looked just like Kuzma's did.

I climbed up on a rock beside the river to watch the rest come down. It was funny, everyone did the same and fell the last couple of meters in shock. Well almost everyone, one of the last guys to come down was not enjoying the canyoning very much, and he was inching his way down at a snail's pace. He saw the end of the rope coming, stopped, and called back up to the instructors to tell them that the rope wasn't long enough! 'I know, just drop,' was the reply that came back. He didn't like that answer too much, but took a couple of deep breaths, closed his eyes and let go.

The next big challenge was more enjoyable. We had to zip line from the top of the next waterfall into the water, everyone got past this without any problems or hold-ups. We had been in the water a long time by now and it was getting really cold, people were shaking from the chill. Every time I had the chance to, I climbed out onto a rock to heat up a little. The guides told us that it wouldn't be long now before we finished. Then the river began to flatten out and we emerged from the gorge into a forest. All that was left was a march back up to the car park where the trucks were.

That night I was so tired and hungry. Being in that cold water coupled with the adrenaline from all those jumps, really took it out of me. I was glad that I didn't have to work in the kitchen with that stressed out corporal-chef, like Doyle. I didn't wait for lights out that night and went to bed straight after dinner.

For the fourth day we didn't have to go anywhere. We would be doing some good old fashioned orienteering right here in Formiguères. Sgt Dsouza and the corporals had been up since the crack of dawn. They had set up a series of control points that we would have to find and punch our score card with. We were each given a map, compass, score card, and a clue sheet. Then we were put into pairs and issued with one mountain bike between us. The course was about ten miles in total and there were fifteen control points to collect. I was paired with Maachi. He told me that I could use the bike the whole time: He was more than happy to run.

We started off looking for the control points that were in the village, and I soon felt grateful for the bike, but even so it was hard to keep up with Maachi. He had one hell of an engine inside him. Our day started off well. We found the first couple of control points near the village and then went up into the hills to get the rest, but somewhere along the way we took a wrong turn. The path we were on got smaller, and smaller, and then it just stopped. It was a dead end. We sat down in a small clearing to examine the map and tried to find out where we were. After twenty minutes of searching we concluded that we had actually gone so far down the wrong path that we had gone off the map! The only solution was to retrace our steps back to the village and start again.

After half an hour of retracing our steps we could see Formiguères again, but we had wasted a lot of time with our mistake. We started off from the last marker that we had got and decided to skip the control points in the woods, for fear of getting lost again, and instead headed for the lakes. We figured that using the lakes as a reference point should make it pretty easy to stay on track.

We soon caught up with some of the others and formed a group with them. Searching together was cheating, but we didn't care. After the lakes we had to go to the ski slopes to find a couple of control points. It was more difficult than we anticipated. The clues that had been written down weren't that clear, even the Francophones couldn't quite understand them. The NCOs could speak French well, but their writing was not of the same calibre, and their vocabulary was limited to military things. After spreading out to search the ski slope we eventually found the markers and punched our cards. All that was left now was a long jog down the other side of the lakes to get the last markers, then we could head back to the chalet.

After stamping the last control point we set off at intervals in our original pairs, so as not to reveal to the NCOs that there had been any collusion between the groups. When Maachi and I arrived back Sgt Dsouza was on duty. He checked our card and recorded the time. He asked why we had missed three of the control points. We told him about getting lost, and he made some remark about us being good at sport, but not so strong in the brain area, then dismissed us. It was true, we had gone too fast at the beginning without planning our route out first or paying attention to the map, but to quote Oscar Wilde: *'Experience is the one thing you can't get for free.'*

Day five, our last full day in Formiguères. Today we were going on a march with Sch Popadynets. We would be visiting the source of the Aude River, which is roughly ten miles from Formiguères. Although the march was going to be quite long. We didn't have much to carry (we had no guns, and only a small backpack with food, water, a fleece, and a waterproof jacket in it). The Chef led the way and we followed him down through the village and then turned off the road onto a dirt path, which zigzagged up the side of the valley that Formiguères was in. We walked along the mountainside until we reached the nearby town of Les Angles. Somewhere near Les Angles we could hear cowbells ringing in the fields below us, and a great deal of mooing too. Sch Popadynets stopped and told us to, say hello to the cows, which we did. As soon as we had greeted the heifers, he gave us a funny look and asked us if we were mad. 'The cows can't understand you,' he said, 'do you normally talk to cows when someone tells you to?' He had a big smile on his face while he was saying this, and was only playing around, trying to lighten up the mood on the march. He often made jokes like that. It wasn't his style to act the tough guy all the time.

Continuing on with our walk. We passed Les Angles and began heading further up into the mountains. It was somewhere along here that I spotted a wild sheep, or goat, with huge curling horns, which I thought for the longest time was a bighorn, or ibex, but while researching for this book I have found out that bighorns are only found in North America, and the Pyrenean ibex was declared extinct in 2000, So what I saw was a mouflon, which is a type of wild sheep, and thought to be one of the two ancestors of all modern domestic sheep. But it still looked cool perched on a rock looking down at us with its big spiraling horns. I just about managed to get a shot of it with my disposable camera before it hopped off.

As we got higher and higher into the mountains, the trees began to thin out. We crossed what appeared to be a ski slope (there wasn't any snow on it at this time of year), then hiked up one last hill. As I came over the crest, I saw the beautiful 'Lac d'Aude,' hidden away in a small valley surrounded by pine trees and grass, with the odd rock sticking out of the ground here and there. The lake itself was a bit on the small side (Wikipedia says that is has a surface area of only thirty square meters, but that sounds a bit too small to me), but it really was a beautiful place.

We walked down a trail that led to the lake, sat down in the thick grass at its edges, and had some lunch. What a great place to take a break this was; the lake was tucked away in a depression that sheltered it from the strong mountain winds. That day the sky was clear and the sun was shining. The view was breath-taking, and to top it off, the grass around the lake was spongy like a mattress. I cooked up my rations, filled my belly, and lay there next to the sapphire blue water. I drifted off to sleep that day, watching the water gently lap against the sides.

As all good things do, the break came to an end, and we set off on our return journey, back to the chalet at Formiguères. Walking back was a lot easier as we were going downhill and our bags weighed next to nothing, now that the rations were empty. We arrived back just before five o'clock in the afternoon. As soon as we arrived, the adjutant called an assembly. We were to put on our good set of combats and get ready to have a slap up meal in town.

It was pitch black when we left for the restaurant (there are barely any streetlights in Formiguères). It was only a short walk down the road from where we were staying. A very charming little place called 'La Tapenade,' which was owned by a local

Catalonian couple. We were the only customers there that night and they had pushed all the tables together so we could sit as one big group. The interior was dimly lit and there was folk music playing in the background. We all had pizza, the adjutant ordered for all of us (this stopped people from wasting time procrastinating over the menu, and besides half the people there couldn't read French anyway). As with any meal in the Legion, there is alcohol involved. The first thing we had to do before eating was toast our hosts. The patron brought out what is known as a porrón. This is a funny shaped glass bottle that looks similar to a teapot. There is a pointed spout out of which a thin jet of wine spurts whenever you tip it up. This enables you to drink from the porrón without touching it with your mouth. Inside was a liqueur called Muscat, which is a kind of dark brown, sweet wine. After the Muscat, we drank a normal glass of red wine, and waited for our pizzas. I was really hoping we would get away with not singing a Legion song, but nope, some fucker couldn't help himself and started one going.

When my pizza arrived I ate it in a matter of seconds. We had to sit in our groups while at the restaurant, and for me this meant sitting with Sgt, stroppy britches, Rakoto, who as usual was wearing a face like a slapped arse. After a couple of glasses of wine, the two guys next to me tried to talk to him. Doyle and I never attempted this, because we could tell from his body language that it wasn't a good idea, but not everyone has the same level of emotional intelligence. Some people just don't pick up on facial expressions, or body language. I can't remember exactly what was said, but they basically tried to engage him in conversation and share a joke. The sergeant really didn't appreciate this and just locked eyes with them in an unblinking gaze, with his brow lowered, nostrils flared, and lips pursed, but they just continued on oblivious to the non-verbal signals he was sending out.

It looked like Sgt Rakoto was going to explode at any minute; and, sure enough, he broke his silence and snarled at them, 'shut your fucking mouths you pair of idiots, maybe you could speak with your last sergeant like that, but don't you ever speak to me again, all I want to hear from you is 'oui sergeant,' now is that clear?' The two guys had finally got the message and they answered him with a, 'oui sergeant' and didn't bother him again. Well, that was a fucking mood killer, I thought to myself, what a way to end the week. The sergeant knew damn well that he was being an unsociable fuck though, as he was careful not raise his voice enough so as to make everyone else at the table aware of what was going on.

After that it was silent for the rest of the evening, at our end of the table. I was glad when it was over. Finally I could get away from that guy. He should have been called Sgt Buzzkill, he really was a joyless, empty man. He hadn't joined in any of the activities that week: He stayed in the truck and waited in the car park every time we went somewhere, like a sulky two-year-old. Needless to say I wasn't looking forward to another three months with him.

The next day we packed our things and waited for the bus to take us back to the 4RE, where we would be taking up service as soon as we got back. Including, for the first time, twenty-four hour guard duty at the gate.

5: 4ᵉ Régiment Étranger

There is nothing permanent except change.
Heraclitus

We arrived back at the regiment late Saturday afternoon, and the NCOs disappeared like a fart in the wind. They must have been missing their partners (except for Cpl Novak, whose partner was his hand). The weekends at the 4RE are pretty uneventful for new recruits. At this stage we were still not allowed out. However, on Sunday you can go to a Church service in the chapel. If you didn't want to go to the church, then you were made to go to the cinema.

The Foreign Legion actually had a pretty decent cinema at Castelnaudary, it was in the same building as our mess. Most of the films we saw there were complete garbage, and people just used the time to sleep. The first time I saw the movie 'The 300' was here, and I can tell you that it just isn't the same when it's dubbed over in French. There was one film that was a genuine thigh-slapper though. It was one of those unintentional comedies, like Orca 2, or Rambo. The film was about Bigfoot, and there was one scene in the movie where the Bigfoot jumps out from the bushes and attacks someone. The best that their special effects team could come up with for this, was to lob an empty Bigfoot suit across the screen. It looked so unnatural, and way its arms and legs were flapping about made the whole cinema explode with laughter.

Apart from the cinema, the only other weekend activity was the occasional trip to the swimming pool, but I was only able to go a couple of times during my four months there. The reason being that those among us who couldn't swim were given priority, and there were a lot of people who couldn't swim.

It was on the weekend after Formiguères that we had our first couple of deserters (we had lost two people to injury so far, but no one had run away). It was a couple of French lads who scarpered that Saturday night. People often criticized the French for making up the bulk of the deserters in the Legion, saying that they were weak and such like, but I never bought into that idea. There are two reasons for the high level of French deserters, in my opinion. The first was that there were more French in the Legion than any other nationality; and the second was that it's just easier for them, we were already in France. All they had to do is jump the wall, and get on the next bus home. The rest of us would have to find the nearest embassy and convince them of our identity, as the Legion had taken our passports. If the number of deserters was an indication of the toughness of a particular group, then the Chinese would take the gold. The Chinese in the Legion, get beasted for not understanding French, picked on by bullies on account of their small stature, and relegated to the kitchens to serve out their contracts. They take no end of shit, but I have never heard of a Chinese person deserting. I can only imagine that if you have worked twenty-hour-days in a factory, for fuck all money, that has nets to stop you jumping out the windows and killing yourself, slept in a single room apartment with nine other people, and lived under the rule of a crackpot government that can decide to imprison you at any moment and harvest your organs, then there is nothing the Legion can do, short of gang rape, that would make you even consider leaving. Not to mention the logistics of getting back if they did ever decide to go. I am pretty sure that if the Foreign Legion was in Russia, then it would be Russians who made up the majority of deserters.

Being back at the regiment was not great, if I am honest. The first week we were back was just pure service. I can clearly remember the first service I had after Formiguères. I was sent to work in the corporal-chef's club, across from the mess hall. It isn't too bad working in there; it's mostly cleaning glasses. But it was the first thing the corporal-chef, who was head barman, said to me, that has stuck in my memory. On seeing my name, he said, 'Hey English, do you know Lenny Kravitz?' Just as I was about to answer, he cut me off with, 'He's a nigger.' Well, how do you respond to that? I thought. I can remember thinking of some snarky comeback like: why how astute of you corporal-chef. But I decided it was best not to reply. I'm guessing that working at the bar, he was, probably, always drunk anyway. Still, coming from the UK, I wasn't really used to that sort of thing.

Most of the time that I was on service I was sent to work in the rank and file mess or the officer's mess. The officer's mess was in a huge chateau, fenced off from the rest of the regiment. You needed a security card to get in there. It looked nice, but it was just as bad as our mess. There was lots to do over there. We had to iron table cloths, set out paper napkins, lay out the cutlery, and stock the tables with bread and wine. It was a pain in the arse because the lieutenants, captains, and colonels all had separate dining halls. The legionnaires who worked over there (mostly corporal-chefs), were the most shameless cocksuckers you could imagine. It was like a competition to see you could kiss the most butt. This meant that we had to work a lot. It wasn't physically demanding; it was just annoying. Having to polish wine glasses and fold the napkins in a pretty way was, in my head, a waste of time: No one noticed. The good thing about the officer's mess was the food you could steal. They had all these fancy cheeses, and loads of wine (I must have stolen a lot of cheese in my time at the Legion).

The first time I was sent to work there, I was half drunk by diner time. I can remember that just as we were taking off the white coats and getting ready to leave one of the corporal-chefs came and told us to wait. The officers were having a garden party with some of the local bourgeoisie and we were needed to help.

For fuck sake, I thought, so we are going to be stuck here until god knows what hour, then we would have to go back to our rooms and go straight to sleep. Then we would wake up the next day and go straight to our next place of service. It was times like this that made me really hate the regimental service at the Legion, it was never ending and at times you had no time to yourself. All your waking hours could be spent toiling away in the kitchens. It was much worse than the farm. I would think to myself at times, I didn't join up for this, to ponce around serving a bunch of inbred French aristocrats; to be a bartender, or a dishwasher.

Maachi and Mejri who were with me at the officers mess that day, looked equally unimpressed, but what could we do? It was worse for them, because at least I could get drunk, they were both Muslim, so they had to remain sober. We helped lay out tables and put up a market tent. Thankfully we didn't have to help with the serving, instead we were sent to the sinks to do the washing up.

We were up in that tiny room scrubbing away when the corporal-chef, who had told us to stay, came up and began drinking some wine (I think he was already quite drunk). I don't know how it started, but a huge argument broke out between him, Maachi, and Mejri. It culminated when one of them called him a 'sale juif' (dirty Jew). What the fuck is going on now, I thought. How had this started and how the hell did they know he was a Jew? Do Muslims have gaydar for Jews, or something? The corporal-chef began shouting back about how he was a proud Israeli, who had served in the IDF, or something along those lines. He then ordered all of us to drop and do press-ups. He stared directly at me and screamed 'pompe putain (do press-ups fucker)'. I stared back at him with a perplexed look on my face, as if to say: What the fuck have I done? I was just a bystander. Before I could say anything, Maachi turned to me and told me not to do it. He was drunk and out of line, Maachi explained, and we didn't have to follow his bullshit orders. At hearing that, the irate corporal-chef shouted at us, 'that's insubordination a direct refusal of an order, we'll see what your chef de section has to say about that.' With that said, he stormed out the door. Oh fuck, we are in shit now, I thought, I had only just got my kepi and now I was going to have a charge of insubordination levelled at me, it didn't look good.

Maachi and Mejri explained that the corporal-chef had been looking for an argument, because he was drunk, and that the whole incident was his own doing. They assured me that nothing was going to happen. We stayed in the washing up room for another thirty minutes and there was no sign of the Israeli corporal-chef, so Mejri decided he would go find another person who worked there and spin them a yarn about us having to go back for some reason. I waited in the kitchen with Maachi hoping that we could get out of there before anything else happened.

A short while later Mejri popped his head in and, told us to drop what we were doing. We followed him out to the gate, where a different corporal-chef was waiting to let us through. He thanked us for helping out and bid us goodnight. Well done Mejri was all I could say. We went straight back to our rooms and hit the hay. Funnily enough, we never did hear another word about that incident. I guess that the corporal-chef must have been in the wrong, and once he had sobered up, he must have decided that it was best to let it go.

It was shortly after we returned from Formiguères that our section began to fall apart. We lost Adj O'Malley, Sch Popadynets, Sgt Dsouza, and Sgt Flaubert. I can't remember the exact timeline of how it happened (we weren't told in advance. We only found out they had left, when they stopped turning up at the morning assemblies). Cpl Novak was happy when Sch Popadynets left. At one assembly in the corridor he delighted in telling us that, there was no one to save us from punishment anymore (he was probably glad that the adjutant wasn't there anymore, to take the piss out of him for being fat too).

Sgt Dsouza was replaced by a Romanian: Sgt Stanescu. They could not have been more different. Sgt Stanescu was an incompetent fool, who was useless at giving orders and instructing people. His response to any problem was to have a hissy fit, and spaz out like a toddler. How he made sergeant was a mystery to me. It wasn't that he had difficulty speaking French. Romanian and

French are both Romance languages and have a lexical similarity of seventy-five percent. He was just an idiot. He also had the habit of speaking only with the Romanians, in Romanian, and would neglect to tell the rest of us what the orders were in French. I always had to ask Banica what the orders were, after he went.

Our new second in command was also a Romanian: Sch Pop, whose face was the spitting image of Popeye the sailor. He was a pretty decent guy. He knew his job well and got on with it 'sans drame'; was good at explaining things in a way that was easy, for us foreigners, to understand; and was approachable. He would listen to what you had to say if you came to him with a problem. All in all, Sch Pop was a good replacement, which was fortunate, because for the next few weeks he was our platoon leader (the Legion was having trouble finding someone to replace the adjutant).

I did, however, see Sgt Flaubert, one last time, shortly after we returned from Formiguères. I was sitting on my bed one evening, when the door flew open. He burst into my room, with a beer in his hand, and ordered me to pompe. While I was down on the floor doing press-ups, he was pacing back and forth, muttering to himself 'it's not possible…it's not possible.…' After a few seconds he ordered me to stand up. 'Do you know what has happened,' he said to me. I told him that I had no idea what he was talking about. 'It's the fucking English,' he said, 'they have just knocked France out of the rugby world cup. We beat New Zealand last week. How is this possible? We beat the best team in the world only to be knocked out by the fucking English, curse them.' He was especially annoyed that now he would have to root for England to win, because the only way he could take the loss was if England went on to win the tournament. Then he walked out of the room, still repeating to himself, his mantra of: 'c'est pas possible.' It was clear that he was just joking around. Sgt Flaubert was, like most French people, a massive rugby fan. There has always been a huge rivalry between France and England, and since they had stopped blowing each other apart with their cannons, and sport being to war what porn is to sex, they had been forced to continue their rivalry on the playing field.

I had my first twenty-four hour guard duty just after all our senior NCOs left. Guard is easily one of the most dreaded things in the Legion. There is just so much that can go wrong, and because you are on the main gate where everyone coming in or out can see you, it is also the most heavily scrutinised thing you will do while being a legionnaire. The guard uniform is a nightmare: everything has to be spotless and in perfect condition (the guard uniform is the one seen in most pictures of the Foreign Legion, which has those red tassely epaulets that look like the kind of thing Michael Jackson would wear).

The shirt is probably the most difficult thing to get right. It has to be ironed with the Legion creases: three above each breast pocket at 3.5cm apart; two down each sleeve at 5.3cm apart; and on the back you must iron one line straight across, going from shoulder to shoulder, then coming down from that line there has to be another three lines at 5.3cm apart. During inspection the shirt is gone over with a ruler to make sure all the lines have the correct spacing, then it is examined for any double-creases, stains, or poor ironing in general. If something is spotted, your shirt will be screwed up and thrown back at you. And that's if you are lucky, if not then it will be screwed up and thrown out of the window onto the dirt below. Some people were forced to go the foyer and buy a new one, because it landed in something unfortunate that wouldn't come out.

Here is a brief outline of what guard duty in the Legion was like: You started by going to the armoury to get the guns and bayonets; then at around 6:00pm (straight after the flag has been taken down for the night), you marched over to the guard house. Once you arrived, there was a changing of the guard ceremony (nothing special, just presenting arms a few times, then the old guard would march away). After that you went into the guard house and the first sentinels got sent to their posts (there were three people to each post; each person would do two hours, and get four hours rest). Then at 6:00am the next morning, all the posts would close (except the main gate), and the people manning them would go back to the section to do mess duty. The guys who were doing the main gate would then get changed into the grey dress uniform (at night you wear normal combat fatigues), and at 7:00am you raised the flag. The rest of the day was spent manning the gate as normal. The last thing to do before changeover was to take down the flag; and that was your standard twenty-four hour guard duty.

I was on the gate for my first round of guard, and I hated it from the start. You stood in a small cubicle next to the road. The main duty was controlling the traffic in and out by using the rising arm barriers. You had to check that all the vehicles coming in had a sticker, or pass. If they didn't you had to record their details, issue them a pass, and make sure you got it back when they left. You also had to salute the cars when they passed, and the people walking past on the path behind you. The amount of saluting was insane, I was constantly flapping my arm about like a spasticated goose. To make it worse less than half the people bothered to salute back, and for a real treat; every now and then, you would come across an absolute fucking arsehole, who, when you saluted, would walk right up to you and look you over to see if there was anything that he could jump on you for, and if there wasn't they would make something up (I once got blasted for not looking mean enough, and another time for having a 'gay face'). The noise would then normally alert the sergeant in the guard house, who would come out to see what the fuss was about, then join in the screaming and promise to deprive you of sleep by sending you to scrub the toilets, once your guard was over. I must admit that garde vingt-quatre didn't fill me with enthusiasm for the Legion.

In the morning I had to get changed into my dress uniform quickly, and go do the flag ceremony. I was lucky in that I didn't have to hoist the damn thing, just present arms while it was going up. In the Legion we don't have to sing the French national anthem, but we are expected to respect the flag, which I pretended to do, but in reality I couldn't have given less of a shit if I tried. It was very important during the flag hoisting ceremony not to let any part of the flag touch the floor while you were unfolding it and clipping it on. That would be a huge banane and you would get severely fucked for it.

It was just after lunch when Cpl Sonking came through to the sleeping area and told me that the plumbing was broken, and that we couldn't use the toilet in the guard house until further notice. If we needed the toilet we could run over to the company building and use the toilets there. No sooner had he gone than Doyle came out of the toilet and said, 'Murray I've just had a massive shit in there and it won't flush.' 'Oh for fucks sake,' I said, then proceeded to tell him what the corporal had just told me. He realized that he would have to get rid of it, without the sergeant finding out, and was trying to think of a plan. Can't you just leave it in there? I asked. To which he replied that, the poo in question was so big that it was rearing up out of the water like the loch ness monster, and creating an inordinate amount of smell. Just as he finished saying that, the corporal came through again and told me that it was time for me to do my guard, and I had to leave Doyle to sort it out himself.

After my guard had finished, it was Doyle who replaced me. I couldn't talk to him with the NCOs there so I would have to wait another two hours. I looked in the toilet and there was nothing there. He must have sorted it out, I thought. That's when it caught my eye, there it was laying in the grass just outside the window. There was no way you could blame that on a dog, and to make it worse the grass was cut to golf course standards. Before Doyle came back in, I had to go for dinner and when I came back I advised him to move it before someone noticed that there was a whopping great Richard III on the lawn. He donned a plastic bag, dashed outside, seized it, and threw it over the hedge. Which wasn't the best idea, because there were cars parked the other side, but there was no thump of it hitting any bodywork, so job done. What a fiasco that had been, but it did make guard duty less boring.

At the end of October we returned to the farm for a week. We pulled up in the car park, got off the trucks, and assembled as usual; and that's when I noticed that a new NCO had joined us. It was our new section commander, a Sergeant-chef from 2REP, but not only that, he had been part of the GCP (le Groupement des Commandos Parachutists), who are the parachute regiment's pathfinders. His name was Sch Taroatehoa, he was a Tahitian, but he didn't look very Tahitian: He looked like a crow actually. He had black hair, dark eyes, a very thin pointy face and nose, and light skin. My guess was that one of his parents was French. Everyone was really excited to have an ex-member of the GCP as our chef de section, and we were sure that he could teach us amazing things.

Once he had introduced himself. He began to lay down his ground rules. It was the normal shit: don't be lazy, obey orders, respect each other, etc. After he had given his talk he demanded to know, who Doyle was. Doyle raised his hand, then the sergeant-chef turned to him and said, 'Toi tu es un bananier (you're a bungler).' 'Oui chef,' replied Doyle. At that everyone burst out laughing. Doyle had become famous. However, I think that it hurt his feelings a bit to know that he was a well-known bananier; he didn't want to make mistakes and he did try hard to be a good legionnaire.

That week at the farm we were introduced to some of the different weapons used by the Legion:

- Browning M2 - 12.7mm machine gun
- AANF1 - 7.62mm machine gun
- The Minimi - 5.56mm machine gun
- AT4CS - anti-tank rocket
- MAC-50(PA-50) - 9mm pistol

We didn't get to fire them. Our task was simply to take them apart, rebuild them, and learn how to operate them. At the end of the week we would be playing the enemy for the people who were doing their corporal's course. We were given some blank rounds for the AANF1, and Minimi. Then we were taken to the same location we had defended a month before after one of the marches, which was handy. The machine guns were set up near the crossroads of the two paths, perpendicular to each other. Something to note about the AANF1 was that it had been in service since 1952, so it had some wear and tear. In fact the bloody thing rattled like a pocketful of change, and you couldn't leave an ammunition band in it, as it had a habit of going off unexpectedly (my theory is that it was caused by the metal changing temperature, with the time of day, and contracting or expanding), and there was no way to stop it. You just had to hang on to the back of it and wait for the band to finish.

Night-time crept in and we settled into our positions. I was halfway up the hill in a fox hole, a little bit back from the crossroads. My group of three just had our assault rifles. We lay there eating rations and talking quietly. Around midnight I awoke to gunfire and a load of commotion down below. The machine guns started up and there was rifle fire coming from the other side of the crossroads. I decided not to bother firing, it would only make cleaning difficult afterwards, and for what? We only had blanks anyway, and there were plenty of people firing already. A few powder grenades began landing in the woods close to my position. One landed in a fox hole below me and covered its occupants in talc. The shooting faded away then stopped completely. Their objective wasn't to storm our position, it was to get to the farm. A couple of hours later we were ordered to quit our posts and walk back to the farm, where we bedded down in the barn.

After the visit to the farm we took up some more service in the regiment. I managed to get another round of guard duty. Someone had been taken ill and I was the replacement. I had forgotten to attach one of the insignias that go on the jacket sleeves. Sgt Stanescu, noticed this during the review and flew into a rage. He punched me a good few times in the stomach for that mistake. Luckily for me he didn't weigh much more than fifty kilos. Guard with him was a nightmare, we were late for the flag ceremony which sent him berserk, and he was stressed out all day after that. It was a relief to get out of the guard house and go to my post, as the mood there was awful. I was certainly happy when that day was over.

Now that we had changed all of our NCOs from the rank of sergeant up, we weren't going running or doing much sport at all. The only time we exercised was when Cpl Novak took us for an aperitif before meals. Also, Sch Taroatehoa seemed to spend all his time in the office. We would see him for five minutes in the morning and that was it. It was the corporals who ran the show now. Cpl Novak was loving it, he could pretty much do what he wanted unchecked. There was a Belgian lad in our section called Klein, he was eighteen and had been in the Belgian under 21s water polo team. He was an amazing swimmer, and could do nearly three laps of a twenty-five meter pool underwater! However, he started to look quite sad and withdrew into himself. He was having issues with his girlfriend back in Belgium. One evening at assembly in the corridor, Cpl Novak noticed him looking down and inquired as to what the problem was. When Klein told him it was girlfriend issues, he laughed and told him to get a grip, because his girlfriend was probably being spit roasted by black guys with huge dicks at this very moment, and that he should forget about her. Klein was in tears after hearing this, but the corporal didn't let up teasing him, and that night, Klein deserted.

Cpl Novak also began to take advantage of my good nature. He had found out that I had a kettle and would send his cup over for me to make him cups of tea all the time. This was an abuse of power, albeit a pretty insignificant one, and he wasn't even nice to me. Well, he obviously hadn't seen any of the films where people are rude to fast food workers. I won't go into detail, but for the last two months of my instruction he was an unwitting urinobibe.

Somewhere around the halfway mark of instruction we were required to perform a series of physical tests. There are four in total and they have to be done three times during basic training. I had missed the first round by being in the infirmary. The first of the tests was an eight kilometre run in full equipment. You must run the distance in under an hour with an eight kilo rucksack (weighed before depart), assault rifle, helmet, and tactical vest. All together this stuff weighs around twelve kilograms. There is a small country lane opposite the regiment for this test. Every kilometre is marked by a painted line. At the fourth line you turn around and come back. I was quite good at this and finished in a reasonable position, but I was really surprised to see that I had finished in front of Maachi. He was a great runner, but not very strong, and the weight had slowed him down considerably. The next test was the obstacle course and this was definitely my strong event and I came first as I had at the farm. The third part was climbing the rope. Most people could do this in around five seconds now, which is a respectable time. The last thing was a hundred metre swim. This could be done in whatever stroke you liked, but the first ten meters had to be underwater. I could do this in around a minute and twenty seconds, but now that Klein had deserted this event was all Doyle's. He was a very good swimmer. After this day of testing everyone was completely knackered, but it was good to do something other than regimental service.

However, the service was never far away, and after the tests we were right back at it. That's how it went after the farm: fifty percent training, and fifty percent regimental service. Sometimes we would train at the farm, and sometimes we trained here at the regiment. The regiment had the better training facilities. At the farm you couldn't shoot live ammunition, but there was a shooting range at the 4RE. I had been a couple of times since arriving and we could train on targets up to a distance of three hundred meters, which was fine for the FAMAS.

Friday through to Sunday there weren't any evening meals, instead we would be given a bag with what amounted to a packed lunch inside, but occasionally the corporals would let us order pizzas from town. However, I was starting to get a little chubby from all the inactivity, and weekend pizzas. Before coming I had worked out six days a week and was very active. Now I ate everything I could get my hands on and didn't really have a chance to burn it off. There was a gym at the regiment, but people on basic training weren't allowed to use it. The Legion didn't want people injuring themselves.

It was near the end of November that we started to hear
rumours of a big regimental exercise, known as the 'raid march.'
The raid march was a hundred and twenty kilometres long, and
ended with a tactical assault (hence the name). It would be spread
out over five days and we would be expected to carry only what
was necessary, so it wouldn't be as bad as the kepi march.
Everyone in the regiment was expected to complete it, and there
were plenty fat old corporal-chefs who would have to keep up too.
The march would be in a place called Caylus, a couple of hours
drive north of Castelnaudary. My section was scheduled to go to
Caylus a week before everyone else for some shooting practice,
but before we departed there were a couple more deserters. It's
normal to get deserters before a big exercise like that: You also got
them straight after payday, and after coming back from an overseas
deployment.

One frosty morning in early December we woke at 4:00am
and departed for Caylus. This time we were going in army trucks.
The trucks only had a tarpaulin cover to shelter us, and bare metal
benches to sit on. The tarpaulin was ripped in a few places and lots
of wind was blowing through the back of the truck, and it soon got
pretty cold. The rock hard suspension made sure we felt every
bump on the road. When we hit a big pot hole you would be jolted
up in the air, and come crashing down smashing your arse bones
on the hard metal seats (sometimes the jolt was so violent that it
collapsed the benches too). However, this was good for me as no
one wanted to sit near the tailgate (that was where the most wind
was, and where you would get bumped around the most, but I
didn't mind as long as I got to stare at things as we drove past).
The Renault GBC 180 army trucks that the Legion uses really are
eight ton lumps of shit and they struggle to get to fifty miles an
hour. If there happened to be a steep hill on the journey then the
trucks would slow down so much that it would be faster to jump
out and run.

At around 7:00am, we stopped for a while to give everyone a
chance to relieve themselves. I discovered that my legs had
become stiff from the cold, so I walked up and down the grass

verge a bit to get the blood back in them. We had already passed Toulouse and it was only another hour or so before we arrived at our destination. There isn't much of anything in this part of France (between Toulouse, Bordeaux, and Limoges) just fields and villages. We got back on the trucks and soon passed by Montauban, which was the last big town we had to go through on our way to Caylus. It is a strange landscape in this part of France; the grass looks like yellow spongey moss, and the ground is littered with white rocks. This area must have been the bottom of an ocean at one point, because it's not hard to find rocks full of fossilized shellfish.

We travelled along some very small country lanes and, eventually, I spotted the sign for the camp. Much to my surprise we drove straight past the main camp and continued on for another kilometre or so. Our lodgings for the next week where not too different from the farm: An old whitewashed stone building, with wooden shutters and no electric. In front was a gravel assembly area (complete with flag pole and a Foreign Legion logo made from painted rocks). The main thing to notice was the terrible smell that hung in the air. It's like when you visit a third world country, and you first step out of the taxi in the capital. The smell hits you like a leather belt to the face. I could see the latrines, fifty meters away behind where we were staying, and I dreaded to think what it must be like inside the cubicles. We, as per usual, lined up for assembly and waited for the NCOs to inspect the building. I had gotten so used to standing in the same place now that it no longer hurt my feet. I could stand for hours, it was the new sitting down.

A little while later we were called into the building. It was pretty barren inside, dusty concrete floors, windows with shutters (no glass), and a rickety old staircase in one corner. Our quarters were upstairs, in the loft. It was a long triangular room, kind of like sleeping in a giant Toblerone box. There was not enough room to stand up straight, and plenty of rafters to bang your head on. Once we had been shown around we set to work unloading the weapons and ammunition. It was all to be placed on the ground floor of our building, where Cpl Sonking could keep an eye on it all.

Once the trucks were emptied, we set off down the road to the main camp. We drove into the main camp at Caylus, past the two WW2 era tanks that were parked by the gate, and headed straight for the munition depot. We were here to pick up the explosives that were too dangerous to take in the trucks with us. At the back of the camp there is a large field with nothing but a few shabby looking tin huts in it, and a small road that passes in front of them. They are all spaced out so that if one catches fire, or something of that sort, the others won't also be affected. After grabbing what we needed the truck took a tour of the regiment. We first visited the shower blocks, this is where we would have to come to wash, as there was only one tap up at our building. Then we passed by the mess hall. We were told that every time we came for dinner here we would have to bring our own cutlery (there had been problems in the past with legionnaires stealing the silverware).

Once our little tour was over we left for our first bit of training, which was learning how to set up and use plastic explosives. This was a fairly easy lesson. First we were shown the different bits of kit: main charge; primer (blasting cap); fuse wire; and detonator. The only scary thing about setting up the explosives was crimping the primer to the end of the fuse. We were shown some photos of people who had tried to do this with their teeth and had the lower part of their face blown off, on one side. My fucking god they were haunting images. We took it in turns to set up a charge then detonate it in, what looked like, an empty car park. There was only enough for one each. The rest of the time we hung out near the trucks.

After we finished with the explosives it was time to eat and grab a shower. The food at this base was much better than ours, and they had a selection of fizzy drinks to choose from too. The showers were a lot nicer too; they actually had individual cubicles here.

Later that night back at our building a guard list was drawn up. There is never any escaping from guard duty. It was freezing cold at night in Caylus, and although I was wearing four layers of clothing, it was still necessary to pace constantly to keep warm. The worst thing was your feet in those bare leather boots. The toes became painfully cold and there was nothing you could do about it.

The next day was spent training with the assault rifle and it was good fun actually. The targets were reactive and they lay down for a couple of seconds, if you hit them. We practiced from a distance of twenty-five, right up to three hundred meters. The first thing you notice about the FAMAS, when you start shooting with it, is that it's not too reliable: It jams a lot and the magazine is prone to becoming dislodged from its housing, or falling out completely. The magazines are so flimsy (they are meant to be disposable, but some have been in service for a decade or more) that if it drops from above waist height it will deform. If that happens, then your gun will jam all the time as the bullets will get sent up at a funny angle and wedge themselves between the block and the side of the barrel.

Another thing that was a bit of a shock was that when we went to inspect the targets, it was clear that the bullets were tumbling and hitting the targets at all different angles, some were going through the target sideways. This is caused by the bullet spinning too much or too little and not gyroscopically stabilizing. My guess is that it was spinning too little, because some of the guns had almost no rifling left inside, after years of being scrubbed to death with wire brushes.

That evening after dinner I was desperately in need of the toilet. I had resisted going since arrival as the smell coming from the latrines was too much to bear, it was enough to make you projectile vomit your stomach out of your mouth. It was really terrible, but I really needed to go, so I walked in the direction of the latrines, then looked around to make sure no one was watching, and dashed for a field that was a little bit further down the path. There was a line of trees that obscured the view from the building, so no one could see me. After walking a few meters down the side of this field, it was evident that I wasn't the first person to have this idea. All along the top of the field and in amongst the trees that ran alongside it. There was shit with bits of tissue paper flapping in the wind, everywhere: It was a true minefield. I walked far enough into the field to find a spot where it wasn't so bad, and left a surprise for the foxes.

During the first week at Caylus I tried to find different places to go to the toilet, but discovered that every inch of the woods and fields around us had been crapped all over. The smell from the latrines was indescribably bad, it was worse than just the smell of shit. It was like Satan had cursed them to smell so bad that they stunk out God and Jesus in heaven. Seriously though, there was definitely a few animals that fallen in there and died, because the smell was a rich bouquet of faeces and rotting carcases; that's the best I can do to describe it.

On Wednesday we practiced throwing grenades. This was good fun and a bit nerve racking: You can't help thinking, what if the grenade is faulty and goes off before it should in my hand. The grenade range consisted of three walls along a three hundred metre long path, with the three walls spaced out at a hundred metres apart from each other, and a concrete trench at the end. Everyone waited at the first wall, then when you were called you ran down to the second, and so on. At the third wall you would receive your grenades and jump down into the trench in front. The NCO in there would then instruct you as what to do.

The grenades were a little bit tricky, you had to pull the pin then shake off the spoon, because if you didn't do that and threw it with the spoon on, the spring under the spoon would push the grenade off at an angle when you opened your hand, and you would miss the target. I saw this happen to one guy: He threw his grenade with the spoon on, and it sprang out of his hand and it came down a few feet in front of the trench (like when a girl throws). It was lucky that the damn thing didn't roll back inside.

One night, at Caylus, I was asleep in bed when I woke up bursting for a piss, but I really didn't want to get out of my warm sleeping bag, get dressed, go down stairs, and walk all the way to those stinking hell holes, or the field, so I decided to try and go back to sleep, but it was no good. I woke an hour later and this time I was bursting for the toilet so bad that I couldn't get back to sleep. After another hour or so I decided to bite the bullet and go: I wouldn't get any sleep otherwise. As I got dressed I was dancing like a fool, so urgent was my need for relief. Halfway down the stairs I had to clamp it off with my hand, my bladder couldn't hold it back any more. I sprinted across to the latrines, kicked open the door, and let it rip from outside like I was a fireman putting out a fire with my hose. Moments later a gargled scream came from inside the pitch black cubicle. Oh fuck! I quickly pinched it off again and ran to the field. There had been someone in there having a dump and I had just urinated all over him. After hiding for a while, and making sure he was gone, I laughed my head off for maybe five minutes.

In the morning after assembly no one had mentioned getting doused in piss last night so I was scot-free. I couldn't wait to tell Doyle, it was fucking hilarious. I mean imagine if you were sitting in a public toilet and someone came in, kicked one of the cubicle doors in, and whizzed all over someone who was having a nice relaxing crap, then ran off.

On our last day of shooting there was a treat in store for us. Our new platoon leader had arranged for some of his GCP friends to come over and train us on some of their weapons. They had a few German guns: a G36, which is almost completely made out of plastic, an MP5, and a Glock 17 pistol. The first thing I noticed about these weapons was just how little recoil they all had. It was much easier to hit the target with them. I particularly liked the G36. It was superior to the FAMAS in every way. Even the magazine was in another league to the French one. For a start it held thirty rounds, instead of twenty-five. It also clipped into the gun securely, and was transparent so you could see how many bullets were left. All of these guns also had holographic sights on, which saved a lot of time when aiming; compared to standard iron sights.

As the first week at Caylus drew to a close we began preparing for the big regimental exercise that would begin next week. Over the weekend Caylus filled with legionnaires from the

4RE. Luckily for me Sgt grumpy bollocks wasn't doing the march. I was, instead, put under the command of a sergeant-chef, who normally worked in the technical zone as a mechanic (I can't remember his name, so I will call him Sch Mechanic). He was pleasant enough on first impression. Cpl Sonking was also in our group, which was good, and so was Cpl Novak.

It was late Sunday night when the exercise began. We climbed aboard the trucks and drove out of the camp. Somewhere down a dark country lane our vehicle came to a stop and we got out. There was so little light on this tree covered road that you could barely see your hand in front of your face. We began walking in single file. The only way to tell that there was someone in front of you was by listening to their footfall.

After walking for a while we began mounting a steep hill. At about three quarters of the way up, I suddenly slammed into the person in front of me, then the two people behind me did likewise in a chain reaction. I cursed the guy in front, why the hell did you stop like that? He answered that he had lost the person in front of him. There were steep banks either side of the road, meaning that they couldn't have turned off somewhere. It was obvious that he had failed to keep pace, so I overtook him and began marching at a good pace. It wasn't long before I could hear the familiar rustling of clothes, and footsteps. Soon enough, the trees died away and we came out onto open fields, which made things easier. The moon didn't provide much light, but it was better than nothing.

After a couple of hours marching we stopped at a farm to take a rest. It was only now that I noticed that the cheek rest was missing from my gun. Shit, it must have come off when I clattered into that guy back at the start of the march, I thought. There was no hope of getting it back. I reluctantly approached Sch Mechanic and told him what I had lost. Unsurprisingly he lost his temper and railed at me for a few minutes, demanding to know why he had been saddled with such an idiot. I can't say that I enjoyed it, but being called a mongoloid, cretin, idiot, waste of space, had its effect, because every march after that, whenever I had a FAMAS, the first thing I did was take off the cheek rest and store it away in the deepest recesses of my bag. It was too easy to lose and caused far too much hassle. My temporary group leader didn't like me much after that, but I was only with him for a few days, so I wasn't that bothered.

Whenever you lose a piece of issued equipment, which can't be brought from the Legion foyer, e.g., magazine, helmet, cheek rest, etc. You are made to write out a formal report in French (compte rendu). The report must not contain any mistakes in grammar or spelling, and it must be done on plain paper (there is a template you have to make with the correct line spacing that is placed underneath). The report is presented to your chef de section. If there are any mistakes, or it doesn't look neat enough, or they just want to fuck you around, it is screwed up and you are made to start again. When the report is done you must purchase a case of beer (24 bottles) for the corporal-chef in the magasin where the new part will be ordered. That's not to mention the standard beasting that you get for any mistake. After the farm, the normal punishment for a mistake was to receive all the shitty jobs for a few days, or until someone else made a banane, and you were forgotten about.

I would like to mention standard the threat that was levelled at you when an error was made, while somewhere it wasn't possible to issue a punishment (in view of the public or the officers, for example), which was: 'tu vas ramasser, comme un chien, quand on rentre au quartier.' This literally means: you are going to collect/gather/pick up, like a dog, when we enter the regiment, but which was always understood as the phrase often used by parents: 'just you wait till we get home.' I would often look up the meaning of words in my dictionary and 'ramasser' was one of those words that took on a meaning of its own in the French-creole of the Foreign Legion. It was always used to denote punishment, but the nearest I could find to it meaning 'to be punished' was the phrase 'ramsser une gamelle,' which means 'to fall flat on one's face.'

After an hour of sitting in the farmyard, the NCOs in charge of each group held a meeting to decide where we should stay that night. They decided on a spot not far from the farm, maybe a kilometre away in some woods. As usual there was guard to be done. When I took my guard in the small hours of the morning there was already a glistening coat of frost over everything. It was very nice to look at, but it didn't do my feet any favours. The large, four season sleeping bag that we had been issued with at Aubagne, was next to useless in this cold. My sleeping bag, I noticed, had been made in 1982. It was four years older than me, and all the fibres in it had been so flattened down by years of use that their ability to trap air had almost completely vanished.

When morning broke, we woke up and began making some coffee. I was amazed to see that a few metres from where we had slept was a high metal fence, and on the other side was a group of massive wild boars. They must have smelt the rations we were eating and came to check us out. It was the first time I had seen a wild boar up close. Their heads are huge and their necks are so thick with muscle that they would put Mike Tyson to shame. I went over to the fence and gave them a couple of biscuits from my ration pack, which they happily snuffled up.

At around eight o'clock we started off on our march again. We were walking alongside the road all day. The colonel had given the order that every time a vehicle passed we had to post ourselves. This soon became tiresome, but we had to keep it up because the colonel was driving around in his jeep and could come past at any moment. That day we spent the whole time walking along the road and diving into the bushes every time a car came by. It was fucking tedious shit.

That night we found another patch of woodland to sleep in. It had begun to drizzle as we set up our camp. I noticed Cpl Novak had pulled his usual trick of not taking anything with him. He only had a sleeping bag, and Gore-Tex cover to keep him dry. I was on guard duty again that night and the sergeant-chef was still pissed at me, now I kind of knew how Doyle felt when he lost his gun at the farm.

In the morning it was good to see that Cpl Novak was soaked again. Seeing him like that reminded me of that old saying 'the second time you make a mistake, it's a choice,' and he had clearly chosen not to give a fuck. Still, it wouldn't be long before he dried off. Today there was a clear blue sky, but it was still rather cold. The tedium of walking and hiding didn't ease up. What made it worse was that we didn't even get the chance to speak. Everyone was spaced out at a distance of five metres apart. Sometimes we would be posted at the side of the road for hours. It was a nightmare. No one knew what was going on, or whether we had enough time to cook our rations, or not. I can recall one time when I was sat in a hedge at the side of the road that day, when Sch Mechanic came by and asked if I was alright. I began to answer, but he cut me off after a couple of words, 'I didn't ask for your fucking life story. Yes or no, that's all I want to hear from you.' I stared back for a second then said 'yes' in a contemptuous manner. He was starting to piss me off now. It was two days ago that I lost that stupid bit of plastic and he was still angry about it. I really wanted to get up and punch him in the face, but that would definitely have seen me thrown out of Legion.

That evening we entered a large expanse of woodland. We walked along a trail that was big enough to get a vehicle down and stopped at a crossroads. Tonight our job was to make sure that no one came past that intersection, but we still had a while before it was dark. Sch Mechanic decided to pass the time by testing our knowledge of the NATO phonetic alphabet (alpha, bravo, Charlie, delta, etc.), so he called us up one at a time to spell out our names. When I went up he made me spell out a load of different things. He said that because I was English, it was easy for me, so I had to do more. However, being English didn't stop him trying to tell that 'Mike' was pronounced 'meek.' There was no point arguing, he would just get angry, so I let it go. The person with the worst luck that day was a Chinese guy called Wu. He was a bright guy and new the NATO alphabet, but his French was bad. He went over and spelled out his two letter name: whisky, uniform, then stopped, but Sch Mechanic thought that he was stuck and began screaming at him, and demanded that he try again. The second time, when the same thing happened, he began beating him and making him do press-ups. It went on like that until one of the corporals saw and told him that his surname only had two letters in it.

That night the guard was a nightmare, there were civilians who used the path we were guarding for cycling and jogging. They must have had the shock of their lives when a foreigner with a gun leapt out from the bushes and started yelling at them. There was another funny moment that night. I had just finished badgering the witness (if you get my drift), when my replacement for guard duty came along and lay down right on top of where I had jizzed. I didn't have the heart to tell him and went back to my sleeping bag. However, karma did catch up with me. It was so dark in those woods at night that instead of walking back to my tent, I walked straight off a two meter bank and fell onto the dirt track, landing face first.

The next day we stayed in the woods for most of the morning, guarding the same crossroad. Then in the afternoon we took one of the paths and continued our journey. It was great not to be diving in the bushes every five minutes when a car came past. Somehow my group found itself at the front of the march and I was marching on point, so there was no one in front of me. It was while I was out in front, walking along a straight bit of path that had a Y-shaped intersection up ahead, that a volley of automatic fire rang out. It came from the small island of vegetation between the two paths in front of me. It was a good ambush and they had picked the perfect spot: If this had been real then I would have been dead for sure. As it was I was just made to post myself and wait, for what seemed like hours. Eventually, the people from behind passed in front of us, including the colonel in his jeep, and my group wound up at the back. After that first contact we inched forward at a snail's pace for the rest of the day, it was excruciating. We did encounter a few more hits that day, but no one was taken prisoner as far as I am aware.

That night, as usual, guard had to be mounted, and owing to the fact that I was a mongoloid, who had lost something, I got the worst guard spot again, in fact I had received the worst guard spots for the whole of that march (right in the middle of the night so I had my sleep broken down the middle). There were enough people in our group that each person would normally get one night on, and one night off, but that's how it is in the Legion: You make a mistake, and boy do they let you know about it. All the same, the lack of sleep coupled with the marching made me incredibly hungry. It is strange just how foggy your mind can get from exhaustion. It really is like being a little bit drunk.

At three o'clock in the morning, everyone woke up. Today was the last day of the exercise (the day of the raid), so we had to be up at the crack of dawn to surprise the enemy before he got out of bed. We quickly got our kit together and started marching. We walked down to a small village, where there were guides waiting for us. They directed us through the village to a hole, in a hedge next to the road. A path had been marked out with Cyalume (glow stick) fluid dripped on the branches.

The path they had chosen was a pain in the arse. There were branches everywhere: It was like walking through the middle of a hedge. You were constantly tripping over, banging you head, getting whipped in the face, and getting your equipment snagged. Some parts were so thick with vegetation that you had to remove your rucksack and gun, pass them through separately, and then clamber through after. If this had been planned as a surprise attack, then it certainly wasn't anymore. We were making one hell of a racket trying to get through that tangled mess of branches. After hours of forcing our way through this path we finally came out onto a normal track (one that you could actually walk along). My face, arms, and legs were scratched to bits from all the snapped branches and thorns.

After we got out into the open, we were told to sit down and wait for the order to move out. It was during this break that I took out my metal gourd to have a drink, but when I tipped it up nothing came out. The blasted thing was frozen solid, but I was hot and thirsty from struggling along through that thicket. The best I could do to melt it was to put it under my armpit, or between my legs, and take sips as it gradually melted.

An hour passed before we were on the move again. The track we were on ended after a few hundred metres and we came out onto a road surrounded by forest. This road looked familiar to me, but I wasn't quite sure where we were. After a short distance we came across a bridge that I definitely recognized and I knew then that we were back inside the military training ground of Caylus. Pretty soon I could hear the faint crackle of gunfire in the distance. Sch Mechanic ordered us to pick up the pace, and we broke out into a trot. Eventually the road came out into open ground, and we could see the combat village off in the distance, so we followed the road as it snaked its way towards the village.

When we were maybe one hundred meters away from the buildings we filed off to the left, into a field with a ridge of earth marking its boundary, and lined up along the ridge to prepare for the assault. We would have to leap frog our way across the remaining open ground. On Sch Mechanic's order we set out. Our destination was the wall of a long farm building in front. When I arrived at the wall I took the corner to the right, and peered round, there was no movement the other side, and no sound of gunfire anymore. I got the order to advance round the building to the farmyard on the other side, but on turning the corner I noticed a Legionnaire standing over the far side of the yard. He looked back at me, raised his hand, palm forwards in a stop gesture, and shouted across 'c'est fini.' I turned back to Sch Mechanic and told him what the legionnaire had just said. He then made a call on his radio to confirm if the exercise was indeed over. The call came back that, yes, the exercise was now finished; and we were ordered to stand down and go wait for the colonel to arrive and brief everyone on how he thought the exercise had gone. I couldn't believe that we had missed all the action. I was sure it had been because of the time we wasted clambering through those fucking bushes on that god awful path. Still cleaning our weapons would be doddle, considering we hadn't fired them.

That evening we had a celebratory meal in a field next to the regiment of Caylus. It was the usual thing: Kronenbourg, crisps, and saucisson. These Legion parties soon become tedious, once everyone had got a few beers in them, you couldn't go ten minutes without some wanker starting a song off. At which you had to stop what you were doing, stand to attention, and sing. If I appear to be less than enthusiastic about Legion songs, then that is because I am. They are, in my opinion, the gayest thing on earth, and by 'gay' I don't mean happy, or homosexual: I mean gay in the way a teenage boy would use it to describe Barney the purple dinosaur. You might say that it's disrespectful of me to talk about their traditions in this way, and I would accept that charge, but I still wouldn't give a flying fuck. I can't stand the songs of the French Foreign Legion, that's just how I feel.

After going through the whole song book a couple of times the colonel, and the other officers, left. Once the officers leave, the party is effectively over, but up until that point you are forced to stay and have fun (we were basically getting paid by the French government to hang out with them). I along with the other new legionnaires were tasked with clearing everything away. This had its upside, as we could finish off the remaining beers, and I needed a drink after that march.

When the cleaning was done, we assembled near the trucks waiting to be taken back to our building. I was bursting for the toilet and our NCOs were still chatting a short distance away, so I did an about turn and started urinating from the back row. Almost immediately after I started, some guy ran across in front of me, took a few steps, stopped, looked at his trousers, and shouted back at me. What was going on with me, I thought, I couldn't stop pissing on people.

6: A Legion Noël

Belief in a cruel God makes a cruel man.
Thomas Paine

After the regimental exercise my basic instruction was almost over. In January we would be leaving for whichever regiment was chosen for us, but there was still the final evaluation to do. This was a test of all the things we had learnt during instruction. The test included sections on: French language ability, shooting proficiency, sporting capability, general knowledge of arms and tactics, history of the French Foreign Legion, and a character assessment.

After the final exam, each person would be graded. The only important thing about the grade was that it allowed you to choose which regiment you went to. Near the end of instruction a list is made of the available places in each regiment. If you wanted to go to the cavalry regiment, for example, and there were only two places, then it was unlikely that if you came fifteenth that those two places would still be available when it was your turn to choose. This wasn't a problem for me, as I wanted to go to the parachute regiment (2REP): The REP was renowned for its harsh discipline and brutality; not to mention the jumping out of planes part. The REP also had the highest number of deserters. There were always plenty of places for the REP. In fact, being forced to go there was the main incentive for not coming last. The most popular regiments for people finishing their instruction were (in order):

- 3REI (Infantry, French Guiana)
- 13DBLE (Mechanized infantry, based in Djibouti)
- 1REC (Cavalry, Mainland France)
- 1REG/2REG (Engineers, Mainland France)
- 2REI (Infantry, Mainland France)
- 2REP (Airborne infantry, Corsica)

There is also a detachment of the Legion in Mayotte, but that isn't really worth mentioning, because there are less than three hundred people there, and places are usually reserved for those nearing retirement.

I can remember talking with the other people in my section about which regiment they wanted to join. I was surprised to hear that many people had changed their mind about joining the parachute regiment. Most notably all the black lads, who at the beginning had wanted to be paratroopers, were now desperate to go anywhere but the REP. On further enquiry I was told that they had been warned that the REP was a racist regiment. One guy, a big Madagascan, told me that it wouldn't be good for him there with all the Russians. I can confirm that you probably shouldn't join the REP if you are black, it just wouldn't be worth the hassle, but maybe the regiment has changed now. Just before I was leaving the Legion I noticed that there were a lot more South Americans (especially Brazilians) arriving at the parachute regiment, so maybe the demographics have changed. However, when I was there it was easily ninety-five percent white and most of them were Russian or Eastern European.

We took the tests over the weeks leading up to Christmas. We had to do the same set of physical tests as we had done twice before. After the physical stuff was out of the way, the NCOs set up little stations around the regiment. We ran from station to station performing tasks, such as: setting up a machine gun, calculating true north, designating an objective, etc. I was confident that I had done reasonably well. The history of the Legion was my weakest point, and, truth be told, I could have been more of a team player: I tended to be a more independent than the Legion would have liked me to be.

When we had the tests done, it was time to prepare for Christmas. As I have mentioned before; Catholicism is the official religion of the Legion, and every year at Christmas the Legion puts on a range of activities to celebrate Jesus' birthday. All legionnaires must spend Christmas day in the regiment. This is to build solidarity and to underline the official motto: 'Legio Patria Nostra (The Legion is our Fatherland).' There is also a series of sporting events where all the companies compete against each other for a trophy. Teams are selected from each company to compete in the different events (swimming, obstacle course, etc.), plus everyone in the regiment must take part in a cross-country run where all the times are recorded. At the end, all the points from these events are added up and the winning company gets to keep the big trophy for a year.

The only, truly Christmas related activity was crèche building. The first time I heard about the crèche, I didn't realize what it was. They only type of crèche I knew was a children's nursery and that didn't seem right, surely we weren't going to look after children: I later found out that it also meant 'nativity scene.' Each section of each company puts together a team of five or six legionnaires and a couple of NCOs to build a large display with models, artwork, music, and a speech. They were usually Foreign Legion, or military themed, in general; and didn't have to depict the birth of Jesus.

I was asked if I would like to be part of the crèche building team, but I said that I was not interested. This came as a shock to the corporals, who stared back at me in amazement, 'but you do realize it will be easy work, and that you will be excused from regimental service while you are working on it,' they said. 'That's fine,' I said in response, 'I would rather go work in the kitchens.' They just looked at me like I was crazy, then said, fine whatever suit yourself. It wasn't so much the crèche building that put me off, rather it was the thought that I would have to spend a whole day round the officers, when they came to inspect it (with all the saluting and other yes-man activities that would include: I hated that stuff). The rest of the crèche team were the most notorious boot-licking-sycophants of the section (e.g. Mejri). However, I did pop down to see the crèche when it was near completion, and I must admit it was impressive. They had taken over one of the downstairs classrooms, and turned it into a scene from the trenches of World War One. There was some moving church music playing in the background to complete the scene, and plenty of fake snow too. I was told that Sch Popadynets had come by to see it and it had brought tears to his eyes (I, naturally, had a good giggle at that). I can't remember if our crèche won a prize, but it was very good.

At this time of year, when you weren't on service, there wasn't much to do and we spent a considerable amount of time up in our rooms. In my room this meant a lot of arguing, usually with Mejri. He would come out with some of the most ridiculous things. I can remember him saying that NASA had a room where they could turn off gravity to train for space expeditions. I tried for longest time (with everyone else in the room) to convince him that this was not the case, and that they trained underwater as it was the next best thing, but he was unshakable in his convictions. One day he was berating Maachi for not being a good Muslim (apparently he had eaten a pizza with ham on it). Maachi's reply was that there is no option to choose your meal at the Legion and he was hungry, which sounded reasonable enough. Mejri, in response, told him that he should have picked the ham off. 'Oh that's ridiculous,' said Maachi, 'we work hard and I need to eat, besides the Koran says we shouldn't take drugs. Caffeine is a drug and millions of Muslims drink it every day, are they bad?' 'I don't,' replied Mejri in a haughty tone, while sitting there with a can of coke in his hand. At which point everyone leapt on him and pointed out that Coca-Cola contained caffeine. It was great to see him get owned like that and have no way of coming back. He would never live that moment down, but it didn't stop him being as pig-headed as ever, mind.

It was around this time too, when I was talking with Raikkonen and he told me that he had observed Kuzma acting very strangely. He would be walking down the corridor normally, then all of a sudden he would freak out in some kind of spastic fit, and run full speed for a couple of seconds, then snap out of it and carry on like nothing happened. I had also noticed this weird behaviour from Kuzma. We decided to go and try to find out more about him, what he did before joining, why he joined, etc. What we discovered was just plain disturbing. It was hard to understand because he was incredibly incoherent, but as far as I could tell, he had been playing a lot of GTA (grand theft auto) and had wondered what it would be like to act out the game in real life. He went outside and lurked around in dark alleyways with a knife. One day he grabbed someone and tried to drag them into the alley, but was spotted by the police and had to flee. This was truly creepy stuff to listen to. Once he had finished, Raikkonen burst out with, 'What the fuck is this weird shit. You better not come to REP Kuzma or I will beat your ass.' Kuzma, looking like a deer caught in the headlights, nodded in fear. 'We don't want weirdos like you coming to REP,' he told him. For my part, I thought that Kuzma should not really be in the army. He was clearly not capable of separating reality from fantasy, and it was a big risk letting him have a gun. I could see him turning psychotic, like Gomer Pyle in the film 'Full Metal Jacket,' and shooting up the base, or something along those lines.

My first Christmas Eve in the Legion was an unusual one. Cpl Pillqu came to my room in the evening and told me that I was being sent to midnight mass at the local church. I tried to protest, but he assured me that it would be a welcome rest from barracks life. All I would have to do at mass was sit down at a pew. If I stayed at the regiment, then I would get caught up in the preparations for tomorrow and there was a lot to do. I took the corporal's advice and went to start ironing my dress uniform for church.

I discovered that Doyle had also been ordered to go to the church service, and I got the distinct feeling that they were just getting us out of the way, but whatever it would be good to get out of the regiment for the evening. We went downstairs and got on the bus that would take us to the church. Once on board it quickly became clear that we were the only two people there who weren't devout Christians. Everyone else was so excited about going to mass, they were like teenage girls going to a pop concert.

The church was near the centre of Castelnaudary, and it was a very nice building, with beautiful stained glass windows. We all filed in and took a pew. It didn't take long for the singing to begin. It was impossible for me and Doyle to join in because all the hymns were in French. I didn't recognized any of the melodies either; the only time I had sung hymns was in junior school and all I knew was: 'all things bright and beautiful,' and 'he's got the whole world in his hands,' but they never came up.

The mass felt like it dragged on forever, and I was happy when it was over. On the way back to the regiment the Christians who were travelling with us, were very hyped up from the service and continued their singing on the bus. At one point they began group hugging, and shouting slogans, such as 'we are all one big family.' This was truly cringe-worthy to me, and I joked with Doyle about jumping through the window, rolling along the road, and making a run for it. I know it's harmless enough, but I can't stand that kind of happy-clappy stuff.

On Christmas day we woke early and stayed in the rooms all morning. Our Christmas meal was in the mess hall. The food was more expensive than usual (not nicer), there were a few bottles of wine per table, and the colonel came and joined us. I can remember that along with the meal, we were each given a small tub of snails. I tried them (just to see what all the fuss was about), and I didn't like them at all. The sauce they were in was nice, a kind of buttery pesto, but the actual snails themselves tasted awful and they had the texture of rubber. So, I put them aside and got on with the rest of the meal. After I was done eating, I asked Doyle what he had thought of the meal. He said, that overall it had been good, but that he didn't think much of the mushrooms in the plastic tub. I let out a roar of laughter and told him that he had in fact just eaten a whole tub of snails, but he didn't seem to mind.

In the afternoon, we were led over to the room below the mess hall. There were tables arranged in groups around the room for each section to sit at, and a stage had been erected at the far end. Everyone filed in and sat down. There was some cabaret, a few speeches, and a comedy act that was as funny as having your colon removed. Near the end everyone was called up to receive their Christmas present. This year it was a small rucksack (a Chinese knock-off version of the American Camelbak hydration-pack, but still better than the standard issue pack). Then, once all the festivities had been taken care of, we were sent back to the rooms. Everyone from the rank of corporal and up left immediately; leaving only one duty corporal per section. For us this was Cpl Novak, which was fine because he didn't give a damn anymore as our instruction was basically over.

Over the next couple of days, while there wasn't anyone around, groups of people from my section snuck out to visit the brothels just over the border in Spain. There was a huge brothel called 'Madame's' which was a favourite destination for sex starved legionnaires. People had gone there before in twos or threes, but now as soon as the last role call was done half the section was gone. It was normally some entrepreneurial corporal-chefs who would take people down there for an exorbitant fee. They would leave at 10:00pm and be back in the small hours of the morning, before reveille at six o'clock. I was told that even though it was a Spanish brothel, all the girls who worked there were Romanian. I decided to save my €300 (that a seat in the car cost), and order a fancy foie gras pizza for €20 instead. Besides, if you were caught sneaking out like that, it would probably earn you some time in Legion jail. Even if you weren't caught you would still be shattered the next day after having not slept, and down nearly a month's wages.

In the first week of January, after everyone had returned from their short break, we only had administrative stuff to do. For a start, the whole section had to pass in front of the company captain to listen to a review of their instruction. The captain was a pleasant enough guy. He would detail your strong points, where he thought you needed to improve, and chat to you about your future in the Legion. Then, a few days after we spoke to the captain, an assembly was called in our corridor. Sch Taroatehoa came out and told us that he was going to announce the results of our basic training, and ordered everyone to line up outside his office. He called us in by order of our passing grade. I finished seventh overall, which I was very pleased with.

When you go into the office to receive your final results there is a strict procedure that you must follow. The most important part not to get wrong is the answer to the question: to which regiment would you like to be assigned? Instead of just telling them what regiment you want to get sent to you must say, 'I am ready to go wherever the Legion sends me.' Apparently that's what used to get said in days of old, so now it has become the official response. Well, when I entered, I began reciting that line, but Sch Taroatehoa cut me off half way through, 'yeah, yeah, I know, but where do you really want to go?' he said (he had obviously got bored of hearing that sentence). I told him that I would like to go to the parachute regiment. He then asked me what my second and third choices were. I told him that if I couldn't join the REP, then I would like to go to Guiana, or Djibouti. He raised an eyebrow at hearing that. There were only ever a couple of places for those regiments, and as I was seventh, so it was highly unlikely that I would get either. I was basically telling him REP or nothing. He paused for a moment before, unofficially, telling me that I was going to the REP (we still had to wait a couple of days for the placements to be confirmed), but that he would write down infantry and cavalry as my other choices because everyone so far had asked for 3REI and 13DBLE, and it was starting to look silly, then he dismissed me.

When the placements came back a few days later, I was pleased to see that I had indeed been able to get a place in the parachute regiment. Doyle and Raikkonen would be going to the

REP with me too. Most of the people from my instruction would be going to the cavalry regiment, and the parachute regiment. However, only around half of the fifteen people going to the REP had actually chosen to go there. Nemet, for example, didn't include the parachute regiment on any of his three choices, but was told to go where he was sent or desert. The rest of the section were split between the infantry and engineer regiments (except for Maachi and Mejri who were going to Aubagne). No one was going to Guiana or Djibouti.

It was strange to see the two groups of people going to the parachute regiment: one happy and one sad. What was also interesting was that seven out of the top ten finishers had chosen REP, and exactly the same number out of the bottom had been forced to go to REP (Doyle was the exception, he had come almost last, but had actually chosen the parachute regiment).There was a good few people who were visibly shaken at the thought of having to go to the REP. You could tell that they weren't looking forward to having to jump out of an airplane; then again…neither was I.

A few days after the placements had been announced, and once we had scrubbed every inch of our floor of the building, we were packed up ready to leave. We would be making the same journey by train back along France's Mediterranean coast to Marseille, then a bus would take us to Aubagne. We would stay there a couple of days before people from our respective regiments came to collect us.

I enjoyed the train journey much more than I had done four months ago: I was now sure of my place in the Legion, and I wasn't suffering from a rotten cold either. All the same, I was anxious to find out what life in the parachute regiment would be like. The way people had talked about it in Castelnaudary made it sound like a mix of penal servitude and storm trooper training. However, I decided that most of this talk was just hyperbole, and scaremongering, and that I shouldn't give too much credence to it. I would just have to wait and find out for myself.

When we got to Aubagne, we all had to go visit the Legion crypt in the museum. This is where the names of the thirty-six thousand men who have died in combat for the Legion are written on the walls. The crypt room is very grand looking: The floor is covered in black marble with an illuminated crucifix in the centre; against the walls, all the way around the room, are glass cabinets with the regimental flags of past regiments inside, which have the names and dates of their famous battles embroidered on them; above the cabinets, on the wood-lined walls are the clear Perspex panels that have the names of the fallen engraved in them. However, the most important thing in the crypt is the wooden hand of Captain Danjou (a relic from the battle of Camarón; the Foreign Legion's most iconic battle), which sits at the far end in a glass box. Everyone is led into the crypt and made to stand in a horseshoe formation. You are made to pay your respects to the dead, then an oath is sworn to serve for five years with honour and fidelity. It is only once this is done that your contract becomes valid.

After the museum visit was over; there was nothing to do but wait. The REP is on the island of Corsica, so we would need to take a ferry from Marseille to get there, and because of this we would be leaving last. It was good fun watching the others getting screamed at as their chaperones arrived and showed them that just because basic training was over, it didn't meant that they could relax. The cavalry guys were the best. They arrived in the carpark at the back of the building and shouted up for an assembly. They put everyone who came out on press-up position, until last person arrived, then gave them five seconds to get on the bus. When our guy arrived from REP, we were surprised to find him quite relaxed. He came up to the room, and introduced himself; his name was Sch Fuentes and he was from the Canary Islands (he was the NCO who would take us through jump school). He told us to relax for the moment, as our Ferry wasn't leaving until around eight o'clock in the evening. He counted us quickly and then left to go have some dinner.

That evening we were taken to the docks at Marseille in an old bus. The facilities there were pretty basic to say the least: Nothing but steel benches, a toilet, and a broken vending machine. Our ferry, was a huge white and yellow thing that was few decades old. We boarded by the back ramp where the vehicles enter, then climbed the steep metal staircase to the lobby. Once we had gotten our room keys Sch Fuentes gave the orders: While we were on the boat we had free rein, as long as everyone was back in the lobby by seven o'clock the next morning, he didn't give a shit what we got up to. Most of the guys saw this as a great opportunity to go to the bar and get drunk, but I didn't care too much about going to the bar, I just wanted to get up on the top deck and take in the view.

We all went to the rooms to deposit our stuff; then went our separate ways. The rooms themselves were ok. There was no window and a broken TV, but the beds were comfy enough. The interior of the boat was definitely an acquired taste. It looked like a bingo hall, with one of those garish carpets that are only designed to make stains hard to spot. I made my way up onto the top deck, which was rather windy. This was the first time I had been on a ferry and I wanted to make the most of it. The city of Marseille is quite beautiful at twilight. The most striking thing is the huge limestone basilica 'Notre-Dame de la Garde,' which is lit up, high above the city on a five hundred foot tall limestone outcrop. French cities really do look better at night (and from a distance). As the ship sailed out of the port there was one more treat in store for me: The Île d'If (Yew Tree island), which is famous for being the site where Edmond Dantès (the main character from Alexandre Dumas's novel, 'The Count of Monte Cristo') was imprisoned for fourteen years, before he made his dramatic escape. In reality though, the island was originally a military fortress that was later turned into a prison, from which, no one ever escaped.

After Marseille and its lights had faded away into the distance, and I had had enough of being buffeted by the wind; I made my way back to my cabin and got my head down early. Tomorrow would no doubt be an eventful day.

7: The Promo

I learned that courage was not the absence
of fear, but the triumph over it. The brave man is
not he who does not feel afraid, but he who
conquers that fear.
Nelson Mandela

I awoke in my cabin, then got washed and had a shave. It was
almost exactly six o'clock; my internal clock had gotten into the
habit of waking me up at that time. I went and deposited my bags
in the lobby then went up to the top deck for half an hour and had a
look around. When I got outside, I was surprised to see that we
weren't far from Corsica at all. The ship was actually following the
coastline. Corsica is a very beautiful place, the island is part of a
mountain chain rising up out of the ocean. There isn't much flat
land, in fact over two-thirds of the island is covered in mountains.
The flora is also very distinct: Most of the island is covered in
scrublands (known locally as 'le Maquis') that have a very strong
fragrance. The water around the island is incredibly clear and there
is plenty of marine life to be seen. Our ship was heading for the
port of Bastia (the second most populous commune on Corsica,

after the capital Ajaccio). The buildings here looked different to those of mainland France; they were more Italian in style.

At seven o'clock, I went back down to the ship's lobby. Everyone turned up on time, although some looked a little hung over. A tannoy announced that we would soon be docking in Bastia. Sch Fuentes arrived and counted us up, then we went back down to wait for the ramp at the rear of the ship to be lowered. When the ramp was down I could see that there was a bus with 'Armée de Terre' written on the side waiting for us.

The Chef told us that it would take another three hours to get to our base. It was in a place called Calvi, on the other side of the island, and the only way to get there was a long winding route through the mountains.

It was a nightmare just getting out of Bastia. It is a long thin town, stretched out along the coast, and there aren't many roads going through it, and you can imagine how busy it gets when a ship arrives just in time for morning rush hour. Once we were free of the traffic, I was impressed (and a little frightened) at our drivers handling of the bus. He drove it at quite a speed. Whipping it round corners like a hatchback. Halfway through the journey we passed through Ponte Leccia, a tiny village tucked away in the mountains, right in the heart of Corsica, as the name would suggest; the main feature of the place was an old stone bridge. After Ponte Leccia we followed the road over one last mountain range, before emerging on the coast. Then we followed the coastline south and passed by the town of L'Ile Rousse, and the small village of Lumio.

Lumio is perched high above the gulf of Calvi, and It was here that I caught my first glimpse of my new home 'Camp Raffalli' the home of the parachute regiment. I can remember feeling very nervous as we pulled up at the entrance. The camp itself was spotless, there wasn't a fallen leaf or pine needle to be seen. Again it appeared as if it was completely deserted, except for the people in the guard house. Our new sleeping quarters were a small, single story, building on the edge of the camp, right next to the drop zone. Inside there was one single room in which we would live for the duration of our jump training. The room was currently undergoing renovations, which meant that we would have to go to the large company building across the road from us to shower and use the toilet.

Now I think is a good time to explain about 'the promo' (short for promotion). This is what is known in English as jump school. It is the training that each new paratrooper must undergo in order to get his parachute brevet. Until we had earned our wings we were not considered part of the regiment, and if you failed then you would go straight back to Aubagne to be reassigned to another regiment. The promo normally lasts three or four weeks. During that time you will learn to equip you self with the parachute, steer it while in the air, and deal with any problems that might arise during a jump. There is also a strict procedure for jumping (inside and outside of the aircraft) that must be learned. Finally there is another set of fitness tests, which were the same as the one's we had done in basic training, but more difficult to pass. For example: the eight kilometre run now had to be done with more weight and in less time, plus you had to complete a timed one mile sprint before you even started, and the swimming test had to done in full combat gear (no rucksack). At the end of the promotion, each person was required to complete at least six jumps (including; one jump with the rucksack harness, one night jump, and one jump where the reserve shoot is pulled) to earn their wings.

Sch Fuentes introduced us to the corporal who would be assisting him on the promo. Cpl Bălan; a well-built, dark haired Romanian, in his mid-twenties. He would be staying in the same room as us and keeping an eye on us at all times. There were also two aspirants (officers in their second year of training school) doing the promo with us. One of them bore a striking resemblance to Rupert the bear (this was mostly due to his white curly hair and milky complexion). The aspirants had it easy, they chose when they would turn up for instruction and when they had enough they would leave. There was nothing Sch Fuentes could say to them as they outranked him.

The first thing we needed to do after getting settled into the room was to go to the foyer and buy all the insignias and patches that we would need for our uniform. However, going to the foyer at the REP was not something to be taken lightly. During my time at the regiment the foyer was manned by the rudest, grumpiest, most sour puss of a man I have ever met in my life. That's a lot of superlatives but anyone who has served at the REP from 2007 to 2011 will tell you that the corporal-chef in the foyer was not a happy man. He fucking hated working in the foyer, and boy did he let you know about it. When you went to checkout he would literally scan your items then throw them down into the bagging area so hard that they slammed into the metal lip at the far end, and god help you if you made him get up from his seat to get something from a locked cabinet, or even made him turn round to get something from the shelves behind him. He would fly into a rage and begin shouting and cursing, slamming everything that he could, and if you got him mad enough he would throw you out of the shop. I once saw a legionnaire ask him to get something from a cabinet. The legionnaire then decided that on closer inspection he didn't want to buy the item after all, and the corporal-chef went completely ape-shit, screamed in his face, made him do a load of press-ups, then threw him out of the shop. That corporal-chef desperately needed some anger management, or to retire. Everyone in the regiment knew about him, and we often joked about him going on a rampage one day like Michael Douglas in the movie 'Falling Down.'

After we were done with the foyer we came back to our barracks and were issued with new helmets. The parachute regiment has its own way of doing everything, including covering the helmet: First you must place a camouflage cover over the helmet, then an elastic web is fitted, finally a section of car inner-tube must be stretched over the rim to hold it all in place. At the back of the helmet a triangular piece of Velcro is sewed on, and a cloth triangle, with the colour of your company, is attached to it. As we were in the promo our colour was orange, so we had an orange triangle on our helmets, and an orange epaulet on our left shoulder. The chaplain also came by and gave us each a small medallion of St Michael, who is the patron saint of paratroopers. We were told to fix the medallion to the inside of our beret by attaching it to our cap-badge pin.

After our attire was sorted out we went over to one of the workshops on base and took some pieces of wood. Each promotion must create a board with some art work, and the number of their promotion, on it. This board gets hung up in the hangar where the jump training is conducted. There are many amazing looking promotion boards, which I think should be part of the museum as they are very interesting. However, the board from my promo wasn't all that, and it has probably been chopped up and used for firewood by now

On my first visit to the mess hall, I was surprised at how small it was (the hall only had around a hundred seats). The food, on the other hand, was of a much better quality than that of Castelnaudary or Aubagne. At the 4RE they used to serve a dish that I christened 'stinkweed and gut sausage.' The sausage was truly fucking awful, it was full of large chunks of aorta, intestinal tubes, and sphincter; and the vegetable that came with it tasted like the smell of farts. Thankfully they never served this at Calvi.

On the evening of our first day Sch Fuentes came back with bad news for us. We were all destined to go to the first company, which in itself wasn't bad news, however, the first company was due to leave for Djibouti in a couple of weeks. This meant that we would have to condense our jump training into one week, and today was over so we had only had six days left. A plane was due to arrive at the start of next week and it was only staying for three days; so we would have to get our six jumps in during that brief window of time. Sch Fuentes told us that he had already booked us on ten jumps (Tuesday alone we were scheduled to make five jumps), but he told us that some of those jumps would get cancelled so we shouldn't expect to do all ten. After hearing that I was a little taken aback. One week did seem to be a very short time in which to learn everything, and do the tests.

I didn't get much sleep that night; I was thinking about the jumps. I had never been in an airplane before and next week when I boarded one, for the first time, I would have to leap out. I was apprehensive about this, to say the least. One can't help thinking about the multitude of things that could go wrong. I can remember glancing around the room as I lay there in bed, and coming across Nemet, who was laying there with his eyes wide open, staring at the ceiling. It was clear that he was not looking forward to jumping next week either.

The next day we went for our first run. It was much more vigorous than anything we had done in basic training. As I mentioned before; Corsica is very mountainous and you can't run anywhere without going up, or down, hill. After the morning run we went over to a large hangar that was near where we were staying. It was empty inside, except for a parachute harness attached to a series of cables and pulleys that could be winched up, and dropped down.

Today we would be learning how to equip ourselves with the main, and reserve, parachutes. This wasn't too difficult; the main thing to remember was to check that none of the straps had become twisted while you were putting it on. The two parachutes weren't that heavy; they weighed about twelve kilograms altogether. However, the harness, which has to be tightly fastened to stop you getting whacked in the crown jewels by the leg straps when the chute opens, compresses your spine. Thus, giving you back ache if you wear the parachute for too long.

In the afternoon, the Chef took us over to a pair of concrete blocks with steps up the back of them (like a concrete diving board). These blocks were roughly a metre high, and in front of them was a gravel pit. We were shown how to land and roll correctly, and then ordered to repeat until it became second nature to us. Sch Fuentes impressed on us the importance of landing properly. The French parachute, he said, fell at a rate of seven metres per second, and that the ground here at Calvi was baked as hard as rock by the sun. That combination, he warned, meant that if we made a mistake, it would be very easy to get injured. He told us that when we were still a couple hundred metres up, we should check which way the wind was blowing; then when nearing the ground, we should put both of our legs together to form one strong leg, and bend slightly at the knee, and tuck everything in. On contact with the ground we were to twist our arses in the direction of travel and roll.

We practiced jumping from the concrete plinths all afternoon. Rolling: left, right, forwards, backwards, and every combination thereof. After the jumping and rolling we wandered over to a full-scale model of an airplane fuselage. Where we were briefly introduced to the procedure inside the plane and had a couple of goes at lining up and jumping out the door, but it was nearly dinner time, so we would have to come back another day.

The next day our morning run took us along the beach. Running on the sand requires a lot more effort than any other type of terrain, as it just absorbs all the thrust that you produce. We passed by the Legion's amphibious centre, which is situated on the other side of a small estuary at the end of the tourist beach. We stopped off there to do some chin ups and stretch. It is an idyllic little place; there are plenty of pine trees dotted around to give you cover from the sun, the ground is covered in white sand, and you can hear the waves crashing on the shore a few metres away. From the centre there is also an impressive view of the beech with the enormous Genoese citadel at the far end.

After the sport was out of the way we were back over at the hangar. Today we would have to learn what to do when we exited the airplane, which meant that we would be using a parachute harness suspended by cables. We climbed up a stepladder and fastened ourselves in the harness (the pulley system was broken so we couldn't lower it). Once you were strapped in you pretended to jump and went through all the checks and procedures that needed to be done: The first thing to do after leaving the aircraft was to count to three. If the main chute hadn't opened by the time you got to three, then you would pull your reserve. Otherwise, if all went well and your chute was open, you had to look up and make sure that the ropes weren't tangled, or twisted, together, and then you would inspect the canopy for and damage. We all went through the procedure ad nauseam, and when Sch Fuentes was convinced that we had memorised it, we put it together with the landing routine we had learned yesterday and repeated the exercise many more times.

The afternoon was spent over at the fuselage. There was a fair bit to learn here. Everything about boarding and exiting had to be done to an exact routine. You entered by the back ramp, which is a fairly big step up and in full gear it would not be easy, so everyone was to mount then offer their hand to the person behind them. Once aboard you would go to the place indicated by the jump masters, unclip, and unfold your seat (if it wasn't done already). Then you would sit down and put your seatbelt on. After that you could have a little rest while the plane took off and the jump masters did their thing. When the red light came on, the order would be given to stand up, fold the seats back up, and clip onto the steel cable running over your head (all done with gestures because it would be too noisy to speak on the plane). After you were attached to the static line you shuffled down towards the door making sure to keep the foot nearest the centre of the plane forwards. When the plane was approaching the drop zone, the jumpmaster would put the first guy on position. Then you knew that it would only be a few moments before the green light came on and a klaxon sounded telling you to go. At that point the jumpmaster would slap the first guy on the back and it was go, go, go. You would then shuffle down towards the door, hand your cable to the jumpmaster and get the fuck out of there. Then, once out the door, we would have to do all the stuff we had learned in the hangar. Again we practised this all afternoon, but it was a lot to remember and we were by no means proficient by the end of that day.

Apart from the short lesson on how to fold the parachute back into its sack once we had landed that was all our jump training amounted to: the suspended harness in the hangar to practice our in-air operations; the concrete plinths to practise landing; and the fuselage to practice boarding, and exiting, the aircraft. Over the next few days we would practice these things over, and over, and over.

The only break from that routine was on one of the mornings when we had to complete the physical tests. If I remember correctly the time limit for the mile dash was ten minutes, and the five mile run was to be done in under fifty minutes. However, because we had no time to practice Sch Fuentes decided that it was best that he ran with us and set the pace. He told us to group around him and not to let anyone drop off. We had no time for errors, everyone had to pass today, so we had to work as a team and help each other out. He would be going as slow as he possibly could to give everyone the best chance. To his credit everyone passed that day and he didn't fiddle with the times or anything like that (I know because I also timed us on my wristwatch).

At the weekend we didn't have any time to rest. While one team worked on our promotion board; the rest of us were put to work cleaning our building (inside and out). Sch Fuentes wasn't around on the weekend so we were fully under the command of Cpl Bălan. Which wasn't great if I am honest, because he had everyone walking on eggshells. At first he had seemed a perfectly charming and normal human being, but it was an act he couldn't keep up for long. He had a volatile temper and was prone to sudden outbursts of anger. Without any warning his personality would flip and he would become very threatening. He never acted like that when Sch Fuentes was around: he was all smiles then. He was like one of those men who seem perfectly amiable and decent, but who, behind closed doors, was a tyrant to his family and pets. Doyle really took a disliking to him, he thought the corporal was just a vicious bully. For my part I got the feeling that Cpl Bălan took things too personally; perhaps he identified too much with his job. Whatever it was, it would only be our problem for the next few days.

Monday morning arrived and we had to be up bright and early at 4:00am. Today there was no time for sport; we had to be over at the airport by six o'clock. The airport at Calvi (Sainte Catherine Airport) is less than five kilometres away from the base. After getting changed into combats and not having breakfast (there is no breakfast served at 2REP) we set off in the trucks. When we got to the airport we found that the gate was locked. We were the first to arrive by looks of things, so we just sat on the grass next to the fence and waited. The military part of the airport was at the start of the runway. There wasn't much there, except for a shipping container; a portable office; and a large area covered in iron grating. Eventually the truck, with all the parachutes on it, arrived and opened the gate. Sch Fuentes made us do a warm-up while we waited for the plane to arrive from mainland France. To say that I was nervous about jumping would be a gross understatement. I felt like I was waiting to go over the top to charge the German trenches. That may be over dramatic, but I was genuinely shitting myself, and we had three jumps to do that day.

After an hour of waiting, more trucks started to arrive full of other people who would be jumping that morning, then the container with the parachutes opened and we lined up to receive our chutes. As this was our first time jumping, and we would be going last. They didn't want us holding up the other people by hesitating at the door or something like that. I was the last in my line. We all sat down back-to-back in the same order we would on the plane, and waited.

It was a while before a tiny black spec appeared way out in the distance, past the citadel. The aircraft that was used by the French for dropping paratroopers was the Transal C-160, which looks very similar to the Lockheed C-130 Hercules except that it only has two engines instead of four. The plane landed, then looped around and parked next to us. We got up and walked over to the back of the plane to line up. When you are standing behind a C-160 like that you get a face full of hot exhaust fumes from the huge pair of propeller driven Rolls Royce Tyne engines, which makes it hard to breathe. Once on-board we were packed in tight like sardines and the heat soon built up when the rear ramp was closed.

The remarkable thing about propeller driven aircraft is the way they take off. They line up on the runway, put all the brakes on and increase the engine speed until the whole aircraft is shuddering like mad and barely staying in place, then the brakes are released, and you are catapulted forwards. It is quite an experience.

Once we were in the air, it wasn't long before the doors were being opened and checks were being made. Because the drop zone is so close to the airport there is only a few minutes between taking off and jumping. The plane simply heads out to sea, circles round, and lines up for the drop. The two inside cables were the first to stand up and get ready to jump. As we approached the first person was placed in the doorway, then the green light came on and that horrible klaxon sounded. Within a few seconds they we gone.

The Foreign Legion doesn't jump like most other armies, where each person takes position on the door, then steps out. That method is sensible and ensures that there is a fair bit of distance between each person, which lowers the risk of in air collisions between paratroopers. In the Legion it is only the first person who touches the door, the rest just run straight out as close together as they can. The reason they do this is that it reduces the time needed to regroup once on the ground, and because the drop zone at Calvi is not very big.

The plane circled round again to make another run. This time it was our turn to jump. From where I was (at the back of the cable) I couldn't see out of the door. All I could see was a rectangle of blinding light at the side of the aircraft. At that time I was about as nervous as I have ever been. My mouth was dry and my palms were sweaty, but I kept repeating to myself in my head: 'you have to do this, there is no turning back now.' As we shuffled forwards towards the door, my heart was racing. It was only a matter of moments now, then the green light came on and the sound of the klaxon broke through the drone of the engines. I shuffled forwards towards the light and stepped out.

The next thing I knew I was outside, suspended in the air, and everything was quiet. I must have closed my eyes when I leapt from the plane, and I sure as fuck didn't count to three. If my chute had failed to open, I doubt whether I would have noticed until it was too late. But now everything was peaceful. I checked my canopy and found which direction the wind was taking me, then I had a look around at the others in the air with me. Some of them had become twisted up and were now spinning around trying to correct themselves, but I didn't have too much time to enjoy the scenery, because the ground was approaching at a rapid pace, and I had to prepare to land.

I made contact with the ground in a rather undignified manner. Instead of rolling into the fall, I slammed into the dirt and ended up in a heap. Landing was quite painful and I was happy for the protection that my helmet provided me. The adrenaline rush that hit me when I landed was huge. I could see the plane circling around up over head and couldn't believe that I had just come from there. I didn't feel worried about my next jump anymore, in fact, I was kind of looking forward to it; parachuting is fun. I got up and set to work folding my chute back into its bag, then began the jog to the rendezvous point (the parachute folding building in the technical zone). As soon as I had handed my parachute in, Cpl Bălan rounded us up and we headed back to the airport for round two.

The second jump was better than the first. I managed to land with the proper technique that time. The only inconvenience was that we had sat over at the airport for hours before boarding, but that was me done for the morning. I could now go get some lunch, then enjoy the two hour midday break, before going back to the airport for my last jump of the day.

On the third jump we had some extra work to do: This time we had to open our reserve chutes. When I got on the plane, for this last jump of the day, there were a load people wearing orange foam helmets. These were jumpmasters doing their freefall jumps from four thousand metres. It took the plane longer than I expected to get up to that altitude, but once we were there you could notice the drop in temperature, which was a welcome relief from the stifling heat that pervaded the interior of the airplane.

After all the jumpmasters were gone, we went back down and got ready for our turn. The plane lined up with the drop zone and before I knew it, I was outside again. I did, however, remember to keep my eyes open this time and saw the plane receding away from me at an incredible speed. My chute opened and I performed my checks, then it was time for me to open the reserve. I was looking forward to this, as with two chutes I could expect a much gentler landing, so I took hold of the red handle in front of my chest with both hands and pulled. However, when the parachute opened it sprang forwards then flopped down and hung like an old man's ball sack beneath me. I tried to get it inflated but it wasn't happening. I landed with only one parachute, and whacked my butt on a big rock sticking out of the ground for good measure. I have never used the reserve shoot since and have no idea what kind of luxurious landing it offers, but the others were all singing its praises.

When we had finished jumping for the day I was incredibly hungry. I devoured every last scrap of my dinner that evening. I was also pretty exhausted, but there was still work to be done after dinner. Tomorrow we would be jumping with full equipment (up until now we had done what is called at the REP a 'tourist jump' with only the two parachutes), so we had to go over to the first company's armoury and get a load of guns. After that we went to the store room, under the company building, and each took a heavy duty canvas harness for our rucksack. This harness was attached to the main parachute, just below the reserve chute, and it could be released by pulling a handle on the top of it, which would let it fall down on a five metre long rope. In this way you could carry a lot of equipment without the weight of it affecting your landing (it was also useful on night jumps, when you couldn't see the ground. You could listen out for the thud of it hitting first; then you knew a second or two later it was your turn). We also took a thick canvas sheath for the gun, which could be attached to either side of the rucksack harness, but this wasn't normally used. The reason was that it was no use searching around for your gun on the end of a five meter rope, then undoing all the straps to get it out. That kind of time wasting could cost you your life. Instead we usually attached the gun to our side by wrapping one of the parachute harness straps around it. This meant that you could be shooting as soon as you landed. The only problem with this was that you could get a nasty injury if the stock hit the ground as you landed and rammed the barrel up into your armpit (that rarely happened though). After we had got everything that we needed for tomorrow we went back to our quarters to prepare it all, which wasn't easy as the rucksack harness had straps going everywhere, but we got it done in the end.

When I awoke the next morning I felt a sudden jolt of pain when I lifted my head off the pillow. My neck felt like it had done an intensive weight-lifting session. I couldn't figure out what had caused it: whether it was from the shock of rapid deceleration when the chute opened; or one of my less than graceful landings. After talking to a few of the others about it I discovered that I wasn't alone, but I would just have to put up with it because today was a big one. We had five jumps scheduled, so it was going to be rough, and the last jump of the day was going to be a night jump.

In the morning we got in the trucks and went back over to the airport. There wasn't much waiting around for our first jump, within half an hour we were already floating down onto the drop zone. I remember that there was still dew on the grass when I landed.

As I was running to go hand in my parachute, I noticed one of the NCOs, who were littered around the edge of the DZ, hollering at someone in the air. 'Release your fucking rucksack you idiot,' he was shouting. I turned to see what all the fuss was about and there was this guy coming in to land with his rucksack still stuck to the front of him. He sailed down and slammed into the ground like a sack of spuds (luckily he wasn't injured). It was quite funny. That guy had obviously understood fuck all of the instruction and didn't know how to release the rucksack, but this is going happen if you employ foreigners. Especially if you beast them for not understanding French, because you will get some people who nod and say that they've understood everything to avoid punishment, in the hope that they don't get found out.

When we returned to the airport for our second jump of the day there was a long delay. Then the Major who coordinated everything came out of his office and told everyone to take off their parachutes and hand them back in. There was a problem with the plane, and the jump was cancelled.

After lunch, Sch Fuentes came over to give us the new orders. The plane was going to leave for an airbase on the other side of the island where it could be fixed. We would be going with it and staying overnight there. So now we had to pack our bags with everything we needed, then after dinner we would be heading back to the airport.

That evening we went back to the airport, kitted up, and got on the plane. To get to the other side of the island the plane takes a bit of a circuitous route around the big mountains in the middle. Twenty minutes after taking off. The order was given to stand up, fold up the seats, and clip on. I was in third place for this jump and I could see out of the door. This drop zone was the complete opposite of Calvi; it was in a huge field full of thick green grass. It was dusk now and I could still see pretty well, but this would still count as our night jump.

It is difficult moving around with your rucksack in front of your legs; you have to waddle rather than walk. The red light was on now and we got ready to jump. The plane levelled out and then it was go, go, go, and out the door. The first thing I noticed when I was outside was that there was a prison right next to the drop zone. It was all lit up with flood lights and covered in razor wire. I wondered if anyone had ever landed in there before and what kind of commotion that would cause. But I couldn't dwell on that for long, I had to get rid of my rucksack, and prepare to land.

This time I managed to effect a half decent roll. The ground here was much softer than Calvi, and the grass was a godsend (Calvi was a dust bowl covered with dead shrub bushes and rocks, and there was also a flock of sheep wandering about it!). The field I was in was huge, and I could just about see a bunch of army trucks parked not far from the prison off in the distance. I went over there, handed my parachute in, and climbed aboard one of the trucks. Before we left, one of the parachute collecting guys came over to our truck to have a word with us. He informed us that the place we had just jumped at was called 'Borgo: b-o-r-g-o', and not

'Burger' as someone had written on their jump slip. This made everyone laugh.

Once everyone was on the trucks we were taken to the nearby Bastia airport where we spent the night on the floor of an aircraft hangar. I was excited about the jump tomorrow as it would be my sixth and that was the threshold for earning your wings. All I had to do was jump out of that plane in the morning and nobody could deny me my wings.

We woke up early the next morning and sat down on a side road, just off the runway, and waited for the plane to arrive. It was during this time that Sch Fuentes came up to me and said, 'You were in prison with someone from my company.' 'Wait…what,' I said. I was shocked for a moment, and I couldn't work out why he would say that or how he knew that I had been in prison, but then it hit me. He must be talking about Frank. He must have come to the Legion when he left prison, and now he was here in the parachute regiment. I nodded back at him and confirmed what he had said. He just laughed and said 'crazy English,' then walked off. That was a very strange moment for me, I had completely forgotten about Frank.

It was not long after that when our plane spluttered into life and began making its way down the runway towards us. A truck had been sent from Calvi last night with enough parachutes for everyone, so we lined up, got ready, and then got back on the plane. I fell asleep on the way back, I find that propeller engines have a hypnotic quality to them and they make me drowsy. However, the cold air rushing in when the doors were opened soon woke me up, and before I knew it I was out the door, suspended in the air, dangling below a green canopy.

After handing in the parachutes we went back to our building. We hadn't been there long when Sch Fuentes arrived and announced that there would be no more jumping for us. There were a lot of other people who needed to jump after the cancellations yesterday and seeing as we already had our six, he had decided it was best if we stopped and got ready to receive our parachute brevets. He told us to iron our dress uniforms, because tomorrow we would be going over to the main parade ground to receive our wings and be officially inducted into the regiment by the chef du corps. He also instructed the corporal to teach us the regiment song that night as we would need to sing that tomorrow too. We were all very pleased at having passed; and without any injuries, which was a bonus: The promo was over.

During that afternoon, Doyle came to speak with me concerning something he had been thinking about. Later that week we would be going over to the command building to be allocated to our company. He was going to ask to be changed to the third company, which specialized in amphibious warfare. He had come to ask me to do the same. He explained to me that amphibious activities were the most difficult and the training that we would receive there would be the best in the regiment. He also mentioned that the third company had its own special group of divers that trained with the regular French army. This all appealed to me, but the thing that tipped the balance was that the third company jumped into the sea. I had already taken a disliking to the drop zone at Calvi and jumping into water sounded like paradise in comparison with that rock hard ground. This all depended on whether there were any places in the third company of course, but it was worth a try and I agreed to join Doyle in asking to transfer there. It didn't matter to me either way; the first company was a descent company and urban warfare was an interesting thing to specialize in too.

The next day, at mid-morning, we put the dress uniform on and got into rows, ready for marching and singing. Sch Fuentes marched us to the parade ground, and we came to a halt in front of the Colonel's building, just to one side of the regiment's monument, which looks like a massive tomb stone, with a bronze winged-sword of Damocles and the Latin phrase 'More Majorum (in the manner of our ancestors)' on the front of it. Cpl Bălan had a rectangular pin cushion with all our parachute brevets on it, and opposite us was a group of senior NCOs. The colonel at that time was the bespectacled Brice Houdet, who looked more like a Dungeons & Dragons enthusiast than a paratrooper, came out,

stood in front of us and said something utterly forgettable. After
that the NCOs came over and pinned the brevets on our chests.
Then the colonel snapped us to attention and went back to his
office. The actual ceremony was no longer than ten minutes. When
it was over Sch Fuentes told us to go back and iron our uniforms
again, because tonight we were going out to have a celebratory
meal at a local pizzeria.

That evening a small bus arrived outside our building and we
all went to town. We stopped on the main boulevard, which runs
along the seafront. Calvi looked so exotic to me, with all its palm
trees and sandy beaches. We piled into the small pizzeria and sat
round one big table. Sch Fuentes was a man after my own heart
and did not request that we sing any Legion songs that night, in
fact he made a point of telling us not to. Legion songs were not for
public restaurants he said, and I couldn't have agreed more. The
meal was great and I had a very good time that night. It was a good
way to end jump school.

The next day, all we had to do was go over to the command
building so that we could be assigned to a company. Neither I nor
Doyle had told anyone else in our group that we were going to
request a transfer to the third company. This was because it might
give others the idea to ask too. If anyone else wanted to transfer
and they got in the office first, then all the places might get taken.
Also if too many asked, the officer in charge of allocation might
just tell us to fuck off and go where we were told.

When it was my turn, I entered the office and stood there in
front of the desk. It was a captain who was in charge of
assignment. He confirmed my details then explained what was
going to happen. After he was finished he asked if I had any
questions. I told him that I had a passion for swimming and asked
if there was any chance that I could go to the third company. He
raised his eyebrows for a second, then said that he would check.
After a minute or two on the computer he told me that it was fine,
they actually needed a couple of people at the third company due
to recent desertions. He then informed me that if I went to the third
company then I would miss out on going to Djibouti at the

beginning of February, and that the third company wasn't going anywhere until October. I told him that it was fine, and he shrugged and said, 'Alright, then you will be going to third company this weekend; you are excused.'

As I walked down the hallway on the way out, I passed Doyle and gave him a thumbs up to let him know that it had all gone to plan, then went to wait outside. A short while later Doyle came out and told me that he had also been successful. Now we could tell the others what we had done. As expected a good few people were amazed that you could actually ask for your preferred company and they wanted to do likewise. A group of people began to petition the corporal to let them repass the office, but he told them that it was too late and that not everyone could change company anyway.

8: La Trois

Military discipline is merely a perfection of
social servitude.
Alexis de Tocqueville

Early on Saturday morning I said goodbye to the rest of my promo and left with Doyle for the third company building on the other side of the regiment. The third company specializes in amphibious warfare, so as you would expect everything over there has a nautical theme. There is plenty of antique diving equipment adorning the walls, and the area in front of the captain's office is decorated to look like a ships deck (there is even a mast and ships wheel). The company colour is black like the sea at night. This is convenient as it make stains less visible. The company badge is a black triangle (point facing down) with a silver trident, and a golden seven flamed grenade (the standard Legion symbol). Apart from the company buildings and sleeping quarters, the third company also had an amphibious centre as well. The centre was on the beach, not far from the regiment. It is where all the amphibious equipment is kept (zodiac boats, wet suits, etc.). It is also where the courses on amphibious warfare are taught; there are three levels of courses with a bronze, silver, and gold badge awarded after each stage.

The first thing you must do when you are dropped off at your new company is talk to the captain. I was enjoying the calm of waiting outside the captain's office before the storm of being sent to my new section. Doyle went in before me and he was sent to the first section. The first section is different from the others, it is what you might call a heavy weapons platoon: They are the only section in the company that has mortars and MILAN guided missiles. The first section is also known for being slightly more relaxed than the other three.

After Doyle had gone I was called into the office. The captain at that time was Cpt Albrecht; a bald, middle aged, and slightly overweight man, who had been a sergeant in the regular army. Legend has it that he used to work at one of France's materiel regiments (RMAT) counting socks into boxes of fifty. He was a good leader in my opinion and he didn't take himself too seriously like some of the other officers (especially those who had been to St Cyr). He told me that I would be going to the third section, which was located on the top floor of the building behind the company. However, before I could go there I would have to pass by the section office and speak with my platoon commander. The office was at the end of the corridor, and my new platoon commander was Lieutenant Bett, a thoroughly inbred, chinless delinquent, whose father was a general, and his father before him, and so on. He welcomed me to the section and told me to report to the on duty corporal.

As I climbed the stairs to me new home I braced myself for what was to come. It is well known by all new recruits that when you first arrive at your regiment the real fun begins. You are constantly reminded of this all the way through instruction. The NCOs never miss a chance to point out that this, or that, kind of behaviour will not be tolerated at the regiment and if you act in that way, you will be punished until you desert, or something of that kind. I knocked on the first door and asked for the corporal du jour. I was instantly screamed at and made to do press-ups. I had messed up the procedure for entering a room with a corporal in it. After a while I was allowed to stand up and try again.

Once I had got the room entering formalities correct, I was giving a chance to state my business. I was taken to my new room where there were two Belarusians (a corporal and a legionnaire first class). The last person to desert from the section had been in this room. The corporal stood up and looked at me with utter contempt, he tried to get me put in another room, but apparently there were no places, so he begrudgingly pointed to a bed and told me to unpack my stuff. I wasn't five minutes into unpacking when I was told to stop and go scrub the toilets. I hadn't done anything wrong he just didn't want to see my face at the moment. I spent all morning scrubbing the toilets.

At lunchtime I was told to get a mop and broom and go clean the company building. In the Legion the cleaning is done three times a day; so three times a day one person from each section must go and clean the company building. Not surprisingly I met Doyle over there. There was a fat Brazilian Corporal-chef conducting the cleaning that day. I swept and mopped my part of the building and reported back to the office that I was ready for inspection. The corporal-chef checked it and gave me the OK.

A short time after, I was talking with Doyle by the steps outside the company when the fat corporal-chef walked by. He stopped and began talking to us. Then, out of nowhere, he grabbed me by the neck, pinned me against the wall, and said to me, 'You're gay, I know you're gay and I'm going to tell your chef de section. I'm going to tell everyone here that you are gay.' After telling me that I was a homosexual and that he was going to out me to the whole regiment, he stared unblinkingly at me, with his chubby face only a couple of inches from mine; before storming back into the building. I just looked at Doyle to make sure that I wasn't hallucinating. 'What the fuck was all that about?' I said. Doyle just shrugged his shoulders and gave a perplexed look. I think that the corporal-chef just wanted to let us know that even though he looked like an Oompa-Loompa, he was actually a bad-ass that took no shit (in his head at least). I decided to brush it off and try my best to avoid that fat sack of crap. Besides, I knew that he was full of shit when he said that he would tell my platoon leader. I wasn't from a third world shithole where that kind of thing was condoned, and I knew that if he told an officer about his homophobic views it would be him that got in trouble and not me. Nothing ever did happen, and I never heard anything more about it.

In the afternoon of my first day at the section, I actually got some time to arrange my stuff in my new room and meet some of the guys in the section. It was an odd section; as I have said, the parachute regiment is mostly Russians and Eastern Europeans (ex-soviet bloc), but in my platoon there were: three Brits; three Japanese; an Irishman; an American; a Chilean; and one of the only five black guys in the whole regiment.

When you first arrive at your company, after you have brought the coloured jumpers and t-shirts, you must buy a crate of beer and go drink with everyone from the rank corporal upwards. The way this goes is you place the crate on the floor and knock on the door, then when they answer you kick the beers into the room and knock again. This time you enter the room and present yourself fully. After that is done you take a beer each. The person you are presenting to will normally whack his beer bottle on top of yours, so that it fizzes over and you have to down it quickly in one. The higher ranking NCOs will normally only drink one beer with you; it's the corporals you have to worry about. I was made to fill my helmet up with beer a couple of times and drink it all without stopping. I ended up having to go and buy another case and was very drunk by the end of the evening. The next day is the worst when you wake up hung over and have to go about your cleaning duties.

A typical day for a new recruit in the parachute regiment goes like this:
- 05:50 Reveille is sounded
- 06:00 Roll call on the parade ground in front of the company
- 06:00 – 07:15 cleaning (room, section, company building)

- 07:15 Corvée quartier (litter picking all around the company)
- 07:30 Morning assembly
- 07:30 – 08:30 Sport (or the start of regimental service if you have it)
- 09:00 – 12:00 Work begins (instruction, or company maintenance)
- 12:00 Lunch (which you must go to marching and singing, and is obligatory)
- 12:00 – 14:00 Second round of cleaning (room, section, company building)
- 14:00 – 17:00 Work continues
- 17:00 Dinner (optional)
- 17:30 – 20:00 Leisure time (or start of guard duty)
- 20:00 – 21:00 Third round of cleaning (room, section, company building)
- 21:00 Evening roll call, and issuance of next day's orders
- 22:00 Lights out.

As you can probably tell, this is quite a busy schedule and you would be lucky to get more than a couple of hours to yourself throughout the course of the day. If you make a banane at some point, then you will be given extra duties and can kiss any free time you might have had goodbye. In a really bad case you might find yourself working at night with just a headlamp on for light. This does get better the longer you are at the regiment, because new people arrive and then they have to shoulder most of the cleaning burden, but the first two or three months are like special forces training for cleaners.

The schedule at the 4RE, had been almost as bad as this, but then there were forty other people with the same amount of service who would also get given all the cleaning jobs. Now I was alone in my new platoon, so I was always singled out for every bit of menial work that came up. In the Legion your army number is everything, whoever has the highest number automatically gets chosen first for all of the work. It is also the end of every discussion (even with people who have a couple of months more service than you).

This constant working all day, every day, for all of your waking hours is, in my experience, the most difficult thing about being in the French Foreign Legion. It is the reason for most of the deserters. It isn't the long marches or tough military exercises as you would expect. Life in the Legion can feel like a never ending stream of pointless jobs that you don't care about, and which are designed to keep the officers happy and you busy. If you could imagine being a prisoner in a McDonalds run by the North Korean regime then you have some idea of what it feels like to be a new legionnaire.

The worst job at the company was working in the club: It took up your whole day. At five o'clock in the morning you would head over to the company building and you wouldn't return until midnight sometimes (the club stayed open as long as the officers wanted it to). In the morning while everyone was running, you had to make sandwiches for when they returned, then all day you would mop up spillages and wipe down tables, which is boring, but not difficult. However, what made it a really undesirable job was being around the officers and NCOs, some of whom were just complete dicks, who would pick on you for no reason other than that they could (I don't think that the alcohol helped matters). I am sure that working in a civilian café or bar is bad enough, but at least the customers don't wield ultimate power over you: They couldn't physically assault you with impunity, or make you do press ups and run round the building while they stood at the window and counted your laps.

The corporal-chef who ran the club (a fat, bald, middle-aged Czech man), was almost as grumpy as they guy from the foyer and was prone to sudden outbursts of rage. However, I didn't blame him for his temperament; I could well understand how I would feel if I had to work in the club every day. It was a thankless job and I would desert for sure, but it still made for a bad atmosphere in there. Sometimes when young legionnaires would come in and order food he would leap upon any opportunity to start screaming and cursing them. He was a deeply unhappy and unfulfilled man, and his face looked like it had given up trying to fight gravity a long time ago; it was sagging all over the place (especially under the eyes). I was glad that I only had to work there a couple of days a week. The corporal-chef on the other hand did that every day: He basically had no life. I did have a lot of sympathy for him, but it didn't change the fact that he was so resentful that he was dangerous to be around.

Apart from the company duty there was, of course, regimental service. There would normally be only two companies present in the regiment at any one time. This meant that you would take service every other week. At REP the service consisted of:

- MDR's mess ('militaire du rang,' rank and file);
- NCO's mess
- Officer's mess
- 24 hour guard
- 12 hour guard
- Night patrol.

The twenty-four hour guard at the parachute regiment was insanely strict. The uniform inspection, changing of the guard, flag ceremony, inspection of the guard by the chef de corps, and the controlling of vehicles in and out all offered plenty of opportunity to make mistakes and get beasted. I don't think anyone enjoyed having to do this service.

The twelve hour guard was probably my favourite type of service. There were three posts: the munitions depot; the technical zone; and the drop zone. The munitions depot was the worst, because it was so small: All you could do was walk in a circle around the depot to pass the time. There was a small watch tower that you could climb into when it rained, but the inside of the tower was covered in sperm from all the legionnaires who had shot their loads in there over many years. The technical zone was my favourite; I would find a vehicle with the doors unlocked, climb in, and lay on the seats. This was dangerous because if you fell asleep and didn't wake up when the new sentinel came to change you, it would land you in big trouble. The drop zone was also a good spot.

It covered the whole side of the regiment, and you only had to pace up and down a couple of times and your two hours would be over. I also found out that the model fuselage, which I had used in my jump training, was a notorious masturbation spot and the inside had been jizzed on more times than George Michaels' face. You had to be careful about going in the fuselage though, because the dog kennels were close by and if you made too much noise they would begin barking. If the officer in charge of security were to discover you on his rounds, it would be highly embarrassing. Speaking of which, there was a tall tower on the edge of the drop zone with a massive search light at the top. There is a tale about one night when the GCP were doing an exercise on the drop zone, and they were carrying out some surveillance of the regiment with a thermal imaging camera. The story goes that when they looked up at the tower, they saw the person who was on guard that night masturbating furiously. Every night at the regiment there was a genocide of potential human life, but what else could you expect from young men who were starved of female company.

The mess work was all pretty much the same: cleaning dishes, scrubbing floors, and emptying bins. The legionnaire's mess was inside the regiment (directly behind my room), but the other two were located outside. The NCO's mess was within walking distance. It was on the other side of the road that ran past the entrance. The officer's mess, on the other hand, was in the citadel at the far end of the town. A van would take you there in the morning and bring you back at night. The citadel is a magnificent building; it was built during the Genoese occupation of Corsica, sometime in the sixteenth century. Its main purpose was to defend the town from raids by Barbary corsairs, who would capture the local inhabitants and carry them away to be sold as slaves.

To get to the mess you had to enter through an arched stone tunnel, then follow the narrow cobbled road round in a spiral to the top. The view from the officer's mess was amazing, it looked out across the bay of Calvi. During breaks I would go outside onto the ramparts and look out at the sea and watch all the expensive yachts.

The officer's mess was a terribly wasteful place, and the lieutenants played these stupid drinking games, and threw their food around creating a huge mess to clean up. They got through a decent amount of wine at lunchtime. It was a wonder how they continued working in the afternoon. However, I didn't have to deal with the officers that much because I would normally get the dirtier jobs like emptying the bins. All the corporal-chefs who ran the mess at Calvi were Russian, and they would line you up when you arrived and look at your name tag. If your name ended in '–ov' or something similar, they would ask if you were Russian. If you were Russian, or you could speak Russian, you would get the better jobs, where the food was. When they saw my name they would screw their faces up in confusion and say something along the lines of 'Murray...what is that...French?' After I informed them that I was British, the response was usually 'OK Engliski, you clean the toilets.' I actually didn't mind cleaning the toilets and moping the floors at the mess, because at least you were left alone.

I have talked a fair bit about the chores and regimental service that a legionnaire must do. This is because it is what makes up the majority of Legion life. Those who join expecting to be practising hand to hand combat, abseiling face-first down walls, and engaging in general 'special forces' type training, will be sorely disappointed when they realize that they are spending more time wielding a mop and broom, than a firearm. I even reworded the first part of the legionnaire's code of honour to emphasize this:

- Légionnaire, tu es un esclave bâtard servant la France avec balai et serpillère.

Later on I will describe all the military stuff, but I wanted to explain the constant corvée of the Legion. It is one of the biggest reasons that people desert and it pervades all parts of Legion life. There is always corvée to be done and you are never finished: C'est jamais fini.

Now I would briefly like to explain the general set-up of the regiment. 2REP is a regiment of twelve hundred people divided among nine companies. The four combat companies are loosely organized like those of the British Special Air Service in that they each specialize in different theatres of battle. After that there are five support companies and one reserve company. I have listed them and their abbreviations below, because they will come up from time to time:

- 1CIE – Combat Company: Specialized in; Urban Warfare
- 2CIE - Combat Company: Specialized in; Mountain Warfare
- 3CIE - Combat Company: Specialized in; Amphibious Warfare
- 4CIE - Combat Company: Specialized in; Sniping & Demolition
- CEA - Support Company: Pathfinders; Snipers; Anti-tank; and Reconnaissance
- CCL – Command & Logistics Company
- CAS – Administrative & Support Company
- 5CM – Maintenance Company
- 6CIE – Reserve Company

All new recruits will go to one of the combat companies (sometimes the CEA will take legionnaires from the promo, but not very often). The other companies are for legionnaires who have, at least, a couple of years' service. They are more relaxed and less stressful than the combat companies, and they don't take part in as much military training or do as many exercises, instead they tend to specialize in certain areas. They are where older, less fit, or less competent legionnaires are sent (as well as legionnaires who are just fed up with the bullshit of the combat companies). These companies are sometimes looked down on by the people in the combat companies.

The CAS is probably the worst company to be sent to. It is the company that all the people who work in the messes belong to. If you make too many bananes, aren't fit, or you have failed a couple of courses you will get sent there to work out your contract in some dark corner of the regiment.

On the flipside, the GCP (group of commando paratroopers) which is part of the CEA, is where the people who excel can go.

The GCP hold a three week long selection once, or twice, a year, which everyone in the regiment can try out for. The third company does have a group of divers called the 'PAT' (plongeurs armée de terre), but there is no selection for them at 2REP, you just have to boot-lick your way into getting sent to mainland France to do a course with the French regular army.

The only other thing to mention about life at the REP is the jumps. A plane usually arrives every two weeks, stays for a few days, then heads back to France. In a year you can expect to do around thirty jumps. For me, now that I was part of the third company, about ten of those jumps would be into the sea, but I would have to finish my level one amphibious course first. Sea jumps are a little trickier than normal jumps and they require extra training.

Shortly after my arrival at the company, we received word that we would be heading to mainland France for a week. The national paratrooper school in Pau, southwest France (where all French paratroopers are trained, except for the legionnaires), was training a new batch of jumpmasters. The problem was they didn't have anyone to jump for them. It would be our job to go over there and jump all day for a week. For me having just finished my promo this was like a baptism of fire. I was told that this sort of thing didn't happen very often. Almost no one had been there long enough to remember the last time the company had been to Pau.

I packed up all I needed into one bag. We would be flying over there and jumping out (no trucks for us, like those candy-asses in the other regiments). When we got over to the airport we didn't put the parachutes on as usual, instead, they were handed to us in duffle bags. We would be equipping in-flight, when we got closer to our destination. Pau is right on the southwest corner of France, near Bayonne. It was quite a distance as here in Corsica we were closer to Italy than France. The journey would have taken two days by land and sea, but by air it was only a couple of hours away.

After a couple of hours flying, the order was given to stand up and start putting on our parachutes. The plane was packed tight with people; this made moving extremely difficult and with everyone moving around it soon became very hot inside the plane. I can remember that when we sat back down again I was feeling pretty sick. I wasn't alone in this, on the seats opposite me a brown paper bag was being passed along in a hurry. After a couple of people had vomited in the bags the smell of sick filled the air and there was no escaping it. When the doors finally did open it was like heaven to have some fresh cold air circulating in the fuselage. A short while after that the order was given to stand up and hook onto the static line. I was still fighting with myself trying not to throw up. My legs felt very weak and wobbly and I hoped that I wouldn't stumble on my way to the door. When the green light came on I shuffled my way to the door and stepped out into the sky. For most of the decent I was just hanging in my harness feeling as sick as a parrot; taking big gulps of the fresh air. However, I did manage to get it together and land properly.

After a short while on the ground I was feeling alright again. I looked around and found the rendezvous point and began trotting over. When I arrived, there was a corporal from the fourth section asking if anyone had seen one of his legionnaires. A corporal-chef from the CAS, who had joined us for this week, arrived and said that he had seen a legionnaire running the opposite way to everyone else, and that he had seen him exit through a gate at the other end of the drop zone. The corporal fell to his knees and thumped the ground, while screaming the name of the legionnaire and cursing him (It was like the ending of the 1968 'Planet of the Apes' film). There is always someone in the Legion who hasn't understood the orders and does something silly like this. It makes for some much needed comedy amongst the long days of stress and drudgery.

After the jump, we secured the drop zone, then once that had been accomplished we were ordered to stand down and board the trucks that had been sent to take us to the nearby base at Pau. The École des troupes aéroportées (ETAP) as it is known in French, is where every paratrooper in France does their jump training and to say that it has better equipment than Calvi is a massive understatement. There is a whole range of contraptions there to cover every aspect of military parachuting. It looks a bit like a military theme park. The school is split into two parts: there is the main camp where everyone lives, and where all the on-ground training is done; then there is the aerodrome that is surrounded by drop zones, which is about five kilometres away. The first thing you notice, as a legionnaire, when you enter any French army base is just how much better everything is. It does kind of make you understand the Legion's obsession with cleaning, and the harsh punishments for losing anything: They don't know when they will get any new equipment so everything has to last as long as possible. For example; my mattress at Calvi was from the 1950's, people were fighting in Dien Bien Phu when that thing was new!

We only had time to pose our bags in the barracks; before we were herded onto trucks again and taken over to the aerodrome for our first couple of jumps. The parachutes here came shrink wrapped in plastic, and the area where we got equipped had a roof over it. It was luxury compared to Calvi. The jumping was more relaxed too, because the jump zones were long, full of thick green grass, and free of obstacles. We did a couple of jumps then came back to the main camp for lunch. The afternoon was the same kind of thing. After dinner, we were allowed to wander around the camp and visit the shop that was on base, but it was strictly forbidden to go outside. I didn't get much time to explore though, being the new guy I had to clean the barracks we were staying in (they weren't up to Legion standards), plus there was always plenty of stuff to prepare for the next day's jumps.

Over the next five days we made all sorts of parachute jumps. I did my first real night jump here. I was worried that everything would be pitch black, but after I got out the door I discovered that it wasn't too hard to make out the trees and the ground. I also jumped with all the different weapons that you could carry (rocket-launchers, machine guns, sniper-rifles). We even practiced throwing large parcels, with mortars or heavy machine guns in them, out of the plane (sometimes they were empty with just some blankets inside to pad them out). For me that week at Pau felt like the second part, and completion, of my promo, and after all that jumping we did I had gotten used to it and no longer felt anxious. I knew then that I would be fine staying at 2REP.

There is one moment that stands out in my memory from my time at ETAP. It was an incident that occurred when we were getting equipped at the airport. A legionnaire from the second section had left something in the truck, and when his corporal discovered this he gave him an almighty slap on the face that reverberated around the hangar. The legionnaire let out a yelp and went sprinting off to get whatever it was. The corporal was quickly taken to the side by a senior NCO for a quiet word. I don't know what was said, but I have a pretty good idea, because to the back of us, dealing out the parachutes, there was a group of soldiers from the regular French forces, and they looked rather shocked at what they had just witnessed. From their faces I guessed that this kind of thing didn't fly in the regular army. The corporal was probably told to control his temper in front of the 'slabor' (slabor is a word used in the Legion to describe the regular French troops. I can find no precise definition of it, and I don't believe that it is of French origin. Just from the sound I would guess that it has something to do with 'slaves' or 'slavery', but, in the Legion, It was used to denote someone who was beneath us; something like the German word 'Untermenschen').

I think that this moment has lodged itself so firmly in my memory, because the image of the legionnaire getting slapped and running off, reminded me of an indifferent farmer striking a pig and it running off squealing. It made me realize just how savage our existence here was, with the thin veneer of civilised society stripped away. I also think that the comparison of legionnaires to mistreated animals is an apt one. I once had a friend remark to me that, 'a legionnaire is like a dog locked in a cage; that is taken out, beaten, and then locked up again; day after day,' and we all know what happens to dogs if you treat them like that.

Once our week of jumping in the southwest of France was over we boarded another Transall C-160 and headed back to

Corsica, and, of course, we were jumping back into town. It just wouldn't be proper otherwise.

9: Stage Amphibie

*Roll on, deep and dark blue ocean, roll. Ten
thousand fleets sweep over thee in vain. Man
marks the earth with ruin, but his control stops
with the shore.*
Lord Byron

Another promo had recently finished, and shortly after
returning from Pau a fresh wave of new recruits entered the
company. This was good news for me as I would get the
occasional day off from swabbing the company decks. It was
announced that there would soon be an amphibious course for all
the recent arrivals. The company only ran these every three or four
months. Most courses in the Legion had to have a minimum
number of participants to make them worth doing, except for the
promo, which could be done no matter what the size of the class
was.

I was starting to settle into my new section now and had got to
know most of the people there. However, I was still far from being
accepted. The NCOs in my section were not too bad, they had their
quirks, but then so does everyone. There was one sergeant-chef,
three sergeants, and five or six Corporals all together. The second

in command was Sch Buttkis, he was from Lithuania. He was in his early 40's, but looked older on account of his silver hair. He wasn't the most intelligent of people, but he was as strong as an ox. There wasn't a person in the company (possibly the regiment) who could match him for brute strength. He spoke a strange kind of French sprinkled with the word 'fucking' here and there (that was apparently the only English word he knew). A typical sentence from him was: 'Hey fucking, go clean the office fucking.' All in all he was a descent and fair chap, and he wouldn't cause you any grief without a reason.

The three sergeants, who were all in their mid-thirties, were a mixed bag. Sgt Cabrão, a Brazilian, was slightly overweight and completely useless at most physical activities. However, what he was good at was kissing butts, fawning over the officers, strutting around like cock of the walk, and blowing his own trumpet. The man revelled in the prestige of being a Legion paratrooper and loved wearing his dress uniform with all the meatal badges and services medals on. It was men like him that Napoleon Bonaparte was talking about when he said: 'A soldier will fight long and hard for a bit of coloured ribbon.' However, in his case I would alter that to: 'A yellow-bellied coward, pretending to be a soldier, will kiss any buttock and suffer any degradation for cheap metal trinkets.' Sgt Cabrão was a typical narcissist who thought that he was more intelligent, and just plain better than everyone. He would do anything to advance his career, and he had the all the moral fortitude of a kapo. The guy wore a mask at all times, and his public persona was an act fashioned with one aim in mind; to make him look good. The real Sgt Cabrão was a worthless coward who lacked even the faintest wisp of integrity.

The next sergeant: Sgt Saito, was Japanese. He was physically in very good shape, despite the fact that he smoked a couple of packets a day and often drank hard liquor. He was a very complex character indeed. He seemed to, at the same time, care and not care, about all aspects of Legion life. He was highly unpredictable, but having said all that, I liked the man and happened to get on well with him. However, that couldn't be said for everyone in the regiment.

Just before I had arrived at the REP, he had been the instructor on a corporal's course held at Calvi (normally you would be sent to the 4RE, in Castelnaudary, but that was slow and expensive, so if the regiment needed a bunch of new corporals quickly, they would run a shorter version of the course on Corsica. However, they no longer do this and Sgt Seito was probably the reason for it ending). During the course there was an exercise, in which les élèves caporaux had to storm an enemy position, where there were a few legionnaires and corporals acting as enemies. After the attack was finished, one of the men playing enemy was laying on the ground pretending to be dead. Sgt Seito walked up to him, pointed his gun at his crotch and blew his genitalia off.

I think that the sergeant must have assumed that because his gun was fitted for firing blanks, nothing would happen, but anyone with a rudimentary grasp of physics will realize that an explosion is just a violent expansion of gases and when that explosion happens in a gun barrel (with a projectile or not) the gases must escape somehow. You may have noticed that when soldiers train with blanks that there is something attached to the end of the barrel (often it is painted a bright colour). This is called the blank-firing adapter (BFA) and its job is to plug the barrel and build up enough pressure to force the block back, and keep the weapon cycling. The French BFA has a small hole in the end of it to let the surplus air out. The thin jet of hot gas that comes out of this is extremely dangerous and will destroy everything in its path (for fifteen centimetres or so). I have been told by the medic who was first on the scene that it was not a pretty sight.

The guy who had his balls blown off was still at the regiment when I was there. What I am going to say now will sound bad, but I will say it anyway: Sgt Seito blew the nackers off the right person. The guy was an utter bastard, who was on a permeant rampage. You might think that I am being harsh and that I would be the same if I had had my nuts blown off, however, I have it from multiple sources that he was always like that. So who knows;

maybe the sergeant just saw an opportunity to get his own back for something, or thought it was better if he didn't reproduce. The Japanese don't fuck around, just ask the Chinese.

The third sergeant: Sgt Tudor; was from Romania (he was my chef de groupe), and he was a good guy, in my opinion. He was competent enough to be able to explain things to us properly, and didn't treat legionnaires badly. He wasn't overzealous about the Legion either. I think that he might have had a porn addiction though, because he was always on PornHub. One time he asked to borrow someone's lap top, then disappeared into the toilets for five minutes with it. Others in the section accused him of stealing equipment from the stores, but I never saw any evidence of that. However, it was true that a lot of stuff went missing from our personal store rooms. We would return from training sometimes to find nearly all the padlocks broken and our personal belongings missing, but that could have been anyone in the regiment from the grade of sergeant up, as they could all gain access to the keys.

There were a lot of thieves in 2REP (I can't speak for the other regiments, but I imagine that it isn't too different) and nothing was safe: some people would even steal your shower gel. You had to be very careful with your money. One of the most common scams was for people to ask for a transfer to a different regiment, or make a plan to dessert, and not tell anyone; then they would borrow money from everyone they could, and go. I don't think that there is a single legionnaire, who has served five years without having something stolen from him. I had all my diving gear stolen from me during my first deployment overseas. I know people who have had their entire savings taken, or who have given a thousand euros to people who vanished the next day, and don't be thinking that it was any nationality in particular; that kind of shit was rife. I know a Brit who borrowed money from his compatriots then deserted. But, the worst case I ever heard of was that of a sergeant with nearly fifteen years of service, who had his bank account, with all his savings in it, emptied. He was just about to retire from the army, but had to sign another contract because of it. That completely broke him, and the change in his demeanour was plain to see.

It was very rare that anyone was ever caught for thieving, and if they did find out who had done it, then the person would just desert and go back to their home country. In my opinion, people who steal from their fellow legionnaires are the lowest of the low (like informants in prison); they are scum; they are lumps of shit.

A couple of months had passed now since I had finished the promo, and I was getting on fairly well with most of the other legionnaires and had even made a couple of good friends. The corporals were strict, as could be expected, but not tyrannical. I actually got on well with a couple of them: Cpl Mazuz, an alcoholic Tunisian; and Cpl Nagasaki, a very calm and thoughtful Japanese man, were probably my favourites. However, that was all about to change. I was about to meet the biggest cockwomble I have ever met in my life (and I've been around): Cpl Frank Bernard, and no one else who I mention in this book will come close to the levels of douche-baggery that he attained. He really had a talent for being a detestable piece of crap. I would bet that when he was born the doctor took one look at him, then slapped his mother.

I had been fortunate, in that when I had first arrived at the company Cpl Bernard had been on his corporal's course in Castelnaudary, but the moment he arrived back, it was clear that he was going to make up for lost time. He set about making himself known to all the young legionnaires straight away. I was in my room one evening when he arrived back and began screaming in the corridor 'rassemblement, toutes les jeunes légionnaires.' As I exited the room he began shouting at me to run, and straight away put me on push-up position with all the others, then, once he had us all lined up, he began pacing in front of us.

Cpl Bernard spent the next twenty minutes threatening and intimidating us as best he could; telling us how easy we had had it up until now, and that we were in for the shock of our lives. He then proceeded to detail all the ways he was going to punish us, in order to make our lives a tortured existence. Not for any particular reason mind you, but just because he could. He spoke really fast, and even made a point to acknowledge this, before saying that he wouldn't slow down for anyone and that it was our problem if we couldn't keep up. I could tell that he was going to attempt to psychologically torture us, because looking at him it was obvious that he was a physically insignificant man (he had a typical dad bod, with thin arms poking out the sides that were the same thickness all the way up), so physical aggression was off the table from the start.

After the assembly he ordered everyone to go stand by the foot of their bed and wait for him. He was going to pass an inspection of all our things. No one got through that inspection unscathed and we all ended up scrubbing the section until the small hours of the morning. He was determined to run us ragged with all the minutiae that he could think of. He would make us iron every bit of clothing we had; arrange our armoires according to a set plan; polish everything that could be polished; and God help you if he found a single scuff mark on anything in your room. He also made us copy out our field manuals from basic training onto plain paper, and laminate them with cello tape.

The guy was on a constant power trip. If the NCOs were present it was even worse, because he would try to impress them, but even they would sometimes tell him to take it down a notch, because he was getting in the way of instruction. For him it wasn't important that we learnt, his mind was focused on finding things that we didn't know. It simply wasn't enough to answer a question that he asked about some item of equipment, because he would keep asking, and asking, until you got one wrong, then he would pounce, and you would end up scrubbing the toilets as soon as you finished work.

Cpl Bernard would have scored high on the psychopathy checklist I am sure, he displayed a total lack of empathy, was extremely egotistical, very cunning and manipulative, and generally abused his position as a corporal, with no apparent signs of remorse for the hurt he inflicted on others. Having said that, he wasn't reckless or impulsive, and he did have a long term plan, which was to climb through the ranks as quickly as he could. However, sometimes, the way in which he was so persistent with his persecution of us, made me wonder if there was some kind of sexual element to his behaviour. There was definitely something perverted about him.

The next couple of weeks with Cpl Bernard were just awful. It was like the farm all over again, but ten times worse. The maltreatment was already beginning to stress people to breaking point: some were considering deserting, and others were getting extremely angry. He wanted the section to be the most disciplined and organised in the company, so that the senior NCOs would praise him and quickly send him off for his Sergeants course.

However, there was a bit of good news that arrived for us legionnaires; in the form of a start date for our amphibious warfare level one course. I was over the moon at the prospect of a month without that boorish pedant. What a welcome break that would be, and that's a messed up thing to say, because these specialization courses were designed to be extremely brutal and demanding, but I didn't mind physical exercise and sleep deprivation at all, because we would be learning new skills, as well as building up our physical strength and endurance. It would be a breath of fresh air compared to folding up your t-shirts in a pretty way, cleaning scuff marks off chair and table legs, and scrubbing an already clean toilet for hours.

At the beginning of March, I packed my bags with all the equipment that I would be needing and walked down to the amphibious centre with the rest of the new arrivals at the company. We would be staying in an old Nissen hut that had a bare earth floor, and sleeping on the same fold up camp beds that we had use at the farm. There were about thirty people on the course altogether, plus one Adjutant who had just transferred from the 13DBLE, in Djibouti, to REP (he did not sleep in the Nissen hut with us). He was a senior medic and occasionally taught us basic trauma care during the course. His face looked like that of a twelve year old boy, and his voice sounded like his balls hadn't dropped. He was terrible at recognizing faces and during the whole month that I was on that course he kept mixing me up with Doyle. He never did manage to figure out who was who.

Before starting the amphibious training, the other legionnaires in my section, who had already done it, told me that I would be constantly wet and cold for the next month (average temperatures on Corsica at that time of year are around 10°C so it still wasn't exactly warm). The company provided us with wetsuits, flippers, and waterproof bags for our guns and rucksacks. The wetsuits weren't that bad, but the flippers were next to useless. They were those 1950's duck's feet things, which weighed a ton and had no flex in them whatsoever.

Our first week of training consisted of regular swims every morning. One of the big Zodiac boats would take us out to a certain distance, then drop us off and we would paddle our way back in. For each swim we had to pack our bags with some basic kit and put it inside a dry bag. The dry bag floated so all we had to do was hang onto it and kick. This was an incredible work out for your hip flexors. The paddling wasn't too difficult, but it was hard to make progress amongst the waves. A kilometre seemed to take forever. However, there were other problems: the motion of the water would rub the bag against your chin, which combined with the salty water would give you a nasty looking graze (this also happened between your legs if you held them too close together). When we had got to within fifty meters of the beech we would line up and take out our rifles, then lay them on top of our sacks, leapfrog our way to the beach, and storm it.

After the morning swim we usually practiced rowing the Zodiacs in teams of six. We would race them up and down the Figarella (the name of the river that ran past the amphibious centre). The Figarella was much colder than the sea; it came down from the snow-capped mountains behind Calvi. Every now and then, while paddling, someone would shout 'alerte avion' and we would have to capsize the boat and hide underneath it.

We ate our lunch down at the centre. A jeep would go up to the mess and collect our food each day. There was an area outside, opposite our hut, which had picnic benches, and was shaded from the sun by tall pine trees. It was very pleasant eating there with the sound of the sea in the background. The only minor inconvenience was the wasps that swarmed us every time we ate. Even though we were on a course, we still usually got the two hour break at midday.

In the Afternoons we would have classes on different aspects of general seafaring, and amphibious assault tactics, such as: tying knots; infiltration by sea and river; bridge demolition; the meaning of buoys and markers; etc. I remember the knot tying vividly. We were shown how to tie a whole range of knots, then you would be called up and asked to tie one of them, on a rope stretched between two trees. If you couldn't, you would have to go jump in the Figarella.

In the evenings there would be more lessons, or sometimes a small exercise that lasted through the night. There was one exercise that will forever be in my memory, which took place in the dead of night. Our mission was to destroy the bridge and train tracks, roughly three hundred meters up the river from the centre. Our leader on that mission was Cch LaVache, a slightly crazy Frenchman who was obsessed with the Second World War, and not too happy that France only fought in it for six weeks. He had been in the French army before the Legion and had around twenty year's military service in total.

We were dropped off five hundred meters from the beech and went through the usual routine: swam in a column; then lined up at fifty metres out, got out the guns, then leap-frogged to the shore and stormed the beach. Once we were clear of the beach we regrouped and struck out for the bridge, leaving lookouts along the way. For the last hundred and fifty meters there was a path that ran alongside the river and under the bridge. We crept along the path and left a couple of legionnaires on guard under the bridge. Then the demolition teams, of which I was a part, climbed up the banks to place the explosives on the tracks, and bridge.

While we were crouched down setting up the explosives, Cch LaVache leapt out from the bushes and started attacking one of the legionnaires on the bridge. He then ran over to the group where I was and began attacking us. He hit me on the back and then grabbed another guy by the collar, rag-dolled him, and chucked him back down the bank towards the river. For some reason everyone just started running. We ran back down to the path and towards the beach. As I came down from the bridge I told the legionnaires on guard to run as the corporal-chef had gone crazy.

As we were all high-tailing it along the path, I looked back to see where Cch LaVache was and what I saw next was one of those priceless moments of hilarity that came from the insanity of the Legion. There were two people behind me, and just behind them, gaining rapidly, was a crazed Cch LaVache. He got within striking distance then hit one of them in the back with his rifle butt. The guy he hit just collapsed and went rolling into the brambles beside the path. I turned my head back around and ran as fast I could. It was like that boulder scene from 'Indiana Jones: Raiders of the Lost Ark.'

The next day, before we went on our morning swim, we had a chuckle with the corporal-chef about what happened during the mission. It turned out that the guy he had hit, and thrown like a ragdoll, was the Adjutant (it's hard to tell people apart when they are all wearing the same wetsuit with the hood up), and he had complained to the other NCOs about it, but Cch LaVache just laughed it off (one of the perks of being a corporal-chef was that you were, in a sense, untouchable; you couldn't be promoted, so you didn't have to kiss anyone's butt).

In the second week of the course, we fixed small twenty horse-power outboard motors to the boats and began learning how to use them. We did a lot of driving around in the bay of Calvi and further south past the citadel, in the gulf of Revellata. There is a fairly large peninsular that stretches out to sea, just south of Calvi, with a lighthouse at its tip. This was typically the farthest we would go with our zodiacs. The first time that I saw wild dolphins was while coming back from there one day. I was buzzing along, when a huge common dolphin leapt from the sea beside our boat. Soon there was a whole pod of them jumping about, but they quickly got bored of us and went to play somewhere else. It was a great experience to see dolphins up close in the wild.

We had a lot of trouble with the boats during that week. Just getting them out to sea was difficult. If you didn't hit the waves straight on, they would overturn your boat. The engines were also a pain in the arse to start, and sometimes they would just refuse to work for no apparent reason. We also had to practice the art of beaching the boats. This involved driving full speed for the beach with one person leaning over the bow to check the depth. When he thought the depth was around a meter, he would raise his arm, and the person driving would yank the motor up, and the boat would slide up the beach (that was the theory at least). There were many times when we would pull the engine up too late and the propeller would hit the bottom, or too early and then the boat would be left floundering in the waves, which would normally turn the boat sideways and capsize us.

At around the two week mark we went on a weekend march into the nearby hills. Normally we would be expected to carry a six man zodiac boat up there, but, for whatever reason, we did not take a boat with us. We simply climbed the highest point in Calvi (around 500m) and took a group photo. All the course photos are hung on the walls of the amphibious centre for posterity.

After two weeks of the amphibious course everyone was looking much fitter and leaner than at the start. The daily swims and constant physical activity had made me feel worn out at first, but now I had gotten used to the workload. I barely had any fat on me at all by this point, but I wasn't feeling insanely tired or hungry. The swims had grown longer each time we did them; we were now swimming around three kilometres each time. Sometimes we would go running to give us a break from paddling.

The downside to the course was that all of your clothes were constantly wet, and putting them on in the cold morning was not the most pleasant of experiences, but this was a minor inconvenience really. Also, the fact that there were no toilets in our hut was a bit of a pain, because it meant waking up in the middle of the night, putting on some clothes, and walking a hundred metres to the nearest bathroom. This led to many people just walking round the back of the hut and urinating against it, which in turn made the hut smell.

I had another accident when I woke one night and was too lazy to go to the toilet. I tried to pee in a plastic bottle, but I wasn't paying much attention and blocked the top. This led to my Johnson inflating like a balloon, then flying out of the bottle, and spraying the guy next to me (a lanky four-eyed French guy) and his sleeping bag with wee, like an irrigation sprinkler. I managed to quickly pinch it off, but he woke up and demanded to know what I was up to. 'Err...nothing...nothing,' I replied, with one hand in my pants and the other hiding the bottle behind my back. 'Then go back to sleep,' he bitched before turning away from me. I dashed outside and relieved myself in the bushes; and had a good giggle about had just happened.

During the third week we went back up to the regiment a few times, to learn the procedure for parachuting into the sea. The main danger with this type of parachuting was getting tangled up in the parachute canopy once you landed and drowning, which would be no fun at all. To solve this problem we would have to undo our harness while still in the air. After jumping and releasing your bag, you would have to manoeuvre in the harness until you were sitting on the leg straps (like you were sitting on a swing), then you could start to undo the harness. First by unclipping one side of the reserve chute and tucking it under your arm, then it was simply a matter of undoing the harness in the same manner that you had put it on. After everything was undone you crossed your arms in front of yourself and held on. At the moment your feet touched the water you would lift your arms straight up and slide out of the harness into the sea.

It was important not let go before you touched the water as, apparently, distances are hard to judge over water (I never experienced this myself, but I think it might be because the waves have a fractal like quality to them). Once in the water you would need to locate your bag and put on your flippers, then you could regroup and head off. We also had a new type of releasable harness for our bag; it was a bit trickier than the land one as it had two seatbelt-type release points that had to be pulled at the same time, if only one was undone, the second would be near impossible to open (in the same way that your car seatbelt won't release sometimes if it's at a funny angle or there's too much pressure on it).

We also learnt how to drop from a helicopter. This was much easier than the plane. There were only two important things to remember: unclip yourself from the helicopter before jumping; and fall holding your bag in front of you at face level. Not doing the first would leave you dangling from the helicopter like a pillock, and not doing the second would result in your bag whacking you in the face when you hit the water.

By now we were spending quite a lot of time on the water and there was no shortage of people getting seasick. This seemed to happen more when we were not moving; after thirty minutes of bobbing around on the waves, people would start losing all the colour in their faces, then begin hurling their dinner into the sea. Afterwards they would be sprawled out on the floor of the boat groaning. I am sure the fish appreciated the extra food. Some people even got seasick while swimming. One person almost drowned because of it. I was close by when it happened to one chap. A young Frenchman, and a good friend of mine, was swimming along with no problem, when he began to feel sick and slowed down; as I passed him he began vomiting into the water over and over again. I think that while gasping for breath he inhaled a fair bit of sea water and choked on it. I, and those around him, began waving our arms in the air and shouting at the control boat. Luckily they got him out of the water just in time and rushed him back to the amphibious centre. I am glad to say that after a day's rest he made a full recovery and re-joined the course.

The last week of the course arrived and we got ready for our tests. The first of which was the final swim. The last swim was six kilometres long, and it had to be completed in under three hours. It began in the next bay, near a marine biology research facility, and the course took us along the coast, past the citadel, then into the gulf of Calvi. It was pretty simple; all you had to do was aim for the citadel, then when you arrived at the citadel you could just about see a tiny white spec in the distance, which was the amphibious centre and you aimed slightly to the north of that (you had to aim north because of the current).

It was incredibly dispiriting, when after what felt like hours of thrashing your legs about in the water, the buildings of the amphibious centre didn't look any bigger. However, when I finally dragged my ass out onto the beach, I was told that I had taken an hour and forty minutes, which was alright with me. It was nowhere near the record, which was something like an hour and six minutes (whoever did that must have been part crocodile). For this course though, I had done pretty well and there weren't many people who had finished ahead of me. Being among the first to finish meant that I could sit on the beach and have a break while waiting for the others to arrive.

It was while I was on the beach watching the others who were still swimming that I noticed that the control boat was picking up the stragglers and dumping them off in the middle of the remaining pack. When I had gotten out there were still people who were near the citadel, which was the halfway point. I guess that either we didn't have enough time to wait for them, or the company couldn't afford to fail them; or both. It was things like this that cheapened the experience of the Legion for me: No one ever failed. It had been the same on the kepi march and numerous other times during my short stay at the Legion so far. There were people who couldn't swim at all in the Legion, and that wasn't an uncommon thing. There were even people in the third company at REP, the 'amphibious company', who couldn't swim; just think about that for a second, it's mad. In my promo Nemet had jumped in the pool when we did our swimming test, which had to be done in combat fatigues, and sunk straight to the bottom. Sch Fuentes had to dive in and save him.

The next day we had a bit of a rest in the morning, while we completed the theory part of the tests. This was the knots, river crossings, first aid, etc. Then when the theory was out of the way we had to do a couple of small missions: one involving the boats, and one where we swam.

The boat exercise was good fun and not too physically demanding. After we had beached ourselves, we had to dig holes and hide the boats. When one of the NCOs came to inspect how well we had done. We directed him to a depression in the ground and told him that the boats were there. He circled it prodding the edges with his foot, then raised his eyebrows in astonishment, and told us what a good job we had done. He said that it looked like no one had been there. That was when we told him that in fact the boats were buried behind him and that what he was looking at was just a dip in the ground. Luckily, he saw the funny side of it.

The second exercise, where we swam and assaulted the beach was done at night and it was very windy indeed that night. After securing the beach, we had to open our dry sacks, change into regular military gear, and then bury everything. This took quite a while and once I had removed my wetsuit, I got very cold and was shivering like mad. When it came time to move out and go on a small patrol, I was put in charge of a two man team. One of the NCOs asked me the names of the two guys who were with me, but I couldn't answer him. I was so cold that my brain had stopped working. I knew exactly what their names were, but I couldn't, for the life of me, turn it into words. It was like my mouth was paralyzed. That was the first time that I had been close to hypothermia, and it was unnerving to say the least. I was ordered to do some push-ups to get my blood flowing, but it wasn't until we started marching that I fully recovered.

The finale of the course was the sea jump followed by a two day military exercise. We woke up at the crack of dawn and put on our wetsuits ready for the jump. As usual, all our equipment had been prepared the previous night. I was felling excited about making my first sea jump. We arrived at the airport at around six o'clock in the morning, got our parachutes and kitted up, but there was a long wait before the plane was ready. I think it was close to midday when we actually boarded. The first thing I noticed, after they closed the ramp at the rear of the plane, was just how hot it was with my wetsuit on. Sweat was pouring out of me. We had all been ordered to put camouflage on that morning, but after a couple of minutes inside the airplane it was almost all gone.

For my first sea jump I was in second place in my stick; Doyle was in front of me and would be the first out of the door. The reason we had been able to get these places was that the nearer to the door you were, the further you had to swim. As was usual, none of the bigmouths and posers, who talked tough wanted to be at the front of the stick, they were too busy fighting it out for last place. I guess those extra few hundred metres were too much for them.

It took the plane a bit longer to get into line for this jump and we had to circle round a few times, but eventually we saw the citadel pass below us and the light went green. As soon as my chute was open, I released my bag, and set to work undoing my harness. By the time I was all done I was still two hundred metres up with nothing to do, but wait, so I decided to have a look around and enjoy the scenery. That was when I caught sight of Doyle, struggling desperately with his bag; it had only released on one side and he was now struggling with it, trying his hardest to free the other side, but it was to no avail. He hit the water with his bag still attached, and fully harnessed into his parachute. Luckily though the control boat had spotted the incident and was gunning for him at full speed.

Shortly after Doyle landed it was my turn. The tips of my feet touched the water and I lifted my arms and slipped out of the harness. Then I got to my sack, took it out of the harness, and put my fins on, and just then the control boat pulled up alongside me to collect my parachute. They made sure that I was alright and pointed me in the direction I had to swim.

It took me around thirty minutes of hard swimming to get to the rendezvous point, but we were still a few people short. Another half hour of waiting, and many headcounts later, we were still missing one person. Doyle had still not arrived, so the NCO in charge of the mission sent one of the control boats to look for him. It was unusual for Doyle to lag behind in the water as he was a very good swimmer, and I couldn't imagine that he had gotten into any trouble, because I had seen the boat go to him when he landed.

Fifteen minutes later, when the control boat came back and dumped him off, I had my answer. It turned out that he had managed to lose one of his flippers while putting them on, and they had found him not far from where he landed. Anyway, now we were all together we could complete our mission: Another round of swimming up to and attacking an empty beach, getting changed into combat gear in the sand, and burying our sacks.

The course was almost over now, all that was left was the two day exercise. We had no time to rest. After doing the sea jump we washed the sand out of our wetsuits, ate, and repacked our bags. Our mission was to infiltrate the coastline by sea, then complete a ten mile patrol inland, and attack a military compound (the amphibious centre). The exercise started at ten o'clock at night; we were driven in the boats to the light house in the next bay. From the lighthouse we had to swim about one kilometre to our target beach at the foot of the peninsular, inside a small cove.

We arrived at the beach and did our usual drill, then posted up in the vegetation and got changed. However, there was no burying the dry bags, and wetsuits, this time; we had to stuff it all in our rucksacks and march with it. The dry bags we used were pretty old and had had hard lives. Many were ripped, or had holes in them, and therefore were not very good at keeping the water out. If you were in the water for over thirty minutes your stuff was pretty much guaranteed to get wet, and this time was no different, but the look on some people's faces when they turned their bag upside down to empty it, and a load of water gushed out, were pretty hilarious. At least five people had completely soaking wet clothes. I was lucky and only the things in the top part of my dry bag got wet. My jacket and trousers were pretty soggy, but the important thing was that my socks and boots were dry.

The first thing we had to do after getting changed was get up to the road, which was about one hundred metres above us. There was a path, but it took a rather circuitous route. Still, it was better that than scrambling up rocks, I, for one, was not feeling very energetic at that moment and was thankful for having a path to walk on. It took an hour, or so, to reach the road.

Upon reaching the road, the next bit of good news was that we would be going over, rather than around, the mountains. We found a path that had been made by wild boars, going through the thick tangle of shrubs that cover the mountains in Corsica. Most of the bushes there have a very strong fragrance and walking among them is like being in one of those natural fragrance shops that women like so much. The path we had chosen was very narrow, and rocky underfoot, one had to be careful not to twist an ankle in a moment of carelessness, which is easily done when tired. When we eventually got to the top a break was given. This, however, didn't last long; the wind was blowing hard, and most of us were wet, either from the swim, or from sweating after the march up the mountain. As anyone who has done any hiking in the mountains knows, you quickly become cold if you stop. So we set off again, towards Calvi.

We were treated to a nice view of the town with its streetlights twinkling in the dark as we descended the other side. We came down from the mountains and cut though the countryside to get to the main road that ran through the town. We had to remain unseen, so we waited for the road to be clear of cars, then dashed across the road, one by one. Now we were in the pine forests that ran the length of the beach, and the end of the mission wasn't far away. We walked along, parallel to the beach, until we came upon the Figarella. To cross it we used a small one person dingy, and by attaching ropes to the front and back we pulled it back and forth to ferry everyone across quickly. Once across, we positioned ourselves around the compound, and waited to spring our trap at the break of dawn.

In the morning we advanced on the building, entered it, and captured the two NCOs, who were playing enemy. The assault only lasted a couple of minutes, if that, and once we had captured our prisoners the mission was over (it was technically a two day exercise, but it in reality it lasted less than fifteen hours).

The amphibious course was over, and I had enjoyed it. This was the kind of thing that I had joined the Legion to do, not to scrub dishes in the mess. For the rest of the day we cleaned all of the gear that we had used during the course (Doyle had to buy a case of beer for the flipper that he had lost). Then we set about cleaning the entire amphibious centre: mowing the grass, raking the sand, and collecting up the pine needles. The next day we would be having a barbeque to celebrate, and there was also the small matter of the finishing ceremony. I was quietly confident that I would finish with a good score, as I hadn't made any mistakes and didn't have any difficulty with the tests.

The next morning we put our dress uniforms on and waited for finishing ceremony, if you could call it that. We basically just lined up in front of the amphibious centre, waited for our names to be called, then went and collected our bronze brevet. I finished in twenty-seventh place (third to last), which kind of pissed on my strawberries. I think that I must have pissed someone off, and my guess was Adjutant squeaky balls, he had taken a disliking to me after I had to constantly tell him that my name wasn't Doyle. He got so angry once that he ended up yelling at me that he didn't care what my name was, but anyway, I wasn't that fussed, my brevet looked the same as everyone else's so fuck it. At least I still got to go to the barbeque afterwards and stuff my face like a fat pig.

10: Camerone

History is a set of lies agreed upon.
Napoleon Bonaparte

Straight away after returning from the amphibious centre, Cpl Bernard was up to his old tricks again. A couple of legionnaires decided that they had had enough and deserted. One of whom was a very friendly, mild-mannered Japanese guy (with tattoos of Jennifer Aniston on his chest and shoulder), had been hounded to near madness. He was nearly forty and had problems picking up French, and Cpl Bernard just wouldn't leave him alone, so one weekend he came to my room and said goodbye to me and told me that he was going back to Japan. I gave him an English ten pound note as a souvenir and that was the last I saw of him.

With the recent desertions it meant that I was now the newest recruit again, and I was back to doing all the cleaning. However, not everyone reacted by deserting, others had reached their boiling points and exploded with rage. At one point Cpl Bernard had to lock himself in his room and call for assistance because a Serbian legionnaire, who he had been harassing was pounding on his door, and baying for his blood. Funnily enough, he never said a word to that guy after that.

Living in the third section at that time was extremely stressful. Cpl Bernard was out of control, and most of the time there was no one to check him. I have lost count of how many times I was made to scrub the toilets for the tiniest of reasons. It did, however, bring the legionnaires of the section together in hatred for him. I can honestly say that if he had gone out to town and been run over by a bus, had his body caught up in the undercarriage and dragged for miles along the roads of Calvi until he was eviscerated, then had his carcass violated by stray dogs; there would have been a party thrown back at the third section. He was truly hated.

It was nearing the end of April now and the regiment was beginning to prepare for Camerone Day, which celebrated the anniversary of the battle of Camarón (30th April, 1963). This is the biggest event on the Foreign Legion calendar, because it celebrates what is considered the defining moment its history. The battle was part of the Second Franco-Mexican war (1861-1867). The war was started by France, because Mexico had had enough of the racketeering by the European powers, and had refused to make interest payments on their loans. The war had originally also been backed by Spain and the United Kingdom, but they pulled out when they found out that France was going to double-cross them and take all of Mexico for itself.

The battle of Camarón started when a patrol of sixty-two legionnaires, and three officers, were escorting a convoy of gold bullion and ammunition to the besieged city of Puebla. On reaching a stopping point at the town of Palo Verde the legionnaires took a break and started brewing up some coffee. A short while after they had stopped, they were attacked by a three thousand strong force of Mexican cavalrymen and infantry. The legionnaires, led by the one handed Cpt Danjou, retreated to the town of Camarón where they tried to escape, but were forced back by the Mexicans, who had encircled them. They took refuge in the nearby Hacienda de la Trinidad (a farm with fifty metre long walls enclosing the buildings) and prepared to fight.

Cpt Danjou then made them swear an oath to fight to the last; and so began the battle of Camarón. The battle lasted for over ten hours. The legionnaires repulsed charges from the Mexican cavalry, and refused three requests to surrender. The Mexicans burnt the roof off of the hacienda, and slowly killed more and more men. Cpt Danjou eventually took a bullet to the chests and died. Then, when there were only five people left, with no ammunition, they fixed their bayonets and charged into the Mexicans. Two were killed during the final charge, and three were taken prisoner. When they were taken to Col Milán, commander of the Mexican forces, he was shocked to discover that only three men were left and, famously exclaimed: 'These are not men! They are demons!'

Every year the Foreign Legion celebrates the anniversary of this battle. Earlier in the week there will be various sporting events, like at Christmas but on a grander scale. The 2REP has a slightly longer cross-country run than the other regiments; they also have a rugby tournament. I didn't get chosen to do any of the activities. The NCO in charge of the assault course came over and asked for volunteers, but when I put my hand up. He took one look at me and said 'absolutely not,' I guess that I didn't look tough enough. All I had to do on my first Camarone Day was the run, which everyone is required to do, and I finished a respectable seventeenth out of a thousand.

On the day of the battle, the officers, and senior NCOs, come to our rooms, and serve us breakfast. The breakfast is always the same: boudin blanc (sausage made from pork, liver, heart, and milk), and coffee. The newest recruit in the section is supposed to give the orders for the day, but this rarely happens. Then everyone will get changed into dress uniform and all the parading and standing to attention begins.

There is usually a parade through the regiment (sometimes you will go through the town, but the Corsican locals weren't exactly fond of us so this rarely happened at Calvi), then a long assembly on the main place d'armes will take place. This was when results of all the competitions would be announced, and the medals were awarded. Then the overall score for each company would be announced and the Camerone day trophy was given to the winning company to keep for a year (on my first Camerone day, it was the third company that won the trophy). Then after the assembly, the regiment opens its doors to the public (30th April is the only day of the year that this happens).

To entertain the members of the public (and earn some money), there are tents set up, on the sports field, with fairground games inside. Each section, of each company, has to set up a tent with a unique game, then the legionnaires of that section take it in turns supervising. There are also fairground rides. However, one year we had to kick them out of the regiment because the people who operated them (gypsies) got drunk and had a mass brawl. The kitchen workers also put on a massive barbeque, and as always there was plenty of alcohol.

My first Camerone day was not enjoyable at all. In the morning, before we were going to line-up and parade through the regiment Cpl Bernard decided to do a last minute uniform inspection. I was found to have a spec of oil on my shirt (and I mean a spec, it was about 2mm in diameter), which was from having the gun stuck to my chest. My shirt had been washed but it would come out. To Cpl Bernard though, it was inexcusable and he promised to punish me for it after we had finished parading.

When the assembly was over, true to his word, he found me and ordered me to write five compte rendus (reports), explaining why I had failed to keep my shirt in immaculate condition. I was forbidden to ask a French person for assistance, and would only be allowed to present the reports to him when I had finished all five. As you can imagine this was quite difficult for a non-native speaker. The first set of reports that I made were ripped up and thrown back in my face, as were the second. This continued until around ten o'clock at night, when he finally let me off, and even then it was only because he was going to go out to town. It still didn't change the fact that I had spent the whole day writing bullshit reports about a miniscule spec of oil on my shirt. What annoyed me further was that I had to start each report with: 'I have to honour to report to you that...' There was no honour in it for me, it was unadulterated pedantry.

11: Training Legion Style

Excellence is an art won by training and
habituation. We do not act rightly because we
have virtue or excellence, but we rather have
those because we have acted rightly. We are
what we repeatedly do. Excellence, then, is not
an act but a habit.
Aristotle

After all the activities of Camerone were done with, I settled back into the daily life of the regiment. I had begun to appreciate regimental service a bit more now, as it got me away from the section for a day. Some new legionnaires were trickling through to the section, which took Cpl Bernard's attention away from me a bit, and lightened my load with the daily cleaning duties. My life at the section was beginning to reach some degree of normality.

One morning, during assembly, Sch Buttkis asked if there were any volunteers to do the GCP selection. I hesitated at first, but when I saw that there were no willing volunteers, I raised my hand and said that I would give it a go. He was just about to write my name down, when Cpl Bernard started his bitching; telling me to put my hand down and know my place. He then reminded Sch

Buttkis that I didn't have a year's service yet. When the lieutenant heard what the corporal said he also chimed in. He told me that I should probably wait until after we had been to Gabon. I tried to argue that if no one else was willing why shouldn't I be allowed, but the lieutenant wasn't going to let me try out this time. However, he did promise to put my name down for the next round of selection. This annoyed Cpl Bernard a great deal and he continued with his snide remarks to me. He clearly had an inferiority complex when it came to physical stuff, and was lashing out at me to compensate. Otherwise, why didn't he raise his hand? If he was as good as he pretended to be, it should have been a walk in the park. It was obvious that he was scared of failure, because that was something that he wouldn't be able to cope with.

Not long after that day, one of the other corporals in the section came to my room and handed me a load of field manuals and information regarding the GCP. He had tried himself, but had not been successful. He gave me a ton of good advice, told me what the selection was like, and what I should study to have the best chance of success. He also told me that it was better that I had to wait, as it gave me time to prepare properly. If I went there now and failed miserably they might not let me have a second try. The corporal who I shared a room with had also tried out, but had failed, and he too gave me some advice. In fact the only person who was being a dick about it was Cpl Bernard, but I didn't expect anything less from a man of his calibre, and took no notice of what he said.

Sometime in May a rumour started to sweep through the regiment: Apparently a Legionnaire had died in Djibouti. At first there wasn't much more information than that. It was strange that there should be a death there, because the legionnaires who were staying in Djibouti were only there to do some training; it wasn't a warzone. I was anxious to know the name of the legionnaire, who had died. Except for Doyle, the whole of my promo, the people I had gone through basic training with, were in Djibouti with the first company.

I eventually found out that it wasn't anyone from my promotion. The man who died was a Slovakian legionnaire who had joined a few months before me. According to what I heard, he had experienced difficulty keeping up on one of the long marches through the dessert, and was, reportedly, a bit overweight and not very fit. The story goes that he had sat down during the march and the lieutenant commanding his section had emptied out his water, and berated him for being a 'piece of shit.' The legionnaire's sergeant and corporal then apparently went to town on him, in an effort to motivate him, but after being forced to march without water in the dessert of Djibouti for a while (where temperatures can reach 40°C), he became dizzy and collapsed. He then suffered massive organ failure, brought on by the heatstroke, and died.

The lieutenant in command was put on trial for the man's death, as were the sergeant and corporal. Unfortunately, the two NCOs fled back to their countries in South America and will probably never stand trial for their part in this young man's death.

You might wonder what an overweight and unfit person was doing in the Legion's parachute regiment, but, as I have mentioned before, the REP has trouble keeping their numbers up, which results in unsuitable people being sent there. That said, I want to be absolutely clear that I am not blaming the legionnaire who died in any way; his death was a tragedy, which could have been avoided. I lay one hundred percent of the blame on the French Foreign Legion. If certain individuals aren't up to the standards required, they should be let go, or put on hold until a place in another regiment opens up.

The third company had a lot of training coming up in the next few months. Our first port of call was to the military training ground at Caylus (the place with the stinking latrines), then we would be going to CEITO (Centre d'entraînement de l'infanterie au tir opérationnel), which is near the world's tallest bridge, in Millau. After that we would come back to the regiment to do some regimental service before heading off again to do some urban combat training at CENZUB (Centre d'entrainement aux actions en zone urbaine). I was looking forward to these trips, because I had just been made machine gunner. This meant that I no longer had to use that unreliable, hunk of junk that the French call 'le FAMAS.' Now I had the Belgian made FN Minimi, which is a far superior weapon in every way. The moving parts in the Minimi are almost identical to the Russian AK47, which is famous worldwide for its reliability. The only down side was that it weighed more, you also had to carry a lot more rounds of ammunition, which often weighed more than the gun itself. Still, it would be fun spraying things with bullets.

We embarked on a, now familiar, Transal C-160 and headed for Caylus. We had to put on our parachutes during the flight again, which always gave people motion sickness. When the doors finally opened we were above a large field with a path running down one side and woodland on the other. Another good thing about being the machine gunner was that you were always third out the door, the order went: platoon commander, radio operator, machine gun. This was because you had a lot of firepower at your disposal.

After landing, one of the guys with an anti-tank rocket noticed that he was missing one of the pieces of rubber from the end of the tube. We spent a good couple of hours walking up and down that field, looking for that piece of rubber that was only worth a couple of pennies. We never did find it, and the person who lost it had to pay the usual case of beers.

I was glad to see that, this time, we would not be staying in that husk of a building with the latrines from hell. We were in the main camp with a whole barrack building to ourselves. I was quick to learn that there were two reasons for our coming to Caylus; we had of course come to practice our shooting, but also we would be collecting a fleet of armoured vehicles, known as VABs. These were four wheeled armoured personnel carriers, with a front turret in which you could mount a 50cal machine gun. They were designed to be amphibious, but after an amour upgrade that added two tonnes of extra weight, this was no longer the case.

The first few days at Caylus were pretty easy, and we just shot at targets from various distances, but after that we began focusing on fire and movement (with live ammunition). It got fairly dangerous at times, and there were a few times when I had bullets come whistling by me.

The usual way we would advance down the shooting range, was in a standard leap frog movement. There would always be someone sitting by the target controls watching us, who would flip the targets up at the worst moment (e.g. when you were halfway through a movement). One group would often be a fair way in front of the other and that was when you normally had bullets whizzing by you. This shouldn't have been a problem, because you were told only to shoot the targets on your side of the range, but there were a few overzealous jerks who shot at every target and that's when you were in danger of getting tagged.

There was one point, when we were advancing down a long shooting range that had a right-hand bend in the middle. I was on the inside of the curve, and the other fire team was behind me and to the left. A bunch of targets popped up in front of my team, so we laid down and began firing at them. There was a low hanging tree branch less than two metres above me and I could hear the bullets smashing through the twigs above my head. It was dodgy stuff, but it didn't matter how many times you screamed at these idiots to only shoot the targets on their side, they would just keep doing it.

Sometime during the first week, all the shooting stopped abruptly. There had been an accident. One of the shitty, cheap cartridges that we had been using had blown up in the chamber: Sending bits of shrapnel and burnt gun powder flying into the face of the person shooting the gun. It was fortunate that he was not blinded. This incident meant that everyone had to stop shooting and turn in all their 5.56 ammunition. I had heard of this type of thing happening before. When I was in the infirmary, during my first week of basic training, there was someone in the next room to me, who had had the same thing happen to him, and his face did not look pretty.

While we waited for the new ammunition to arrive we practiced shooting on the computer. In most regiments in France there is a room, rather like a cinema, with a large screen and weapons that have been fitted with electronic motors and sensors. It was like playing the game Doom, but with real guns instead of controllers. The rest of the time we practised throwing grenades, and other non-shooting activities.

During a bout of grenade throwing, I noticed that there was a load of branches that had been cut down and stacked up, just to right of the area where we were throwing the grenades. When it was my turn to throw, I aimed for them and threw the damn thing as hard as I could. The grenade hit the ground just in front and bounced right into the pile. After it had exploded I stood back up and saw that the pile had vanished, and the branches were scattered all around where it had been. Sch Buttkis, who was supervising, found it quite amusing.

One evening, while we were waiting for the new ammo, I went over to the club that had been set up. There were a few NCOs in there getting drunk. When I stepped up to the bar one of the guys sitting there, a big Czech sergeant, slapped me round the head with his great bear paw of a hand. I turned round and stared at him, and asked if there was anything that he wanted to say to me. He didn't answer and just sat there, swaying on his barstool. I turned back round to order my food, and he did it again, then again. I then turned round as he was swinging again, caught his hand, and threw it back to him. He swung again but I stepped back to avoid it, then decided it was best to leave. What a fucking nuisance that guy was when he got drunk, in any other army that type of thing would see you kicked out on your ass, but not here.

There are plenty of jerks in the Foreign Legion, a lot of good people too, but the jerks outnumber them and they ruin it for everyone. The decent people usually get fed up and leave, whereas the arseholes stay because they know that, in civilian life, their behaviour would be unacceptable; they would get fired, and end up living under a bridge somewhere. Even if I had complained about that sergeant, it would have been me who got moved to another regiment, because a sergeant was too valuable to them. The Legion was having trouble keeping hold of legionnaires for more than a couple of years, never mind convincing them to sign a second contract.

When the new ammunition arrived we continued our shooting. The new bullets were much better than the old ones, and they hardly tumbled in the air at all. The first couple of nights after we received the new ammo we went out to do some night shooting, which is great fun. The French army uses green lasers that can be fixed to the guns, and are invisible to the naked eye. To see them you must put on the night vision googles. You can only shoot up to a hundred meters or so, but it's so much easier.

Over the weekend we had some free time to get our things in order. There were no washing machines so everything had to be washed by hand, in the sinks. However, the free time soon came to an end when one of the sergeants spotted a legionnaire putting the wrong type of rubbish in one of the recycling bins. The legionnaires then had to gather all the bins from our part of the regiment, empty them out on the grass, and sort the rubbish correctly.

When we emptied them, it was clear that almost no one had bothered respecting the recycling rules. Still, it wasn't that bad. There was a section of the CEA, who had also come to Caylus, at the same time as us, to do their long range sniper training. Two of their legionnaires, a black guy and a white guy, had been hidden away somewhere talking and avoiding work. When they were caught, the white guy was ordered to put boot polish all over his face, and the black guy was ordered to cover his face with shaving foam, then they had to climb into the trees next to their barracks and make owl noises every quarter of an hour. Given the choice, I would have picked the bins any day.

On Sunday an orienteering challenge was hosted. Everyone from the company paired up and set off at ten minute intervals. I drew the short straw and had to team up with Lt Bett, which was fine with me. He did all the map work, and I just had to follow him around and go into the undergrowth looking for the marker when we stopped. It was one hell of a long course though, and we must have covered fifteen kilometres that morning.

During the second week at Caylus, we focused on weapons other than the assault rifle. We had training on the big 50cal machine gun, as well as the mini mortar. I found the mini mortar very difficult to aim, the tiniest movement when firing it, would send the thing off the target by tens of metres. I also spent a lot of time training with the other light-machine-gunners that week. We had our own special types of targets to practise on. There were moving targets that raced across in front of you, and there were also targets in the shape of helicopters, and jeeps. These were bigger, but we had to shoot them at much greater distances.

Once all the shooting was over we had to sort out the VABs. Radios had to be installed in them, and of course they had to be cleaned. We also had to strap everything down inside; the suspension in these vehicles was hard and that made the ride particularly bumpy. No one wanted loose boxes of ammunition flying around inside, so it all had to be strapped in place. I heard a story about a group of soldiers, who were travelling in a VAB, which unfortunately came off the road and rolled over. They had a spare barrel for the 50cal in the back (a lump of metal that weighs around twelve kilos), which they had neglected to tie down. The barrel flew around inside the vehicle and killed two men. Ouch!

Now that I was the machine gunner, I had to sit right next to the back door of the VAB, so that I would be first out in a combat situation. I was also right under one of the back hatches, which meant that I could stand up and do a bit of sightseeing as we drove. Most people were happy just to be able to sit down and sleep for the journey, but I always wanted to look around and take in the scenery.

There was quite a journey ahead of us. It was roughly one hundred miles to La Cavalerie (the town where CEITO was located), and the VAB was not known for its speed. The journey took a scenic route through great swathes of French farmland, before beginning the climb up to the edge of the Tarn valley. I was treated to one of the most spectacular views in France as we crossed the huge bridge that spans the valley, over the city of Millau (the bridge at Millau is the tallest in the world, but the actual road that you drive across, at two hundred and seventy metres above ground, is only the twenty-first highest deck).

After crossing the bridge we continued on a little further before arriving at the town of La Cavalerie, in the Aveyron department. It is a medieval looking place, steeped in history, with stone towers and battlements that sits atop a huge limestone plateau. There is a castle at its centre that was, at one time, home to the knights Templar. It had been badly damaged in the wars of religion, but later rebuilt and is now a hotel. The town, and surrounding area, is also renowned for being the home of Roquefort cheese.

The camp we were staying in had the look of a Victorian workhouse about it. The buildings were long and rectangular. They were four stories high, and the sides were covered with windows. The insides were damp and mouldy, especially around the windows. However, we didn't have much time to settle in as there was plenty of shooting to be done (CEITO is slightly different from Caylus in that it doesn't have so many traditional shooting ranges, instead it has courses that you progress over).

From the moment we arrived, the weather was awful. There was constant drizzle and a howling wind. The terrain around the camp was pretty barren; nothing but yellow grass and mud, with the odd gorse bush here and there. On the first shooting session, I was using my backpack as a rest; when the wind blew one of the straps in front of my gun barrel, as I was firing. I didn't realise until I went to put it on and noticed that one of the straps had been shot in half. I had to implement a quick fix and sew it back together with some bootlace.

Somehow we ended up having to do service in this regiment, but it was quite nice actually. While on service here you were under the command of the regular troops and they were no way near as strict as the Legion: It was a nice break from being treated like a whipping boy all day. On guard, when the security officer came round at night to check the posts, he didn't break your balls with an impromptu quiz on your equipment and make you do press ups in the middle of the night, instead he just asked if all was well and continued on his rounds.

Every day that we were at CEITO we would go out shooting in the wind and drizzle. By the time you returned you were soaked through, covered in mud, and halfway to getting hypothermia. The living conditions there weren't great. There were only a few sinks for the sixty men on our floor of the building, which caused problems in the morning when everyone needed to get washed and shaved at the same time. I was alright because I didn't have that much facial hair at that time so I could get away with shaving before I went to bed; as long as the corporals didn't catch me (Cpl Bernard would have had a field day with that).

It was difficult to get enough rest as well; there was one guy in my room, who had an incredibly loud snore (even people outside would comment on it as they walked past during the night). This guy would regularly wake up the whole room during the course of the night. People soon got fed up with this, and after a few nights, instead of the usual, waking the culprit up and telling him to sleep on his side, a boot would fly across the room towards his head. I once awoke to see someone calmly walk across the room to his bed, lift it up to eye level then drop it. The funny thing was that this guy who had ruined our sleep every night, collapsed with exhaustion one morning, before we started shooting, and had to be wrapped in a space blanket and sent to the infirmary. Well that's a bit fucking rich, I thought at the time. To be honest that guy was a lazy fucker and I suspected that he was just pulling a fast one to get out of a couple of days work.

As the week came to an end we prepared for a two day exercise, on the windswept limestone plateau of Larzac. On the first day of manoeuvres we only marched a few kilometres. We had to stop quite often to engage targets, or wait for another part of the company to get into position.

In the evening we took up positions along a ridge and I camped down for what was probably be the worst night of my life. We had been told not to take our sleeping bags with us, but to instead take only our tarpaulin. As night fell the wind, and rain, picked up. The wind was so strong that you could barely hear the person next to you. In between guard duty, I would roll myself up in the tarpaulin and try to get some sleep. However, this was a futile exercise if there ever was one; apart from the cold, the main thing that kept me awake was the wind hitting my tarpaulin and making waves ripple along it at an astonishing speed. This made it whip me in the face, twice a second, for the entire night, whilst making an annoying rustling noise at the same time. Being wrapped in plastic also meant that I hadn't dried off at all; all the water from my clothes, and the moisture from my breath, just circulated inside the tarp and made me damp all over. I was most definitely not feeling refreshed in the morning.

The second day we manoeuvred until the whole company was lined up facing the main shooting course. We then advanced through various stages, shooting all types of targets. At certain points along the course there was detonation-cord laid across the ground, which blew up when we got within a certain distance. There was one memorable balls up that day; when a target in the shape of a tank popped up. The ERYX (guided missile) team took aim at it and fired their missile, which flew for thirty metres, then slammed into the ground, rebounded and went spinning up into the air, it then came back down again, hit the ground a second time, and went spinning off over the hill. It was a spectacular miss, but great fun to watch.

Once the day was over, we returned to the start of the course and the supervisors came over and announced the score. We had set a new record, which surprised everyone. The regiments that were on mainland France surely had more opportunity to come here and practice than we did: for the REP this was a once a year thing, if that.

As our time at CIETO came to a close we cleaned the whole building that we had been staying in and readied the VABs again. To my surprise we were treated to a little town visit before our departure. We got in the trucks and drove down to Millau. When I say little town visit, I do mean little. We parked in an industrial estate and were given an hour to do some shopping. The only thing there of any interest was a super market, so I went and brought some food for the journey back. A few people were late returning to the trucks and we ended up doing a load of press ups in the car park, which entertained the locals.

After we returned from Millau, we went out to a pizzeria in La Cavalerie for a meal, and what's more, we were actually allowed to order for ourselves. Seeing as we were in the home of Roquefort, I had a Roquefort and honey pizza, which I thoroughly recommend to anyone who gets the chance to try one. The officers showed themselves for the spoiled brats that they were, by chanting 'nous avons faim' while banging their cutlery on the table while waiting for the food to arrive, and, once again, the evening didn't pass without someone starting a fucking Legion song. It's bad enough having to sing them in the regiment, but we didn't need to embarrass ourselves in public.

The next day, early in the morning, we loaded up the VABs and set off on the long drive back to Calvi. We would have to drive all the way across France to the port at Marseille. The trip back was very cold for the time of year, and it took slightly longer than anticipated (due to a couple of breakdowns), but we still managed to arrive in time to board the ferry to Bastia.

Once all the vehicles had been embarked, an assembly for all the legionnaires was called. A guard would have to be mounted for the VABs; this was to stop the other passengers tampering with them. My guard slot was at one o'clock in the morning, so I decided that there was no point going to sleep and waited in the bar until it was time for me to start.

Sometime around midnight, a legionnaire came into the bar and called us all outside. Someone had drank too much, and was now smashing up everything he could get his hands on. When I went out onto the deck I saw that this guy had climbed up a tower with a foam cannon on top, and was spraying everything with foam. Including our VABs, which were parked on the lower deck. A member of the ships security arrived, but had to make a hasty retreat when he too was sprayed with foam.

The drunken legionnaire then climbed down from the tower, ripped a fire extinguisher off the wall, and began smashing the benches to smithereens with it, then he got hold of the life rings and began throwing them overboard. The guy was in a crazed state and there was no talking to him. I along with the others just went back into the bar. It wasn't worth hanging around at the scene of the crime, because anyone found loitering around there was likely to be associated with what had gone on, or at least interrogated for information. Besides, the security guard would have surely notified the right people, who would soon be on their way to deal with the situation.

When I went back outside to take up my guard the place was still a mess, but there was no one from the ship's security, or any of our officers hanging around. I changed over with the previous guard and asked him what had happened to the legionnaire, who had wrecked the ship. He told me that by the time that the security had come back with our captain, he had disappeared. They searched around for a while and inspected the damage, then gave up and went back inside. I spent my guard duty wondering what would happen in the morning; there was going to be hell to pay for this that was for sure. It would be bad enough to do this in the regiment, but in public was on a different level, because it made the whole regiment look bad. I went to bed that night wondering what time I would be woken up by the shitstorm that was coming.

At six the next morning everything was still quiet, but then came the call for assembly out on the deck where the VABs were. We all got dressed as quickly as we could and went out onto the lower deck. All of the NCOs were there waiting for us. As we came into sight they began shouting at us to run. The whole company was there, assembled by section. Sch Buttkis, who wasn't normally violent, was incensed when we were one person short. He demanded to know who was sharing a room with the missing person. When someone put their hand up, he called him out of the row, and punched him full force in the chest as he approach. He then gave him one minute, an impossible time, to go find the missing legionnaire.

The same thing happened in the fourth section: A couple of their legionnaires were sent to go find their missing guy; a regular bananier who understood zero French (the same person who had run the wrong way on the drop zone). When he arrived, ten minutes later, one of their NCOs roundhouse kicked him a good few times, before he was allowed to join the rows. It was a tense situation and people were getting hit left, right, and centre. Nobody dared move.

Once everyone was accounted for, the captain arrived. The extent of the damage done the previous night was worse than we thought. As well as the benches being smashed up and the fire extinguishers thrown overboard, the ships flag had been stolen, and the captain of the ship was refusing to dock until he got it back (apparently there is an ancient law that prohibits ships from docking without a flag). Also, the life ring that had been thrown overboard had a signal buoy attached to it, which alerts the coastguard when it is deployed, and they had sent a boat out in the middle of the night to search the sea; fearing someone had fallen overboard. Not surprisingly, the coastguards were pissed about being jerked around like that.

The captain asked for whoever was responsible to be a man and own up, or he would punish everyone, as long, and as much, as he could. Unfortunately, no one put their hand up to take responsibility. The NCOs began interrogating us, people were being slapped in the face and shouted at. As I had been on guard last night, I had some questions to answer. Fortunately, when the captain was explaining what had happened he gave a timeframe for the events, and I told Sch Buttkis that by the time I had taken up my guard everything was already smashed up and covered with foam, and he had to accept it. I knew exactly who had done it, so did many others, but we didn't rat each other out in the Legion; it was up to the person in question to come clean and face the consequences. If he decided that he didn't want to own up, then we would all have to take our punishment, then wait for an opportunity to enact our own form of justice on the culprit.

For the time being our punishment would have to wait, Cpt Albrecht had convinced the ship's captain to dock and let us off the boat. There were a fleet of buses waiting to pick us up in Bastia, and a group of corporal-chefs from the maintenance company, who would drive the VABs back to Calvi. My hopes of enjoying a comfortable bus ride were dashed when I discovered that I would have to act as co-pilot in one of the VABs.

I was teamed up with a, laid back, Brazilian corporal-chef for the journey home. Most of the way back we chatted, and he told me some stories from his time in the Legion. He had heard rumours about what happened on the boat, and I filled him in on the rest of the story. When I finished, he shook his head and said, 'that is too much, whoever did that was probably going to get kicked out.'

When we arrived back at camp Raffalli, I was ordered to go straight to the head of security's office. All the legionnaires from the company were already lined up with a couple of MPs guarding them. When I arrived the MPs demanded my bag and straight away began searching me. Once our numbers were complete the head of security (a fat Portuguese sergeant-chef with no neck and the temperament of a spoiled toddler) came out and began shouting at us. He told us that until the offending party was found we would not be allowed to go anywhere. We were to stand right here on this spot, day and night, without eating, until someone came forward and accepted responsibility. He then went back into his office with the two MPs.

As soon as he had shut the door, everyone began chastising the guilty guy, and telling him to go into the office and confess. He didn't feel like doing that, and we began to argue back and forth. The volume of the argument gradually increased until the Security officer stuck his head out the door, and asked if we had anything to tell him. To everyone's surprise a voice replied, 'Yes chef, I do, it was me that smashed up the boat.' Straight away the two MPs came out and bundled him into a jeep, then took him off to the dungeon over at the citadel. After that the security officer released the rest of us back to the company.

As soon as we went back to our section, all the corporals and sergeants were waiting for us, desperate to know who it was. They couldn't believe that just one person had wreaked all that havoc. They also thought that he would probably get kicked out of the Legion for this. However, that didn't happen; all that was dished out in the way of punishment was a month's hard labour in the Legion's prison (the maximum sentence that they can give), then he was returned to his section. There was never any explanation as to why he did what he did that night on the boat; it was just hooliganism for its own sake.

The first few days back at the regiment were spent cleaning everything we had used at Caylus and CEITO, then we took up regimental service. There was a bunch of new legionnaires, fresh from the promo, ready to join the company and help out. This was great for me, because I was slowly moving up the food chain. Now I could go a few days without being sent over to clean the company. There was also a new legionnaire in my room, which meant that I only had to clean that every other day.

The new legionnaires had a lovely surprise when they first met Cpl Bernard, if they had thought Castelnaudary, or the promo, was bad then they were in for a shock. As usual we had a couple of deserters, not long after returning. It was a constant struggle in the REP to keep the numbers up; it was two steps forward and one step back. The company was always changing: People got sent to other companies or regiments, finished their contracts, went on courses, or deserted. At the same time, new people would arrive from various different places.

Some of the desertions were quite spectacular. There was one guy who, before a jump, emptied his bank account and packed his rucksack with everything he needed to take with him. Then when he jumped out of the plane, he steered his parachute as close to road as he could, landed, changed into civilian clothes, and disappeared. When his sergeant noticed that he was missing, they went looking for him. At first fearing that he might be laying on the drop zone injured somewhere. When they finally found his discarded parachute and other belongings, they were surprised to see that he had folded up his parachute, and combat fatigues, then stacked them in a neat pile with his helmet on top, and the gun resting next to it. Only a legionnaire would fold everything up, and arrange it like that, before doing a runner.

After all our training was done, my section got ready to change our commanding officer. Lt Bett had finished his two year stint at Calvi, and would soon be promoted to captain. He was going off to command a company of his own, in the regular army. As you can imagine, there is a ceremony that has to be done on these occasions, and we had to put on our dress uniform and parade around a bit in honour of his service. However, it was not a huge affair, and we got to have a few beers in the club at the end of it.

While we waited for our new commanding officer to arrive, Sch Buttkis was put in charge. He immediately called a team of legionnaires over to the office so that we could arrange it in the way he wanted, before the new lieutenant got here. He also decided to repaint the whole of our section. It wasn't all bad though, he did finally manage to get the mattresses changed. Now instead of having a mattress from 1954, I had one from 1978. Sch Buttkis seemed to have an obsession with arranging our store room. He kept changing his mind and making us do it again and again. It became a running joke at the section.

The new Lieutenant arrived a month later, and introduced himself to everyone. Lt Petry was his name, he was a small man of mixed race (French-Moroccan), and he had the air of a smug twat about him; his face looked like he was permanently trying to squeeze out a fart. He had been a fireman before going to officer school. Being brown skinned, he stood out from all the other officers, who were white French upper-class types.

The bootlicking brigade wasted no time fastening themselves to him like remoras to a shark. They would make any excuse to go over to the office and ingratiate themselves with him, by laughing at his crappy jokes, and nodding their heads like those imbecilic toy dogs that people put in their cars. It was such a blatant and cringe-worthy display of sucking up. The rest of us would amuse ourselves by making jokes about them going over there with their knee pads on, and taking up the 'deux genoux au sol' shooting position upon entering.

Not long after our new lieutenant arrived, we had to head out on some more training. This time we were travelling all the way up to the Sissonne, in north-east France, to train in urban combat techniques. CENZUB, as it is known, is a purpose-built facility for training in urban combat, and the largest facility of its kind in Europe (many other nations, besides France, also train there; including Germany and Britain).

Once again we boarded a transport plane early in the morning, bound for France, and once again we would have to equip in flight. A few hours of nap-of-the-earth flying, and many full sick bags later the doors opened and the fresh cool air of northern France filled the fuselage. It was a pleasant drop into a large meadow, full of long grass to cushion the landing. I had to help collect one of the parcels that we had thrown out of the plane, and by Jove was it heavy.

The regiment at CENZUB was huge, and all the buildings were spread out. Our buildings were old, but they had everything necessary: showers, heating, etc. The first thing we had to do, after unpacking, was head over to the technical area to have our guns fitted with lasers. I was back to using a FAMAS as there were no laser systems for the Minimi at that time. We also received a waistcoat and helmet cover that had sensors all over them.

In the afternoon we were treated to a few demonstrations by the urban warfare teams at the regiment. They are known as 'Les Bleus' on account of their blue camouflage. They looked very impressive as they demonstrated how to enter buildings. There was one demonstration where they used a ladder to enter the upstairs window of a house that was done with great speed. The combat village at CENZUB looked like a Hollywood film set; from the street the houses all looked pretty normal, but round the back you would discover that only the ground floor had been built. On the first floor of the roofless houses was a steel walkway for the instructors to observe you, and direct the enemy, from above.

Over the course of the next two weeks we took instruction in the morning, and put what we had learned into practice in the afternoon. It was an eye opening experience into the dangers of urban warfare. There was one exercise where we had worked our way through the terrace houses in a street and we had to assault a building that was maybe thirty metres away. Between us and it was open ground. We launched a series of charges, but our whole section of thirty people were hit before getting within ten metres. The smoke grenades that we threw to hide our advance were completely useless.

There was also plenty of internecine killing due to confusion; if you didn't constantly update your position by radio, you were likely to get shot by your own side. There was also a fair bit of cheating going on. Some people would cover up their sensors. There were a few NCOs who removed the helmet cover altogether (my sergeant included). Les Bleus were a good enemy, they knew the combat village inside and out. Sometimes they would wait for you to enter a room then run past the window and throw a grenade in. I must admit that it was great fun, it was like real life 'Call of Duty.'

The first weekend in Sissonne, we were given permission to go out into town. You would have thought that after the fiasco with the boat that everyone would be on their best behaviour, but that was not the case; it was as if a pirate ship had docked in town that weekend. The evening began well with the Anglophones treating the French to a show of 'flaming arseholes' outside the local bar. It is a pretty harmless tradition, which involved sticking toilet paper between your butt cheeks, lighting it, then downing a pint before it burnt you. However, as the night wore on and people got drunker, things turned sour and fights broke out among legionnaires and the locals, then fights broke out between the legionnaires. It culminated with one legionnaire stabbing another in the neck.

The next day, the guard on the front gate found bodies strewn in the bushes, where people had tried to walk back to base, but collapsed drunk just outside and slept where they lay. Fortunately, no one called the police and nothing was made of it.

To finish off our time at CENZUB we held a two day exercise. A group of army engineers came along to join us, and we also had an AMX-10RC, which is a light-reconnaissance-tank with a 105mm gun on it. This provided excellent cover as we advanced over open ground. For two days we chased Les Bleus from house to house. They did a good job at shooting us, but our numbers were too great.

On the second day my group was ordered to block the escape route, while the rest of the company flushed them out. I was alone in the downstairs room of a building when I heard the enemy team arrive in the kitchen (I knew it was them because they were speaking French too well to be legionnaires). I quickly climbed inside of a large metal armoire, set my gun to fully automatic, and waited for them to come. A few minutes later I heard one of them enter the room, then a second, then a third. At that moment, I burst out of the armoire with my gun trained on them. They turned and all tried to get through the door at the same time, but I was too fast. I pulled the trigger…and…nothing, the fucking gun wouldn't fire. I quickly turned and ran out of the other door cursing my FAMAS. Les Bleus began firing at me as soon as they realized what had happened, but I managed to escape out of the building and get back to the rest of my group.

I couldn't believe it, what a fucking piece of shit the FAMAS was. If that had been a real situation, the shitty manufacturing of the French would have cost me my life, and the other guy would be claiming that Allah had stepped in and performed a miracle to save him. Later on that same day I managed to get shot by another legionnaire, so it definitely wasn't my lucky day. However, the third company did finally manage to kill all Les Bleus before the two day time limit was up.

I had a great time at CENZUB and it was a worthwhile training exercise. It is the next best thing to real combat, in my opinion. To return from Sissonne we would be flying back and jumping into Calvi. I am pretty sure that Corsican Ferries were relieved that we wouldn't be travelling with them again. We went to the nearby Reims-Champagne Air Base in the afternoon, grabbed some parachutes, and flew back to Corsica. The journey was much better on the way back; there was no nap-of-the-earth flying this time. It wasn't all plain sailing though; when we got back to Clavi we discovered that the wind speed was too high for us to jump. Some of you reading might think, well that's no problem, just land the plane at the airport and get off normally. Unfortunately, the REP doesn't work like that. The geography of Corsica with its spine of tall mountains bisecting it down the middle, from north to south, means that if one side of the island is windy, then the other, generally, is not.

The plane turned around and flew back across the island to Borgo, near Bastia. As luck would have it the wind was good and we jumped out. The only thing was that we had to wait a while for the trucks to arrive from Calvi. It was quite late when we finally rolled back into camp, but to everyone's surprise we weren't done yet. The NCOs set us to work cleaning everything; all the guns and equipment that we had used. The reason for their eagerness was simple: it was Friday night, and they didn't want to have to come in on Saturday, which is understandable. We didn't get finished cleaning until early in the morning, but the NCO's didn't break our balls with the inspection this time; as long as the guns were relatively clean, they got a pass.

After all the equipment was done, we could finally go upstairs, have a shower, and take care of our affaires, or so I though. The corporals had already taken over the washing machine and it would be a day or two before the legionnaires would get to use it. This was often how it was when we got back from training, and there was no point waiting by the machine and quickly getting your stuff in before anyone noticed, because they would just cancel the wash and pull it out. The corporal who I shared a room with was particularly bad for this and would do it whenever he needed to wash anything. Many a time, have I collected my clothes, thinking they were done, only to find that they still stank to high heavens, when I put them on.

After finishing our training in France my company didn't have much to do for the next few months. Our captain decided to use this time to get some marches done. We would be doing a few exercises right here on Corsica. These exercise focused more on building up our endurance, than they did on tactics. Corsica has some difficult terrain, and now that it was summer the heat would make it even more difficult.

The first exercise that we went on was the epitome of a Legion death march. We set off from the regiment at night and marched up towards Lumio (the closest village to Calvi). We passed Lumio and at the far end of the village took a path that went up into the mountains. It wasn't long before the path came out onto a Roman road that was paved with huge great stone slabs and had small walls either side of it. The paving stones were worn down in the middle by the centuries of people walking on them. I couldn't help thinking about the amount of work that must have gone into building something like this all those years ago, without the use of machinery. Shaping and then moving those huge slabs must have been backbreaking work. These ancient roads went all over the island, so it must have taken a century or more to complete. It was a truly amazing achievement.

At the top of the first hill was an abandoned fifteenth century village. The last inhabitant had left at the beginning of the twentieth century and the only inhabitants today were sheep. We stopped off there for a few minutes, but the howling wind soon forced us to move on. From the ruined village we marched up and around the mountains that are behind Calvi.

The farmers on Corsica just let their animals roam around freely, and every so often you would bump into a group of cows. Even worse was when you came across the rotting carcass of a cow that had lost its footing and fallen to its death. If the animals died up on the mountainside, just like the cars that had come off the road and fallen onto the rocks below, they were just left there to decay.

I encountered one incidence of this just after we had crossed over the ridge into the next valley. A couple of guys had stopped and were staring at a strange looking object, beside our path. As I approached they asked me to look at it and say what I thought it was. They couldn't tell if it was a cow, or a rock. I stared at it for a while, but it was hard to tell. We only had the moonlight for illumination, but it wasn't enough to make out what this object was. However, I could just about make out the shape of it and it looked too round to be an animal. Then one of the others kicked it, and his foot went straight through it; like kicking a giant Easter-egg. That kick answered the question for us, and it was indeed a cow; more precisely a calf that had died, swelled up like a balloon with decomposition gasses, had its insides eaten by insects, then dried out while retaining its bloated form. It was so strange, it was just the shell of a cow.

During the daytime on these marches, we would hide up somewhere and set up lookouts. It was pretty hard to get much sleep between look-out duty, due to the heat coupled with the sparse cover provided by the vegetation. When the night came, we would start marching again. We marched all night, non-stop.

On the third night of marching up and down the Corsican countryside people started hallucinating from tiredness. It was really spooky: you would be marching along, thinking that you were following the person in front, then they would vanish into thin air, leaving you completely lost. I can remember hallucinating and seeing groups of people stood around talking, a few metres to the side of where we were marching. I knew they were hallucinations because who would be out at three in the morning, talking with their friends on a cow trail, but it didn't stop me seeing them.

On our last night of marching, there was a heavy rainstorm. It hardly ever rains on Corsica, and not many people had taken waterproof clothing (myself included), so we all got soaked. As dawn broke on the final day of the march we didn't stop as usual, but kept on going. We had to get to our objective today, so there was no time to rest. We had marched all night, and now we would be marching all morning.

While marching along a bit of road leading up to the village we would be attacking, I actually began falling asleep while walking. I had read about this in books, but didn't think it was possible. How could you fall asleep while you were doing a physical activity, I thought, it just didn't seem right. What I discovered was that you can get so tired that you fall asleep mid-step, and fall flat on your face. Fortunately for me, the sensation of falling woke me up in time to catch myself, but others were not so lucky: we would be walking along and someone would just keel over, out of the blue, shake themselves off, then get back up again like nothing had happened. It was crazy stuff.

In spite of our state of near exhaustion, we did successfully reach our objective and root the enemy out. Then, after all the action was over, we retired to a nearby piece of scrubland and slept in the bushes while we waited for the trucks. At the end of that march, I had lost a good few inches from my waistline: I had actually lost so much weight that I needed a belt to keep my trousers up.

The next exercise was a bit easier, and more exciting too. There wasn't so much marching this time. We started the exercise by helicopter. The French Puma helicopters landed on the drop zone, and we got in and flew towards the interior of the island, then touched down in a field somewhere. From our drop off point we went straight up into the mountains. I did wonder why they hadn't just put us down in the mountains to begin with, but these exercises are supposed to be hard, I guess.

The enemy were of a different type this time. They weren't located in a village, instead they were a small roving band of guerrilla fighters that we had to chase around mountains. It was pretty difficult to corner them off when they had plenty of forest to hide in and a whole mountainside to escape into. Also, the people playing the enemy had been dropped off a few days before us and had plenty of time to set up their ambushes, and plan their escape routes.

The last couple of days of this exercise were hell for me. I had developed an abscess on one of my teeth; it was throbbing and sending jolts of pain up through the nerve. I was very jealous of the guy, who got to play the wounded soldier, and was evacuated by helicopter from the mountains. Watching the skill of the French pilots was amazing though, they evacuated this guy from a rocky outcrop that was barely large enough for the chopper to touch down on. The blades were centimetres away from the mountainside as he came down, and the spot was so uneven that the pilot had to keep in a half-hover: The helicopter was bouncing off the ground and it looked very touch and go, but hats off to the guy for his flying, because in spite of everything he pulled it off. That's the kind of pilot you want supporting you in somewhere like Afghanistan.

There was one small moment of pleasure for me on this exercise, amongst the constant pain from my tooth, when Cpl Bernard collapsed with exhaustion, just a few metres in front of me. I didn't bother offering my hand to pick him up and just walked past him. He stared up at me with a look of desperation in his eyes, but I looked away and kept on walking. He wasn't going to get any sympathy from me, especially after the way he had behaved in the regiment. He never showed any compassion when he hounded that Japanese legionnaire until he deserted, and I wasn't a Christian so I didn't have to turn any cheeks. If he didn't want to get up and finish the march, then he could lay there and get his eyes pecked out by the birds for all I cared.

It was often the way that those who shouted the most and acted tough were all mouth and no trousers; and there was nothing better to expose them than a good old Legion death march through the mountains. Anyway Cpl Bernard was lucky, because the exercise was almost over: All we had to do was get out of the mountains, and find an open area for the Helicopter to land and take us back to base.

When the company had no service, and no exercises planned, I was sent off to do a couple of ceremonies around Corsica. These were to commemorate important dates in military history. Even though your dress uniform had to be ironed to perfection, I didn't mind doing this type of thing. It was nice to get out of the regiment for a day. It was also nice to be out in public, and see women for a change: There were only three women at Camp Raffalli, they were a detachment from the French army (they wore red berets instead of green) and they were, to put it bluntly, cock-repellingly ugly. They were all senior NCOs, and they worked over at the parachute folding building, where they sewed up holes in the parachutes.

The ceremonies weren't difficult; it was just a lot of standing still and presenting arms. The only real downside was that the kepi hurt like crazy after a couple of hours; the edges of the visor dug into your temples and the pain would just build up. There was also the danger of getting heat stroke. At one ceremony in Bastia, we were commemorating something to do with World War One, and next to us was a group of French marines; half of them were women so this attracted our attention. Right in the middle of the ceremony they began dropping like flies; they just kept fainting. The first to go was a ginger bloke (typical gingers, can't handle the sun) then a couple of the women fell down. For us that was out of the question, if one of us had fainted, that person would get beasted like the damned, for bringing shame on the regiment.

Not long before we were scheduled to leave for Gabon, I was told that I would be going back to the 4RE, in Castelnaudary. I would be going to do my driving licence, known as 'stage VL' (light vehicle course). There were only a handful of people from the REP, who would be going at the same time as me. Going to Castelnaudary again would be like a holiday compared to life at Calvi, and I was looking forward to it. The Legion pays for all your travel, to and from courses, but they expect you to be in dress uniform at all times throughout the trip.

We were driven to the port at Bastia, and as soon as the bus was gone we all changed into civilian clothes. This wasn't just because the dress uniform was uncomfortable, but also because travelling in it was sure to make it dirty, and if any of the stains didn't come out you would have to buy a new uniform, which wasn't cheap. After getting on the boat, and sorting out the rooms, we went our separate ways. Most people went straight to the bar as usual; and, as usual, I went out onto the deck to watch Corsica drift off over the horizon.

The next morning we arrived at Marseille, and took the Metro to Gare de Saint Charles. I took the chance to grab a Big Mac meal while we were there. It had been a year since I had eaten any fast food (fast food restaurants are banned from the island of Corsica, because the people fear that it will cause too much litter, and spoil the natural beauty of the place). The train journey from Marseille to Castelnaudary was packed, and there were no free seats, so we had to sit on the floor in the space near the doors.

Before the train arrived at Castelnaudary, I changed back into my uniform. I got in a taxi outside the statin and went straight to the regiment, but the majority of people decided to make the most of their weekend and bought a ticket to Toulouse. When I got to the regiment, I had to go over to the buildings at the far right of the regiment. The rooms for the people doing the driving tests had as many bunk beds in them as was possible. There weren't many others there when I arrived, but that was normal. All courses in the Legion start on a Monday and you would be released by your regiment on Friday night. This means that you effectively have two days leave (the latest you can arrive for a course is midnight on Sunday, any later and you might get sent back to your regiment, and then sent to jail). I used the rest of my weekend to visit the regiment's internet café, and hit the gym.

On Monday morning we had to go to the big regimental service, then the course started and we went over to the test centre. There would be no sport during the two weeks that we were here: our one sole mission was to pass the driving test. The course was simple enough; we had a four hour session in the morning, and a four hour session in the evening. We would do practical for one of those sessions, and theory for the other. Then in the evening there was on last session of revision from 18:00 – 20:00. It was a long day.

I had already bought the two books that you needed to pass the theory, read them both twice, and highlighted the bits that I thought would be useful. This turned out to be a successful strategy. On the first practice test we did, I was only two questions short of reaching a passing grade (35/40 questions answered correctly). This was a great relief to me, I could now focus solely on the practical aspect of the test. I had never driven a car before. I had ridden motorcycles, but I wasn't that interested in cars. I knew that it would be a challenge for me, and to make it worse I was from a country that drove on the left side of the road.

The first few days we spent driving around the course inside the regiment. The car we had to drive was a relatively new Peugeot 206. I had trouble getting used to the clutch at first and kept stalling it, but after a few days it was not so bad. My driving instructor was a Madagascan corporal-chef, he was quite patient and generally a good instructor. However, some of the others weren't so lucky. There was a huge Polish corporal-chef, who looked like he ate a bowl of steroids for breakfast every morning. He would go insane at the smallest mistake, start beating the hell out of the dashboard, and shouting his head off. You could hear him shouting from inside his car as you drove past!

After a few days of driving inside the regiment we went outside. I had gotten used to the car by now, but I still stalled it every now and then. The theory test was whole different story, by now I was consistently getting near perfect scores, so I wasn't at all worried about that. However, many of the others in the classroom were struggling. It was due to their lack of French. Most of them only knew the vocabulary that we used in the Legion; they had no idea what any of the driving terminology meant. Also, a lot of the legionnaires, while fairly competent at speaking French, were very poor at reading it. They just couldn't read the multiple choice test. This lead to some funny moments with people just randomly guessing the answers, or pressing all the buttons in an attempt to gain the system.

After the last lesson of the day, we were free to do as we liked (well, as much as you can in the two hours before lights out). I would go straight over to the gym and get in ten kilometres on the rowing machine, then do a bit of weightlifting to finish off. I didn't like the fact that we had no sport scheduled for the entirety of this course. At the weekends we had to do regimental service. Fortunately, I didn't get guard duty while I was there. Instead, I was sent to work in the mess, which was fine by me.

The legionnaires from the other regiments would ask me about the parachute regiment. They mostly wanted to know if all the horror stories were true. I told them that most of the stories were exaggerated, and if they did happen that it was rare. But I told them that the workload at Calvi was truly insane, and that we seldom had a free evening or weekend; there was always some bullshit to do, so the regiment's nickname of 'Alcatraz' was warranted. They, in turn, told me how at their regiments most of the legionnaires had apartments in town and that hardly anyone slept at the regiment. They said that on Friday they would sometimes finish work at midday, and that many of them would go to Paris for the weekend. This sounded unreal to me: Even if I happened to have a day off, it was hard enough just going out to Calvi town, and when you did get out there was hardly anywhere to go. The Corsicans hated the legionnaires and we were banned from all their bars. There were only two bars that we could go to and there were no women in there, except for the two wrinkly, old, sea-hag prostitutes: Patricia and Lorena, and boy were they disgusting, I can't even describe how bad they were, but they still managed to get a lot of business. The descriptions that I heard of the other regiments seemed like a different world to that of the parachute regiment: They were allowed to have lives there.

The second week of the driving course we went on longer and longer journeys out of the regiment. We also started to drive through some built up areas with a fair bit of traffic. My driving instructor told me that I was doing well and had a good chance of passing the test on Thursday. He had looked at the theory test scores, and told me that there was no problem at all for me there, and if I didn't stall on the day of my test, he would pass me. I was glad to hear that, because I didn't want to have to stay an extra week here. I had my first holiday coming up soon, and would miss the start of it if I had to stay longer than two weeks.

Driving back to the regiment one time during the second week, I saw another white Peugeot 206 from our fleet parked up, next to the road. As I drew closer I could see that Cch Roid-rage, had ordered his students out of the car, and into the ditch at the side of the road. They were all down there in the ditch doing press-ups, as he stood on top of the bank shouting at them. I was so glad that I didn't have that guy for an instructor; stressing people out, who were learning to drive, was surely not the way to get the best results, but this is the Legion.

On the day of the test, I had to do my practical first. There were two of us going in the car together and each would drive for roughly two hours. The corporal-chef came over and asked who was willing to go first. When we both put our hands up he decided that whoever had the most service would start. The other person with me only had eight months of service, so I got to go first (I had over a year's service at that time), but when I told the corporal-chef this he stared at the place where my rank patch should be, and said in surprise, 'You have over a years' service and you're still a second class legionnaire! You must be a bananier?' I just laughed and shrugged my shoulders. 'Well alright,' he said, 'but no bananes today please.'

Two hours of driving around trying not to make a single mistake was a tiring exercise, but I got it done, and didn't stall the car once, so it was looking good for the first part of the test. In the evening I went in to do the theory test. Normally, when we were in the classroom we would do some revision, then do a couple of practice tests at the end. Today we would have six opportunities to take the theory test, and you just had to pass one of them. I was very pleased when I passed on the first attempt, but I wasn't allowed to leave, and still had to take the test another five times.

After three tests had been done we were let outside for a break. While I was standing around outside, I was approached by a Chinese guy named Wang. He was struggling with the test and spoke almost no French, but he did speak some English. He told me that this was the third time that he had been sent for his driving test, and that if he failed this time he would get a month in prison. He wanted me to tell him the answers to test. I agreed to help him and we worked out a plan: I would sit in front of him and use hand signals to tell him what the answer was (one finger for A, two for B, and so on).

When we went back inside, I sat in front of him as planned and waited for the test to start. I signalled every question to him, then at the end of the test, as always, the instructor read out the results. He started at the back and worked his way forwards. When he got to Wang his eyebrows disappeared round the back of his head, as he announced 'Wang 38/40…wait a minute…how the hell, did you do that?' Wang had consistently got shockingly low scores all week (in the range of 10/40), the instructor wasn't dumb and he knew something was afoot. He peered back at his computer screen for a couple of minutes, smiled, and said to Wang, 'You got the same two questions wrong as Murray, who is sitting in front of you. You sneaky bastards.' Wang began protesting his innocence, but the instructor told him save his breath, he wasn't going to do anything. He was impressed that we had managed to pull it off under his nose, because he prided himself on being able to spot any foul play.

After all the testing was over we headed outside to line up for dinner. Wang came up to me, thanked me for helping him, and stuck fifty euros in my hand.

Friday morning the results were announced. I had passed, which was great news as I now had the evening off and could return to Calvi. Those who failed either of the tests had to stay another week. It is worth noting that the angry Polish guy's students didn't pass, and Wang, unfortunately, had managed to fail his practical exam, and had to stay on for the extra week as well. I don't know if he ever did pass test, but I hope he was successful.

When I arrived back at Calvi, I was told to prepare for some jumping. We were going on holiday the coming Wednesday, but we had jumps scheduled for both Monday and Tuesday. I went over to the company building to see how many I had. I was shocked to see that I had two on Monday and three on Tuesday. Five jumps right before going on holiday! I had been in the Legion over a year now, without a break, and they wanted me to jump five times before I had my first holiday. There was a good chance that I would get injured, but there was nothing I could do. I would just have to jump and hope for the best. A more cynical person than I would think that they wanted a few of us to get injured so that they had people to stay behind and do the cleaning.

The Sunday evening before the plane arrived was pandemonium at the section. Orders were given then retracted and changed five minutes later. I remember Cpl Bernard entering my room in a crazed state, and upon seeing that I hadn't prepared my kit as the newest update commanded, ran up to me and punched me in the chest. I took his punch, raised my eyebrows at him, and stared with an unimpressed expression on my face (now I was the one playing mind games). He shouted that I had better get myself sorted or else, then stormed out. The stress was getting to him and he was starting to lose control; it was great.

The two days of jumping went alright for me. Though, I did manage to lose my helmet a couple of times. The Velcro on my chin strap had worn out, and when my parachute opened it would hit the back of my helmet and rip it off my head; sending it spinning to the ground below. This was bad for me, but worse for anyone who happened to be on the ground below. A metal helmet dropped from 300 metres would sting a bit if it caught you. I hit my head on a rock during one of the landings and had a large bump on my head, and my helmet also had some considerable dents in it. To stop my helmet falling off I had to jump out of the plane with one hand on my head holding it down.

After all five jumps were done. I finally got to go back to the section. We scrubbed our whole floor of the building until it was spotless, then I locked everything I wasn't taking with me away, and prepared for four weeks of vacation.

12: Gabon

The mountains, the forest, and the sea,
render men savage; they develop the fierce, but
yet do not destroy the human.
Victor Hugo

After returning from a much needed holiday, the company still had a fortnight before we left for Africa. This was be a very busy time: We had to put everything that we needed into crates, clean the whole company, pack our bags, empty the rooms, and lock everything away in the stores. Once all the equipment that we needed for Gabon had been packed away and put in a shipping container, it was sent on ahead of us. For the last few days at Calvi we lived out of a small bag with only our personal affairs inside.

To get to Gabon we would first have to go to Solenzara air base, which is on the other side of Corsica, below Bastia. For some reason we couldn't fly directly from here, instead we would have to fly to another airbase at Istres, in southern France. Then from Istres it was a non-stop flight to Libreville, Gabon.

We arrived at Solenzara air base mid-morning, we had a long wait for our plane to arrive with nothing to do except stand around and chat idly. The plane touched down just after midday and we walked across the runway and got on board. I was excited about this plane journey; it would be the first time that I would be in the plane when it landed. I had been in a plane thirty, or more, times by now, but had always jumped out.

It was nice being in a civilian plane for a change; that had proper seats and air conditioning. We took off from Solenzara and after only an hour we began descending towards Istres. I must admit that I was a little apprehensive, and was bracing myself for landing. However, I needn't have worried, the landing was much smoother than I had imagined. The plane taxied to the terminal and we all got off and went into a small waiting room. Our next flight wasn't until tomorrow. Tonight we would be staying in a nearby army base, so we had to wait for some trucks to come pick us up.

About half an hour after getting off the plane from Corsica, a member of the flight crew came and spoke with our captain, then an assembly was called. The cabin crew had counted the blankets and discovered that they were quite a few short. The captain demanded to know who had taken them, but there was total silence, and nobody raised their hand to admit guilt. The captain spoke again, 'I know that some of you have those blankets. We can do this the easy way, or the hard way. I will give you one more chance to own up, if you have taken a blanket from the plane then raise your hand now, and there won't be any repercussions. If you don't own up, or we don't get all of the missing blankets back, then I will order everyone to empty their bags out on the tarmac and I will conduct a full search with my officers. If it comes to that, then those found with any stolen items will pass report and go to jail as soon as we land in Gabon. Now, for the last time, whoever has taken those blankets from the plane come to the front and place them in a pile next to me.'

What happened next was truly astonishing. Around thirty people left the rows and went and placed a blanket next to the captain. It was far more than anyone expected, and it was quite funny to watch people come and dump their stolen booty in a pile next to the captain (especially the guy who had taken two blankets). I must admit that I was tempted to take a blanket. I had never been on a commercial airplane and was unaware that they counted them after each flight, but I decided against it at the last moment: It was not worth the risk of getting caught in my estimation.

After all the blankets had been recovered, our transport arrived to take us to the base we would be spending the night in, which was just a couple of miles down the road, in a place called Miramas. The base itself was huge (there was even a train station in it that was maybe ten tracks wide). However, most of the base was empty carparks that stretched off into the distance.

We would be spending the night in cheaply built, plastic, pop-up buildings. To everyone's surprise the captain allowed us to go out on the town that night. The only condition was that we were back before midnight. I wasn't going to miss an opportunity like that, so I went out with a couple of friends to grab something to eat and maybe buy some supplies for the long flight to Gabon. However, I needn't have bothered, because nearly all the shops were closed, and the only places open were bars and restaurants.

The next day we went back to the airport at Istres. Before the flight, everyone was given a temporary French passport, and a Gabonese residence permit. It was cool having a French passport with all your fake Legion details on it; it was like something out of James Bond. After we had our passports we could go board the Airbus A310 that would take us to Africa.

The journey took around seven hours in total, and there wasn't much to look at out of the window as we took a route straight over the Sahara dessert. As we neared Gabon the sky began to fill with clouds. When we hit the tarmac in Libreville it was raining pretty hard. On exiting the plane, the heat and the humidity hit you like a brick. The air felt heavy with condensation, which made breathing feel weird, it was like you weren't getting enough oxygen into your lungs.

As soon as everyone was off the plane, our passports were collected in again, then a small buss arrived to ferry us to Camp De Gaulle (our new home for the next four months). It was a fairly decent place that had everything you might need inside of it: It was like a little village inside an army base; there was a restaurant, mini-supermarket, barbers, and a small market area where locals could sell their wares. The rooms we would be staying in were slightly better than those at Calvi; they had a balcony at the back, a fridge, and they were also air-conditioned. The beds had iron poles at each corner and a mosquito net that fitted over top. I was on the top floor of our building, which had a good view of the surrounding area. I was very excited to be in Africa and wanted very much to go out and have a look around. I had been a very fond of nature programs when I was a small boy, and was desperate to see some of the local wildlife, but that would have to wait.

The day after arriving, we were taken for a tour of the camp and shown all the facilities, then we had to go for a lesson on how to conduct ourselves while in Gabon. The lesson could be summed up as follows: If you have sex with the prostitutes in town, wear a condom; don't buy any ivory or animal skin products; and agree a price with taxi drivers before getting into the vehicle.

Our first couple of weeks in Gabon were pretty uneventful. The first week we spent waiting for our guns, and other equipment, to arrive. We mostly took lessons on how to live in the jungles of equatorial Africa. There was a reptile house in the regiment that had most of the dangerous snakes, and insects that you were likely to come across while in Gabon. When my section visited, it was feeding time, and we got to witness the big python eating a live chicken. They also had the beautiful Gaboon viper that has two little horns on its nostrils, and a camouflage pattern that looks like dried leaves. It is an amazing creature; a contender for the largest venomous snake with some growing up to two metres in length. They also have the largest fangs (2in), and venom sacks, of any poisonous snake. However, its bite is not usually fatal to full-grown humans, but the symptoms include such things as: rapid swelling, intense pain, uncontrollable defecation and urination, and such extensive tissue necrosis that you may need your leg amputated, which I think you'll agree is no picnic, and to be avoided at all costs.

Apart from the insects and reptiles there were other animals that we had to be careful of: gorillas, chimpanzees, mandrills, leopards, and forest elephants. It was chimpanzees that I was most scared of; those motherfuckers are smart enough to know what you value and go straight for that; hence they normally attack your genitals, fingers, and face. I don't care how endangered chimps are, if one came to bite my balls off, I would bust many caps in its ass, especially if it was a bonobo, because we all know about them; the kinky devils.

In the mornings we did some light sport. When we jogged into the outskirts of town, I was surprised to see the level of poverty that existed here. There were many houses that consisted of nothing more than some rusty corrugated tin and wooden posts. Many of the roads were unpaved, and the ones that did have tarmac often had huge pot holes in them. There was one hole in the footpath that was a couple of metres deep!

Sometimes we would go past the airport on our runs. It was shocking to see their lack of security; the fence at the back was completely destroyed and was just lying in grass. You could walk straight into the airport, and onto the runway. Doing sport in eighty percent humidity was difficult at first. The sweat didn't evaporate off your body, so you couldn't cool down. Occasionally, we would go down to the beach for a bit of swimming. The beach at Libreville is very nice indeed; white-ish sand and palm trees.

We had no washing machines in our building, there was a laundrette in the regiment, but the officers and NCOs usually got their first. This meant that it would take too long for us to get our clothes back, so every morning, after sport, and every evening, the legionnaires would wash their clothes in the sinks. If nothing else, it was a great workout for your forearms. Another inconvenient thing about being in Gabon, was that we couldn't drink the tap water. The French army had supplied us with bottled water, but only for when we were in the field. While we were on base we had to buy it from the minimart, and it was so expensive there that the owners should have been thrown in jail for extortion. To make matters worse, the corporals, not wanting to go down three flights of stairs, walk three hundred metres to the shop, then return back with fifteen litres of water; would send legionnaires to the shop for them. This was a piss take, they did this at Calvi, but now, instead of a can of coke, you were ordered to go buy two packs of water and lug them up to the top floor, without so much as a thank you.

The rain here in Gabon was nothing like European rain. In the UK it can rain for three days non-stop, but the rain drops are small and it takes you a while to get really wet. Here, by contrast, it would bucket down for thirty minutes at a time, and if you were caught outside you had to make a quick dash for the nearest shelter before you got soaked through. I had anticipated that there might be a lot of rain in the rainforest, and brought myself a camouflage umbrella. However, the first time that I used it, I was spotted by Sgt Cabrão. He called me into his office and gave me a right bollocking. He told me what a pussy I was for having an umbrella, that it was unbecoming of a legionnaire paratrooper, and banned me from using it again. To this day I think that he was just resentful that he had to get wet and I didn't, what a wanker.

During the first few weeks, we also did a lot of training on how to enter and exit helicopters. We didn't actually have any helicopters to practice with so we used a gazebo with two rows of chairs in it. It looked kind of silly, but it was good enough to practice our drills. There was, of course, the dreaded regimental service to do. This, however, was nowhere near as bad as in Calvi. Here in Gabon the regiment employed civilians to work in the kitchens. All we had to do was guard duty, and this could be done in regular combat fatigues. We did, however, have three different types of guard to do: the regiment, the military airbase, and the prisoners (military prison). There was also a convoy escort duty, which was really fun: You sat in a pickup, drove to the airport, collected whatever it was that needed escorting, and then delivered it to its destination.

Two weeks after we had arrived, the fourth company joined us. This was good news, as it meant that they could now take over regimental service and we could head out into the terrain. The first thing we did was get ready to do some parachute jumps. We would be jumping at a place called Point Denis, which is on a peninsula that lies between the Gabon Estuary and the Atlantic Ocean. It is Gabon's top seaside resort, it has large white sand beaches and is a breeding location for leatherback turtles. It is also a good place to see humpback whales. There are no roads leading to Point Denis, the only way to reach it is by boat, or, if you are in the Legion, by parachute.

We went over to Libreville airbase, which is next to the civilian airport, and got our parachutes on. For these first jumps we would be jumping with a local parachute regiment. The plane was half filled with Gabonese paratroopers, and half filled with legionnaires. It was very hot inside the plane, and thankfully the jumpmasters opened the doors as soon as we had taken off. It was only a short, ten minute, journey to Point Denis. The Gabonese troops would be jumping first. I don't know if it was their first time jumping, or if their superiors didn't bother to train them, but they seemed to have no idea what was going on. Some of them had the static line cord wrapped around their necks (which is a sure-fire way to decapitate yourself), others hooked on the wrong way, or put their fingers in static line clip (a good way to lose your finger).

When they began jumping it was hilarious; one guy covered his eyes with his hands and ran out the door like that, another sat down in the doorway and scooted out. The best part was when the light turned red, to signal the end of the drop zone, and they kept jumping. The jump master tried to stop them but they were determined to go. They jumped out over houses! God only knows what kind of grief they came to at the bottom.

The plane circled around again, and this time it was our turn to jump. The drop zone was a huge stretch of beach with a bit of grass here and there. Landing on the sand was like a mattress compared with Calvi. After the jump, we had to wait on the beach while the plane went back to the airport for the rest of our company.

For the journey back we had to take a barge, and it was a rusty old piece of shit that was coughing out clouds of thick black smoke as its engine spluttered along. We had to wade out a bit to climb aboard. It would be a two hour journey back, and there was no shelter from the sun. It was not an enjoyable journey at all, and the mixture of being baked in the sun and breathing in exhaust fumes gave everyone a headache after a while.

Once we arrived back at Libreville there was no time to hang around. We had to get back to the regiment, iron a set of combat fatigues, and head over to the Gabonese paratrooper's base. We would be doing a ceremony where we exchanged parachute brevets, then there would be a party afterwards.

At the Gabonese base, there were tents set up all around their parade ground. First the Gabonese guys lined up, and our Officers and NCOs pinned French brevets on them. After that we reversed the roles and did the same thing. Once all the pomp was finished with we settled into the beer and food. After having a couple of beers, some of the Gabonese soldiers broke out into song and dance. It was quite a thing to behold. It started off as a small group; that group then danced over to another bunch of people, who weren't dancing, and sang at them until they joined in; then, finally, once they had gathered up all their soldiers into this dancing band; they danced over to their colonel and sang at him. He didn't want to participate, and kept on protesting, but they sung louder and louder, until he agreed to join in. Then they went around the regiment dancing and singing. It was great to see.

Our first experience of the rainforest would be a two week long stay near the equator. The main purpose of this trip was weapons training. As you can imagine, for two weeks in the jungle you need a lot of stuff. I went out to town and brought my own food supplies (mostly corned beef, and tinned fish) and a load of water purification tablets.

My bag was already full just with my personal stuff and the ammo for the Minimi, when, the night before we set out, I was given a load more stuff to carry. I had to find space for a load more bullets, plus a couple of mortar shells and 40mm grenades. As usual, the NCOs didn't carry any of this stuff. My rucksack was now so big that it was a job to fit it in the harness for parachuting. It was heavy as well (I would guess somewhere around forty

251

kilos). It was insane how much stuff we had to carry, but we had to do what was ordered of us.

The day of the depart we got dropped off at the airport and put our parachutes on. The weight of the parachutes, combined with our bags and weapons, must have weighed nearly as much as we did. You could only stand up for a little while. People would take a few steps, rest, then take a few more steps. Getting to the plane was like doing the farmers walk. Some people almost had tears in their eyes from the strain of the weight pulling down on, and compressing, their back and shoulders. On the plane it wasn't much better, the pilot decided to do some nap of the earth flying, and boy did he go for it. We were pulling some serious Gs on the turns; one moment you would be stuck to your chair, then you would be up in the air. I was close to the door, and could see out the window. We were flying along a river, and sometimes the pilot would go so low that we were just above the trees! It wasn't long before the sick-bags were out.

After an hour of flying, the plane levelled out and we were given the signal to get up and prepare to jump. The doors opened, but all I could see below was jungle. Then I caught sight of it; a patch of grass in the middle of all the trees. It was about the size of two football pitches. We flew over it, then circled back round, and prepared to jump. However, jumping was hardly an apt description. With all that weight the best I could manage, was to hobble out of the door. It felt great to be in the air, because now the parachute was taking all the weight and I could just hang there and let my spine recover. It wasn't much of a break though, the ground was approaching rapidly. As I got closer, I started to see these brown dots all over the place. When I got even closer I could see that they were, what looked like, huge toadstools made of mud, but I soon got a much closer look.

After the briefest descent that I have ever experienced, I hit the ground hard. I rolled into one of the mud mushrooms, and broke it. Once I had folded away my parachute, and heaved all my equipment onto my back. I took another look at that strange mud structure that I had just smashed into, and I finally realized that it was a termite mound. The termites were not too pleased that I had just wrecked their home, so I got out of there and started off for the rendezvous point.

The going was a little tricky, because the area we had jump onto was quite boggy, but if you kept to the high patches of ground it was alright. I had been lucky to land on a dry bit of ground, and was one of the first people to arrive at the meeting point. When I looked back I could see people struggling to make it across the bog. Now and then, someone would disappear up to their waist in it. I dropped my stuff and went back out to help guide people to the RV. One guy was walking towards me when his leg sank in the bog, and he collapsed on the ground. He didn't even try to stand up, and he looked like he just wanted to give up and lay there.

There were a couple of injuries from the jump, but that was to be expected given the weight of the equipment, and the unevenness of the ground. It took a while for everyone to wander in, but an hour later we were still one person short. After a short search, the missing man was located at the far end of the drop zone. He was up to his neck in the bog and being attacked by angry ants. A helicopter was called in to get the wounded back to Libreville, and once we had put our parachutes on the truck, we set off for our campsite.

It was a short march, maybe five kilometres, to the place we would be staying (a piece of jungle halfway between the drop zone and the sea). We set to work clearing an area of forest, digging a fire hole and latrine, and setting up our hammocks. I positioned myself at the edge of our camp (deepest into jungle). Another English guy in my section had a nice surprise when he opened his rucksack. All the tins of sardines that he had brought had burst from the impact of landing, and had covered all his clothes in smelly fish oil. I found this very amusing, and it got even better; just after we had set up our camp, he hung his fishy clothes out to dry and it started to rain. Now, not only did his clothes smell like a fishmonger's shop, but they were soaking wet to boot.

Every day, we would march back up to the drop zone and practice our shooting (we also practiced the usual fire and movement drills as well). Before I had experienced the jungle, it was the big scary animals that I was worried about. However, after a few days of living in it, I realized that it's the small things that seem to have it in for you the most. You couldn't stop for five minutes without being attacked by ants. They would climb up your legs, get inside your clothes, and start biting you. It was a strange, sight to see people dancing around in pain, hitting at their own bodies, for no apparent reason. At night it was the turn of the mosquitos to attack. If you had a plastic hammock the mosquitos would sometimes be able to bite you through the plastic. Some people woke up with over a hundred bites on their backs. Prickly heat was also a big problem; it drove those afflicted with it crazy with itching. My biggest problem was that the heat had turned my corned beef from a solid into a liquid.

On the weekend we went to the coast to see if we could find any fishermen. We came across a couple of guys who had just got back from a fishing trip, and bought a huge barracuda from them. On the way back, I and a few others found a mango tree and went to collect the fruit. I ended up getting burnt on my face by the acid that squirts out from the stem when you pick the fruit. In the evening we cooked up the barracuda and all sat round the campfire. The truck that had come on the barge to collect the parachutes had brought a few cases of Kronenbourg with it for each section, so we got to have a beer while in the jungle. As we sat around the campfire the NCOs told stories from their time in the Legion, and, of course, there was the usual bit of singing to be done, but not too much.

However, the good times were interrupted, by Sgt Cabrão. Earlier that day I had taken a beast of a shit in the forest. I didn't like using the latrine, so I just walked into the jungle a bit and had a dump where I thought no one would find it, but, during the meal, Sgt Cabrão had wandered off and come across my handiwork. He came back in a rage, and demanded to know who had committed such a dastardly act. I didn't own up, so to shame the person who had done it, he began to rant; saying that whoever had done it had to be a homosexual because it was so big that it must have come from someone with a loose arse. I couldn't help myself, and burst out laughing. I was dying with laughter hearing him go on and on, describing it. Sgt Cabrão noticed me laughing, but he didn't get suspicious.

Sunday morning I woke to a tremendous racket coming from the direction of the latrine. I rushed over to see what was going on and found a very angry forest elephant. It had destroyed the latrine and was busy ripping off tree branches and thrashing them around with its trunk. It tried to charge me a few times, but the forest was too thick. I went back to my bivouac, got my camera, and returned to take some photos. The elephant did not like that at all and made a lot of noise. Meeting a wild elephant that wishes to crush you, makes you realize just how powerful they are, and how powerless you are to stop them. Luckily, humans have bigger brains than our pachyderm cousins, and I used mine to stay behind some trees that it couldn't get through.

After two weeks in the jungle, and being constantly tormented by insects, everybody was looking forwards to going back to base. For the return trip we would be using the barge again. There were tracks through the jungle, but that would take too long, and they often got blocked by fallen trees. Going by helicopter was also out of the question, because it was too expensive. So we all marched down to the beach and waited for that floating rust bucket to arrive.

It was a hot day, without a cloud in the sky, the day we had to go back. The return journey was estimated to take around eight hours. If the last trip on the barge was anything to go by, this time would be pure hell. Eventually, the barge arrived and we waded through the sea and climbed aboard. No one had thought to erect any kind of shelter and we would have to sit in the baking sun for the entire journey. The best you could do was cover your skin to stop it getting burnt, but the heat was intense and it wasn't long before I had a major headache. I was surprised that no one passed out with heat stroke. Eight hours of painfully slow going under the hot sun of equatorial Africa later, we docked in Libreville. I was glad to get off that floating oven and into the shaded back of an army truck. Oh, how I never wanted to see that barge again.

Every time we came back to base, after being in the field for an extended period, no one was allowed to shower or attend to their personal belongings, before the guns and equipment had been cleaned and stored back in their proper places. This only applied to legionnaires, and corporals; sergeants and above would seldom clean their own weapons. They would instead head straight to the laundrette, then shower, and relax. You would see the officers and senior NCOs heading out to town while you were still scrubbing the guns in your stinking clothes that you had had on for two weeks. You quickly realize that being in the Foreign Legion is only difficult as long as you are a legionnaire. Once you make it to sergeant, you don't really have to do anything, because you can order the legionnaires to do whatever you want (just being a corporal reduces your workload by ninety percent). Of course, this all depends on whether or not, you are OK with being a piss-taking so and so, who doesn't mind abusing his authority.

For the next couple of weeks we had to take up regimental service while the fourth company went shooting. I went out on town the first weekend back. I had fantasized about what I was going to eat after being stuck in the jungle and drinking liquid corned beef. There was a seafood restaurant in Libreville that I liked very much, and they gave you huge portions of food. I was particularly fond of their gambas (prawns), which were a good 5-7 inches long; they were like small lobsters. I also managed to procure a nice bag of weed while out. The weed wasn't strong, but it did the job. Drugs were quite easy to get in Gabon, you just had to ask the taxi drivers. Cocaine was the most readily available, but I wasn't interested in that.

In between all the service we did a few more jumps. We would jump over small aerodromes and practise assaulting the control tower and securing the runway, then the plane would land and we got back in and flew back. Our next trip out into the rainforest was going be a long one. We would be doing, the infamous, commando training. The commando training boils down to: a lot of training; and very little food, or sleep. When the other company returned to base we set off. This time we would be going in trucks to our destination, somewhere deep in the jungle.

It didn't take long, after leaving Libreville, for the roads to get pretty damn awful. The journey wasn't that long, but the state of the roads made any progress difficult. How people got around in normal cars was beyond me. After the terrible mud roads we came to the bank of a wide river. There was no bridge spanning it, instead there was a barge that ferried you across. Eventually, after some more terrible roads and a couple more river crossings, we arrived at our new home for the next few weeks.

Our camp this time was much better than the last place we stayed at; each section had their own clearing with a long wood frame hut in it. There was also a large, sheltered seating area to eat in, and a couple of fire places with huge logs around them. The only thing missing was a place to wash, but in the rainforest you can just wait for it to rain then go out with your bar of soap and have a shower. A note of caution to anyone who finds themselves in the rainforest: Avoid washing in streams and rivers, because they are the favourite hiding places of large snakes. Not long before we arrived, an aid worker had gone down to a stream, by himself, and disappeared. Only to be found, a couple of days later, inside a huge python. If you do have to visit a body of water in a region with large snakes, I would recommend going in pairs. If that isn't possible, tie a knife to your wrist with a bit of string, so that you don't drop it if you get attacked, and cut the motherfucker in half.

For the first half of the commando course (I am not being pretentious, it really is called that) we learned a range of techniques for living and fighting in the jungle. We learned about: what you can and can't eat; which plants have medicinal properties; how to navigate; etc. We also spent a fair bit of time learning how to make booby-traps (most of these were from the Indochina/Vietnam war era). There were some pretty nasty booby traps. All the booby-traps with spikes on were covered in faeces to infect the hapless person who triggered it. After the booby-traps, we learned about tracking and searching. Lastly we learned a few ambush, and fire and movement, techniques that were particularly effective in the rainforest. Then we had a few guys from 1RPIMA (French SAS) come and instructed us, but they didn't really teach us that much. I got the feeling that they didn't want to be there, and one of them seemed a little unhinged; he kept lecturing us about Afghanistan, and how he had lost three quarters of the two hundred Afghan soldiers that he was mentoring. He just kept going on long winded rants that led nowhere. In-between all the lessons we did a fair bit of sport, and there were also plenty of hand to hand combat sessions thrown in for good measure.

The second half of the course we spent putting into practise what we had learned. We also began practising for the big obstacle course. To get your commando badge you must complete the obstacle course without failing more than three obstacles, and complete a three day exercise. The obstacle course was very long, and the fastest time recorded was just under two hours. Apparently, the US marines had refused outright to do it, saying that it was too dangerous, but I don't think that ever happened and was probably just French propaganda.

Before we tackled the obstacle course we had to do a bit of shooting. There was a course set up in the jungle, where you would walk along a river and have targets pop-up in front of you. It was fairly easy to tell where the targets were hidden as all the foliage in their vicinity had been clipped back by bullets. The only thing that made it difficult was having to use a FAMAS. The one I was using kept blowing the magazine out of its housing after every couple of shots, forcing me to reload all time. The beach, near to where we did our shooting, was an interesting place. There were enormous logs strewn all over the shore. I would guess that they came from a wrecked ship.

After the shooting was done the next thing on the agenda was the obstacle course. We would be competing in groups of ten. Each group set off at intervals of around twenty minutes. My group had received a couple of guys from one of the support companies (I don't think that they did any other parts of commando course, they just turned up at the end). For the obstacle course we each had to carry a small backpack filled with sand, and an assault rifle. There was also an ammunition case filled with concrete that we had to lug around with us, but this was carried by four people at a time.

The course started off in the jungle with some fairly standard obstacles. I knew that we weren't going to get a good time when one of the guys who had been added to our group at the last minute (a guy who worked in the armoury) couldn't lift himself onto a one and half meter high beam; he was a real life Gomer Pyle. Fortunately, you are only allowed three attempts at an obstacle, before you are failed, so we didn't have to wait too long.

After maybe ten obstacles we came to a river area. You had to cross this river three times: first by setting up a tyrolean traverse; then by crossing a wobbly plank and rope bridge, high up in the trees; and lastly by crossing a bridge made from floating plastic barrels. The first two weren't that difficult, but the floating barrel bridge was an absolute bastard. It was so easy to fall off. Naturally, Gomer Pyle managed to fall from all three. Watching him try to hang onto the rope for the tyrolean crossing was very amusing: It was like a cartoon. Each of his fingers slipped off, one by one, then he splashed into the muddy water below. He must have been feeling pretty demoralized by now, because he had failed to complete half of the obstacles, and had, therefore, failed the course. However, there was no backing out; he had started, so he had to finish.

Once we had done the three crossings, we went to a wide stretch of the river for the next obstacle. There was another crossing, this time it was a series of ropes, with little metal triangles at the end, which you had to swing across to get to a set of monkey bars. The monkey bars started off close together and got further apart, then the last three were like a set of steps. You had to do a pull up, then let go and try to grab the next one up, before you fell. It was a fairly difficult obstacle, and the last part required some decent arm strength. If you didn't do it on the first try, then you were done for.

Sgt Tudor (my group leader) got his foot caught in the metal at the end of one of the ropes on that obstacle, and when he went to reach for the monkey bars, was pulled back and fell. He was left dangling upside down with his head under the water. Unable to reach the bottom and push himself out, all he could do was hang there and flail about like a fish on a hook. Lucky there are always a couple of instructors nearby, ready to act if anything like this happens and they quickly got his foot free, but he could have quite easily drowned.

Once everyone had crossed the river for the last time, we started on the most difficult part of the course; the mangroves. In this part we had to travel through a thin channel that had been hacked out between the mangrove roots. The water usually came up to your waist, but sometimes it got so deep that you had to swim. Under the water there were roots all over the place and it was easy to trip over; the silt was also very deep and this made walking even more difficult. To top all this off, the water was a thick brown soup that smelt like eggy farts (this is because the silt has no oxygen in it and this causes the build-up of hydrogen sulphide from all the decomposing mangrove fruit, and leaves). It was so bad that I saw people fall over, get a mouthful of the water, and instantly begin vomiting.

The obstacles in the mangroves usually involved climbing up something, traversing a gap, then jumping off into the water. The most difficult obstacle of the course was in this part. On first glance it didn't look too bad; there was a river running perpendicular to the course, and on each side there was a metal pole sticking out horizontally from the mangroves. The poles overlapped slightly in the middle, and the idea was that you walk along one pole then jump to the next. This sounds simple enough, but the poles were maybe two metres apart and very slippery. The only way of hanging on was to dive at the second pole so that you hit it with your armpits, then you had to bring your arms down and grab onto your clothes. Trying to grab the pole itself won't work because it was too slippery. My first attempt at this obstacle failed miserably. I didn't want to do it the way that the instructor told us to, because it looked painful, so I tried to hang onto the pole, but it was impossible, and before I knew it I was in the water. For the second attempt I tried it the instructors way, but I didn't jump far enough and was unable bring my arms over the pole. So far I had passed all the obstacles and I was aiming for a perfect score. I had to get it on this third attempt, because there would be no fourth. I climbed onto the first pole one last time and made my way down to the end, determined to be successful. I eyed the distance to the next beam and threw myself at it with all my might. As soon as I felt it contact my body, I brought my arms down, and grabbed the first thing they came into contact with. After a couple of seconds, I realized that I hadn't fallen into the water. I was ecstatic that I had made it. All I had to do now was get my legs wrapped around it and make my way to the end. That obstacle was really tricky and around half of those who tried failed to pass it.

The course gradually got easier after that, and the water got shallower. The last part of the course was just moving through a dry forest of mangroves. Eventually we came out onto a beach and the obstacle course was over. It had taken us a little over two hours to do, which wasn't too bad. I was happy that I had achieved my goal and completed every obstacle (Gomer Pyle was happy to be alive).

The last part of the commando course was a short exercise in the jungle. This was more a test for the officers, than for the rank and file. There were a few rules for working in the jungle, the two big ones were: don't move at night; and always stay within sight of each other. It is incredibly easy to get lost, or separated, in the rainforest. The vegetation is so dense that you can only see for a few metres. Unfortunately, my new lieutenant decided to break these rules on the first day.

We started the mission off in style: A couple of Puma helicopters arrived to take us to our starting point. I had my Minimi machine gun back now, and this meant that I got to sit in the doorway. The view from the helicopter was amazing; everywhere you looked there was jungle as far as the eye could see. The journey didn't last long though, and within fifteen minutes the pilot had found a clearing, and landed. Once the helicopter was gone we started out on our march. I was surprised to see that there were people living out here; they must have been the people who had cut down the trees and made the clearing that we had landed in.

The march started off in the jungle, but after a while we came out onto a logging trail. At first all seemed well, but at some point along the journey the lieutenant realized that he wasn't where he thought he was. He stopped us, while he studied the map a bit, then we started off again. We repeated that exercise of stopping and starting many times trying to find our location on the map, but to no avail. We were still wandering around in the jungle, trying to find the right path, when it began to get dark. Instead of stopping and making camp for the night, the lieutenant decided to plough on. At one point while we were walking along there was a tremendous crash, just off to one side. Going over to inspect we saw that an enormous rotten tree had collapsed. One thing you will be sure to notice if you stay in the rainforest for any length of time, is the sheer amount of falling rotten branches and trees that there are. Every few minutes you can hear something crashing down onto the jungle floor.

Not long after the falling tree, we were walking along when a voice called out to us. We had stumbled upon one of the other sections. Their lieutenant came over and explained where we were, and where we should be heading. That was good, I thought, at least now we know where we are, we should be able to get to our bivouac site fairly quickly.

Not long after meeting the other section, we went off the path and into the jungle. In my section there was a Belarussian corporal, who was the biggest skinflint you could ever meet: He never bought anything. He only ever used the equipment that was given to him by the army, always ate at the mess hall (or rations if we were in the field), and stayed at the Legion's (€5 a day) hotel in Marseille for his holidays. He also stunk of B.O because he only used the army issue soap, and didn't buy deodorant. The last time we had been out in Gabon this cheapskate had constantly borrowed everything from me and the other legionnaires, and he didn't even respect the things that you lent him: He used up all the gas in my camping stove, drained the batteries in my headlamp, and ruined the file on my Leatherman. This time, just to fuck with him, I too brought noting, except the bare essentials, with me.

Now that we were making our way through thick vegetation, constantly tripping over roots, and getting caught by branches. This fucking pinchpenny, who of course didn't have a lamp, asked me if I could get out mine and walk behind him to light up the ground in front of his feet. When I informed him that I did not have it with me he got quite irate, and told me that everyone was required to have a lamp, as it was on the equipment list, and demanded to know why I didn't have mine with me. I simply threw the question back at him and asked where his lamp was, which elicited the expected response of him telling me to watch my mouth, because he outranked me. It was true that he outranked me, but as arguments go that was a pretty poor one. To be honest I was enjoying watching him get flustered. It had been worth going without a few things, and eating cold meals, for the last few weeks, just to see his parasitic game plan fall apart. He was a real Scrooge McDuck.

After hacking our way through the jungle, and getting bit to death by bugs, we stumbled on one of the other sections again, and once again our lieutenant asked for directions to our encampment. The other lieutenant advised that it would probably be better just to camp next to him tonight as it was already late and moving in the jungle at night was not advisable, but my platoon leader was determined to get to the designated spot, and we set off again.

It was nearly midnight when we finally got to our campsite. I managed to get the second guard slot so there was not much point in me going to sleep; I would only have to wake up again, in less than an hours' time. Once I had done my guard, I went over to the next person's hammock and woke him for guard. Five minutes passed, and there was no sign of my replacement, so I went over to see what was going on and found him fast asleep, so again I woke him up, and told him that he had to get up and do his guard. I waited another few minutes, and it was clear that he had fallen asleep again. This time I went over and handed him the guard list, I told him that I wasn't going to keep waking him up; I had already finished my guard, and was going to sleep. Now it was totally up to him, he could get himself out his hammock, or go back to sleep and face the consequences in the morning, but I wasn't wasting anymore time. He told that it was fine and I could go to sleep, and assured me that he would get up and do his guard.

The next morning, I was awoken by one of the corporals. It was nearly 8:00am and we were supposed to be up at six. The corporal was demanding to know what had happened to the guard last night. As soon as he told me that, I knew exactly what had happened, but I didn't squeal, I just told him that I had finished my guard and passed it onto the next guy, so it must have been somewhere after me that the chain had been broken. Sure enough, when the corporal went over to the person who was after me, he told him that he had fallen asleep while on duty. I'm sure the guys who were on guard after him where happy, at least they had had a descent night's, uninterrupted, sleep. Me too, I had got to sleep in an extra couple of hours. In the end it didn't matter that we had slept in, because we didn't move out until midday anyway.

Today we were going to find a jungle camp with some fake enemies in it. We didn't have to march far, instead we spent most of the day setting up the trap that we would spring, first thing the next morning. My section used a river to get as close to the camp as we could. We had to go slowly as the place was riddled with booby traps, which had to be located and disassembled without setting them off. Once we had got as close as we could, we set up firing positions. The place where I was, really stank for some reason, but no one could find out what was causing it.

At dawn the next day we sprang our trap and attacked the enemy camp. My section didn't take part in the offensive, our job was to cut off possible escape routes. The attack went well, and the instructors were satisfied with it. As the sun rose and lit up the forest, I finally found out what was making that horrible smell. There was a huge cane rat that had been caught in a snare, it had been dangling there, right next to us all night, just stinking and rotting away. It had been impossible to see it last night, the forest canopy blocks out so much light that it gets as dark as a cave on the forest floor.

After the attack, our next task was to exfiltrate to the beach and get on another barge. However, to make it more difficult the instructors designated one injured person per section, who would have to be stretchered there (and they didn't pick the smallest people). It was four or five kilometres to where we would catch the barge, and that is a long way to be stretchering someone. We had to move as fast as we could (if someone was really injured you don't want to hang around), even so, It took us nearly an hour to reach the beach with the stretchers. When we did arrive everyone was exhausted. However, the barge was nowhere to be seen, so we set up a secure perimeter and waited. There were a few local Africans going about their business who looked a little surprised to see the place fill up with foreign soldiers. Pretty soon after that our barge arrived to take us back to the camp.

After spending the best part of a month in the jungle. The first thing that most people did on returning was to head out into town for some drinks. I also went out, but in my case it was to get hold of some more weed. Having a joint on guard duty made the time pass so much faster and it eliminated a lot of the boredom. However, this was not to last. Not long after getting back to camp, someone was caught smoking a joint outside the guard house. The dog handler had been walking past, when his dog started barking at someone sitting on the bench behind the guard hut. He then smelt the cannabis and apprehended the guy. As soon as I found out about this, I flushed all my weed down the toilet, and not long after that, all the rooms were searched with dogs. I was sure that I would be called into the captain's office, because Sgt Cabrão, had caught me and a French guy rolling a doobie on our first trip to the jungle, but the French guy was a fast talker, and spun him a yarn about it being a cigarette that had got wet and broke, but I think he knew what it was. However, in spite of that, I never was summoned in front of the captain, nor was anyone else, instead the whole company got a bollocking the next morning at assembly.

Shortly after the reefer debacle, my company was due to take part in a regimental exercise. An amphibious assault ship, called the FS Foudre, was arriving from France, and we would be heading off in helicopters (somewhere into the surrounding jungle) to complete a four or five day mission involving the ship. We would be working alongside the French marines, and French special forces.

The day before the depart we had everything ready, all the guns were out, the ammunition had been distributed, and we were packed and ready to go early the next morning. However, when we awoke the next day there wasn't any movement. There was no sign of the officers, or senior NCOs. Then at around seven an assembly was called. What was said at the assembly was truly shocking: The exercise had been cancelled, because the previous night a helicopter, with a group of French special forces soldiers on board had crashed into the ocean, killing all but one. The lone survivor had been saved because he was thrown from the helicopter into to sea when it began spinning out of control. The ship (SF Foudre) was now at the crash site conducting a search.

Now there was a new mission, we needed to send a couple of search teams out to the crash site, in order to help collect the debris, so that the cause of the accident could be determined. I wasn't selected to go out and search the ocean, instead I had to iron my dress uniform and get ready to take part in a ceremony for the dead. Later on in the day I found out that two more survivors had been found, but unfortunately one of them later died in hospital. The final death count was eight (out of ten). The flags in the regiment were lowered to half mast, and the French president Nicolas Sarkozy ordered his minister of defence to fly out to Gabon to oversee the search.

Over the next few days, parts of the downed helicopter began to arrive at the regiment. The way that the metal was mangled and deformed, gave you some idea of the forces involved in the crash. Every piece was examined for any evidence of what might have caused the accident, but, to this day, the cause is unknown. It was just a tragic accident that cost eight people their lives.

The next thing on the agenda, after the regimental exercise, was what is known as 'tour des provinces.' This is where we go out into the sticks and help out the local people by digging a well, fixing roofs, providing basic medical assistance, etc. A few days before going, I started to get really sick. At first I thought that maybe I had caught the flu. I had been taking my malaria tablets everyday so I was reasonably confident that it wasn't that. Just before we were ready to go I noticed that a red lump was developing on my inner thigh, and I asked if I could go to the infirmary to have it checked out. At the infirmary, the doctor took one look at it and told me that it was an abscess, which had most likely been caused by an infected mosquito bite on my ankle. I was ordered to stay at the infirmary until it was better, and therefore I missed the tour des provinces.

However, my stay in the infirmary wasn't uneventful. A couple of days after being admitted, I ran into Adjutant squeaky balls (from the amphibious course). He was now the company's medic, and had been breaking everyone's balls about not forgetting to take their malaria pills. Well, guess what? He had malaria! You couldn't make it up, it's like those preachers who rail against homosexuals, but who are then caught in cheap hotels with rent boys. Needless to say, he was a bit quieter after he got out.

The infirmary was run by the French regular army, and was therefore more laidback than I was used to, but this soon changed. At first we were allowed to serve ourselves when the food arrived, but all the food kept disappearing rather rapidly. I too noticed this when I went to get my meal and there was hardly anything there. It wasn't long before the culprit was apprehended. It was a rather stupid guy from the fourth section of my company (the fourth section had all the biggest dumb-asses for some reason). This guy was a total idiot; he had been in the Legion a little bit longer than me but spoke almost no French. He maybe had a working vocabulary of twenty-five words, and that's no joke. This fucker would wait for the food to arrive, then fill up his plate as much as he could, eat it, then go back and do the same thing again. When I say fill his plate, I mean it: One of the orderlies showed me the plate they had caught him with, it was a fucking pyramid of food. You couldn't physically put any more on there. The strange thing was that this guy wasn't even fat. Anyway, the doctor soon signed him out of the infirmary, and that was the end of his feasting days. I spent nearly two weeks in the infirmary, and was let out just before everyone returned from the tour.

The next thing on the list for my section was to go to a place called Port-Gentil. We would be spending the rest of our time in Gabon there. When we came back to Libreville we would pack up and go. However, before we left for Port-Gentil the lieutenant wanted to make preparations for our return to Calvi. He would be sending a lot of people away on courses, because a lot of people would be finishing their contracts and there was already a load of new legionnaires waiting for us back on Corsica. Everyone was asked to think of three course that they would like to do and then go and pass before the lieutenant and tell him. The courses I had chosen were: medic, signals, and the amphibious level 2 course. When it was my turn I went into the lieutenant's office and told him my choices. He noted down what I had said and told me he would see what he could do.

I had one hell of a shock a couple of days later when I was informed that I would be going on a course to learn how to fold parachutes. I had been well and truly shafted; everyone knew that parachute folding department was like a forced labour camp, and there was no fucking way I was going to work over there. I would rather take the month in jail for refusing the course. After speaking with a few other guys in the section it was clear what had happened. All of the bootlickers had taken the good courses, and those of us that just got on quietly with our work had been given what was left. I got together with another Englishman, and an Irishman from my section who had been condemned to the kitchens, and trumpet playing, respectively. We all decided that we would refuse to go on the courses. We were all young fit guys in our early twenties, who spoke French well, and we didn't join the army to work in the kitchen, fold parachutes, or play the fucking trumpet. It was better to refuse these courses, have no specialization, and just concentrate on combat training, even if it meant getting passed over for future courses.

It didn't take long, after letting our intentions be known, for us to get a visit from an irate Sch Butkis. He went nuts, shouting and screaming at us; telling us that we were going on those courses whether we liked it or not. However, the main reason for his enraged state, was not so much that we had refused the courses. He was actually more concerned that that our display of insubordination might reflect badly on him and affect his chances of promotion. He even accused us of plotting to get him thrown out of the company. We did try to explain our real reason for refusing the courses, but he was stuck in his way of thinking, and couldn't appreciate that we might have other motivations for acting as we did, but, in any case, we stood firm and told the him that we would not be going on those courses, and that he could deal with us as he pleased. He told us that refusing to go on a course would land us in military prison, and we reiterated to him that we were willing to accept whatever punishment came our way.

After he got the message that we weren't budging, he calmed down and tried to play good cop and reason with us a little, but that didn't work either so he gave up and went back down to his office. However, that was not the end of it. Before going to Port-Gentil we were called in front of the company sergeant-major to explain ourselves. Fortunately, the company sergeant-major was British and understood our motivations for not wanting to go on the courses. He got it that we had joined to be soldiers and didn't want to get stuck in the kitchens. This didn't mean that we wouldn't be punished, but at least we had made our point.

A few days later, I was at the airport, parachute on, loaded up with equipment, ready for the flight to Port-Gentil, which is Gabon's second largest city, and it is also the home of its petroleum industry. The city is on a peninsula, just below the equator, and it is not connected to the mainland by road. The flight to Port-Gentil didn't take long, and before I knew it, I was out the door and heading for the earth. We had jumped out right next to the airport. I could tell, as I was descending, that there was a fair bit of wind, but just how much would be made clear to me when I landed. I hit the ground with such force that my helmet shot off my head, then my parachute began dragging along the ground towards a giant puddle. I managed to pull one of the shoulder releases just before getting soaked. When I got up I saw others being dragged around the drop zone. People came in diagonally, hit the ground, let out a groan of pain, and then got dragged along by their parachute (I later found out that we shouldn't have jumped that day as the wind speed was too high). There were a couple of injuries; one guy had his head cut open, and was badly concussed, but no broken bones.

Our camp was right next to the airport. It was a tiny place and there were only around seventy people staying there. Apart from us there was a group of French special forces divers, who didn't seem to do anything except lounge around in sports gear. While we were here our main job was to do regimental service. Being a small base there wasn't that much to do; the main thing was guard duty. The rest of the time we could go shooting, jumping, or explore the surrounding area. We spent the first few days at the tip of the peninsular doing a fair bit of shooting. It was great fun, because we had all the ammunition you could dream of. We even had a load of shotgun shells, which was a rarity in the Legion.

The first weekend after our arrival, we went to the beach to help the local fishermen drag in their nets. It was an amazing sight, to see the sheer amount of fish that they caught. In my estimate there was well over two tonnes of fish. The variety was also interesting. There were half a dozen different species of shark (including hammerheads). After helping the locals we put a few fish on a stretcher and took them back to camp for a barbeque.

On Sunday we went to visit the local zoo, which was a big disappointment. It was the most squalid, animal prison I have ever seen in my life. The cages were tiny, and there was nothing stimulating for the animals to do. It was clear that most of them had gone mad: They just paced back and forth, or stayed on the same spot rocking like lunatics. That zoo was an affront to decency, and should have never been allowed to open. I was glad when we left, looking at those animals made you feel sad; especially the chimpanzees, which were in tiny cages, on their own.

After the visit to the zoo we went to a nice stretch of beach to relax. I amused myself by digging crabs out of their burrows. They would pop out at last moment and scurry for another hole. It was fun chasing them, but they were too fast and always went down another hole before I could get them.

The second week of our stay, there was an overnight exercise. Thankfully I had twenty-four hour guard and didn't have to go. When the section returned I was told that the lieutenant had brought a couple of local prostitutes, who he had met in a nightclub last weekend, along to play the hostages. I was also told that he managed to get lost again. Many were beginning to suspect that the lieutenant didn't know how to read a map, or was incompetent, or both. He had made a series of gaffs since taking over the section, and didn't appear to know much about the equipment, or tactics, that we used. He was also an insufferably condescending prick, who thought that he was très cultured, and that we legionnaires were uncivilized brutes who had grown up in a field. At least that's the impression that I got from him.

When our time was up in Port-Gentil we got ready to fly back to Libreville. Thankfully we didn't have to jump this time. It was less than a week now until we would be returning to Corsica. Overall I had enjoyed Gabon very much; it had been a unique experience, and very different to anywhere that I had been before.

When we got back to Libreville, everyone began clearing out the rooms and packing everything away into crates for the return journey. The locals who worked in the regiment must have guessed that we were leaving and were waiting by the bins. They would go through all the rubbish and take whatever they could use, or sell. There were a few people who didn't like the fact that they were getting stuff for free, and that they were black, so they destroyed whatever they had before putting it in the trash. One NCO went out to the bins with a pair of trainers that he was going to throw out. The locals were waiting at a distance, watching and waiting for him to leave, so they could grab the shoes, but before he placed them in the bin the NCO produced a pair of scissors and began cutting away at the shoes thus making them unwearable, while staring at the Gabonese locals with a smug grin on his face: It was an act of pure malice. To deny people, less fortunate than yourself, something that you were going to discard, and to actually gain some sadistic pleasure from it was so spiteful that it bordered on perversion. Unfortunately, in the Legion, that type of thing wasn't uncommon.

A few days later we left Gabon, and after another eight hour flight, touched down in Corsica, at Solenzara airbase. It was the beginning of March and, compared to Gabon, it felt rather cold on Corsica to say the least. There were buses that had arrived to take us back to Calvi. However, I had to stay and wait for the equipment to arrive, then load it onto the trucks. This meant journeying back to Calvi in the open back of an army truck. By the time I got to camp Raffalli I was frozen stiff.

A couple of days after arriving back at Calvi I was ordered to take a 'randomized' drug test. Coincidentally the only other person from the company to be chosen was the French guy who had been with me when Sgt Cabrão had caught us rolling up. I hadn't smoked since our rooms had been searched, and my test came back clean and so did the other guy's. I knew that Sgt Cabrão wouldn't be able to resist snitching on us in order to curry favour with someone, but those negative results sure pissed on his bonfire, and a good job too, because he was a no-good dirty rat.

13: La Grande Randonnée

Walking is the best possible exercise.
Habituate yourself to walk very far.
Thomas Jefferson

After my holiday, I was straight away called back over to the command building for another not so random drug test, which I again passed. This time I was a little surprised, because I had visited Holland during my break and smoked a fair bit of high quality skunk.

My section had changed completely after returning from Gabon. Many had gone away on courses, others had changed company, or deserted. There was a load of fresh faces too. I was now among the more senior legionnaires and as such did not have to do as much menial labour. The only thing that I had to clean was my room, and since passing my driving test I was also able to do other types of service, besides working in the mess. Things were starting to turn out alright, but I was sad to see that Doyle had not returned from holiday. I guess he had got fed up with being labelled a bananier, and the constant punishment that came with it.

At the beginning of summer I was sent down south to a place called Galeria. There had been an oil spill and the government didn't want it to effect Corsica's tourism, so a group of legionnaires was tasked with cleaning up the beaches. This wasn't a spill from a tanker, but instead from a ship's fuel tank being ruptured. I had visions of scrubbing sea birds, but in fact all we did was walk up and down the beach in a line picking up clods of tar. This was all kept quiet and didn't get mentioned by any media outlets.

Every year on the 14th of July (Bastille Day), one of the regiments of the Foreign Legion goes to Paris to take part in the parade, and marches down the Champs-Élysées in front of the president and the French public; and this year it was the REP. I was not looking forward to this at all. It would be like a commando course in ironing and marching in step. Bastille Day is the biggest regular military parade in Europe, and it was important that there were no mistakes. This meant that we would have to drill, drill, and drill again, until the day of the event. I was not a big fan of the dress uniform or parading, so this was like my worst nightmare. However, as luck would have it, I was called into the lieutenant's office not long after it was announced that we would be taking part in the parade. I was informed that I would be going back to Castelnaudary to do my HGV licence. The lieutenant told me, with a smirk on his face, that he knew that I would be disappointed about missing out on Paris, but that he would try to make it up to me at a later date. While he was saying this, I was thinking, you clueless bastard, you are trying to get back at me for refusing your shitty parachute folding course by not letting me go to Paris, but you have inadvertently given me the greatest gift that you could have possibly bestowed upon me at this point in time. I maintained a straight face and nodded in agreement, but as soon I got out of the office I punched the air with joy. I couldn't believe that I had got out of having to do all that pointless bullshit. Instead I would be going back to the 4RE for a nice break.

Before leaving I went to talk with Sgt Tudor, I had been in the Legion for a year and a half now, and was still a legionnaire second class. Everyone with the same amount of service as me, and many people with less, had been promoted to the rank of first class already (this normally happens after a year of service). I was sure that with the change of platoon leader I had been forgotten. I did not want to go to the 4RE as a second class, as I would get all the shitty jobs. It was always, 'we need someone to do this or that. All the second class legionnaires stay here. The rest of you can go.' So I asked if he could remind the lieutenant about it before I left. He agreed that I was long overdue for promotion, and said that he would see to it that I got my first stripe ASAP. The sergeant was good to his word, and few days later I was promoted to legionnaire first class.

Getting my truck driving licence was a lot of fun. The course was pretty much the same as before, except that the book was a bit thicker and the vehicles were larger. We spent most of our time learning how to reverse around a series of cones. By this time I had quite a bit of experience driving and it didn't take me too long to get the hang of it. I passed the test on my first go again, and after two weeks was on my way back to Calvi.

When I arrived back at Camp Raffalli a big announcement was made. At the beginning of next year we would be going to Afghanistan, and it was the second and third companies that would be going. This meant that our whole schedule had to be changed, because we were going to have to get some serious training done before we went. Fortunately the terrain of Corsica is not too dissimilar to that of where we would be going. The mountains were smaller and temperatures weren't quite as extreme, but it would have to do. We were also going to have to learn a whole new range of techniques for dealing with things, such as IEDs. Not to mention all the new equipment we would have to familiarize ourselves with.

While I had been away in Gabon the regiment had changed its commanding officer. We now had the highly regarded Colonel Éric Bellot des Minières as our commander in chief. He was a thoroughly decent chap, and a good leader who had a lot of experience. At the beginning of his career he had spent nine years with the third company here at REP (1986 – 1995), which he ended up commanding for his last two years, and had taken part in many operations overseas with the Foreign Legion (Chad, Rwanda, Somalia, et al.). He knew exactly what to do and it wasn't long before all the new equipment began to arrive and plans were drawn up for exercises that would help us get an idea of what would be expected of us. Being chosen to go to Afghanistan also meant that we finally got rid of those museum piece bandages.

Not long after returning from Castelnaudary, I was chosen to go as part of a group to Fontainebleau, near Paris, for a couple of weeks. We were sent there to be the punching bags for a hand to hand combat course. It was a tough course and they wanted some tough opposition, so they thought who better than the REP, and asked us to put together a team.

Fontainebleau is a picturesque area of France, just south of Paris, and every garden there is immaculate and full of flowers. The palace of Fontainebleau is a UNESCO world heritage site, and well worth a visit. There is also a large forest there that is a popular weekend destination for people living in the capitol. The regiment where we would be staying was the French national centre for combat sports, and it had every kind of sporting facility that you could imagine. The rooms we were staying in were very comfortable and the food at the mess was in a different class to what we were used to.

Each day, while at Fontainebleau we were given a different scenario to act out. Sometimes we would have to attack with a certain weapon, other times we would attack en masse like in a riot situation. My favourite day was when I got to wear the 'black man suit,' which is a full contact, padded suit that covers your whole body and makes you look like an ice hockey goalie. The people doing the course would patrol in groups of three, and you would have to jump out and attack them. They had batons and rifles that they could hit you with so it was important to have to have the suit so that you didn't get injured. It was great fun attacking people all day, but having your arm twisted behind your back fifteen times in a row did take its toll on you.

The people doing the course were from all over France. There were people from the police, and gendarmerie. There was even a couple of guys from the GIGN, which is the gendarmerie's special forces unit. When we weren't getting beat up we were allowed to join in on the lessons that they were taking. It was interesting stuff, and I learned some descent self-defence techniques.

At the weekend I went out to Paris with a couple of others to do some shopping, then on Sunday I visited the palace, and museum, at Fontainebleau. The palace rooms were breathtakingly beautiful and the palace grounds were just as impressive.

The second week would be the final test for those on the course. They would have to walk round the camp and deal with a range of different situations when they arose. Each day we changed our position and method of attack so that those who went before couldn't tell the others what to expect. At the end of the course we took a group photo together (except for the GIGN guys, who couldn't be photographed). I was surprised when the instructors handed out elementary certificates in self-defence to us for taking part. It was a nice gesture, even if we didn't really deserve them.

When we arrived back at Calvi there was a nice treat lying in store for us. We would be going on a long march, and not just any march, but one of the toughest in Europe. It was the height of summer now in Corsica and daytime temperatures were in the low thirties. The march we would have to complete was the GR20 (Grande Randonnée; great hike). The GR20 is one hell of a march; it is one hundred and eighty kilometres long and has over ten kilometres of ascent and descent. The northern part of the trail often climbs to over 2,000 metres above sea level. To make it even more difficult, we would be doing it in full equipment. For me this meant taking the Minimi along for the journey. Even though it would be difficult, I was looking forward to the march. I enjoy hiking and being out in nature, especially in the mountains.

Just before we set off on the march, I was called into the lieutenant's office. I was told that after the march I would be going on holiday. The company didn't have holiday scheduled until Christmas, but I was to go on holiday early, because afterwards I would be going straight to Castelnaudary to do my corporal's course. I was a little surprised, I had only been promoted to first class two months ago. The reason for me being sent off so early was our deployment next year. The company was a little short on man power, and it needed new legionnaires and new corporals to train them. I was happy about going off to do the course, but it did mean that I would have to miss out on the selection for GCP, which I had been preparing for ever since our return from Gabon. The next opportunity I would get to do it wouldn't be until after we had returned from Afghanistan.

The start of the GR20 is only ten kilometres behind our camp, in the small town of Calenzana. Our bags were pretty heavy, as we needed to carry a lot of water with us, but not unbearably so. The trail we were about to hike takes roughly two weeks to finish in full, but we would only be doing the Northern part, so we had to cover just over fifty miles through some of the most difficult terrain in Europe, in five days. No problem.

The trail started off with a gentle incline. There was a little bit of tree cover to begin with, but we soon emerged onto open scrubland. It didn't take long, marching in full equipment, before you were wet with perspiration. We took regular breaks; every hour we would stop for ten minutes. The whole day was spent walking up hill. Eventually, we got to place high enough to be able to see Calvi, and the sea. I amused myself along the march by taking photos with my new camera that I had bought after Gabon.

Our destination for the first day was to reach the Auberge de la Forêt (one of the small refuges located along the trail). Thankfully the scrubland we were walking through began to disappear as we got higher, and we entered Corsica's high-altitude pine forests. Some of the trees up there were enormous; they looked like they had been growing for a thousand years. The mountain began to get much steeper when we entered the forest, and clambering up rocks with a gun hung around your neck is rather annoying, because it swings around, snags on branches, or in the rocks, but most irritating thing is that it hits your knees when try to step up. The only solution to this is to climb with one hand, and have the other hold the gun, but that is not always possible.

After a few hours of climbing, everyone was tired and soaked in sweat. When a break was called people would just flop on the floor. I made a point of not drinking water as soon as we stopped. Instead, I would wait a few minutes for my heartbeat to slow down a bit, and the sweat to stop pouring out of me. I didn't feel as thirsty that way, and could make better economy of my water.

Sometime around late afternoon we reached our destination. The Auberge de la Forêt is a medium sized compound that has a restaurant, bar, shop, and even rooms to rent. All this at around a kilometre above sea level is pretty impressive. There is a single road leading to refuge, but for some reason they chose to restock by helicopter. Sadly we didn't get a chance to use any of the facilities; our sleeping area was in the nearby forest, alongside a river.

I didn't bother setting up a tarpaulin as there wasn't a cloud in the sky, and it rarely rains on Corsica. I just slept in my sleeping bag under the stars. Before sleeping I went over to the river to bathe. It was very cold water and I didn't stay in for too long. After washing I went to eat some food; for this journey I didn't bother taking the army rations, instead I had gone out to town and bought some dried meat, bread, and boiled sweats. I also had some salt and sugar, which I would put into a litre of water and drink before sleeping (like a homemade sports drink). As always, when we stay outside, there has to be a guard mounted, and as usual I was on sometime around midnight. That night, I remember, was particularly beautiful. It was a full moon and everything was bathed in silvery moonlight. The only sound was that of the river running beside our camp. It was a good time to be on guard duty.

The next day we set out bright and early. We started off by crossing a wire bridge that spanned the river we had slept next to. Today we would have to cover a lot of ground. Our route wound its way up a valley that was covered with pine trees. The incline was quite gentle at first, but it kept getting steeper, and steeper. As the day wore on, the sun began beating down on us, and the pine forest was getting thinner the higher we climbed.

A little further on, we came to the scenic 'Passerelle du Lamitu,' a thirty metre long, and very wobbly, cable bridge. As we passed over I saw that, sat on the rocks by the river below, we had a casualty. It was the Captain, and he had twisted his ankle. We were treated to a nice long break while we waited for him to get back on his feet. However, it wasn't long, after starting to march again, that we had our first case of heat stroke. There were no roads up here so heat stroke, or not, you would have to march. The only thing that we could do, was to cool the person down, rehydrate them, and empty their rucksack.

Just after midday we rounded the last bend in the valley, and we could see what lay ahead of us; Bocca di Stagnu, a two thousand metre high ridge. We stopped for lunch near another refuge, and refilled our water bottles for the climb ahead. When we began again after lunch, the real fun started. There were no pine trees anymore, in fact there was no cover whatsoever, just bare granite. It was incredibly steep, and the sun reflected off the rocks and right into your face, burning you from every angle. At times we had to climb up huge boulders, not an easy thing when you are weighed down with twenty kilos of equipment. The nearer we got to the top, the steeper the mountain became.

After a couple of hours of marching up that oven of a mountainside, and a couple more heat stroke victims later, we reached a small plateau, with the bluest lake I have ever seen in my life. While I was waiting for the rest of the company to arrive, I climbed up a little further, to a patch of snow and filled my hat with it, then plonked it back on my head. I also managed to find a little stream to refill my water bottles with (we were forbidden from taking water from streams, but I gambled that it would be ok). The cold mountain water, coupled with the snow on my head, was just what the doctor ordered. By the time that the company had regrouped, I was feeling totally refreshed. There was a small hundred metre climb left, to the top now, and once we got there we took another short break, before heading off, along the ridge.

The most difficult part of toady's journey was over. All we had to do now was go along a short section of ridgeline, cross over, then go down the other side. The walk along the ridge was precarious, to say the least, and the load that I was carrying didn't help matters. There were a couple of times when I leaned back a bit too much and almost got pulled of the mountain by my rucksack. After we had walked along the ridge and crossed over, I could see the next refuge from the top of the mountain. It was straight down from where I was, at the foot of the mountain. However, between us and it was a very sharp descent.

An hour or two, of controlled falling down the mountain later, we finally arrived at the refuge where we would be spending the night. This place was huge and it had road access, a hotel, and plenty of log cabins. However, for us there would be no log cabins. My room for the night was a boggy field, inhabited by cows, and there wasn't an inch of that field that hadn't been crapped all over. Many people had picked up some nasty blisters from the two days of marching. I had learned a good trick for avoiding blisters; this was to put adhesive bandage on my feet before marching. I simply bandaged up the places where blisters usually occurred and the bandages took all the friction. The old saying 'prevention is better than cure' is one worth heeding. That night in the cow field was frightfully cold, and there was one hell of a wind blowing through the place all night. It was great for drying your clothes, but it chilled you to the bones.

The next morning there was a thick mist permeating the valley. This was a welcome change from the glaring sun of yesterday. The first hour of the march was fairly easy; there wasn't much of an incline. Though, eventually, we did have to begin the climb up to Col de Perdu, which was one of the highest points on the march at well over two thousand metres above sea level. The bit of mountain we were walking up now was north facing. It was hidden from the sun, and snow was still thick on the ground.

When we reached the top, there was a fantastic view; most notably, we could see Monte Cinto, the highest mountain on Corsica, which stands at a whopping 2,706 metres high. However, we didn't have much time to admire the scenery. In front of us was a huge challenge. The next part of our journey was the infamous

Cirque de la Solitude; a deep, snow-filled, valley that ran right up the side of the mountain. It was a steep four hundred meter climb down to where we could cross, then another four hundred metre climb back up to the other side, and for a little bit of excitement the middle had a meltwater river running through it with lots of ice and wet slippery rocks around it. One false move would see you tobogganing down two kilometres of mountain into boulders and trees. Cirque de la Solitude was very tricky, but there were cables, and iron bars, fixed to the rocks to aid your climb.

The ridge on the other side was the highest point on our journey so far, which meant that from there on in the hiking would get a bit easier. We marched down the mountain again to another refuge, stopped for a bit of lunch, and then continued our descent. When we reached the bottom, we crossed over the river that ran through the valley, and started to climb up the other side. The sun was beating down again and it wasn't long before some more people fell with heat stroke. The climb was nothing, in comparison with the previous two days, but everyone was tired, and many were struggling to keep up.

It was late afternoon when we arrived at our camp for the night; a piece of bare mountainside with no shelter from the elements. It was so windy up there that those, who had brought army rations, gave up trying to cook them and just ate their meal cold. Word went round the camp, that tomorrow we would be cutting the march short and returning to Calvi. This was because of all the heat strokes (one guy had collapsed twice in the same day); and the captains bad ankle. This was a shame, because the mountains had started to get smaller now, and I was curious as to what lay further along the trail, but it was asking for trouble to push on.

The next day we woke a little later than usual, but by eight o'clock we were on our way. Before we came down from the mountains, we took a picture of the third, and forth, sections together, which was done with my camera and I still have the picture on my hard drive. After the group picture, we walked down into a valley and followed its river. The river led to a series of beautiful waterfalls and pools with crystal clear water. There were quite a few tourists enjoying themselves in the water, and sunbathing on the rocks at its edge.

A bit further on from the waterfalls we entered a thick pine forest. It was great to be out of the sun. A few hours, of walking through the forest, later we emerged onto a car park (much to the surprise of the people there). Then we followed the road up to the second company's mountain training base, in Vergio. It was a great relief to know that the march was finally over. There was nothing to do now but wait for our transport to arrive and take us back to Calvi.

14: Stage Corporal

Nearly all men can stand adversity, but if
you want to test a man's character, give him
power.
Abraham Lincoln

I came back to the regiment a couple of days before the end of my holiday; so that I didn't have to rush around packing my bags and getting everything ready for my trip to Castelnaudary. There was one other person from my company going with me: a French legionnaire called Durand, who I liked very much, and got on well with. There were another two legionnaires from the regiment who would also be joining us, but they were from the support companies. One was a short middle-aged Frenchman, who worked in the kitchens, and the other was a tall Russian in his late twenties, who was a mechanic. They had both been in the Legion for nearly five years and were being sent as a reward for their years of service. We all met up one Friday afternoon, outside the security officer's building, and as always there was transport to take us to the port at Bastia.

The next morning we arrived in Marseille at rush hour. It was a nightmare taking the Métro with the two massive bags that we each had. When we got to the train station, I went to withdraw some money from the ATM, but the blasted thing swallowed my card. That was all I needed, now I would have to go two months without any money, just like basic instruction. I was planning on getting some high energy sports bars and other supplies, but now I would have to make do with the French rations. There was no time for me to go to the bank and get another card, besides it would be sent to my address at Calvi even if I did.

We got to Castelnaudary later that same day, and went over to the CIC (compagnie d'instruction des cadres). The others who came with me dumped their bags in the rooms then went out to town. I was planning on doing likewise, and going to Toulouse, but given my financial situation I was forced to abandon that plan. Still, it wasn't that bad, I could still go to the gym, and there was now a huge bar/pizzeria in the camp, where I could go and watch TV. There were already a couple of guys from the other regiments up in the rooms and I got chatting to them. Most I found out were from the infantry regiment at Nîmes.

Sunday at midnight everyone had to go out onto the parade ground and line up to be counted. There were around forty people on the course altogether, and only three instructors. However, the NCOs who would be training us didn't have much to say for the moment. The real fun would begin in the morning. It is well known that the corporal's course is the second toughest course in the Legion (the most difficult is sergeants course, which is the same kind of thing, but a month longer), and everyone was speculating on what tomorrow would hold.

The next day we got up and went downstairs to line up at six o'clock, and the three instructors introduced themselves to us. There were two sergeant-chefs, and a sergeant. The chief instructor was a tall thin Frenchman; the other sergeant-chef was a grumpy looking Irish guy, who never smiled; and the sergeant was a sneaky Russian, who seldom spoke, but who watched everything like a hawk. One thing to note was that they were all from 2REI, and ever since the parachute regiment has existed there has been a fierce rivalry between them and the infantry. This was made clear

285

during the initial briefing. All the parachutists were asked to raise their hand, then the head instructor looked at each of us before speaking, he told us that he fucking despised the REP, and would like nothing better than to see us all come last, but he was fair man and if we performed well we would be ranked accordingly. He then issued a warning to the infantry guys, telling them that it was their duty to triumph over us, and not to let us beat them at anything, no matter how small.

The first thing we had to do as part of the course was a series of fitness tests. We had to complete the rope climb, obstacle course, and do an eight kilometre run in full equipment. No one cared about the rope climb, the real competition was for the obstacle course and, most of all, for the run. I decided to take it easy for the first series of tests. I had just come back from a month's holiday where I did nothing but eat fast food and ice cream, and I knew that we would have to do the tests another two times during the course. It would be no good if I went hell for leather, injured myself at the start, and then got sent back to Calvi. Having said that, I was surprised when I came first on the obstacle course with a time of three minutes flat, and nobody was within thirty seconds of me. I hadn't even been trying, so that one was in the bag. As you can imagine, this made our chief instructor happy when he asked the person who had made that time to raise their hand and saw that it was one of the REP men. However, on the run I trotted along at a safe pace and kept to the middle of the group; finishing tenth or thereabouts.

Later on in the day, after the tests, Durant came to my room to have a word with me. He said that the infantry guys where gloating and mocking him non-stop about how they had destroyed the REP on the run. He was not happy about it and said that he, and I, needed to get our acts together and make sure that next time we opened a can of whoop-ass on them. I told him that I had seen the winning time and could easily beat it, and that today I had taken it easy so as not to injure myself. I assured him that on the final test I would shut them up.

We had just finished speaking, when a group of guys from the infantry burst into my room with the Tunisian legionnaire, who had come first in the race, on head. They began trying to wind us up by rubbing their victory in our faces, and true to Durant's word they were being class-A pricks about the whole thing. I kept my cool and calmly asked the leader what time he had finished in. He told me that he had done it in forty-two minutes. I congratulated him, and wished him luck for next time. The group of legionnaires then made some comments to the effect that this proved the infantry was superior to the REP and left. After seeing just what colossal arses they were being about the whole affair, I told Durant that I would not wait until the end of the course and would beat them the next time we conducted the tests. He said that he hoped I would because they were insufferable and his room was full of them.

Over the first few days it was made clear what would be expected of us on this course. We would have to learn every song that the Legion sang; know every detail, of every piece of equipment that the Legion used; memorise the complete history of the Legion; learn to identify every military vehicle in use today and know what weapons it had; keep our rooms and clothing immaculate (everything ironed, everything spotlessly clean); complete every physical activity within the given time; and display perfect discipline.

Our days would start out with a good dose of sport, then we would normally take instruction during the day, and at night we would have a mission to complete. You got to sleep when you finished the mission. If you didn't finish, you didn't sleep. The tinniest mistake would result in you and everyone else on the course being punished. One of the favourite punishments was compte rendus. They would give someone an insane number to write, and the deadline would be at six o'clock the next morning. There was no time during the day to do them so this had to be done at night, and no one could write fifty in a night so we would have to split them between everybody.

After a few days of this constant harassing, something dawned on me. I had experienced this before. This was exactly how Cpl Bernard had treated everyone when he arrived in the section, after returning from this same course. He had simply remembered how the instructors had acted, and mimicked their behaviour back at the section. This turned out to be handy for me as I had already learned most of what we were expected to know on the course. The only thing that I hadn't been forced to memorize was the vehicle identification, but I had learned that myself, while preparing for GCP selection. The one part of the course that I would have to revise was the songs. I fucking hated the Legion songs and thought that they were retarded, but now I would have to learn every last one. Oh, happy days.

On the third or fourth night, after starting the course, the lights came on in our corridor, and one of the instructors began shouting for us to assemble. I jumped out of bed and ran to the hall. Once everyone was there, we were given five minutes to pack our bags with ten kilos of stuff and assemble in the parking lot. In the parking lot everyone's bag was quickly weighed, then we were bundled into a truck with the flaps rolled down and driven out of the camp. I guessed that they were going to dump us somewhere and make us march back, so I went to the back of the truck and looked through a gap in the plastic. I was looking at the road signs and remembering the names of the villages that we went through. When the truck stopped we were ordered out onto the side of the road and given a map. They told us to find our location and get back to the regiment before role call at six the next morning.

Once the truck had gone, I looked in the direction we had come from and found the lights of the village that we had last passed through, then I went over to the people with the map, and told them that the lights over in the distance were a village called so and so. They quickly found it on the map and we worked out the fastest route home. It turned out that we were around thirty kilometres away from the camp. Marching with rucksacks on, we could expect to cover five kilometres in an hour, so the journey would take around six hours if all went well, and it was already eleven o'clock, which meant that we had a seven hour time limit.

It was clear that we had to get a move on and there would be no time for breaks. Someone suggested cutting across the fields, but I insisted that the chance of getting lost, or coming up against an impassable barrier, was too great. This time I was able to win more people over to my way of thinking and we took the road.

After just a few hours of marching people began to drop off, and we were forced to take a break. During the stop we pleaded with the guys at the back to try and keep up, so that we could get back on time. They agreed to try their best.

When our short pause was over we took up the march again, and after another couple of hours we reached the Canal du Midi. This lifted everyone's spirits; the canal was the last part of our journey and it ran right past the regiment so all we had to do was follow it along.

By the time we finally got to the fence at the side of the regiment it was half past five in the morning and the sky was starting to get lighter. In thirty minutes we would have to be lined up outside the company, ready to start the day's instruction. The course was often like that; just when you thought you could relax, you would be taken away on some godforsaken mission. I would say that on average, one night out of three we didn't get any sleep.

At meal times we would have to march to the mess and sing a couple of songs, and every day it was different songs. If our singing was not up to par then we would march round and round the regiment until it improved, only then would we be allowed to eat. There was no time during the course when you weren't being harassed. It was tough, but we all knew that after the two months were over, there would be no more mopping and sweeping, no more being sent to the shop to buy coke, and no more guard duty. Instead, we would be expected to make other people do these crappy jobs.

As our first week drew to a close we prepared to go to the farm. We would be spending over half of our time at the farm while on this course. The CIC's farm (known to everyone as

Bertrandou) was located on a plateau overlooking the medieval town of Carcassonne. It was much more basic than the farm that I had stayed at as an engagé volontaire. For a start there were no rooms for us to sleep in. We camped out in the woods the whole time we were there. There were no toilets either, we had to dig a latrine and shit in that. However, it did have some things in abundance. The place was littered with obstacle courses and stone pyramids: Making stone pyramids is a common punishment in the Legion, as is painting rocks and arranging them in the shape of the Legion logos (these arrangements of rocks can be easily seen on satellite images. If you want to see one, put this into Google Maps: 43.177111, 1.884056).

As you would expect for a course like this we would be marching to the farm. Our commanding NCO was leading us on this march so we didn't have to worry about finding our way there the first time, all we had to do was keep up. We started off marching along the canal at the back of the regiment. The head instructor was a tall man with long legs and he marched at a decent pace.

At the begging of the journey everything was fine and everyone was managing to keep up, but I knew that it wouldn't take long for people to start dropping off. There were a lot of people on this course who worked in offices, kitchens, etc., and they weren't used to marching. A few had already picked up a load of blisters from the last time. Laffon, the French guy from the kitchens, who had come with me from Calvi, was in a particularly bad state. After a few hours of marching he was clearly in a lot of pain. When the sergeant-chef noticed this he gave him a good tongue lashing and ordered him to march near the front where he could keep an eye on him.

The route that we took to the farm was longer than necessary, but it passed by a lot of interesting places. The sergeant-chef had obviously walked around this part of France hundreds of times, and knew it like the back of his hand. At one point, we came off the road and passed through the garden of a derelict house, before going through some fields. The people who had lived in that house must have had a herb garden, because the place was covered in sage and thyme. There was a really heavy scent that hung in the air all around it. We also passed by a Thales Alenia space centre that had a load of huge white radar dishes. It looked very out of place in the French countryside.

Eventually, after passing a few villages and cutting through some woodlands we arrived at the farm of Bertrandou. At the entrance to the farm there is a large triangular piece of land with two obstacle courses, and an old tank, on it. The obstacle courses were nearly falling apart and almost completely worn down from years of constant use. A bit further in, down a dirt path, is the main farm building. The farm building is surrounded by woodland, and as I have said before there are no facilities, except for a classroom.

Our campsite wasn't too far from the farmhouse; it was a couple of minutes' walk up a trail. The camp was not that bad: there was a wooden shack for the instructors to sleep in; a kitchen hut with a long wooden table in front of it; and a sheltered classroom area. We slept on a bare patch of ground with our tarpaulins for shelter. The first thing we had to do after arriving was to dig a latrine, then we set to work tidying everything up.

Once the camp was in order one of the instructors took us on a jog that ended in front of one of the many obstacle courses, which we then completed three or four times. After the obstacle course everyone was really worn out, and hungry. For the entire time that we would be at the farm we ate army rations and bread. The kitchen consisted of a gas stove and a couple of large pots. The designated cook would empty all the ration tins into one of the pots, add some pepper, and heat it up. It wasn't great but when you are hungry you don't care.

That evening, after the meal, there was some orienteering to do. We had to go round and punch bits of paper with the fifteen markers that were hidden in the surrounding countryside. The course was around ten kilometres long and the markers were well hidden: It would have been a challenge in the daytime. The land around us wasn't exactly easy going either. It was mostly woodland, but there were a few quarries that we had to be careful of, and a huge gorge at the southern end. There were more than a few people who nearly ran straight off the edge of a cliff in the middle of the night.

The orienteering courses were designed to take us all night, and the instructors had made it as hard as possible to cheat, but we still managed. There were in fact more than fifteen markers to get, and the instructors would give each person a different set to collect, they would also send half the people in a clockwise direction, and the rest in reverse. However, if you stopped every time you came across someone else, and copied each other's punch marks (we did this by taking the pin from our cap badges and laying one piece of paper on top of the other then carefully piercing the holes), you could reduce the time it took by up to a third.

We did a lot of orienteering while we were at the farm and after the first week, when the sleep deprivation really started to set in, some people began hatching schemes to gain some extra sleep. We were normally sent out in pairs and some guys would run five hundred metres away from our camp, then one of them would curl up and sleep in the bushes while the other went and did the orienteering then came back to wake him up, and the next time they would swap over. Others went balls to the wall and both curled up in the bushes, then came back at six the next morning, and said that they got lost and didn't find any of the markers. This worked because it wasn't that rare for a couple of knuckle heads to get completely lost and wander off the map (I've done it). It was good when people genuinely did get lost as well, because we would have to go and search for them in the morning, instead of doing our exercises.

If we weren't doing orienteering, or getting taken miles away in the truck and dumped off down a back lane, the night-time was normally spent learning a new song and marching up and down the path being forced to sing it like North Koreans forced to wail over the death of the dear leader. It was an insane experience; we were in the woods, in the middle of nowhere, marching up and down a path singing at the top of our lungs while being screamed at, and threatened, from the side-lines. If we screwed up then we would normally have to run around the farm while holding our guns above our heads, do an obstacle course, or just anything that would tire us out really. One time we were told to dig a trench in front of a row of trees with pickaxes and only candles for lighting. Once we had dug down a metre, the light from the candles didn't reach the bottom of the trench, so we had cut out little shelves in the sides and place them in there. It was like a scene from the First World War.

In the daytime at Bertrandou, we would learn things from our field manuals, or practice tactics. The sport that we did in the mornings was tough; some of the runs were like half marathons and we wouldn't get back until nearly midday. All the physical activity, lack of sleep, and the constant harrying from the instructors soon wore you down, and the strain from this would cause some people to completely break down. That was not good news for them, because instructors were like wolves following a herd of caribou; if they saw any sign of weakness they went in for the kill.

With the people who didn't react well to stress, you could have these positive feedback loops arising, where because of the hectic and demanding nature of the course they would make a mistake, then the instructors would jump on them and give them a good beasting, which would stress them out further, thus causing them to make additional blunders, and on it went; until the legionnaire collapsed quivering on the ground in the foetal position. What I've just described could be a pretty good summation of the course: The more the instructors went berserk, shouted and punished us, the more we ran around like headless chickens, making ever bigger bananes. However, you had no choice, but to get used to this state of affairs. As I have already mentioned, when one person makes a mistake everyone is punished, and someone would always fuck up, which meant that we were always being punished for something (sometimes there would be another banane made during the punishment). I am sure that you can imagine that if being around the instructors was like that, then the long marches and all night orienteering soon became something to look forward to, because, even if it was physically demanding, at least we were out from under their scrutinizing gaze.

We also did quite a few short missions while at the farm. What would normally happen was that we would be split into three or four groups, and each group would have a designated leader. After that, each group would be driven a good distance away from the camp and dumped off. Our mission would be to locate ourselves on the map and find our way to a rendezvous point, by a designated time. At the RV we would meet up with the other teams, then from there we would go on to our objective and set up an attack. The task of getting to our destination was made more difficult by the fact that we would have to get there undetected. What this meant in practise was that we couldn't use the roads.

Most of the time the missions went well and we managed to get in place on time and pull off the attack, and not being able to use the roads had its perks. On our journeys through the fields we would often came across vineyards and orchards that we could pillage for their fruit. If an exercise took place at night we could sometimes phone a local taxi service and get them to take us to the RV. The look on the taxi drivers faces, when they turned up and saw us in camouflage, carrying machine guns and rocket launchers, were priceless, but they didn't refuse to take us.

It was extremely risky taking a taxi, if we were spotted, we would be beasted like we had never been beasted before. The last group to be caught had to push a scrap car, that didn't have any tyres, around the farm with the instructors inside it, for hours.

I came close to being caught once. I had been dropped off with my group by truck; we decided to hide in the undergrowth and sleep for a few hours, then call a taxi to take us to the rendezvous point. We arrived at the RV with a couple of hours to spare, so we sat down in the bushes to wait for the other groups. However, unfortunately, a couple of lads were making a bit too much noise and one of the instructors found us. Luckily, he didn't question why we had arrived so early, because one of our group had nothing on but his boxer shorts and he was too busy going ape shit at him.

However, we still got fucked over for being unprofessional and making too much noise.

After two weeks of torture at the farm we were ready to return to the 4RE. We would be marching back, during the night, without the instructors. We left the farm in three groups, but unbeknownst to the NCOs we had planned to meet up and walk back together. Opposite Bertrandou was a derelict farmhouse; each group went straight there and hid, while they waited for everyone to arrive. The house was a complete wreck and covered in human faeces. I don't know why people feel the need to defecate in derelict houses, but it seems to be a common thing. Maybe it's how squatters mark their territory, but you would think that they would go outside and do it, or at least hang their arse out of a window.

Once everyone was together we waited for the instructors to leave in the vehicles. Not long after arriving at the farm I had started a trend. After the first few days of constant running and marching I had developed some nasty blisters. Physically I was fine, but the tough leather boots that we had to wear were blister factories, so I started hiding my trainers in my bag. Any time we had to do a march, or orienteering, I would get out of sight of the NCOs and change into my trainers. It solved the problem of getting blisters that's for sure. At first people were not too happy with me because they were worried about getting caught, but as time progressed more and more people began doing the same thing. Now for this march back after two weeks at the farm, nearly everyone was wearing their trainers: It was a strange sight to behold.

We started out on the march just after eight o'clock in the evening, but some of the guys had almost been destroyed by the last two weeks, and even with their trainers on, they couldn't keep up. After a few hours on the road there was a group of people who were shuffling along and staring at the ground in front of their feet. They were slowing us down no end. The understandable eagerness of some people to get back quickly and get some rest in a real bed, mixed with the inability of others to march soon led to fights. However, the fights were broken up before they got too serious.

It was early the next morning when we arrived back at the regiment. We just about had time to have a wash and change our clothes before starting a fresh day of work. Luckily, all we had to do was clean the guns and equipment, then put them back in the stores.

Now that we were back in the regiment we focused much more on the administrative side of being a corporal. It was a welcome break from the madness of the farm. However, there were always the occasional marches thrown in for good measure. We also did an incredible amount of classroom work. The most difficult part of the classroom stuff for me was identifying the Russian military vehicles. There were hundreds of them and all the vehicles looked the same. If you want an example of this, type 'BTR' into a search engine. It's a Russian/Ukrainian armoured personnel carrier and there are around fifteen models of the damn thing.

At the end of our first week back we were given weekend leave. This came with a few conditions of course: we had to perform well in the classroom and scrub the whole floor of our building, top to bottom. When I got my scrubbing brush out to clean my room, one of the other legionnaires took it from me and held it up for the others to see. The bristles on it were worn down to nothing. The people in my room saw it and gasped with horror. They asked me if it was common to be made to scrub the toilets at the REP, and I told them that I had spent many a night in the toilets scrubbing away until dawn. They were shocked and said to me that at their respective regiments it was rare for someone to be punished like that; they would have to have done something quite bad. In fact, most of them said that they hadn't been majorly punished since finishing basic training. One of them joked that living at the parachute regiment must be like doing this course all the time: The scary thing is that he wasn't far wrong.

I was the only one who stayed at the regiment over the weekend. I had no money so there was no point going out. I had borrowed €20 from Durant so that I could get a pizza on Sunday, and that was good enough for me. On Saturday I went to the back of the regiment, climbed over the fence and went for a nice long run along the canal. We had the second round of tests coming up on Monday and I wanted to be in good form. My plan was to go on a long run, empty my muscles of their glucose, then eat like a pig over the rest of the weekend, and hope that on Monday I would be fully charged.

As usual everyone left it until the last minute to return from their break. As we were lined up on the parade ground at midnight on Sunday there were people running from gate to make it back on time.

On Monday we had our second round of tests and like the first time we did them in order of easiest to hardest. We started off with the rope climb, then moved onto the assault course, and finally we had the eight kilometre TAB. The infantry guys were jubilant and completely sure of their success. Durant was eager that one of us beat them this time, and I again assured him that I would do my best.

The mistake people make with long distance races is that they start off too fast, then they build up an oxygen debt and can barely move. The best tactic is to start slow then build up your speed to the point where you are at limit of you aerobic endurance range, then you stay at that speed until you get within a couple of kilometres of the end, and that's when you give it all that you've got. As a general rule, you should only be giving it a hundred percent for the last fifteen percent of the race.

The race began, and sure enough everyone ran ahead of me. For the first kilometre I was almost in last place, but as the race progressed I started passing people. By the halfway point I had passed around three quarters of the group. From there I slowly worked my way through the lead group until, at around the six kilometre mark, I came upon the lead guy. He heard my footfall as I approached and looked over his shoulder. He was startled when he saw me, and tried to speed up, but it was no use. I passed him then went flat out for the finish. Over the last couple of kilometres I ran like my life depended on it, I really wanted to put as much distance between the infantry guys and me as I could.

I ended up finishing that run in thirty six minutes, which is a respectable time. Once I had crossed the line one of the paramedics, who were on standby, shouted over to me; he wanted to know which regiment I came from. When I told him that I came from the REP he smiled, rubbed his hands together, then went over to his colleagues to collect his winnings; they had been betting on the outcome of the race. The next person came in nearly five minutes after me, and when he asked for my time his face dropped. I could tell that he knew that he wasn't going to beat that. I extended my hand to him, to shake on a race well run, and that was the last of any obnoxious bragging.

After the second round of tests were finished we packed up the trucks then watched them leave for Bertrandou without us. We had to march there. However, it was an easy march for us now; the route was so familiar that we didn't even need the map.

Our second visit to the farm was just as intense as the first. However, we were over halfway through the course now and we had gotten used to how things went. We were making far fewer mistakes and working much better together. In fact we made so few mistakes that the instructors had to make things up.

Every morning while we were at the farm, the instructors would get a delivery from a nearby bakery, and each morning someone would have to go down to the farmhouse, meet the van, and bring the pastries back to the camp, then set their breakfast table. Well, one morning they called an assembly and claimed that one of their pain au chocolats was missing, and because we were thieving bastards they were going to beast us into extinction. From morning until noon we did the big obstacle course that ran through the woods, non-stop. After lunch we marched and sang for four hours. Then in the evening we were given another trench to dig. We had until six the next morning to dig a two metre deep trench that was big enough to fit all of us in. As soon as the instructors were gone, there were many among us who were ready to tear Laffon to shreds (he had been the one who was tasked with collecting the pastries that morning). He had also consistently slowed us down on nearly every march, and it was he who had been in his boxers when the instructors found us before. Most people would have taken any excuse to give him a hiding, but the more level headed among us, realized that it was all a ruse. The instructors couldn't not punish us because we were following all the rules; this was the corporal's course, we had to be run ragged twenty-four seven. Eventually everyone calmed down and realized that not even Laffon was stupid enough to steal one of their pastries and think that he could get away with it.

During this second outing to the farm, we did a lot of training on how to command a fireteam. This is not too technical, but it is important to get right; fireteams are the atoms out of which the modern infantry is built. It is also the main role of a corporal in a combat company, but practising fire and movement drills gets pretty tiring after a while. You are constantly getting up, running, and then laying back down, over and over again. In a way, it's similar to doing burpees. All that activity builds up a healthy appetite, but no one was looking forward to meal times. At the start of the course we had gone to the stores and taken all the rations that we would need for our time at the farm in one go. Unfortunately for us, every box of rations we had taken was the same menu. All we had to eat was cassoulet: It was cassoulet for lunch and cassoulet for dinner, every day. Cassoulet is beans and sausages, so you can imagine the flatulence that it produces. At night you were constantly assaulted by foul smelling gas clouds that crept through our camp like mustard gas. It was pretty awful, and a fart cloud would always hit you just as you were drifting off to sleep; and let me tell you that inhaling a lung full of retched fart gas woke you up like a bolt of electricity.

Having to eat the same food every day was just another straw on the camel's back. It made the farm just that bit harder. There were people who lost it at times and times and flew into a rage or wallowed in despair. However, sometimes, when we were tired from days of not sleeping, being beasted, and eating the same food. Times when you thought things couldn't get any worse; that everyone would just burst out into hysterical laughter. Sometimes it was at the absurdity of our situation, other times it was at something that was said. Things that wouldn't cause much laughter under normal circumstances. Those were the good times at the farm, and they are the moments that have stuck in my memory.

When our second visit at the farm came to an end we were split into four groups and told to walk back. So that we couldn't meet up, like the last time, each group was driven a short distance away and dropped off. My group was dropped off on a hill, located a couple off kilometres from the main road that ran between Carcassonne and Castelnaudary. All we had to do was reach the main road, then follow it back to base. However, to get there by road we would have to take a rather circuitous route, whereas if we took a shortcut through the fields we could considerably reduce the journey. As always, I advised that we should take the road because it was guaranteed to get us there, but I was outvoted and we started off across the fields.

The route started off alright, we got through the first field with no problems. The second field was full of sunflowers and didn't pose any problems. There was a small hedge at the other end of that field, but we found a gap and got through. Now there were only two fields between us and the main road. As we walked down the third field the ground began to get wet, soon it was a complete bog. We managed to find our way to the edge of the field, even if it did get everyone's trainers wet and covered in mud, but, alas, it was all for nothing; there was a huge thick hedge that ran the length if the field with no gate and a sizable ditch in front of it, full with water. There was nothing for it but to turn back.

When we reached the road, where we had started off, the feeling among the group was one of despair. We had wasted a fair bit of time and effort trying to cut across the fields, and it was now questionable if we would make it back in time for assembly the next morning. We decided that the only thing for it was to get to the main road, then try to hitch a ride with a lorry driver.

We got down to the main road and began the march towards Castelnaudary. Every time we saw a truck approaching we all stopped and stuck our thumbs out. To everyone's surprise, after only the third try, someone stopped and offered us a lift. He had just finished a delivery and was on his way back to Castelnaudary. We all climbed in the back of his truck and fifteen minutes later we were outside the regiment. It was not long after midnight, but we couldn't just go in now because someone would know that we had cheated, so we lay down on the grass next to the back gate and got some sleep. When the first of the other groups arrived we got up and entered the regiment with them.

There was now roughly three weeks left of the course. The first of which would be spent at the 4RE. That week would be mostly spent doing classroom work. For the second week, we would be going to Caylus to practice using all the weapons that we needed to know. The last week would be spent at Castelnaudary, doing the final tests.

The first week back at base was pretty mundane. The one notable thing was that there was a bit swine flu doing the rounds. The infirmary was full of people suffering from it. By the time I caught it there was nothing to do but wait for it to pass. I couldn't understand what all the fuss was about; swine flu didn't seem any worse than most colds that I had caught before and within a week it was gone.

After a relatively relaxing week back in the regiment we set off for Caylus. We would be staying there for almost a week, and at the end of the week we would do our first couple of tests.

When we arrived at Caylus, we went to the back of the camp; to an area where I had never been before. There was nothing in this part of the camp except for a wooden barn and a small wooden shed. However, we wouldn't be sleeping in either; as usual we slept outside.

This week was one of the easiest for me and the other lads who were in combat companies. Most of us had been made to memorize every detail of the weapons, and had no problem using them. Every night we also had some orienteering to do while we were here. The training ground at Caylus was enormous and these orienteering courses didn't leave much time for sleep. There was one night that was particularly difficult, and nobody found all the markers; we spent the whole night searching.

At the end of the week we took the arms test. This was pretty straight forward; you had to be able to assemble, disassemble, load, and fire, all the weapons. You also had to know all the specs for any given firearm. The instructors would also present you with a FAMAS that wouldn't fire, and gave you a few seconds to fix the problem, and fire it (this is child's play for anyone who has used a FAMAS, because the damn thing malfunctions so often that you soon become a black belt in sorting out problems with it).

After the weapons tests were done with, we had to do our orienteering test. For this we would be split into pairs. I was in one of the last pairs to be sent out. As I ran up the road leading away from our camp area, I heard a couple of people thrashing around in the bushes just off to the side. They were shouting and cursing at each other for not being able to find the marker. I could tell that this course was going to be difficult.

An hour later, when I had just finished collecting all the markers that were in proximity to the road, I came across another pair who had been going the other way around, and, of course, we copied each other's markers, but luck just so had it that we had the same sheets. I was now complete, but it was too soon to go back, so we walked back down to our sleeping area and climbed into our sleeping bags and rested for a while. Then after a few others had finished and passed by the sergeant, I went over to the little wooden shed to hand in the sheet.

I entered, presented to the sergeant, and handed over my sheet. He studied it with a fine-toothed comb, trying to spot any evidence that we had cheated. Then he looked over at the sheets of the people who had already finished. He came to one sheet, raised his eyebrows and said 'you're sheet is the same as so-and-so's.' It was clear that he was trying to trick me into making a response that would be tantamount to admitting that I had cheated, but I was one step ahead of him and answered that, I wouldn't know what was on anyone else's sheet. Maybe I was too blunt, because the expression on his face changed instantly. He was clearly aware, that I had just checkmated him, and he didn't look too pleased about it. He stared at me with contempt for a few seconds, trying to think of a way that he could come back at me. He knew that I had cheated, and I knew that he knew I had cheated, but I had given a watertight answer. He eventually broke eye contact and dismissively waved me out of the room. He was obviously annoyed that I had outfoxed him, but fortunately this was the end of the course and he couldn't exact his revenge on me; or so I thought.

When we got back to Castelnaudary we were given the weekend off. That Sunday I was over in the on-base pizzeria with Durant. We were enjoying a meal and watching the final stage of the Tour de France on the big screen TV that was hung on the wall. Durant, who was a keen sports fan, proudly told me that an Englishman had never won the final stage of tour, in Paris. What happened over the next couple of hours was priceless. The British rider Bradley Wiggins, gradually worked his way to the front of the race, and as he did the look of disbelief on Durant's face got starker and starker, until finally he cruised over the finish line on the Champs Élysées. I turned to Durant, once he had finished cursing, and said, 'that's your fault that is, you should have kept quiet.' He was not impressed.

The last week of the course started just like the first; with the physical tests. I was confident of getting a good score on these. We did all three in a row again, and again I came first on the eight kilometre run. There was however a surprise with the obstacle course. I had consistently finished this in around the three minute mark, give or take a few seconds. This time however my time was read out as four and a half minutes. This shocked me at first, until I remembered that the person doing the timing was the sergeant who I had pissed off during the orienteering. That sneaky Russian bastard had found a way to get me back, but I couldn't be mad about it. It was my own fault for cheating in the first place; but I sure as hell didn't see it coming.

The rest of the final week was spent in the classroom. Some of the tests were rather difficult. One of the questions on the Legion history test was: *In what year did the infantry regiment move its base from the previous location to the current one?* What the hell kind of question is that, I thought. I don't think anyone, not even

303

the Francophones, got a hundred percent on that test. The classroom exams were tough, but for the people who didn't understand written French they were near impossible. To make it worse, the tests weren't multiple choice or anything like that; you had to pull the answer from your brain and write it down. A few poor bastards scored a big fat zero on some of the written tests.

During this last week one of the groups doing their sergeant's course had finished and were having their end of course ceremony. They needed a few extra people to help with the proceedings and I was chosen to go hold the pin cushion with all their brevets on. This meant I had to go over to the officer's mess for the days leading up to it and drill. On the day of the ceremony as I was stood opposite the group of corporals who were about to be promoted to sergeant, I spotted my buddy Cpl Bernard. He had been here the whole time that I was, but these courses keep you so busy that you don't have time to notice anything else. My job in the ceremony was to wait for the guys who came first, second, and third to get called out of the row, then I had to walk up to the colonel with them. After that I just had to move along with the colonel as he pinned their brevets on them. Once the first three were done the colonel read out the results for the rest of the guys. It made me smile when I heard Cpl Bernard's name get called out at around the halfway point. I knew that an egotistical narcissist like him would hate not coming top, but he always was a mediocre piece of crap.

A couple of days later I had my own finishing ceremony to attend. To my surprise I finished in second place (I think that this was mostly due to me dominating on the physical tests). Durant had finished in first place, and he deserved it; he had given it his all on this course. More importantly we had maintained the reputation of the parachute regiment. We had slogged it out with the infantry guys, and the chief instructor had been true to his word and marked us on our merit. The other two guys who came from Calvi had also managed a nice one-two, but at the other end of the spectrum. Which was, in my opinion, an even more impressive feat, because there was far more competition for last place than for first.

No one failed the course. The Foreign Legion couldn't afford to fail anyone, because the desertion rate was too high. They only way that you could have failed this course was to get injured and not be able to complete it. There is a joke in the Legion that goes like this: *What do you call someone who came last on their corporal's course? – A Corporal.*

15: En Taule

Stone walls do not a prison make,
nor iron bars a cage.
Richard Lovelace

When I got back to Calvi my company was getting ready to go on holiday. While everyone was away I would be staying with a bunch of new recruits in the amphibious centre. My job was to take them through a bit of basic training and familiarize them with life at the REP. I was officially promoted to corporal a couple of days my return from the course. There is no increase in salary for being made corporal (that doesn't happen until you make corporal-chef, or sergeant), but life in the regiment was completely different. No longer did I feel like I was trapped in perpetual basic training. The sergeants spoke to me like normal human being too (except for Sgt Cabrão, he was still a massive dick-cheese). There was no more working in the mess, or sweeping and mopping to do, but there were other jobs that I could now do. My first job as a corporal was to go and work in the company office. This work isn't hard but the day is long (seventeen hours long to be exact). Thankfully the service only lasts a week and you only have to do it once every three months or so.

When the company went on holiday, I moved down to the amphibious centre with the new guys. It felt good to be training the next bunch of legionnaires for the company. It was as if I had come full circle. With the company on holiday there wasn't much to do, and the time I spent down at the amphibious centre was a holiday in itself.

When the company returned, I re-joined my section. I didn't have much time to hang around though, because I was sent off on another course. However, this time I would be staying on Corsica. I had to learn to drive the VAB. The course was only two weeks long, and although it was a driving test, we still had to spend most of our time sleeping out of base.

Driving the VAB was a bit tricky. Inside it looked like an airplane cockpit; there were switches and dials everywhere. Just starting it up involved flipping a series of switches in the right order, and it was a pain in the arse to drive once you did get it going. It wouldn't drive in a straight line so you had to constantly adjust the steering, and the shape of it meant that you couldn't see anything behind you.

After the first week, which we spent familiarising ourselves with the VAB and getting accustomed to driving it. We got ready to depart for the military training ground of Frasselli, which is on the southern tip of Corsica. It was one hell of a trip to make in the VABs, which were not built for speed. Frasselli is a large training ground, with plenty of difficult terrain for us to test our skills on. The building where we slept was an old cow shed, and even though it had been thoroughly cleaned, the stench of cow dung was overpowering.

While at Frasselli we put our VABs through their paces. Each day we would go out and find somewhere to get stuck, then we would have to get ourselves out. The nights were spent practising driving with night vision googles on. This was difficult because the googles restricted your field of vision. As with all the other driving tests there was a book to go with this one, and I spent my free time doing my best to memorize what I thought would come up on the test.

Over the last couple of days that we spent down at Frasselli
we took our theory and practical tests. Then when the testing was
over with we formed a convoy and drove the long journey back up
to Calvi. It was a relief to get out of the concrete shed that was
haunted by the ghosts of cowpats past. However, after spending a
week in there, all my stuff now smelt just like it.

A couple of days after returning from the course all the
participants had to line up in front of the company building to get
the results. I was shocked when they read my name out first.
Apparently I was the master at driving VABs. It was nice to come
first on a course at last, but I would have preferred if it wasn't this
one; I was worried that the company might mark me down as a
driver for Afghanistan. I didn't want to be stuck in a vehicle: I
wanted to be out on foot where all the action was.

After the VAB driving was over with I finally got to go back
to my section and relax. For the first few weeks I took 'corporal du
jour,' which basically means that you give the orders, and make
sure that everybody goes where they are supposed to and does their
job properly. If you aren't corporal du jour, then you can pretty
much just stay in your room all day (unless you have service, or
there is some kind of instruction). However, corporal du jour was
not to remain easy for long. Some new legionnaires had arrived at
the section. Among them was a Russian named Marshall.

Marshall was in his mid-thirties and from his mannerisms I
would guess that prior to joining he had been living on the streets,
or in prison. He was on the take for everything that he could get.
All he wanted to do was eat, sleep, and wait for his salary. He
made out that he understood no French whatsoever, and just stared
at you blankly whenever you gave him an order. However, that
was easy to get around because seventy percent of the people at the
REP spoke Russian, but, even when the order was explained to
him in Russian, he still managed to get it wrong. My guess was
that he was trying to gain the system, he thought that if he
pretended not to understand, and made a terrible mess of
everything that people would stop asking him to do things.

It was unreal how stupid he was. I would send him off to clean the company but he would never make it over there. The sergeant from the company office would then come to me and demand to know why I hadn't sent anyone. I would send people from the section to find him but it was no use, and I would end up sending someone else in his place. The bastard was probably curled up in the grass somewhere having a kip, or hiding in the bins. I once sent him to work in the club and, a couple of hours later, had to change him. He had been tasked with making the sandwiches, but people began to complain that there wasn't any ham in them: He had eaten half of it, and filled his pockets with the rest! The corporal-chef beat him all the way back up to the section and banned him from entering there ever again. So that was one bit of work he got out of doing. He also got banned from working in the mess for the same reason.

A good example of the mentality of the man, is a story from when he was on guard duty. He had been placed on guard over at the munitions depot, but no sooner had he been dropped off than he scaled the fence and appeared outside the guard house demanding a coffee. When he did stay at his guard post he would just go and find somewhere to sleep and not bother about waking up in time for the changeover. This meant that you had to search for him in every nook and cranny. He was completely useless as far as the military was concerned. I don't know how he managed to make it past the initial tests at Aubagne and all the way through basic training.

Marshall soon became famous for his blundering and stupidity. He was the laughing stock of the regiment and this did not go down well with the other Russians. He was giving them a bad image. One day he was invited to big get together of Russians somewhere on the base. He went along quite happily; thinking that he was going to have a drink and play some cards. However, when he came back it was clear that a trap had been set for him. His head was twice its original size. He had been beaten black and blue for disgracing the name of Russia, but it didn't change him, he was still his old useless self. After that incident, the other Russians refused to speak to him in their language. He would have to understand French, or desert.

Not long after Marshall had had his head beaten in, he was kicked out of his room. Sch Buttkis called me over to the office and told me that he was going to be staying with me. I don't know why I was chosen; perhaps they thought that I would be a positive influence on him, but I wasn't happy at all about this. Having him in the section was bad enough, but having him in my room was pure hell. His personal hygiene standards were worse than those of a heroin addict. When he took his boots off the smell from his feet filled the room. He never washed his clothes, brushed his teeth, made his bed, or woke up in the morning. Having him in my room was like looking after a child.

One evening, after I had returned from guard duty, I came back to my room to find the place in a mess. It was like there had been five people squatting in there. When I told him to clean it up he told me that he couldn't because he had to go clean the company building. I waited for him to come back, but he didn't appear. He was trying to avoid coming back to the room before lights out, so that I had to clear up his mess. This really pissed me off, and if he thought that he was going to get one over on me he was wrong. I sat down and tried to think of the best solution. Then I noticed that his locker didn't have a padlock on it. I took all of his stuff out of his locker and put it in the closet that was between the toilets and showers. The closet had a light and plenty of pipes for him to hang his clothes on. It was also more than long enough for him to lie down in; I thought that it was perfect for him. Then I went back to the room and waited.

He came back not long after lights out. I was sitting at the table near the door, and I watched him walk in and go to his locker. He opened the door, and seeing that all his stuff was gone, looked over at me. I stood up and motioned for him to follow me. I led him into the toilets and opened the closet door. When he saw his new room, he was not best pleased, to say the least. He tried to argue, but I told him to shut his mouth, and warned him that if he came back in my room during the night, I would kick ten bales of shit out of him. Yes, it was mean to make him sleep in the closet, but I wasn't picking on him for no reason. He was a freeloading piece of crap, who expected to do as little, and take as much, as he could. The Legion wasn't going to kick him out, because they needed to keep their numbers up, so it was up to me to get rid of him.

After a week or so of him sleeping in the toilets, I was called over to the company building: Marshall had reported me for bullying (it was to be expected I suppose). Later that same evening he came back over to the room with a sergeant from the first section. The sergeant explained to me that I had to take care of him and there was to be no more banishing people to the toilets. When the sergeant left, Marshall grinned at me and asked which bed was he to sleep in. 'Which bed motherfucker?' I snapped, 'which fucking bed, you've got to be having a laugh? Get the fuck back in your closet now.' He tried to protest by reminding me of what the sergeant had just said, but I told him that I didn't give a shit what the sergeant said. He was going to sleep in the closet and that was that. He got angry with me and gave me a look that said he wanted to kick my ass. I wasn't having that, so I asked if he would prefer sleeping in the infirmary instead. He got the message and moped off back to the toilets. He had gambled that by going to the captain and reporting me for bullying that he could hamstring me, and I would be forced to let him stay in my room, but he had lost.

A few days after his return to the toilets, I sent Marshall to go clean the company at midday. A while later the company office sent a legionnaire over to ask why no one from my section had been over to do the cleaning. This was a fairly normal occurrence with Marshall; he would often wander off somewhere in the regiment when you sent him to do a job, then return a short while later claiming that he had misunderstood and gone to the wrong place; but this time he didn't come back. He had finally deserted, and he had taken the cleaning equipment with him. I chuckled when I imagined him wandering around Corsica with his mop and broom offering to do odd jobs for people.

As soon as anyone deserts from the Legion people descend upon their belongings like a plague of locusts. As I had been the first to know of his disappearance I was the first to see what he had left behind. There wasn't much, and certainly nothing worth taking. The only items that he had left were his clothes, so, just for some fun, I got some scissors and cut all his trousers into assless chaps. It would have been hilarious if they caught him, and he had to come back; he would have to walk round the regiment wearing them.

The next day when the NCOs came by to see what they could scavenge from Marshall, there was another priceless moment from my time at the Legion. Sch Buttkis came over to look through his stuff, and I'll never forget the look on his face, when he pulled out a pair of his trousers, spun them around, and saw that the ass had been cut out. He was gobsmacked and didn't know what to make of it. After a couple of seconds of staring at the trousers with a perplexed gaze, he put them back and said to me with a straight face, 'Well, I don't know where he thought he was going to wear those. What a strange lad.'

It wasn't until two or three weeks later that I found out what had happened to Marshall. A report came to the regiment from the local gendarmerie that he had been arrested after a farmer spotted a man hanging around his sheep, and called them to come get him. It turned out that he had been bedding down in the sheep shed for the entire time since he left (hopefully he wasn't fornicating with them during that time, but I wouldn't put it past him).

Up until now the company had been doing a lot of training in preparation for our deployment to Afghanistan early next year. We had recently changed captains and my section had changed Lieutenants. I don't think that our previous Lieutenant was up to the job so they shipped him off.

Our new captain a serious man; he was very strict and a bit of a fitness fanatic. People who had gotten away with being lazy slobs and making their subordinates do all their work were in for a shock, and the new captain didn't give a shit about your rank. If you weren't pulling your weight he would tell you. This made a lot of people dislike him, but, for my part, I liked the man.

Now that it was coming up for Christmas we stopped our training and began to prepare for the festivities. As I was alone in my room I had to give it up, so that it could be made into a bar. In the REP each section must also make a bar, on top of all the other Christmas activities. I was tasked with painting murals on the walls. It was easy work and when the bar was finished it looked quite good. I painted a Viking long ship along one wall and painted the shields of the warriors with the flag of each nationality that we had at the section. I covered the opposite wall with cave art, copied from the famous caves at Lascaux. The rest of the bar was decorated with camouflage netting and coloured parachutes.

On Christmas day we had to go over to the technical zone and have our meal in one of the hangars. There is a cabaret show where each section does a comedy sketch, satirising daily life in the Foreign Legion. NCOs aren't allowed to take part in the sketch, and those doing the sketch aren't allowed to make fun of anyone under the rank of sergeant. There were the odd performances that were funny, but on the whole I didn't enjoy them. There was always a few Legion songs (the bane of my life) that had to be sung, and of course there were Christmas presents to be dished out. Normally the presents were pretty decent: a piece of equipment, or something useful, but that year it was a big A4 sized book about the Foreign Legion. It seemed very questionable to me. They were probably given money from the government to produce that book, and then they made us buy it as a Christmas present (the presents were bought with the profit from the company club). After the meal we returned to the section and began drinking in the bar, but it wasn't long before fights broke out. Our bar was shut down early, and everyone sent to bed.

Once Christmas was over and done with we got to go on a four week vacation. I had already been to the British Embassy in Paris and received a replacement passport, so I decided to go to Southeast Asia for my next holiday and enjoy a bit of winter sun. However, this turned out to be a bad decision because I ended up returning late from my holiday. This earned me a month in Legion prison, which meant I would miss the departure of our deployment to Afghanistan. The prospect of not going to Afghanistan with my company was bad enough without a month in the Legion's prison, but there was nothing I could do.

If you ask anyone from the officer class about Legion prison they will probably deny that there is such a thing, but there most definitely is. In fact there is a saying in the REP: *'You aren't a real legionnaire until you have been in the prison.'* The prison itself is hidden away inside the guard house. The guard building is long and thin, and it goes round in a square. There is a concrete courtyard in the centre and that's where the prison is. The front two faces of the building are where the guards stay, and the back two are the prison. There are no doors from the prison to the outside. The only way out is through the guard house or over the roof, but that has barbed wire on it. Only grades up to corporal-chef go to prison (although it is rare for a corporal-chef to be given time in jail). If a sergeant commits a punishable offence and he lives in the regiment, then he would be made to stay in his room on evenings and weekends. If you live outside of the regiment then there is fuck all they can do to you. The rules in the jail are pretty harsh, you aren't allowed to: listen to music, watch TV, read, sit down, walk, or speak to anyone who isn't associated with the prison.

While in prison you are not allowed to wear anything that shows your rank, and you will be worked from sunrise to sunset. The day normally begins with everyone putting all of their belongings in their rucksack and running round the parade ground. Then the prison, and prisoners, will be inspected by the head of security. After that the day will begin. The work is mostly sweeping and gardening, but you will have to do other maintenance work such as: repairing damaged gates and fences, painting, etc. The last job of the day is to clean the command building. After the work is done, sometime around eight o'clock, you will be issued with a single blanket and locked in the cell, which is just an empty room with a toilet a one end, and a long thin window on one wall, just big enough to put your arm through.

During my time in jail, the first job we had to do every morning was sweep all the roads in the regiment. Then in the afternoon we would be given some more interesting tasks. The second week I was in jail we were tasked with clearing out the old library. I wasn't aware that there had ever been a library in the regiment. The inside of it was full of dust and mould. It appeared that the place hadn't been in use in over a decade. While we were clearing everything away I had a look at the books, and I found a small section of English ones. Among them was 'The Elegant Universe' by Brian Greene. I love science books so I secreted it about my person and took it back to the jail with me. I read it during our lunch break, when the people guarding us went to the mess. It didn't last though, and a couple of days later I came back after working to find that our quarters had been searched and the book was gone.

The prison was infested with rats; there was a hole in the concrete next to the sink to let the water drain away, and inside was an army of the furry bastards. If you left any food uncovered for a second they would run out and snatch a morsel, then dart back into their hole. I had great fun trying to catch them. I would put a scrap of food out and wait just inside the door to our eating area with a broom ready to spring out and hit them, but the rats were too smart. They never ventured far enough from their bolt hole for me to be able to get them. If you placed the food too far from their hole they wouldn't take it. I once managed to whack one of them on the rear end with a broom, but that was the closest I ever got.

The prison was the only place in the regiment that had a rat problem. The rest of the regiment was overrun with feral cats. The prison yard was completely sealed off from the outside and the roofs around it were covered in barbed wire, so it was like a rat citadel. The feral cats were also a giant pain in the arse; they hung around the bins and scavenged for scraps. They were infested with fleas, and their faces were scared up from being cut by tin cans and fighting. They most definitely weren't cute. The worst thing was when they would give birth in the bins. You would go to throw away your rubbish and, when you opened the bin to dump it off, a deranged mother cat would fly out hissing and clawing at you. It's unfortunate that they chose the bins as the place to have their litters because the number of kittens that must have been crushed to death in the back of a garbage truck was surely pretty high.

You can be sent to prison in the Legion for pretty much anything, for example: failing a course, wearing civilian clothes, not wearing your uniform correctly, going to a town other than Calvi on your weekend, getting married, getting a second passport, owning a computer or telephone without permission, and leaving France during your holiday. There are many ways that you can land yourself in Legion prison and the chances are that over the course of your five year contract you will go there at least once. I have a friend who went mountain climbing on holiday. During the holiday there was an alert and everyone was called back to the regiment. There is, of course, no signal up in the mountains and he didn't find out until he came back down. When he arrived back at the regiment, a day or two late, he was given a month in jail.

If you rack up over a certain amount of jail time (which I think is six months, but I could be wrong) you will get discharged from the Legion, but because of the manpower problem this rule is not strictly enforced. While I was in jail I met a Polish legionnaire who had nearly a years' worth of jail time. He got out, halfway through my time in there, and a couple of days later was back. I later heard that he had another month added to his time for smuggling in alcohol, so he ended up with over a year of jail time in total.

Some people actively tried to get sent to jail. While you were in jail you weren't required to jump or go on exercises. So if you heard that there was a week of intense jumping coming up, or an exercise that involved a hundred kilometre death march; all you had to do was stay out in town all night and miss the morning roll call, and you would miss it. It was also a good way of saving up some money, because you can't go to the shops, but still receive full wages.

When my month in jail was over, I was sent to the CAS (Administration & Support Company). There was a small contingent of the third company there who had stayed behind to train new legionnaires while the company was away. I moved into a room in one of second company's empty buildings. I was glad to see that Sgt Saiko was there too (the Legion obviously didn't want him shooting off any ball sacks in Afghanistan). There were roughly thirty new legionnaires that we needed to put through their paces while the company was away, so we had our hands full.

I was now part of CAS for the foreseeable future and this meant dealing with their captain; Cpt Pavilhard. The captain of the CAS was a French guy who had worked his way up from the rank legionnaire, and he was a roaring bastard. He had a permanent chip on his shoulder, and thought that he was the most badass swinging dick to ever walk the earth. His attitude was most likely due to the fact that he had started out as a 'Fut-Fut' corporal, which meant that he had gone through an accelerated promotion program. If you show 'leadership qualities' (good deep-throating technique) during the basic training at Castelnaudary you have the opportunity to stay there an additional eight months and become a corporal after only one year of service.

Fut-Fut corporals are generally not respected in the Legion (especially in the parachute regiment), because they haven't been through the hardships that most legionnaires face when they first arrive at their regiment. Cpt Pavilhard would have really had to prove himself to the people at his new regiment, and it was more than likely that he was subject to bullying, insubordination, and probably had the crap beaten out of him on a regular basis.

Cpt Pavilhard thought of himself as the ultimate warrior, and he was not happy that he had ended up captaining the CAS (legionnaires who become officers aren't allowed to command combat companies). It was clear that he held most of the people there in contempt. He tried to run the company like it was the Spetsnaz; arranging as many training exercises, and jump days, as he could. This didn't go down well with the people at there, who were mostly older legionnaires who had left the combat companies precisely to get away from all that kind of thing, and who just wanted to serve out the remainder of their contracts working in a supporting role rather than on the front lines.

The captain of the CAS was also the biggest supplier of fresh prisoners to the jailhouse. Every Monday there was a line of people waiting outside his office to pass review. I feel confident in saying that there wasn't a single person in that company who had anything positive to say about him. However, he didn't break my balls that much, or any of the other NCOs from the third company. I think this was because we were still in a combat company and he didn't consider us lazy. Also I think he was pleased to have a platoon of new legionnaires attached to his company, because it gave him a chance to come on training exercises with us and feel like he was a soldier.

The first time that Cpt Pavilhard came out with us, was to a nearby shooting range. I think a few of the guys will have PTSD about that day. There was one Scandinavian legionnaire who he developed a particular disliking to. We were practising fire and movement drills and this Scandinavian legionnaire, who was new to the military, kept making mistakes. The captain started off by shouting at him, thinks like: 'you suck caribou dicks,' 'stop thinking about caribou's arseholes,' and, 'all that caribou sperm that you've drunk must have rotted your brain, you caribou fucker.' It was pretty harsh stuff, but the shouting was not enough, and the captain escalated to physical assault. He ran over to this poor guy and beat him while screaming 'putain sucer des caribous' at him, then he picked him up by his rucksack, and threw him. This happened all throughout the day, and that legionnaire's name became (as far as Cpt Pavilhard was concerned at least): 'Sucer des caribous.'

Fortunately for everyone, on the second day of shooting we had a journalist turn up and the captain had to wind his neck in. The journalist was an American who was writing a book on the Foreign Legion. He looked a bit like a hippy (smelt like one too), but he was nice enough. I was given the job of explaining what was going on, during the training exercise to him, and we got chatting. He told me that he had spent a little bit of time at Castelnaudary. He had also spent time at some of the other regiments. Now he was staying at the REP for a week, before he flew out to Afghanistan.

The next time that I did some training that involved Cpt Pavilhard was a day of jumping. We were scheduled to jump at three airports in a day. The first two were on Mainland France, and last was our own airport at Calvi. I was the only corporal in our platoon, and the guys that I was training had just finished jump school. It was a lot of work making sure that they put their parachutes on correctly before the jump, and after we landed I would also have to make sure that no one got lost. Fortunately, I had done this type of exercise many times before, but the captain, of course, had to go the extra mile. We were told to treat the exercise like the real deal. No one was to fold their parachute after landing; we were to leave it wherever we landed, and complete the mission first.

The first jump went well and the landing was nice and soft due to a thick blanket of snow that covered everything, except the tarmac. There were a couple of injuries from people landing directly on the runway, but all in all it was a success. Then we lined up at the end of the runway, got back on the plane, and set off for the next airfield. This time after landing I could hear the captain going nuts at someone for folding up their parachute, but it wasn't anyone from my platoon, so that was OK. The second airfield that we jumped at was only a stone's throw away from the 4RE, in Castelnaudary. We had travelled all the way across France from east to west. The injured people were starting to build up now. There was a group of about seven guys sat at the back of the plane who couldn't jump.

We had started the day early at the airport of St Catherine in Calvi, and by the time we got back for the third and final jump it was almost dark. Everyone was exhausted after that day. We had equipped in the airplane for each of the jumps, which always adds to the fun. However, there was no time to rest as tomorrow we had an even more difficult exercise to go through.

The next day I was back over at the airport. This time we would be jumping out over Lac de Nino. Lac de Nino is a lake that sits almost two kilometres above sea level. The lake is frozen over during winter. It is fairly safe to parachute onto; the difficult part is getting back down from the mountains. The lake is one of the prominent features of the GR20, but I didn't get do see it as it is about ten kilometre south of Vergio (the place where we finished the march).

My day didn't start off too well, as I received a torrent of abuse from the captain at the airport. He spotted that the green top I was wearing under my uniform wasn't the French standard issue one. I had taken the effort to order my cold weather gear from Norway. The shirt I had was made from Merino wool and had a second layer made out of net material that trapped air. It really kept you warm. From the outside it looked almost identical to the French one except that it was a darker shade of green. The captain noticed it the moment he laid eyes on me. He walked over, grabbed my collar, and yanked it up. Then began screaming about how unprofessional, and what a disgrace to the Legion, I was. Luckily he didn't make me pass report for it at a later date. In the Legion everything has to be 'règlementaire.' You have to be careful what equipment you buy, because you might not be allowed to use it. I think this was mostly due to the insurance company, but it was also a good excuse for jealous and bitter people to exert power over you. There was definitely an element of, 'if I don't have it, you can't have it either.'

After staying with the CAS for around a fortnight, I was told to put on my dress uniform and report to the captain's office. I went over and lined up with the others who were passing report that day. When I got inside the office I was surprised to find out that I wasn't being punished, instead I had been called over because someone had fallen down a mountainside in Afghanistan and injured their shoulder, and I was being called up as a replacement. My orders were to go and pack my bags, then pass by the transport office and get my ticket for Paris. I would be travelling with group of French soldiers in a couple of days' time. I was thrilled that I would finally be going to re-join my company in Afghanistan. Up until then I was convinced that I would have to spend six months at the CAS.

Two days later I was again on board the ferry from Bastia to Marseille. I had to meet the French regiment that I would be travelling with in Charles de Gaulle airport the next day. I had no trouble getting to Paris and locating the group of soldiers that I would be travelling with, but then I received word that our flight had been cancelled, and we would have to wait until tomorrow for the next one.

That night everyone was put up in a nearby hotel at the expense of the French government. Now that I was with the regular army, things were a bit more relaxed, and everyone was allowed to go out and visit Paris. I grabbed that opportunity with both hands, and headed straight for the nearest KFC, then had a couple of pints in an Australian bar.

The following day we went back over to the airport at around midday and after a few hours wait, we were allowed to board the plane. When I arrived at passport control, I handed my passport over to the customs officer and he straight away took issue with me. 'This is a temporary passport, why don't you have a full one?' He asked. When I opened my mouth to explain he became more alarmed. 'Wait, you're not even French! What the hell is going on here?' He said to me. He was just about to get up and go find one of his superiors, when the colonel who I was travelling with entered his cubicle from behind, put his hand on the guy's shoulder and sat him back down in his chair. The colonel told him to let me through, but the customs officer kept protesting, 'but…but…this isn't right.' The colonel didn't take any notice of him, and just looked up at me and waved me through.

16: Afghanistan

Bombing Afghanistan back into the Stone
Age was quite a favourite headline for some
wobbly liberals. The slogan does all the work.
But an instant's thought shows that Afghanistan
is being, if anything, bombed out of the Stone
Age.
Christopher Hitchens

I touched down in Kabul at the beginning of March 2010.
Osama bin Laden was still alive and the war in Afghanistan was in
its ninth year. The first thing you notice about Kabul is how
colourless it is. The buildings are the same beige colour as the
ground and mountains that surround them. After landing I was
driven to, the aptly named, 'camp warehouse' on the eastern edge
of the city. It was a NATO camp and was home to soldiers from
many different countries. Everyone had their own sealed off
compound and there was very little opportunity to mix. I stayed in
a pop-up plastic building at the western edge of the camp. I was
told that I would have to wait a couple of days for a convoy to
arrive from the Legion base, in Surobi.

While at the camp, I wandered around and went to each country's PX (shop) to see what kind of equipment they had. I quickly found out that I wasn't allowed to buy much from the stores that weren't French. I guess that they only have a limited supply and they don't want everyone clearing them out in a couple of days. Camp warehouse was pretty boring. I spent most of the day in my room. The only thing I did while I was there was escort a French colonel to another nearby base. The colonel was shitting himself about having to drive through Kabul. He already had a full guard, but he wanted me to come along so that I could sit in the boot and protect the rear.

After a few days, a convoy from the Foreign Legion base arrived at the camp. I was told to gather up my things and go wait by the main gate. While I was waiting to be picked up I saw a couple of armoured vehicles approaching. There were quite a few bullet-proof cars parked around the gate area, but it soon became apparent that whoever was driving couldn't see them, because the last APC ploughed straight into one of the parked pickups and ripped the front end off. The person driving the APC didn't even stop; he got the fuck out of the camp as quickly as he could. The driver of the pickup was flabbergasted when he returned to see his truck looking like it had just been skull-fucked by Optimus Prime.

Not long after that incident, I was picked up by the guys from the Legion. Every time you travel in Afghanistan you must wear body armour and a helmet. I was also handed a gun before getting in and told to stand in the back turret. I was told that although the FOB (forward operating base) was only around sixty kilometres away, the journey would take two or three hours, because our route was a difficult one to navigate.

We left the camp, got out of Kabul, and then followed the turquoise waters of the Kabul River into the mountains. The mountain pass that we were now on was the most difficult part of the trip. Kabul sits on a plateau that is almost a kilometre higher than the nearby Surobi district we were heading to. To one side of the road there was a solid rock face, and on the other was a rather steep drop with plenty of jagged rocks, and the Kabul River, at the bottom. Down in the river valley you could still see lots of evidence of the Soviet war, in the form of rusted up tanks and personnel carriers that had fallen down in there and never been recovered. Once we were out of the mountains, there were a few other tell-tale signs of the 1979-89 war. Dotted all over the landscape were deserted villages that had been left in ruins by Soviet bombing raids.

A bit further on, the road began to climb again. On one of the corners along that climb there was a wrecked Soviet t62 tank sitting next to the road like a trophy. At the top of the hill we turned off the road and went along the dirt path that lead to FOB Tora. The path snaked its way along a ridgeline that lead up to the base. The FOB itself was built on a large mound, which was surrounded by open ground. There was a large rocky outcrop at the back corner of the camp that was around two hundred metres tall, and on top of that was an observation post. All in all the base was in a good location: it had a commanding view of the surrounding territory and occupied the high ground. Any Taliban attack on it, would have been tantamount to suicide.

FOB Tora was a fairly decent camp. It had a mess hall, gym, internet café (with only two computers), pizza restaurant, shop, and an Afghan market (the market was just outside the entrance, but still protected by bastion walls). The camp had a good few people staying in it. Besides the Foreign Legion, there was another company of French troupes, a group of American green berets, and a load of drone operators. However, we didn't get much opportunity to socialize as we were all pretty busy.

The convoy, that I had arrived with, dropped me off in the technical zone and told me to go and find my company on my own. I walked around the camp until I saw some familiar faces, then asked them where our company was staying. I was informed that the third company was out on a mission in the nearby Tagab valley, but there was one section that had been left behind. I went over to the buildings where the third company was staying and was glad to see that the section that had been left behind was my own.

I eventually met up with Sgt Tudor who told me that I would be going up the hill at the back of the camp with him to do some guard that night. It was nice to see the guys from my section after three months away. I spent a long time chatting with them about Afghanistan. I learnt that, the newly promoted, Sgt Bernard had just recently had a breakdown and had to be sent back to France. The reason for his breakdown (supposedly) was that he had discovered that his girlfriend was having an affair while he was away. I also found out that Sgt Cabrão was too much of a coward to be of any use here, and had become the laughing stock of the company. The story was that at the first sign of danger he would leave his equipment and his team, and run back to the armoured vehicles. Even while in base, he would hear a loud noise and dart under the nearest table.

That evening I met up with Sgt Tudor and prepared to go up to the observation post behind the camp. The outcrop, on which the OP was located, was pretty steep. There was only one thin path leading up to the top. The rest of the outcrop was covered in barbed wire, booby traps, and human faeces. At the top there were three posts to be manned that would give us a 360° view of the surrounding countryside, and we could probably see for ten kilometres in each direction. Our main duty up there was to look out for people firing rockets at the camp. The Afghans had these old Chinese rockets that dated right back to the Mao era. However, they didn't seem to have the proper equipment to launch them with. This made the rockets difficult to aim and unpredictable, but no less deadly.

Later that night, while on guard, the sergeant called everyone over to his post to tell us that a legionnaire had just been shot and killed in the Tagab valley. A Slovakian legionnaire had been struck in the head, just below the rim of his helmet, by a stray bullet from a 'pray and spray' (poking your gun over a wall, or round a corner, without aiming and emptying a clip). Most of the time this technique doesn't work, because you can't see what you are shooting at, but sometimes you'll get lucky and tag someone. That was the first person that the REP had lost on this mission.

Afghanistan was starting to warm up now and that was sure to mean that there would be more activity from the Taliban. I think that this news shook a few of the guys. It made them realize that they might not come back from this deployment.

The next day we sat up on that hill and waited for the next group to come and relieve us. I passed the time between guard slots by exploring the hilltop. The only problem was that if you went more than a few metres from any of the posts you were confronted by a minefield of shit, and soiled toilet paper flapping in the wind. However, I did manage to find a few snakes that were basking in the sun. I later heard that all the poo had to be cleared of the mountains by the prisoners (yes, that's right, the Legion had its own little prison in the base. Where anyone who misbehaved would go and be made to do hard labour). I felt sorry for those guys because that was a whole lot of shit to clear up, and there wasn't a toilet up there so it would just reappear in a few months. Those poor bastards must have felt like Sisyphus endlessly pushing his boulder up the hill, only to have it roll back down to the start.

When the rest of the company returned from the field, I had to report to the captain. He assigned me to the fourth section (the section that had just lost a legionnaire). I wasn't that happy about being sent to the fourth section. I didn't know anyone in that section, and there were a couple world class idiots over there to boot. I went over, introduced myself to the platoon commander, and installed myself in one of the spare beds. While I was busy sorting my room out a young Frenchman named Gillet, with whom I had been through basic training, came in. I went straight over to him and gave him a hug, it was great to see him again. He had gone to the first company with the rest of my promotion, but had been lucky enough to secure a place with the third for Afghanistan. I sat and talked with Gillet for a while. It was good to catch up. However, our conversation was cut short because I had to go and get the last of my equipment. I still didn't have a gun, or any protective gear of my own.

I went to the room at the front of the barrack building and met the sergeant that I would be working with. He was a fairly new sergeant, who had been doing his course at Castelnaudary at the same time that I was there. Sgt Conti was his name, and he was a tiny Italian man, who wasn't much over five foot. At first we got on well, but that wouldn't last long. I was issued with: Kevlar helmet, body armour, machine gun, 2000 rounds of ammunition, and a load of grenades.

I hated the body armour from the get-go. It was the American style armour, which was better than the French, but I was not in favour of body armour in general. The damn thing weighed over fifteen kilos on its own, which slowed you down a fair bit. It also made you hot, and made it difficult to throw grenades. I would have preferred to fight like they did in Vietnam; with only combat fatigues. The armour weighed you down too much and, in my opinion, the protection you gained was outweighed by the fact that it turned you into an obese person. It was like sending people to war in those fat man suits. The Afghan fighters, on the other hand, wore light clothing with a small tactical vest thrown over top. They were much more mobile than we were, which meant that they had no problem escaping.

The rest of the equipment was great. My Minimi machine gun now had a telescopic M4 stock, and a red dot sight with a 3x magnification lens that could be flicked on and off. I was the only corporal (outside the GCP) to have anything other than a FAMAS. I suspected that this was because the section had just lost a man and now they needed someone to do two jobs. This was later confirmed when I was introduced to the fireteam of one that I would be commanding. I didn't mind having the machine gun. I had been using it for that last two years and preferred it to the FAMAS in every way. The only downside was that gun and the bullets added a load more weight to what I had to carry: The two thousand bullets actually felt heavier than the gun! All in all I would have to carry around thirty to forty kilograms of equipment each time I left the base and went out on a mission.

Later that evening I was told to get ready for my first trip out into Afghanistan, early the next morning. It was only a two day operation, and I would be going with yet another section. I had been chosen to go because everyone else had just recently returned from a long stay out in the field, which was fine with me. The truth be told, I was itching to get out and see just what Afghanistan was like.

The mission was simple enough; we would be taken by helicopter to a mountaintop that overlooked a pass, which was used as a supply route by Al-Qaeda. Our job was to make sure that nobody came through that pass and into the Tagab valley, where the French regular army was. Then after the French had finished their business in the valley, we would be picked up and flown back to camp.

I gathered my things and walked up to the helipad at the back of the camp. It was still dark when we climbed on board the helicopter. As soon as we got on, the pilot took off. We flew round the back of the large rocky outcrop where the guard post was, and as soon as we emerged the other side we were hit by a huge gust of wind that violently knocked the helicopter back. It was such a strong hit that you could hear the chassis creaking under the strain as we were thrown about. Fortunately, our pilot quickly regained control and we were back on our way.

The helicopter touched down on top of the mountain just as dawn was breaking. In a couple of seconds everyone was out, and the helicopter was on its way back to Kabul. My first foray into Afghanistan was rather uneventful. Over the two days that we were sat up on that mountaintop all we saw was a couple of young Afghan men driving their goats along the pass. Somehow one of the goats made it up to where we were. It trotted over to where I was. I was struck by the weirdness of its pupils. I had seen goats before, but I had never paid any attention to their eyes. They have these long, thin, horizontal slits for pupils that have wobbly edges. It looks just like the pupils of the hypnotoad from Futurama. While I wasn't on sentry duty I had a look around the mountain top to see what I could find up there. It didn't take me long to stumble on a load of spent AK47 rounds, and I just kept finding them. This place had witnessed a battle or was the scene of an ambush, at some point in time.

The Legion was very strict about leaving any evidence of our presence behind when we went out into the field. Everything had to be taken with us, and I mean everything. You were supposed to crap in a plastic bag, tie it up, and put it in your rucksack. These are good rules to follow, because if the enemy knows where we have been, then they can reasonably assume that we might return there again at some time in the future, and place booby traps all over the area. However, most people didn't follow these rules, and would often lift up a rock and put all their rubbish under it. I wasn't any better. I usually took all my rubbish with me, but carrying around bags of shit was a bit much. Far better just to leave the locals some fertilizer.

When I got back to camp the third company was on guard duty. There was a lot of guard to do at the FOB. I liked guard in Afghanistan because you didn't have to wear your dress uniform or ponce about with the flag twice a day. There were guard posts every hundred metres or so along the bastion walls. The standard length of guard duty was two hours, and once you entered the post you were forbidden to leave until the next person came to relieve you. There was no toilet in the post and most people relieved themselves in the corner, which made the place smell a bit. Also there wasn't anyone who made sure that everyone made it to their guard duty on time. There were many occasions where you would end up doing four, or six, hours of guard, because the next guys didn't wake up, didn't give a fuck, or were too lazy and self-centred to do their jobs.

Most people passed the time, while on guard, by listening to their iPod. I had plenty of audio books that I would listen to when I was on duty. Others would write defamatory statements about the French, or other legionnaires, all over the walls. This eventually turned into a graffiti war. The French regular troops and the legionnaires took it in turns to do guard week by week. One week the French would write a load of stuff, then the legionnaires would answer. On, and on, it went like a YouTube comment thread, and it was just as toxic. The writing would get scrubbed off now and then (normally when someone wrote something about one of the officers), but it always came back with a vengeance. However, the graffiti wasn't even the worst thing people did on guard. Some people would just curl up and sleep on the floor as soon as the previous guard left!

My most memorable moment from guard duty happened early one morning. I had been on duty for over an hour and I was in desperate need of a number two. As I have mentioned there is no toilet and no chance of you being relieved so that you can go to the toilet. It eventually got so bad that I was bent over in pain. I decided that there was nothing for it, but to cut the top off my water bottle, and do my business in there. My plan was going well, at first, and I soon had plastic bottle with a behemoth log in it. The only problem now was how to dispose of it. In front of every post was a hoard of plastic bottles filled with urine, which were fermenting away in the hot Afghan sun. I decided to do as everyone else and chuck my bottle out with the rest of them. However, there were two problems:

1. My bottle had no top so I would have to be careful that nothing spilled out when I threw it.

2. It was now the time that everyone did their morning sport and there would be groups of people running around the outside of the base.

I climbed up on the bastion block that the machine gun was on, and got as close to the edge as I could. I scanned around for anyone who might be jogging around the camp, but I was on a corner and I couldn't see if anyone was coming, so I listened for the sound of footfall and, when I was confident that the coast was clear, threw the bottle out. At the moment that the bottle left my hand, a French soldier came round the corner, and I watched in horror as the bottle turned upside down and began emptying its contents as it flew, within a hair's breadth, of this guy's face. I quickly dove back down into the guard post and lay on the floor. The man outside skidded to a halt and began shouting up at me. After a few seconds, he stopped shouting and continued on with his jog. I was terrified that he was going to come knocking on the guard post door, take my name, and report me to the captain. Thankfully that never happened, because a British legionnaire flinging bottles of faeces at unsuspecting Frenchmen out on their morning jog, would, definitely not, have sounded good at a report hearing.

Once the company's week of guard was over, I began preparing for my first trip out into the Tagab valley. We would be spending a few days down in the valley, and our main objective while there was to push the Taliban out, one parallel at a time. This time I would be going in a VAB, instead of a helicopter. Now that I had the machine gun my job would be to stand in the back turret every time we went in the VABs. The convoy lined up at the main gate and once the final checks had been done we set off.

We drove in the direction of the nearby town of Surobi, but turned off just before the town centre, and went down a small road that lead to a place where we could cross over the Kabul River. As we drove along by the river the mountains began to rise up on each side. It felt like we were going down into the underworld. Every now and then I would notice a patch of mountainside that had rocks that were painted white. These were minefields laid down by the Soviets. The Afghans didn't want to risk trying to clear them, so they painted a perimeter of white rocks around them to warn others. At the end of the road was a small wooden bridge that was barely wide enough to get the vehicles across and only strong enough to support one vehicle at a time. On the other side of the bridge was a walled compound that had fifty, or more, broken down Soviet BTR armoured personnel carriers.

Shortly after crossing the river we climbed the road up to the huge Naglu dam, which houses the biggest power plant in Afghanistan and supplies most of the power to Kabul. After passing by the dam we drove round the edge of the reservoir to the far side, where the entrance to the Tagab valley was located. Afghanistan has a lot of pristine natural beauty. The country has remained virtually untouched by the industrial revolution and the information age. The Tagab valley was a good example of this. The valley was around half a kilometre wide in places, and the sides were bordered with some pretty formidable mountains. A river ran through the valley and on either side of the river was where the locals lived and farmed. The whole scene looked like something out of the Bible. The houses were made from mud and had no electricity or plumbing. The fields were tended by hand or with oxen, and the locals dug an intricate network of irrigation canals that were reminiscent of those I had learned about when studying ancient Egypt. They had pomegranate, and mulberry orchards as well as plenty of watermelons, and cereal crops. There were a lot of chickens that lived free range in the villages. However, the number one thing to grow was opium poppies. They were everywhere, for as far as the eye could see. Second to the poppies were the cannabis plants some of which were like small trees, and you could detect their sweet smell from a good distance away. The Tagab valley was like a little Garden of Eden; except for all the warring and drugs that is. The fact that everything else was so colourless and beige made the ribbon of green that ran through the valley stand out so much more. It would be a nice place to visit if the country wasn't so damn dangerous.

As we drove deeper into the valley people began taking pot shots at the vehicles. This gradually intensified and pretty soon there was a constant stream of bullets passing by just over my head. Eventually, we reached our start point and got out of the vehicles and began to walk. I was marching in second place, in front of me was a guy from the bomb detection squad, who was scanning the ground with a metal detector. My job was to look out for him while he was concentrating on his work.

Less than ten minutes after starting out on foot, the man in front of me walked past a gap in the mud wall that ran alongside the road, and just as I was approaching an almighty boom rang out and an RPG came flying through the gap, went across the road and hit the bank on the other side. Fortunately, it didn't explode so there was no danger of shrapnel. After that we moved along further, until we found a good place to enter the village. Waiting for us was a local militia group who we were supporting. I may be a bit of cynic, but I didn't trust those militia guys one bit and I didn't want to be anywhere near them. The way they were looking at us didn't exactly fill me with confidence.

We crossed over a couple of fields, then the river, and entered the village itself. The village was a real labyrinth of mud walls and tiny paths. If you had to choose a place for an ambush, then it would be near perfect. I ended up on point again and began patrolling through the near side of the village. It is eerie how deadly quiet everything is when you are on point. At any moment all hell could break loose, and being the guy on head normally meant that you would be the one getting shot.

The hours dragged on and we slowly worked our way through the village. I was a bit surprised when I first learned that we weren't allowed to check inside any of the houses; only the ANA (Afghan army) or the ANP (Afghan police) could do that. It seemed a bit of a waste of time if I'm honest; all an attacker would have to do is launch an ambush, then throw his gun away and go in the nearest house. As long as we didn't see him enter he would be fine.

The village looked totally deserted, all the windows had their shutters drawn and there wasn't a soul to be seen. The only living things that didn't seem to mind our presence were the chickens, who were too busy scratching around for bugs to notice us.

A couple of hours into the march we had our first contact with the enemy. It wasn't anything special just a small group of guys sticking their guns over the walls and emptying their magazines. As long as you quickly found some cover you were usually all right. The problem was that it slowed us down a great deal. Sometimes you would get pinned down for an hour with people spraying bullets over the top of your head.

It was near impossible to catch the guys who were shooting at us. They knew this place like the back of their hand and wore only light clothing, which meant that they could outrun us any day of the week. The best chance we had of nailing those bastards was with artillery (every time we went into the valley there was always at least one group up on the mountains looking over us). If they could get eyes on the insurgents then they would be toast.

We had some pretty fierce artillery backing us up each time we went out. The single most impressive piece of equipment that we had at our disposal was the CAESAR (Camion Equipé d'un Système d'Artillerie) a 155mm howitzer gun mounted on top of a six wheeled truck. It never left the base, but it could deliver rounds, with pinpoint accuracy, up to a distance of forty-two kilometres. Weighing in at eighteen tonnes, it truly was a beast.

However, for the moment we would have to flush the enemy out ourselves. All we could do was keep up the pressure and keep going forwards. We had been slowly moving through the village all day and it was now starting to get dark. The colonel gave us the order to get out of the village before night fell. My section was ordered to stop and cover the rest of the company as they left the village. To get back to the safety of the VABs, they would have to cross two hundred meters of open ground. I climbed up onto the roof of a large mud building so that I could get a good view over the tops of all the mud walls (some of which were over three metres in height), and found myself a good firing position.

The first load of people left the village and set out, in single file, across the flooded fields. Just as the first person reached the far end of the fields, the sound of gunfire filled the air. I could see bullets slamming into the water all around guys who were out in open ground with nowhere to hide. I could tell where the gun fire was coming from; a tree-filled, walled garden about fifty meters in front of me, but I couldn't see the guys doing the shooting. I decided to send a few rounds in their general direction with the aim of making them take cover, which would give the guys under fire a chance to get the hell out of there. So I began shooting over into the walled garden. I was trying to skim the top of the wall with bullets so that they would think twice about poking their heads up. I also sent a few rounds through the middle of the trees in case they had climbed up in there. I had gone through around thirty or so bullets when one of the guys out in the field fired off a rocket launcher and blew the front wall off the garden, and that was the end of that of their ambush.

After that brief engagement, everyone got out of the village safely and re-joined the vehicles. Then we drove back down the valley, crossed the river, and drove back up the other side to where there was a small COP (combat outpost) that housed the second company. We parked the vehicles in a defensive line and got out to have some dinner. There isn't much to do in Afghanistan once the sun goes down. There was no electricity in the Tagab valley, and the Taliban fighters knew that with our night vision goggles and infrared lights they would get a serious ass whooping if they tried to attack us when it was dark. Even so, we still made regular night-time patrols through the village. I enjoyed these forays into the village at night, everything looked so peaceful when it gave off a lustre of silvery moonlight, and it made you feel like some kind of predatory cat prowling through alleyways while the people slept in their houses only metres away.

The next day we were up early and back into the village, but today we would be staying put. There was a group of doctors who would be setting up a field clinic in the area that we cleared the previous day. All the rest of us had to do was set up a secure perimeter and make sure that no bad guys spoiled the day. Then once the doctors had done their business we could head back to base.

I was pleased with my first outing into the Tagab valley: I had handled myself well, and wasn't overcome with fear when the bullets started flying. However, I did receive a bollocking from my new lieutenant for opening fire without first clearing it with him, but I didn't really care about that. He was only trying to suck up to the colonel, who had impressed upon everyone the importance of the controlled use of fire, and even of being fired on by the Taliban without responding in kind. These are decent guidelines if your aim is built rapport and win over the hearts and minds of the locals, but it's bloody frustrating for soldiers.

Back at camp we cleaned all the equipment then got ready for another week of guard. When you weren't on guard you were free to roam around the camp. Most people set up local networks and played Call of Duty in their downtime. At that point in my life I wasn't interested in video games very much, but there were other things to do in the camp, for example: you could get as drunk as you liked. As far as I am aware the French are the only nationality who allow you to purchase alcohol while deployed on operations. The American green berets who I spoke with were gobsmacked when they heard this. If they were caught with so much as a can of beer, it would earn them a one way ticket back to the USA, and possibly a dishonourable discharge from the army. Whereas I could go the PX, buy a bottle of Jack Daniels, then go sit down the pizzeria, and drink it in front of the French officers. Despite that fact, I never did buy any alcohol while I was there. Instead, I went to the gym, or visited the Afghan market at the side of the camp.

The Afghan market was a funny place. The people there would sell anything. You could find American equipment, such as night vision goggles, which still had the previous owners name and number written on them. They had untold amounts of Soviet badges, medals, watches, and all other sorts of things. There were even First World War era bayonets and rifles. Apart from all the plunder, the Afghans at the market also sold clothes, bedsheets, food, and little touristy souvenir items. However, it was a nightmare trying to haggle with them. Once you started haggling, all the other shop keepers would gather round and gang up on you; but, we did figure out a way to gain the upper hand. If you went down to the market with a data stick that had a couple of gigabytes of porn on, you could pretty much get whatever you wanted. It was funny to see their faces when they first saw Western pornos. You half expected their heads to explode. They couldn't believe that stuff like that actually existed. Up until the Western soldiers arrived they had to make to with fucking adolescent boys, and goats (not a nice thing to think about, but true).

It was around this time that I found out that the base was full of hash. You could get a huge chunk of cannabis resin for next to nothing. As soon as night fell there was a lot of stoned legionnaires in FOB Tora. Most people just smoked their hash, but I thought that it was too risky, because of the smell. So, instead, I ground my hash down to powder with the file on my Swiss army knife and sprinkled it in my tea. This way I could walk around drinking my cup of tea and no one was any the wiser. You might think that it wasn't a good idea to get stoned while in a war zone, but, as I have said, the Afghans never attacked us at night, and even if they did I don't think that being a bit stoned would hamper my fighting abilities that much. Besides, it was perfectly OK to drink alcohol, which would have much more deleterious effects on one's ability to fight effectively.

Life in Afghanistan carried on in this same fashion: one week you would be in the valley, the next you would be guarding the FOB. If you were lucky, you might get to go on a trip to one of the main bases in Kabul, but that was quite rare.

The next time I went out into the valley, I was taken by chinook helicopter to the backside of the one of the mountains that bordered Tagab. All I had to do was climb up to a position where I could observe what was going on in the valley below. This was easy work, but pretty boring and a bit frustrating. I can remember that I was up on top of a mountain looking down into the valley. I could see the rest of the company advancing north. In front of them was a small group of Taliban, they were searching around for a place to mount an ambush, but they were spotted and came under sniper fire, so they fled to the mosque. Whereupon everyone was told to stop firing and forbidden from calling in artillery. You can't touch the mosque we were told. I am an atheist with a pretty low opinion of religion (especially that fascist, totalitarian, supremacist, death cult of a religion, called Islam) and I would have been more than happy turn that building into a fucking crater, but alas it was not to be.

The next time I went into the valley, I decided to take the Kevlar plates out of my body armour. It felt great to have all that weight off, and I could actually run and climb over walls. However, my fun wasn't to last; at one point during the mission my sergeant came up and tapped me on the side to get my attention. He noticed that I didn't have my armour plates, and he got seriously annoyed with me. He demanded to know where I had put the armour plates, and when I told him that I had left them back at the base, it made him even angrier. The sergeant continued his tirade of verbal abuse, then began to lecture, me on why I should have the armour on, and how stupid I was to take it out. It did kind of annoy me that he thought that I didn't understand why some pussies felt better with the armour on, or that the insurance company required us to wear it, but I didn't bother arguing back and just waited for him to finish ranting. In an effort to calm him down, I said that when I got back to base, I would put it back in and never take it out again. To be honest, I didn't think he would get so irate about it; from the way he reacted anyone would have thought that I had taken the plates out of his armour. What a bitch.

After the tongue lashing I had received in the field, I assumed that it was over, but when I got back to base I found out that the sergeant had snitched me up to everyone he could. I was called to the lieutenant's office and given a royal bollocking by him and the second in command. They threatened to send me back to France if I took the plates out again, and all the while the sergeant was standing there with his arms crossed, looking smug, and chiming in every now and then with some extra info for the lieutenant. That was moment I lost all respect for the little Italian bastard. He could have handled the incident himself, but he chose to rat me out for brownie points. There was no reason for him to go to the lieutenant. If I had refused to put the Kevlar plates back in, and told him to go to fuck himself, then I could understand, but that wasn't what happened.

It wasn't long after that incident when I had my next bust up with the sergeant. However, this time it involved the lieutenant too. We were driving along a dusty road that ran from the back of our camp to the Jalalabad/Kabul highway, when the Lieutenant stopped the vehicle and ordered everyone out. He told us to climb the hill next to the road and take up defensive positions on the ridge. I tried to point out the white rocks that were dotted around the hill, but I was still in his bad books and immediately got shouted down, told to obey orders, and get my arse up there. Me and the legionnaire in my fire team just stared at each other in disbelief. Then shrugged our shoulders and got on with it. It was pure madness, I couldn't believe that I was now walking through a fucking minefield. I was cursing the sergeant and lieutenant all the all to the top. Luckily, there was some instant karma on its way.

Shortly after I reached the top of the hill, the command vehicle with the colonel came along, then skidded to a halt next our vehicle. The colonel, who was in the middle turret, was furious: 'what in God's name are those two doing up there? That's a fucking minefield. Get them down from there right now,' He yelled. It was great.

The Tagab valley seemed to be getting more dangerous each time we entered it. The fire fights became more frequent, and were lasting longer too. Fortunately, we hadn't suffered any losses since the legionnaire died shortly after my arrival. In fact, the scorpions were doing a better job at fighting us off than the Taliban. I think two or three people were flown back to France because of scorpion stings. Often we would smash our way through the mud walls because we were carrying too much weight to climb over them, and that was when people got stung. The scorpions loved to hide in the cracks.

After a while, getting shot at loses its effect on you. As soon as you hear shots ring out, you take cover and try to return fire. It happens so often that it becomes an automatic response: no different from realizing that it's starting to rain and putting up your umbrella. Firefights were often a good time to catch up on some rest, take a dump, or cook some rations. If you could get into a small group then one person can keep lookout while the others take a break. It was hard work running around with all that equipment in thirty degree temperatures, and it wasn't like you could rest at night, because at night you had to do guard and go on patrols. You might think it's impossible to sleep in the middle of a firefight, when bullets are whizzing by a couple of metres above you, but it all depends on how exhausted you are and we were pretty worn down after a few days out in the field.

The Afghan locals (by locals I mean the men, you hardly ever see, let alone speak to, the women, and the women don't make any decisions anyway) didn't like having us in their village one bit. I can't imagine that many of them understood the reason for us being there, and they probably sympathised more with the, self-described, Mujahideen of the Taliban. A poll carried out in the

south of the country found that ninety-two percent of Afghans
didn't even know what 9/11 was. Add to that the fact that seventy
percent of them were illiterate, and had to believe everything the
local imam said was in the Koran and you had a right task on your
hands, for trying to win the 'hearts and minds' of the local
population. The only feedback we ever heard from them was in the
form of complaints about the destruction of the walls and crops,
the litter that we left, and them finding huge turds all over the
place. Eventually, we were banned from breaking walls or
defecating in the village, but no one took any notice.

However, there were some people in the villages, who didn't
mind our presence as much; whenever we were conducting
operations in the inhabited zones, and all the men had fled, the
children (mostly girls; I think the young boys worked or went with
the men) would stand in the doorways and stare at us. Sometimes,
if you smiled and waved at them, they would wave and smile back;
other times they would get startled and dart back in their houses. I
think that they were just glad to be free for a short time, while the
men were gone. It was probably one of the few times they were
able to look out the front door. They were too young to understand
what was going on anyway. All they knew was that all the men had
left, and when they looked outside they saw strange people, in
weird clothes, carrying all these strange contraptions.

On the next big mission, we did our usual routine of entering
the village and pushing the insurgents up another couple of
parallels; and the insurgents did their usual trick of ambushing us
then running away. As we were leaving the village, I heard
someone shouting and as I turned to see what all the commotion
was about, a machine gun opened up on us. The bullets were
slamming into the wall that bordered the path and getting closer to
where I was standing. I moved to the other side of the path and was
covered by the wall. I took up a defensive position, but I couldn't
see back down to where the shots were coming from. It was funny
to see how some people just shat themselves and ran leaving the
people at the back without any cover. Sgt Cabrão would have
given Usain Bolt a run for his money that day.

When we got out of the village, we went to the vehicles that were parked around five hundred metres away, sat down behind them, and began to eat. We were sat in a circle behind the VAB enjoying (I use the term loosely) some rations when a sniper round skimmed the ground right next to us. At that everyone dived into the back of the vehicle. We had thought that we were out of range of small arms fire, but someone had fancied their chances with their Dragunov sniper rifle and had nearly pulled it off. After getting sniped at we left the vehicles and went further back away from the inhabited zone. We moved right up to the foot of the mountains and made a semi-circle with the command and medic vehicles for protection. We were now about a kilometre away from the village and there shouldn't have been much chance of getting hit by sniper fire here. Besides, there was someone in the turret of every vehicle who was now scanning the houses for anyone who might like to take a pot shot at us.

Feeling somewhat protected people began to relax. We took off our body armour, ate, and tried to get a bit of rest. However, our peace and quiet was rudely cut short by a large boom and a hiss. The next thing anyone knew, a rocket was coming straight for us. It happened so fast that nobody had time to react. We all just stood there, mouths agape, while this thing hurtled towards us. Then it slammed into the ground, about ten metres in front of where we were, ricocheted, and bounced over our heads. The rocket then flew towards the mountainside and smashed into the ground, right next to someone who was going to toilet, ricocheted off the ground again, and span off up into the mountains. The poor guy who was up on the mountainside having a pee was so shocked that he came running back down the hill with his wedding tackle out, which gave the rest of us a good laugh. All this took place in a matter of seconds. All I can say is thank goodness for shoddy Chinese workmanship, because if that rocket had exploded, there would have been a few people going back to France in a box that day.

Shortly after the rocket attack, the Afghan national army rocked up in a rickety, beat-up Russian T55 tank that was belching out clouds of thick black smoke. They parked on top of a large earthen mound overlooking the village, and, seemingly, picked a house at random and began firing at it. As you can imagine, that didn't sit to well with the colonel's plan of 'trying to win the hearts and minds of the locals,' so off he went flapping his arms and shouting at the Afghans to stop. I'm not a fan of the ANA. In my opinion they were more of a hindrance than a help. They had zero discipline, didn't listen to anything we said, and couldn't be relied on in a firefight. Every time you tried to explain something to them, they would be playing on their phones or chatting amongst themselves. This meant that they barely knew any tactics or how to use their weapons properly. That's why you hear of things like someone standing behind a rocket launcher when it's being fired and getting their head blown off. They were fucking useless bastards.

That night we didn't sleep. Instead, we loaded up on water and climbed up into the mountains. The plan was to climb up into the mountains then come back down, further up the valley, and encircle a part of the village where some Taliban fighters were. Then in the morning an attack would be launched by the GCP with the rest of us acting as backup. It is easier than you might think to sneak through an Afghan village at night, because there are no dogs in Afghanistan (the prophet Muhammad didn't like dogs; especially black ones).

The next day, when dawn broke, the morning quiet was interrupted by machine gun fire. I could clearly hear a Minimi and a PKM going at each other. The firefight went on for thirty minutes before our guys decided that it was time to call in some mortars on those goat fuckers. I was posted about fifty metres away from the building where all the action was taking place when the mortars started dropping. It was so close that I could feel the ground shaking with each hit. I remember thinking that if one of those is just the tinniest fraction off then I've had it. It makes you have a lot of respect for the guys in WW1 who went through months of not knowing whether or not the next shell had their name on it. The stress must have been incalculable. After the mortars were done, a Eurocopter Tiger (European version of the Apache) arrived and began firing on the insurgents with its 30mm canon. Finally after all that the baddies were dead, and we could get the fuck out of the Tagab valley and go back to Tora for some rest.

On the 30th April (Camerone day) a special guest arrived to celebrate with us: General Stanley McChrystal, the ISAF commander in Afghanistan. He had been trying to promote the same strategy, of maximizing civilian safety and minimizing collateral damage from aerial bombardment, as our commanding officer: Colonel Bellot des Minières, and was eager to come and see how things were going in Tagab.

All the English speaking legionnaires (myself included) were told to iron our dress uniforms and get ready to do a presentation of arms for the general. The first time I laid eyes on McChrystal, I remember thinking that he reminded me of the man in the painting 'American Gothic' (minus the glasses and bald patch). It was clear from the get-go that the general was a polished politician who had rehearsed all his lines. He passed in front of each legionnaire, said the same insincere drivel, and then moved on.

After the presentation we went into the tent that normally served as the officer's mess. Inside there were tables full of boudin blanc, croissants, and coffee. Gen McChrystal read out a short speech and was presented with a kepi blanc. Then…you guessed it…we sang some Legion songs. After the singing was over the General began going round the room, shaking hands, and repeating 'it's an honour to meet you.' I can't stand this kind of political schmoozing, so when the General came my way I thought that I would ruffle his feathers a bit. He came up to me, looked me straight in the eye, shook my hand, and told me that it was an honour to make my acquaintance. I looked him straight back in the eye and said 'I just met you outside, five minutes ago.' He squeezed my hand tight, moved his face a little closer to mine and just repeated his mantra 'it's an honour to meet you,' and moved on. I really hate all of that fake political shit where you have to pretend to like things and people that you don't. Still, it was all over and done with quickly enough.

A couple of months after that meeting, I heard that McChrystal had been forced to resign after being overly critical of civilian government officials in the US; including Joe, I touch kids too much in photo ops, Bidon. So, it turns out that McChrystal wasn't too fond of diplomacy either.

It was June now and the height of summer in Afghanistan. During the summer months there are huge dust storms that roll across the landscape like mega tsunamis. It was a spectacular site to see the enormous walls of dust approaching, there was something apocalyptic about it. I remember one dust storm that was so violent that it snapped and electricity pylon and sent it crashing down onto a portable toilet with neon blue sparks flying everywhere (fortunately, no one was using the toilet at the time).

We had been continuing our regular trips to the Tagab valley and we were having a fair bit of success: we had already exceeded our objective of clearing six parallels and were now on parallel seven or eight. The valley was starting to get really wide and the inhabited zone was no longer a thin strip next to the river. The attacks started as soon as we entered the valley and didn't stop until we left, or the insurgents were dead.

On one outing, in early June, things went very badly for us indeed. We had set up another field clinic and the doctors were busy treating the locals, when a group of Taliban came to crash our party. As usual the GCP were out in front of the main group, and it was them who bore the brunt of the attack. As they were advancing down a narrow alleyway, between two tall buildings, they were fired on, from in front with an RPG. Then insurgents, who were hiding on the roofs of the houses, got up and fired down onto the rest of the guys trapped in the alley. As soon as the rest of us heard what was happening we rushed forward, swamped the area where the ambush had taken place, and drove the enemy away. However, we were, unfortunately, too late to save the life of the guy who was hit with the RPG and he died on the way to hospital. The other three were in bad shape, but they all pulled through. As if all that wasn't bad enough, another member of the GCP was stung by a scorpion while trying to rescue the people in the alley.

What made Tagab so dangerous was that the valleys to the east, and the Hindu Kush to the north, were places where the Taliban had free reign and could act with impunity. Not to mention that fact that Pakistan was less than a hundred miles away. All this meant that there was no shortage of new fighters and munitions flooding into the area. There was also no one stopping the insurgents from walking back into the areas that we cleared as soon as we went back to base. It wasn't uncommon for you to have enemy fighters in front and behind you.

Back at the FOB there was also a few problems in the last month of our stay. Maybe it was due to stress, boredom, or just plain old human stupidity. One of the members of the GCP shot himself in the foot whilst cleaning his gun, and another got into an argument with a Pilipino legionnaire, who, to stop himself getting beat up, pulled the pin out of a grenade and threatened to let go if anyone came near him. This obviously earned him a one way trip back to France. There also seemed to be more people who were getting sent to jail. It was as if they didn't want to go out and risk getting shot in the last month of our stay. However, I am sure that this was merely a coincidence, and that I am being far too cynical.

One of our last missions was a joint operation with the Americans. An Afghan informant had disclosed the location of an arms cache somewhere high in the mountains to the east of Tagab. The arms cache was located in such an inaccessible area that the only options were walking or helicopter. The Americans, wisely, chose to go for helicopter. The Legion, on the other hand, had to demonstrate how tough they were by marching there. This meant that we would have to start the mission a day earlier so that we arrived at the same time as the Americans.

The afternoon before the mission began we drove in the VABs to COP 46 in the Tagab valley, got out of the vehicles, and began to climb up into the mountains. The march started off hard and just kept getting worse. The mountain appeared to have no end; every time we got to what we thought was the top, there was more mountain to climb. The going was tough and we regularly found ourselves clambering over huge boulders. Just walking was difficult on account of the vast amounts of scree that littered the mountainside. One sloppily placed step could easily see you twisting an ankle. The march dragged on throughout the night. The only rest that we got was when we had to wait for those at the rear to catch up.

It wasn't until the break of dawn that we finally caught sight of our destination, down in the valley below. We left the snipers and the guided missile teams up on the mountain, then walked down. We walked through a two hundred metre wide corridor in the middle of the village. There were houses and walled compounds either side of us. If the enemy had been coordinated enough to launch an ambush from both sides, we would have been pretty fucked. Suddenly, the sound of automatic rifle fire pierced the quiet stillness of the early morning, but it wasn't coming from the locals. I could see tracer fire streaming down from the mountain, into a walled compound off to my right. Then, a few seconds later, I heard the most horrible blood curdling scream that I have ever heard in my life, and I just knew that someone had come outside to see her husband lying in a mangled heap, full of bullet holes.

It was a tense few moments after that, because you didn't know if things were going to kick off big time (there was an arms cache up here somewhere so they had the means to attack us). Nothing more did happen though, and we walked through the village and crossed the river at the far side. We set ourselves up, on top of a large embankment that was on the other side of the river and waited for the Americans. However, there was one small problem with the place we had chosen to install ourselves: There was no cover from the sun whatsoever. In the early morning this wasn't too bad, but by nine o'clock it was starting to get quite uncomfortable. There was nothing for it but to try to cover up as much exposed skin as you could and just sit there baking in the sun.

At around 10:30am, I took out my water bottle to have a drink and was shocked that there was only a mouthful of water remaining. I had taken seven litres with me yesterday (a two litre hydration bladder; two, one litre gourds; and two, one and a half litre water bottles), but now it was all gone. I asked around and discovered that nearly everyone was either out, or nearly out, of water. My sergeant overheard me talking with the others and asked what the problem was. I told him that I was out of water and he just grinned, waved his bottle at me, and said 'I have plenty of water,' then took a sip and went back to his post.

After another hour of sitting in the sun I was getting desperate. I was incredibly thirsty, and starting to get a headache too, so I decided that I wasn't going to blindly follow orders until I collapsed from heat exhaustion. I came up with a plan to fill up a bag with empty bottles, sneak down to the river, and fill them up. We all had water purification tablets that came with our rations so there was no danger of getting sick. Somehow, word got around about what I was planning and a couple of guys from the other sections came over with backpacks full of empty bottles too. Even one of the junior medical officers came over, the medical team was out of water as well!

I set off with three others for the river that was twenty metres down the embankment in front of me. We filled up all the water bottles and began our march back up. I was feeling quite pleased with myself and it didn't appear that anyone had noticed us leaving our posts and going down to the river. As I reached the top of the embankment I saw the sergeant-chef, who was second in command of my section, standing there. He didn't stop the junior medical officer (who outranked him) or any of the others, but when I approached the top it was a different story. He straight away began punching me in the face, and he kept on punching, and punching.

After getting hit twenty or thirty times in the face (no exaggeration) I began to feel dizzy, so I put my hands up to protect myself. At that moment he stopped hitting me and began screaming at me, 'who the fuck do you think you are, I give the orders round here. You could have got everyone killed.' That I was taking a risk was true, but it was a calculated one. In my opinion (and of course I am biased) I saved the Legion from a huge scandal that day. If they thought that having one guy die in Djibouti from heat stroke was bad, then how do they think thirty plus cases of heat stroke would have looked? Because that's what they were facing whether anyone knew it or not. The people who had used up all their water might have been able to sit out in the hot Afghan sun all day, but what would have happened when they had to march back the way we came. Because a ten hour march through the mountains of Afghanistan with no water and carrying thirty to forty kilos of equipment sounds like a recipe for disaster to me.

The sergeant-chef told me that as soon as we got back to base, I was finished. He would make sure that I was sent back to France and was expelled from the Legion. I didn't mind so much being hit and shouted at. I knew that if I was caught, I would get one hell of a punishment. What pissed me off was that little Italian pipsqueak of a sergeant standing next to the second in command, and doing his usual trick of acting like a self-righteous prick with his arms crossed, adding his two-cents each time the sergeant-chef finished a sentence. However, the thing that really got my goat was when he said to me, 'why did you go down to the river for water? You could have asked me, I have plenty.' I couldn't believe the nerve of this guy. He knew full well that we were out of water and all he had done was tease us. Oh, how I would have loved to put a bullet in his smug face at that moment.

I continued to be lectured for a while, and I was getting pretty bored of it to be honest. It wasn't that I didn't understand the implications of what I had just done. I knew full well, and I did it anyway. All that needed to be said had been said; I had acted without their permission, and they were now going to kick me out of the Legion, so what was the point of banging on about it.

Sometime around mid-afternoon, a couple of chinook helicopters appeared on the horizon. They landed on top of the embankment and the American soldiers got out, blew up the weapons cache, and flew off again. They were there for two hours maximum.

After the Americans left, we waited for dusk, then set out on our way back to base. The march back wasn't without incident: four or five people began to suffer from the effects of dehydration and had to have an intravenous drip put on them. One guy got so thirsty that he ripped the drip bag open with his teeth and tried to drink the saline solution. This had the effect of making him vomit, thus making him more dehydrated than before. By the time we got to the end of the march there was a troop of people who were on the verge of collapsing.

Funnily enough, I never heard another word about what happened in the valley that day. It was never brought up to me again. Perhaps the sergeant-chef thought that giving me a hiding was punishment enough. However, I tend to think that he didn't report me because he didn't want to risk the fact that he had used me as a punching bag coming up over the course of the inquiry, which would have been bad for his Legion career as well, but hey, I don't have much faith in humans. Oh, and that same sergeant-chef got kicked out of the company not long after returning from Afghanistan, for refusing a direct order from the captain, so make of that what you will.

I would like to offer a short comment on the use of paid informants in Afghanistan. To my eyes the whole thing was a complete charade. It was patently obvious that the Taliban were just selling us their faulty, and broken, equipment in order to finance the purchase of new stuff. The weapons caches that the informants told us about were always full of rusty old mortars and rockets that looked like they had been in the ground for thirty years. I have seen WW2 era bombs that have been dug up in better condition. So next time you hear on the news that so and so has found and destroyed a weapons cache, you should first wonder how much they paid to find it, and second if it was worth blowing up, because it was most likely a bunch of dud rounds anyway.

The last mission that I took part in wasn't in the Tagab valley. For our last outing we would be going to base Rocco in the Uzbin valley, which is one of the most volatile parts of eastern

Afghanistan. Only two years earlier, on August 18th 2008, the French suffered heavy casualties there.

Previously the Uzbin valley had been hailed as a success story and was considered a quiet and, relatively, safe area. Since 2006 it had been under the control of the Italians. However, unbeknownst to the French, who took over the area at the start of August 2008, the reason for the apparent calm in the region was due to the fact that Italian secret services had been bribing the local insurgents into inaction. This meant that the French went into the valley with a false sense of security, despite being warned by locals of large numbers of Taliban fighters that were operating in and around the area. To make matters worse, it appears that some interpreters who had deserted from FOB Tora prior to the mission had alerted the local Taliban, and militant leaders to their plans.

On one of their first forays out of the base, the French planned to enter the Uzbin valley and advance towards the village of Sper Kunday. When they were only fifty metres from the village they came under heavy attack from a large, well equipped, and well prepared group of insurgents. Straight away the insurgents killed the second in command of the lead section, the radio operator, interpreter, and a medic who was from 2REP. The insurgents kept the French pinned down with mortar, RPG, and sniper fire.

After receiving four wounded the ANA fled the scene and left the French, and a group of twelve American special forces soldiers, behind. Ninety minutes into the fight, the French began to run low on ammunition, and had to be resupplied by land, which was tricky owning to the sheer numbers of Taliban in the area (~140). The battle dragged on and the Taliban attacked both flanks of the French column in an attempt to encircle them in a pincer like movement. The rest of the French troops, along with some backup that had arrived from FOB Tora tried to rush the insurgents and link up with soldiers who were pinned down, but were unsuccessful.

The Americans called in air support, but the enemy fighters were too close to the French troops for the jets to fire on them. The insurgents were then joined by another hundred, or more, fighters, and that's when the jets decided to throw caution to the wind and bomb them anyway. The aerial bombing lasted an hour, then two Blackhawks were called in to evacuate the wounded, but were driven away by enemy fire.

Two hours after the fighting began the support group managed to set up and fire their 81mm mortars. Then, four hours later, another group of French soldiers arrived with 120mm mortars, and as night fell predator drones began circling in the sky above the battlefield in order to guide the mortar fire.

At 21:00 the French support groups began to make their way up to Sper Kunday to evacuate the dead and wounded, while an AC-130 Spectre and an OH-58 Kiowa helicopter pounded the ridges around them. It wasn't until midnight, nearly nine hours after the fighting began, that the French took control of the situation and drove the enemy away. Later on, at around 02:00, Norwegian special forces arrived to help locate wounded, and collect the bodies of the dead. Most of the bodies had been looted, some had been mutilated, and one had been killed with a knife.

The next morning the last of the bodies were found, then the remaining French soldiers were transported by helicopter up to the ridges that the Taliban occupied. They came under attack once again, but now were able to drive the insurgents off. By midday the last of the Mujahideen had fled. However, that wasn't the end of the carnage. One more French soldier was killed, and two injured, when the road they were on collapsed under the weight of their vehicle. All together ten French soldiers were killed and twenty-one wounded.

In the days after the battle NATO forces bombed the shit out of three villages, where the insurgents were thought to be hiding, for three days. One village was on the receiving end of seventy bombs! It's estimated that the bombing destroyed 150 houses, killed 40 civilians, and displaced 2000 others. Afghan security forces claimed that most of the casualties were women and children, which, they said, proved that the men had been away, taking part in the battle.

Now I think you'll agree that this is a pretty fucked up story. The French government would dispute pretty much everything I have written here, but that's to be expected. A NATO report that came out shortly after the battle heavily criticized the French for: lacking supplies and preparation, running low on ammunition early into the fight, and only having one radio. The French also left behind a treasure trove of goodies for the insurgents including:

- 4 FAMAS assault rifles
- 2 Minimi light machine guns
- 2 FR-F2 precision rifles
- 1 LGI grenade launcher
- 6 Pairs of binoculars
- 9 Flak jackets

So not a good day for the French under any stretch of the imagination.

Given this history of the French in the Uzbin valley, you could understand why I was a bit apprehensive about going there, especially during the lasts weeks of my tour. However, I needn't have worried. We encountered far less resistance than we were used to in Tagab. The only heavy fire I remember was when some insurgents fired at the command vehicles, who, used to being far away from the action, promptly shat themselves and retreated.

After all the missions were over we packed our things and went to Hamid Karzai international airport, but we had a couple of days to wait in the American base that covers the northern part of the airport. I couldn't believe how good the facilities were in the American base. They had by far the best mess hall (and it was self-service), their gym was better than anything I have seen in Europe (civilian or military), and they even had a Pizza Hut for God's sake.

On our return from Afghanistan we didn't fly directly back to France, but instead stopped off in Cyprus for a week of 'decompression,' which basically meant seven days of enforced fun, meditation, and stress management classes. We stayed in a five star hotel while in Cyprus, and some of the activities were fun, but others were just plain bizarre. For example; we spent a whole day riding around on a pirate's galleon that was like a floating disco. The highlight of that day was when one of the ship's crew got into hot water for being flamboyantly gay. He started commenting on the attractiveness of some of the Russian legionnaires, and had to be locked away below deck for his own safety.

While in Cyprus, we were forbidden from leaving the hotel grounds, unless we had a day trip planned with the decompression staff. As you can imagine this frustrated everyone a fair bit. Most of us just wanted to get back and go on leave, so that we could go out, have a drink, and meet some girls. To stop people going out at night there was a security officer who patrolled the roads around the hotel in his jeep, as well as a designated group of legionnaires who mounted foot patrols around the hotel grounds. However, in spite of the orders from the decompression staff, almost everyone planned to sneak out in small groups and make their way to the nearby bars and clubs in Pathos.

I also planned to sneak out of the hotel at the first opportunity, so at night I and a few others changed into civilian clothing, and snuck our way through the trees and bushes in front of the hotel. Just as we were approaching the road, a jeep came hurtling towards us and screeched to a halt. The security officer jumped out, shone his torch into some bushes on the other side of the road, and shouted, 'come out of there now.' In an instant, that quiet road that ran past the hotel turned into Omaha beach. Legionnaires sprang from everywhere; they jumped down from the roof of the bus shelter, popped out of bins, crawled out from underneath cars, emerged from every bush and tree in sight, and ran in the direction of Pathos. The poor security officer just stood there in amazement. There was nothing he could have done anyway. It was an amazing sight to see. I was laughing so hard that I could barely run.

Later on, we all met up in the bars of Pathos. A couple of Polish guys arrived covered from head to toe in scratches. It turned out that when we had run away from the security officer, they had gone in the direction of the beach and followed the coastline along, but had run into a forest of thorn bushes. Being legionnaires, and paratroopers to boot, they didn't turn back, or find a way around, but instead bulldozed their way through it.

The next morning I arrived back at the hotel, just before six, and still drunk from the night before. I was happy to find out that the day's activities included nothing more strenuous than sitting down and talking. I think that I fell asleep during one of the yoga classes that day.

After Cyprus, we finally flew back into Solenzara airbase, on Corsica. As soon as we were back in Camp Raffalli I was sent back to the third section, and I couldn't have been happier. I hated the fourth section and it was clear that the feeling was mutual.

Before being sent on leave, I was called into the lieutenant's office. I was told that there was going to be another GCP selection in couple of months, and asked if I was still interested in trying out. I confirmed that I was very much still interested, and the lieutenant put me down on the list. I was ecstatic, at last I would get to try out, and it had only taken a little over three years.

17: Downfall

It takes many good deeds to build a good
reputation, and only one bad one to lose it.
Benjamin Franklin

I spent my holiday training for selection. I went up to Norway
with a friend and hiked round the famous Lysefjord, near
Stavanger, which had some amazing cliffs that were over a
thousand metres high. It's popular with base jumpers, but there
was no one jumping when I was there as a Russian base jumper
had recently died there.

After Norway I went back down to Chamonix, in France, and
did the Tour du Mont Blanc: a one hundred and seventy kilometre
long hike that circles the Mont Blanc massif, and passes through
France, Italy, and Switzerland. The hike is a tough one and it has
over ten kilometres of ascent and descent. After all that running
around in Afghanistan, with all the extra weight that I had to carry,
I was in pretty good shape and It only took me three and a half
days to complete the hike round Mont Blanc.

When I got back to Calvi, I continued my preparation by
reading every field manual and studying all the SOPs I could get
my hands on. In the evenings, I went to the running track behind

the infirmary and trained for roughly an hour each night. At the weekend, I would run the thirty kilometre course that was part of the selection process, or swim the two kilometres out and back, to the fish park in the bay of Calvi. The thirty kilometre run was part of the selection process and would have to be completed in under four hours, while carrying around twenty kilos of equipment. Unfortunately, you weren't allowed to run in combat fatigues, or with a rucksack, on your own, so I had to settle for shorts and t-shirt, but it was better than nothing. After a few weeks of this training regime I was in excellent shape. I was completing the 30k run in around two hours (give or take ten minutes), and was able to do a hundred push-ups with relative ease.

However, my preparation had to be put on hold for a while, because our commander in chief, Col Bellot des Minières, was leaving, so we had to put on a big ceremony for that. It was a shame the he was leaving, he was the best colonel I ever served under. Sure, I might have disagreed with him on minor points, but he knew how to get the best out of people, and never appeared aloof or condescending. I would not at all be surprised if he ends up commanding the entire French army one day.

Our new commander was his polar opposite: Colonel François Plessy was a jumped up remnant of the French aristocracy, who thought that he was part of some master race, and that the legionnaires under his command were dogs. He was a small man with grey hair, leathery skin, and a permanent scowl. I always suspected that he was an alcoholic and a sexual sadist, who paid prostitutes to kick him in the nuts, or had dungeon back at his house where he would truss his wife up like a Christmas turkey. Oh…and yeah…he fucking despised the British, and anyone who came from an English speaking country for that matter.

I had my first run in with our new colonel when someone vandalized a sign at the front of the camp. On the wall next to the front gate was the name of the regiment, spelled out in one foot brass letters. Someone had gone out, gotten drunk, then came back and ripped some of the letters off the wall. In response the colonel called all the Anglophones over to his office for questioning.

I entered the colonel's office and he began his interrogation. It was obvious that he had taken a course with the police and he was feeling pretty confident about being able to get whatever information from us that he wanted. However, unfortunately for him I had been in trouble with the police since I was twelve and was well used to all their tactics. This infuriated the colonel, but what really pissed him off was when I called him out for asking the same question multiple times with slightly different wording. He eventually got so mad that his face turned bright red, and he began shouting and screaming at me.

My first encounter with him ended with him throwing me out of his office. He really lost his temper with me, but it was worth it. The man was just a total plonker. In the end it turned out that it was Sgt Conti, the Italian sergeant that I had worked with in Afghanistan, who had taken the letters.

The colonel continued to blame the Anglophones for everything that happened in the camp. Every time someone did a poo on a piece of cardboard and left it outside his door, or spray-painted penises on the walls of the command building with the words 'Nique Plessy' next to them, he blamed the British. However, I was never questioned by colonel again. Each subsequent time I went over, I was always questioned by the security officer, who didn't let you speak, and was one of the biggest arseholes in the regiment, but he hated everyone equally. He shouted and screamed a lot, but he didn't try and trick you into admitting to things that you hadn't done, so that was fine.

I soon came to regret my trolling of the colonel. A couple of days before the GCP selection was due to start, I was told that my name had been struck from the list and I would not be allowed to take part. It was obvious who had done it, because the list had to pass by the colonel before the selection could start, but I still couldn't believe that he had done it just because I had been cheeky with him. He let Sgt Conti (the guy who actually stole the brass letters) do the fucking selection.

I was quite depressed for a while after that, but I eventually got over it. I did, however, receive a bit of good news. I had been designated to receive La Croix de la Valeur Militaire (Cross for Military Valour) for actions in Afghanistan. Although, I didn't feel like I deserved it. I was only getting it because I was one of the few people who had actually fired their weapon in combat. It wasn't because I did anything particularly brave.

Shortly before Christmas, I was called into the section office to speak with the lieutenant about what training courses I would like to go on in the following year. I told him that I would like to go on the sergeant's course, but he said that although he had no doubt that I could finish the course and get a good passing grade, he thought that I wasn't mean enough to be a sergeant. This added insult to injury, and I had just about had enough of hearing that crap. It was clear to me now that the Foreign Legion didn't want leaders, they wanted bosses, who would stand at the back, shouting and threatening the legionnaires into doing their bidding. I didn't agree with that way of running things at all, and I wasn't going to play that game to appease the lieutenant.

It began to dawn on me at that point that I should probably start thinking about what I was going to do after the Legion. The military life wasn't for me, and I didn't have a future here anyway; five years was enough. I told the lieutenant that I didn't want to go on anymore courses, I just wanted to serve out my contract. That was all.

The months rolled on, and soon enough it was Christmas time again. Christmas was the usual combination of forced fun and the singing of Legion songs. Then just after New Year everyone was given a month's leave. I had spent my last holiday training so this time I was going to make up for it, and party my ass off. However, this plan didn't work out so well. I boarded a flight whilst high on acid, got paranoid, and freaked out. I ended up running to back of the plane, opening the door, and jumping out while it was still on the runway. I then got chased by the airport police, who I escaped by climbing the two perimeter fences, and running across a busy motorway.

I was eventually arrested, and interrogated as a suspected terrorist. I was, however, still hallucinating, and in no state to be interviewed. So they decided that I was nuts, put me in a strait jacket, and locked me in a padded room. The next day I was sent to an insane asylum just outside of Paris. Where I had to convince the staff that I wasn't crazy, and was, in fact, just high. This didn't go well, because when they gave me blood test to see if I was telling the truth, and it came back clear. The test must not have been able to detect LSD.

After a few days observing my behaviour, the staff decided that I wasn't crazy after all and arranged for me to be handed back over to the Legion. I was sent to Fort de Nugent in Paris, where I waited for someone to come from Calvi and collect me. I had almost got away with the Legion not knowing about my adventures on holiday, but one of the police officers, who arrested me, found my Legion ID card and phoned them up. I was certain that I would, at least, get some jail time, and possibly even be sent to Castelnaudary with all the other bananiers, but what did end up happening to me was worse than that.

Upon arriving at Calvi, I wasn't sent to the prison, instead I was confined to the infirmary for a month (they must have been worried that I really was crazy). All I had to do was lay on my bed all day and wait. It was while in the infirmary that I started smoking cigarettes again. It was just so boring, and I needed something to do. I was allowed to go to the Foyer once a day and that was it. I did however manage to have some fun. I had brought some milk and breakfast cereal, but some thieving bastard kept drinking my milk. One day, on seeing that someone had drunk almost all my milk, and left only a few mouthfuls, I took the bottle to the toilet and filled it back up with urine. It was easily a 70/30 mix. The next day I couldn't believe my eyes when it was nearly empty again. I hope that whoever it was, enjoyed their cornflakes.

My company was still on holiday when I arrived back. When they returned I was told to pass report at the captain's office. The captain then told me to pass report at the colonel's office. I went over to the command building, but didn't speak to the colonel. Instead, I saw the security officer who told me that I would be facing court martial, and that most likely I would be getting kicked out of the Legion. The officers thought that I had scandalized the name of 2REP, but the NCOs, on the other hand, thought it was the funniest thing they had ever heard. A couple even shook my hand and congratulated me on my banane. They couldn't believe that I had opened the door of a civilian airliner, jumped from four or five metres onto the tarmac without getting hurt, then got up and outrun the airport police, and finally scaled two massive fences with barbed wire on them and escaped the airport. I must admit that I couldn't believe that I had done it either.

The court martial would take a fair bit of time to organize, so in the meantime I was to remain at the company. I was deemed to be mentally unstable and was not allowed to parachute, or use a gun. I either worked as corporal du jour in my section, or over at the company office as corporal de semaine. I was also forbidden from doing any physical exercise. It was pretty god damn boring. I liken it to being in limbo, I was still in uniform and still at the company, but I already had one foot out the door.

Sometime in March the regiment got ready to do another tour of Afghanistan. The third company was broken up: Half joined the first company and got ready for another trip to Afghanistan, and the rest were spread throughout the rest of the regiment. I was left with the legionnaires who had less than a year's service (they couldn't go to Afghanistan), and was sent to live down at the amphibious centre. I was happy to see that Sgt Seiko would also be staying behind and working with me to train the new guys. The poor bastard had been in the same situation I was now in ever since his ball exploding incident. There was another sergeant, a couple of corporal-chefs, and a couple of corporals who were staying behind also. They were either injured, or coming to the end of their contracts. It was a good bunch of people and we all got on well together.

There was only one problem at the amphibious centre, and that was sergeant-chef Bartos, the centre's head. He was a knuckle dragging ape if there ever was one. If I had to guess I would say that he had an IQ of around seventy. His answer to every problem was to get mad, make a lot of noise, and hit things. He had been in the military for fifteen years, but couldn't read a map to save his life. He was the epitome of what was wrong with the Legion. He was what someone like my lieutenant thought was the archetype of a Foreign Legion NCO; he had a hair-trigger temper, a big mouth, and was quick to use his fists. The problem was that he barely understood the orders given to him by the officers, let alone how to put them into action. I have seen trained crows that had better problem solving abilities. He was the kind of guy that never got the hang of putting the shapes through the holes as a toddler.

Fortunately he wasn't around that much, most days he was only there for a couple of hours in the morning. He hated me with a passion, but he never got violent with me. At that time I had sixteen inch biceps and I'm guessing that he didn't want to risk me fighting back and beating him up. His pride would never recover from that, but he never missed an opportunity to tell me how much he despised me. To be honest, I didn't mind, at least he was up front about it and I knew where I stood, and it wasn't as if he could wreck my career anymore that I had done myself.

In spite of Sch Bartos, I had a good time at the amphibious centre. The young legionnaires were a good bunch of guys, and the other NCOs were a pleasure to work with. Most days were spent training the new recruits in basic combat techniques. Sometimes we would do mini two-day missions, or go on a march to one of the nearby shooting ranges, do some live fire and movement drills, then march back.

I ended up doing the GR20 again while staying down at the centre. This time we marched all the way down to the train station at Vizzavona (roughly twice as far as the last time I had done it). It was a bit more frustrating, however, as Sch Bartos had the map and managed to go off track twice. You didn't even need a map for the GR20. There were little red and white markers painted all along the trail; all you had to do was stand at one marker, look for the next one, walk over to it, and repeat. However, I wasn't going to tell him that. It was far too much fun watching him get frustrated and have a hissy fit up on the mountainside. I also refused to share his tent with him and just sleep out under the stars. He paid me back at the end by refusing to let me be in the group photo. It was quite cute how much he disliked me.

Later, around August, word came back that two legionnaires had been killed by friendly fire in the Tagab valley. One of them, a Nepalese legionnaire, was a good friend of mine, who had stayed in the same dorm as me. He was only thirty years old (the same age I am as I write this book) and had left a wife and young child behind in Nepal. I was called up to the company by the captain, second in command, who asked me to write a speech for him to read out at the funeral.

I was sad to have lost a good friend. It was especially unfortunate that it was friendly fire that killed him. I couldn't understand how you could mistake a French soldier for the Taliban (they didn't wear helmets or uniforms), but maybe I am being too harsh. I wasn't there, so I will withhold my criticism.

When the regiment returned from Afghanistan, I went back up to stay at the company, in my old room. It was completely empty now, but then there came a knock at the door. I answered it to see one of the guys who had been in the amphibious centre with me. A young Macedonian legionnaire, who was a giant of man. He used be a bodybuilder before joining. The guy had quads that were the same thickness as my torso, but he couldn't have been a kinder, gentler, human being. I had gotten on well with him during our stay at the amphibious centre and was happy to have him stay with me in my dorm. I wasn't around much, however, because as soon as the company got back I was sent to work in the company office. I was to work from five o'clock in the morning until half past ten at night, in perpetuity.

A few months later there was some more bad news, when the new guy in my room went out drinking with friends in Bastia, on the other side of the island. On the way back their car careered off the road and plummeted down the cliff onto the rocks below, killing everyone inside. It was terribly sad, just a tragic accident, and to make it worse they were in their late teens and early twenties. It was a terrible waste of life.

A month later I got ready to pass my court-martial. It was to be held in the museum, opposite the guard house at the entrance to the regiment. It was to be made up of two officers and two senior NCOs. One of the NCOs was from Manchester and said he would put in a good word for me. I had to be in full dress uniform for the hearing. One of the rooms in the museum had been cleared and there was a row of tables with the officers and NCOs sitting behind it.

I had to stand just outside the room and wait to be called. When I heard the call, I entered and presented myself. After presenting they refused to let me stand at ease, and made me stand to attention for twenty minutes while they chatted idly. This really pissed me off and I was ready to tell them just where to stick their job. The proceeding began, and I tried to make it as difficult as possible. I refused to affirm my earlier testimony that I had taken drugs, and said that there was no evidence, except for my word, and I wasn't trustworthy. They just brushed that aside and said that they thought I was telling the truth the first time so they would go with that. Then they tried to get me to grovel to stay in the Legion, but I told them in no uncertain terms that if this was going to be held against me for the rest of my time here, and I was to be passed over for promotion that I would rather leave. I told them that I didn't need the Legion to survive and had no qualms about entering back into civilian life. By this time the Adjutant-chef from Manchester was shooting daggers at me, but I didn't care, he had been in the Legion for nearly twenty years, so of course I expected him to side with them.

I had had enough by now and I was tired of being lectured to by these people. Take them out of their uniforms and they were just tired old men with saggy man boobs, besides what did they know about life (the officers I am speaking of) most of them had gone straight from private school to military academy, then straight into the army. They knew fuck all about fuck all. They had been living in institutions all their lives, sucking on the nipple of the state, and I was fed of being talked down to by them.

The hearing ended with me denying everything and them getting annoyed and declaring that I was guilty of everything they thought I was guilty of, and that I was a disrespectful arsehole. It was pretty obvious that they were going to throw me out on my arse, but I didn't give a damn; I would be free.

A few days later I got confirmation that I was to be dishonourably discharged from the Legion. I was also stripped of all my medals, and would never get my valour cross. I didn't care about the medals, they were just shiny bits of metal on the end of a piece of ribbon, and it didn't change anything that I had done. I had still been to Afghanistan even if I didn't have the medal to show it, besides having medals doesn't make you a better person; I know one guy who closed his hand in a VAB door, blamed it on the Taliban, and got the valour cross; so fuck those poxy, pendulating, pieces of crap. I was also told to hand in my driver's licence, so that it could be turned into a civilian one with my real name on it. However, that never happened, they just took my driver's licence, destroyed it, and never gave me a civilian one, which was nice.

One evening while I was in the company office I was told that the order had been given for me to be sent back to Aubagne the next morning. They gave me next to no time to prepare my things. Luckily, I had expected them to pull something like this and had already sold all of my equipment, except for a couple of sets of combat fatigues, and my dress uniform. I had been ready to go for some time.

The next day I was taken to the ferry at Bastia for the last time. I got on board climbed to the top deck and said my final adieu to Corsica, as it faded into the distance.

18: Aubagne Again

You only have power over people so long as
you don't take everything away from them. But
when you've robbed a man of everything, he's no
longer in your power - he's free again.
Aleksandr Solzhenitsyn

I arrived at Aubagne mid-morning and was sent to the same building that I had stayed in when I was waiting to go to my regiment after basic training, four years ago. I just about had time to dump my things in one of the rooms, before I was called down into an office on the second floor. Inside, behind a desk, was the most jacked Arab I have ever seen. This guy was definitely on the juice; he was damn near popping out of his uniform, but I guess some drugs are acceptable in the Legion. This guy had some serious anger issues, and it was clear that he didn't like the British or Americans.

He began ranting about how unfair it was that I had been to Afghanistan, when he had been in the legion for fifteen years and no one had offered him the chance to go. I listened to his bullshit, then when he was finished I asked if I could go out into town to take the fifteen thousand euros I had saved, out of my bank account before my name was changed back to my civilian one. He told me that there was no chance of that happening and that I was to stay in my room and only come out for meals. I tried to argue with him that what he was doing was dick move of the highest calibre, but he flew into a rage, pounded the table with his fist, then got up and confronted me. He was ready to kick my arse, so I decided to stop arguing with him and just go jump the fence as soon as I left the office. However, he was a crafty bastard and guessed that I would pull something like that, and demanded that I hand over my Legion ID card and all other forms of identification.

Normally, I would have been screwed by this point and would have lost all my savings from four years in the army, but I was also a crafty bastard and had already made copies of my Legion ID using my printer back in Calvi, and because the Legion ID was not that common, most of the bank clerks didn't know what it was supposed to look like and so didn't bat an eyelid at my photo copy stuck to a piece of card. Even so, I had already tested it out in Calvi to make sure.

I handed over my ID and left the office. After that, I went to lunch, then came straight back to my room, changed into civilian clothes, put my fake ID in my pocket, and went to the far end of the regiment to jump the fence. I went down to the technical zone, which was closed over lunch, climbed over the gate, then walked to the far end and climbed out of the regiment and walked down the road to the bank.

When I got to the desk, I told the lady that I would like to empty my account. She took my ID, looked at her computer, and told me that I would have to wait twenty-four hours for that amount of money. Then she froze, and stared at her computer screen with a perplexed look on her face and said 'oh no, sorry I can't give it to you, because your savings account was opened in Calvi. If you want to take more than €800 you will have to do it there.' I was lost in despair by this point. I was going to get kicked out of the Legion with no driving licence, money, or proof of where I had been working for the last four years.

I pleaded with the lady to see if there was any way that I could take my money out. I filled her in on my situation, and told her that the Foreign Legion would change my name and freeze my account, in a week's time. If I didn't get the money out of the account before then, I would lose it forever. She told me that it might be possible to transfer the account to here in Aubagne, but it was risky, because that would take five working days and today was Monday. Risk or not, it was the only chance I had, so I told her to go ahead and request the transfer. She assured me that she would do her best to get it done on time, and she also put in a request to take out all the money on the same day. If everything went to plan, I could come back on Friday afternoon, take my money, and go. However, in the meantime there was nothing I could do, but fret about it.

I thanked the lady profusely, then set off back in the direction of the regiment. I got to the fence, climbed over, and went back to my room. I was obviously extremely anxious. The uncertainty of my financial situation was doing my head in, but there was nothing I could do until Friday.

My day didn't get any better after that. Just before dinner time I was called back down to Osama-bin-injecting's office. Unbeknownst to me, he had driven past when I was walking down the road, coming back from the bank. When he got back to the regiment, he went straight to the head of security, and demanded that I be kicked out the regiment for insubordination. I was handed a letter stating that 'as of now I was banned from all Foreign Legion property,' given five minutes to pack my bags, then escorted to main gate, and kicked out. I was told to return to the front gate on Friday to receive my discharge papers and that was it.

I caught the train to Marseille and stayed in a cheap hotel opposite the train station. I fucking hate Marseille, it is a crime-filled-shithole. The first thing I saw as I walked out of the train station was a young man run across a patch of grass and snatch a bag from a woman who sitting down. The place looked more like North Africa than Europe.

The next morning, I woke up and went to have a wash in the shower that was shared by everyone on the floor of the hotel that I was staying in, and was confronted by a whopping great Richard III. I mean who the fuck takes a crap in the shower? Some people are worse than animals. I pity the staff who had to work in that place.

Friday morning I woke up bright and early. I hadn't slept much the night before. I had been worrying too much. If it turned out that my account couldn't be moved before Monday I would be left with barely enough money to make it back home. Not that it would have done me much good, because my parents had immigrated to Australia, so I would have been homeless. I couldn't go to Australia either because I had a criminal record. They would have just stopped me in the airport and put me on the next flight home.

I caught the train over to Aubagne, and went straight to the main gate of the 1RE and got my discharge papers. When I had a look at them, I noticed that not one of them had my real name on, they were completely useless to me. After that I walked over to the bank. The clerk, who I had spoken to on Monday told me to wait until the afternoon, so I went and had some McDonalds to pass the time. I missed American fast food, and it doesn't get any better than two double cheese burgers put together to make one giant quadruple-burger.

At two o'clock in the afternoon, I went over to the bank. There was a massive line reaching all the way out of the door. This is just what I fucking need, I thought, but that's life; it never stops kicking you when you are down. Eventually, after an hour of waiting, I got to the counter. The lady, who I had spoken with on Monday wasn't there. I approached the counter and explained my situation. One of the other clerks overheard me and handed a letter to the lady dealing with me. The clerk from Monday had left a note explaining everything. Sweat was rolling down my face as the clerk checked to see if my account had been successfully relocated to Aubagne.

After clicking around on her computer for a bit, she looked up at me, smiled, and said, 'everything is in order sir, can I have your ID.' I was so relieved, it was like my death sentence had been overturned. She checked my ID, then called me over into a private room at the side, where she counted out my money and handed it over.

I was over the moon. That steroid freak had tried to fuck me over, but I had outdone him in the end. I walked down the road cursing him, 'Fuck you, you fucking jacked up, hateful piece of shit. I won...I fucking won.'

19: Afterthoughts

In this book I have tried my best to give you the reader an honest and accurate, account of life in the French Foreign Legion. I have tried, not to glam anything up, or make myself, or anyone else, look better or worse than they really were. I hope that you will note that I didn't use the word 'elite' once in this book (except where I translated the legionnaire's code of honour, but those weren't my words). I believe that word has been bandied about so much that it has lost all meaning. If everything is elite, then nothing is. However, I realize that although I have tried to give an honest and unbiased account that this is not really possible and that everything I experienced is filtered through the lens of my own subjectivity, and that I have plenty of conscious, and unconscious biases. I think George Orwell summed what I am trying to say up best, at the end of his book on the Spanish civil war:

'I hope the account I have given is not too misleading. I believe that on such an issue as this no one is or can be completely truthful. It is difficult to be certain about anything except what you have seen with your own eyes, and consciously or unconsciously everyone writes as a partisan. In case I have not said this somewhere earlier in the book I will say it now: beware of my partisanship, my mistakes of fact and the distortion inevitably

caused by my having seen only one corner of events. And beware of exactly the same things when you read any other book...'

I hope that this book won't come across as too negative. I realize that it is easy to criticize and I know that I have done my fair share of that. It was not my aim to paint the French Foreign Legion in a bad light. I was simply trying to describe my experiences, and how I felt about them. I hold no grudges against the Foreign Legion and am thankful for the valuable lessons that serving in that prestigious institution has taught me. Even though life in the Legion was tough, I had many good times there, and was lucky enough to meet a bunch of great people from all over the world. People who I would never have known existed otherwise, and who are still good friends of mine to this very day.

Everyone's experience of the French Foreign Legion will be different. For my part, I would have to say that my personality is not one that is suitable to military life. I have almost no respect for authority or tradition, and I question everything, no matter who said it, or how long people have been doing it for. However, I don't wish for anyone who might be reading this book, and thinking of joining, to be discouraged. If you are thinking of going to France to sign up, then I would recommend that you also read:

- Fighting for the French Foreign Legion: by Alex Lochrie. He was an ex-policeman who joined the Legion in the eighties, and has a completely different take on things to me.
- Legionnaire: by Simon Murray. A bit dated, but still the number one book, in my opinion, for anyone looking to join the ranks of the Foreign Legion.

Read these books, then join or don't, but whatever you do; don't procrastinate. Besides you can always desert after a year, if you don't like the way things are going. Nobody will come looking for you (unless you desert with a gun) and you won't be arrested if you enter France in the future; there are way too many deserters for them to do that.

Now, would I question some of the practices that the Foreign Legion engages in? For sure. The big one would have to be the

371

general treatment of legionnaires, which, at times, borders on physical and mental torture. I am not against corporal punishment in the military, but it has to have limits. There are definitely some people, who need a good slap to wake them up, but the question is: How much is too much? Is it too much when you drive people to the point where they come into a room with a loaded rifle, shoot their sergeant, corporal, and a random Togolese soldier, then run outside, shoot a farmer, steal his horse, and ride off into the sunset? I would have to say yes. When things like that start happening, or people are dropping dead from heat exhaustion, then something needs to change. In my opinion, the Legion goes over the top at times, and ends up traumatizing a fair proportion of its soldiers to the point where they become either useless or dangerous. I would say that if someone needs such a severe level of punishment to bring them into line that it ends up psychologically damaging, or killing, them then it is better to mark that person as unfit for military service, and show them the door.

The second thing that I would call into question is whether half of the people in the hierarchy are fit for purpose, because the Foreign Legion is, in my opinion, a bit of a mess. If I wanted to be insulting I would label it a totalitarian kakistocracy: There are high levels of incompetency at all levels, and they aren't promoting the right people for the right reasons. It also seems to have strayed from the path of being a purely military institution. Many times, while working there, I began to question whether it wasn't just a plaything for the French aristocracy. A place where they could relive the good old days of pre-revolution France. It felt at times like you were more of a serf, than a soldier: You were a perpetual dogsbody. The fact that there are no civilian workers in the legion, meant that everything had to be done by the legionnaires. In my opinion, this was to save money, so that the officers could have a better standard of living.

What are my thoughts on the future of the French Foreign Legion? Well, I think that Legion has become more concerned with its continuation, than with its effectiveness. If I had to guess, I would say that in the near future it will be severely reduced in numbers, or disbanded altogether, but that fate awaits most traditional armed forces (in the West at least), because the robots are coming to take our jobs, and that is not a joke. I think that in my lifetime, I will see the first war in which one side has no human boots on the ground, but, instead has an army of killer robots that never sleep, have no fear of death, and are far more deadly than humans ever could be. If there are still Islamic terrorists around at that time I would love to see the look on their faces as the robots hunt them into extinction. Unless they become really good at making EMP bombs that is. If I was them, I would start practising now.

And so, this little window into a brief period of time in the French Foreign Legion closes. I hope that you have enjoyed reading this book as much as I have enjoyed writing it.

THE END

Made in the USA
Coppell, TX
19 October 2021

64338837R00218